DATE DUE

DEMCO 38-296

Recharting
the Thirties

Recharting
the Thirties

Edited by
Patrick J. Quinn

SUP

Selinsgrove: Susquehanna University Press
London: Associated University Presses

tocopy items for internal or personal use,
clients, is granted by the copyright owner,
ght cents per page, per copy is paid directly
Rosewood Drive, Danvers, Massachusetts
'96 $10.00+8¢ pp, pc.]

iversity Presses
gate Drive
Cranbury, NJ 08512

Associated University Presses
16 Barter Street
London WC1A 2AH, England

Associated University Presses
P.O. Box 338, Port Credit
Mississauga, Ontario
Canada L5G 4L8

The paper used in this publication meets the requirements
of the American National Standard for Permanence of Paper
for Printed Library Materials Z39.48–1984.

Library of Congress Cataloging-in-Publication Data

Recharting the thirties / edited by Patrick J. Quinn.
    p.   cm.
  ISBN 0-945636-90-3 (alk. paper)
  1. English literature—20th century—History and criticism.
  2. Literature and society—Great Britain—History—20th century.
  3. Great Britain—History—George V, 1910–1936. 4. Great Britain—
History—George VI, 1936–1952.   I. Quinn, Patrick J., 1946–
  PR471.R44   1996
  820.9′00912—dc20   96-3539
                                                             CIP

For Bartholomew P. A. Quinn

Contents

Acknowledgements

Permission to quote from Cyril Connolly's *The Rock Pool* is granted by permission of Rogers, Coleridge, & White Ltd.

Permission to quote from Jean Rhys's *Good Morning, Midnight* is granted by permission of Penguin Books Ltd.

Permission to quote from *The Dying Gaul, The Sleeping Lord, Epoch and the Artist, and In Parenthesis* by David Jones is granted by Faber & Faber Ltd.

Permission to quote from the letters of Irene Rathbone to Louise Morgan Theis is granted with the permission of The Beinecke Library and of Rathbone's literary executor, Patricia Utechin.

Permission to quote from the works of Edward Upward was generously granted by the author.

Permission to quote from the works of William Empson was granted by Random House Ltd.

Introduction

Very few critics and academics would disagree that English literature in the thirties centered around the person and writings of W. H. Auden. Three major commentators of the period, Bernard Bergonzi in his *Reading the Thirties,* Samuel Hynes in his *Auden Generation,* and Valentine Cunningham in his *British Writers of the Thirties* each see Auden as the focus of their respective studies of the period. He was the pollinator of thirties literature in England; many of his ideas were borrowed and developed by writers such as Spender, Isherwood, Day Lewis, and Mac Neice, as well as lesser-known authors of the period.

The ensuing problem, however, was that Auden's legacy is so immense and his influence so profound that other writers have had difficulty emerging from the shadow of his reputation. Those who survived the cast of Auden's shadow were often writers closely connected with Auden such as Christopher Isherwood or Stephen Spender or those who have been rediscovered in the revisionist critical atmosphere of the last quarter of the twentieth century where one's gender, politics, or sexual tastes are often more important than the quality of one's writing.

On account of this concentration on Auden or writers associated with Auden, the teacher or student of twentieth-century literature faces a difficult time finding many of the less popular works of the dedicated writers of the period. Part of the reason for this is that many of the writers of the thirties espoused Socialist and Marxist political philosophies which were unpopular outside the intellectual circles they inhabited, and as the decade unfolded, sympathetic publishers and writers lost faith in the promises and dreams they held, and the literature was forgotten as the inevitability of another devastating world war grew more certain.

Perhaps another reason for the lack of interest in many thirties writers is that after the Second World War the perspective of literature changed significantly. When Auden and Isherwood left England for the United States and the Germans and Russians joined forces and marched into Poland, the core of political unity was lost. By the time the war was over, new dreams were in the air, and the feeling of literature was largely neoromantic, not only to escape the deprivations of the war but also to avoid dwelling on the future of the individual in a new world order which offered the icons of Buchenwald and Hiroshima as realities to ponder. The writings of the thirties seemed to have little relevance in the atomic age.

Even by the Festival of Britain celebration, the thirties for many British people represented a rather unpleasant reminder of the forlorn years during The Great Depression: poverty and squalor covering the industrial cities and rural villages of England alike. The memory of haggard-looking laborers and miners with their families marching across grimly lit landscapes presided over by massive impersonal factories was too vivid to dwell on amid the glittering promises of a new generation of politicians. The stark images of bodies left to rot in the parched fields of far-off Spain had been replaced by the horrors of a more destructive aerial bombardment where civilian and soldier alike were fair game. The thirties were grim years, and many of the realistic writers of the period attempted to capture with a strong social conviction the pain, suffering, and deprivation of the times. The postwar world chose to look ahead rather than back.

The purpose of this book is largely to revitalize the awareness of the reading public with regard to a number of writers whose books have been largely ignored by publishers and scholars since their major works first appeared in the thirties. The selection is not based on a political agenda, but encompasses a wide and divergent range of philosophies; clearly, the contrasts between, say, Empson and Upward or between Powell and Slater indicate the wide-ranging vision of the period. Women writers of the period have been too long marginalized, and the writings of Rathbone and Burdekin, for example, not only present distinct feminine voices of the period, but also illuminate how much good literature has been forgotten. In fact, this very diversity of opinion is what makes a collection like this useful, for it helps to break down some of the fatuous preconceptions of the period.

Each chapter is devoted to the neglected work or works of one particular writer of the thirties. The purpose is to give an overview of the writer's work through an in-depth study of a small representative sample of prose, poetry, or drama. Each chapter also contains a brief biographical introduction to the author concerned and a comprehensive bibliography of his work during the thirties as well as the significant critical studies of his work to enable the reader to follow up on ideas raised in the chapters themselves.

In attempting to rechart the map of thirties literature in this collection, I am aware that only three of the eighteen essays deal with poets, and the addition of essays about John Cornford or John Lehmann, for example, would have given a more balanced feel to the book. In fact, I received over fifty essay submissions for inclusion in this book, and over twenty were centered on poets. But an editor's task is oftentimes full of compromises and difficult decisions, and I felt I had to sacrifice balance in genres for quality of insight and freshness of thought. The essays included all offer an energy and enthusiasm which was in keeping with the spirit of the collection as I first conceived it.

Ideally, this book will allow lecturers and teachers to have access to materials with which to build courses around the period. I have found while piecing together this book that many academics feel that worthy literary figures of the period have been marginalized far too quickly by publishers who have failed to see the market for fiction, poetry, and drama written in the thirties. If this book goes partway to address this injustice, it will have served a useful purpose.

This book is indebted to the large number of people who submitted essays on writers of the thirties, which confirmed that there was a great deal of interest in the period. But, in particular, I'd like to thank Nene College for awarding me a grant for some teaching remission during the academic year 1994–95. Secondly, I'd like to thank Ian Firla, my postgraduate student who followed me from the University of Toronto. His knowledge of computer technology and second pair of eyes made the creation of this book far easier than it could have been. And, of course, in Catherine Quinn, I have found not only the psychological and moral support, but an editor who gently reminds me that "haste makes waste" and that my style of writing is slapdash.

PATRICK J. M. QUINN

Recharting
the Thirties

1

We Shall Act: We Shall Build: The Nomadism of Herbert Read and the Thirties Legacy of a Vanished Envoy of Modernism

JERALD ZASLOVE

Through all the mutations of these years
I have relied upon a weapon which I found
in my hand as soon as I was compelled to
abandon my innocent vision and fight
against the despairs of experience. This
weapon was adamantine and invincible, like
the sickle which at the beginning of legendary
time Earth gave to Cronus and with which he
mutilated the divine father. The Furies were
born from the drops of blood which fell in that
fray.

—Herbert Read, "The Adamantine Sickle"

Wounds dried like sealing-wax
upon the bond
but time has broken
the proud mind.

—Herbert Read, "Envoy"

A Brief Biographical Sketch of Herbert Read (1893–1968)

HERBERT READ WAS BORN ON 4 DECEMBER 1893 AT MUSCOATES Grange, in the Vale of Pickering. Read's early school experiences stamped him with a Dickensian childhood. He joined his mother in Leeds and while attending evening school there became a voracious reader of European and English writers and also became familiar with modern painting. He enrolled at Leeds University in 1912 where his characteristic unwillingness to be pinned down to a par-

17

ticular field is evident in his wide variety of studies. Read's contact
with the circles around A. E. Orage and futurist and syndicalist
causes already marked his outlook with the magical aura of social
transformation. In Leeds he established many important, lifelong
friendships with poets and artists. From 1914 until 1919 Read fought
in the war as an officer and frontline combatant. Throughout the war
he wrote poetry and maintained relationships with the visionaries,
partisans, and practitioners of poetic modernism who seeded British
modernism. Read was hired by the Department of Ceramics at the
Victoria and Albert Museum in 1922—a position he kept until he
took the Watson Gordon chair of art history, which he held until
1933. Disappointed when his hope for a renaissance of art history
and theory modeled on Bauhaus perspectives was not fulfilled, he
resigned and returned to London. London gave him a vantage point
to continue the literary writing of the twenties on poetics, influenced
by Hulme, Eliot, and Wordsworth, as well as by Freud, Nietzsche,
Kropotkin, and Marx. In London he was able to defend modern art
and radical connoisseurship by appropriating the quarrels between
art and social ideas of the thirties and by placing the controversies
squarely in the studios of Moore, Hepworth, Nicholson, Gabo, and
the surrealists. During and after the war the turns and twists of his
writing, lecturing, editing, collecting, and advocating for the poetics
of contemporary art practice were firmly entrenched in pacificism
and in the social and educational values associated with an evolving
anarchist outlook. His attempt to bring technology and material
design into some utopian alignment with social change was informed
by depth psychology. His work with the Institute of Contemporary
Arts (ICA), the British Arts Council, the publisher Routledge,
Kegan, Paul, the Bollingen Foundation, as well as continual lecturing and traveling gave him an identity as a public intellectual in the
service of modern poetry and art. He was knighted in 1953 "for
services to literature." He accepted, not without some reservations.
He died at Stonegrave, the mythical pagan-Christian dwelling of his
childhood, on 12 June 1968.

* * * * *

1

Herbert Read vanished sometime after his death in 1967. "Neglect" is almost too honorific when applied to the now-disappeared
Herbert Read. It suggests that his achievements in his own time
might still be remembered but perhaps have been discounted, mini-

mized, assimilated into a tradition, or have even been superseded by a more adequate political aesthetic of modernism. But this is not the case. He is not "the last modern," the title of a comprehensive 1990 biography of Read, but the archetypal lost modern. A retrospective examination of the historical vagaries of British modernism since World War I, which would attempt to locate Read within the current controversies over modernism and postmodernism, would have to account for the almost total amnesia which has settled over the remains of this poet, anarchist, and partisan of a comprehensive radical aesthetic modernism.[1]

Understanding the shape of Read's literary work in the thirties and his break with his past in that decade should begin with his attempt to construct an aesthetics of memory and continuity with the ruins of the past, themes, present in his collected poems of 1926, and in his study of Wordsworth in 1930. In the Wordsworth study he made peace in his personal synthesis of Wordsworth and Godwin by turning his thoughts to the creative process without sacrificing his political outlook as Wordsworth did. Read's march through the thirties ends with the publication of *To Hell with Culture; Democratic Values Are New Values* (1941), the war itself, and his choice of anarcho-pacifism as the resolution of his engagement with the politics of modernity. But the militancy of his postures does not reveal at first glance the nature of his *inner and personal pilgrimage* into the world of modernism, which started with his discovery of poetry and philosophy at Leeds before World War I, and carried him through the philistine and conventional British art worlds, where the formation of a national literature based on the values of Arnold or Ruskin—the rites of passage that would lead either to honor and gentlemanship or Newman's world of intellectual power and the cultivation of an elite—had been forever damaged by turn of the century modernisms and the mutilation, death, and homelessness suffered by over a million people in Europe during World War I.[2] It is not an overstatement to say that a quality of inner nomadism marks Read's life and also marks his way of looking at pictures. This is characterized in the way he ascribes both a sense of foreignness and hermetic rationality to both art and literature.[3] The picture for Read was a situation, an event, not unlike wandering into a Talmudic book which both located and resisted authority, power, and insight at every turn. Art and poetry for Read always maintained a condition of separateness and individuality that has something to do with the sacredness of the image, conceived as if it were a person. Read revered the almost tabooed quality of the individual utterance or image that he claimed was a spiritualized otherness. Needless to add that this often looked like mysticism or religion to antiromantics.

By the 1930s Read was at the center of the new revolutionary movements where gallery, museum, and publishing were working together to constitute a new art public. The world of the vanguard contemporary art journals like *Unit One, Axis, Art Now* and *Circle,* enabled artists, educators, and left-wing politically engaged intellectuals to form a brotherhood, a syndicalist inspired intelligentsia with roots in the constructivist and surrealist antifascist art movements of England and Europe. Read's own aesthetic values were tempered by a deep self-scrutiny of his own artistic controls and a continued preoccupation with the relevance of the *failed* revolutionary British social movements to effect social transformation based on artistic practices in England and Europe. In his own way he became part of the impulse to reconcile the art and power movements of the thirties. He recognized that any revolution in deed would ultimately have to be communicated through a thorough knowledge of the laws of the visible and material universe as revealed in the way particular communal conditions must evolve out of the reciprocity of nature and praxis. The urban grotesque as a violent pictorial norm for the phantasmagoria of modernity would have to be reformed and made into more relativized precise materials: the thing-representations of the unconscious. The unconscious would be processed by abstractions which could then conceptualize art itself as a representation of the social history of the individual. Thus his use of the term *superrealism* displaces the violence of the grotesque which prevents modern life in its misery to be linked to the beautiful rationality of our art susceptible inner selves and worlds. This enabled him to develop a new theory of the grotesque and phantasmagoria based on a new receptive attitude toward nonrepresentational subject matter. Read construed this art movement as the mimetic expression of modernity itself.

At his death in 1968 Read was arguably the most significant international public spokesman for literary modernism that the English-speaking world had produced since romanticism. Moreover, the economic analysis that accompanied his aesthetic rationalism—wrongly conceived by many commentators as a brute synthesis of pure literary romanticism and classicism—enabled him to critique the postromantic aesthetic social pragmatism of Ruskin, Morris, or Fabian-styled Bloomsbury, although this aspect of his thought has been widely ignored, sadly and most centrally by Raymond Williams, who is paradigmatic of critics who attempt to place him into a unitary, single modernist tradition. Williams's rejection of Read, and

E. P. Thompson's silence about him, is in fact exemplary of the narrow sectarianism of the British modernist tradition that saw culture subsumed into the laborist traditions which were in turn historically placed as a struggle between Morris and Marx.[4]

This vanished legacy of a cultural revolution deeper than the venerable clash between two cultures, or between Christianity and guild socialism, has surfaced since the crisis of European Marxism is played out in the British schools of cultural studies, whose roots clearly coexist with Read's own populist, communitarian, and regional modernism. The historical consciousness in cultural studies is far more indebted to purely academic institutions and their languages than Read's tradition ever was. Read, to be sure, is not a part of cultural studies.

The pinnacle of Read's public recognition does not coincide with the depth of his influence in the 1930s. His knighthood in 1953 which was awarded for his contribution to literature and to the cultural symbol that literature had become was inevitably and correctly scorned by his fellow anarchists. This episode in Read's life, certainly plays a role in the perception of him as an establishment figure. This is a condescending stereotype continued to this day by those who never recognized that his pacifism and anarchism were deeply philosophical and moral forms of subversive anarchism that enabled him to speak against the liberalistic state while protecting and nurturing artists and artistic practices which were seen by the cultured public as cultural Bolshevism or appeasement, for example when pacifism is rendered into being pro-Nazi, an accusation leveled at Alex Comfort by George Orwell in an exchange in *The Partisan Review* in 1944. His subworldly anarchism[5] was not symmetrical with accepting a knighthood. But his quixotic and idealistic, perhaps opportunistic acceptance of the knighthood did not stop him from speaking out against what his fellow anarchist and poet, Alex Comfort, called, in *Art and Social Responsibility* (1946, dedicated to Herbert Read), our "megalopolitan civilisation living under a death sentence" which, for Read and Comfort and their fellow anarchists like Louse Berneri, Vernon Richard, Nicolas Walter, and George Woodcock, included a cultural struggle against professionalizing art in the name of sycophantisms of all kinds. Ironically, Read is now accused of being a conformist modernist.

Read's form of anarchism is grounded in his experience of a consensus about the widespread denunciation of the social and political barbarisms active in the dictatorships and mass cultures of the 1930s, which were developing new forms of obedience and accommodation to the very state which liberal cultural epigones thought would safely

steer a welfare state through capitalism and fascism. While Read
never accepted liberal solutions to the psychopathology of power,
he never made the step to becoming an absolute enemy of society,
as did, for example, Blake, or Céline, Mann, Kafka or Brecht.
Read's search for a radical humanist intellectual tradition which
would enable him to bridge his pre-World War I Nietzscheanism, is
illustrated, for example, in his *The Sense of Glory; Essays in Criticism*
(1929), where figures as diverse as Froissart, Malory, Descartes,
Swift, Vauvenargues, Sterne, Hawthorne, Bagehot, and James are
linked to a personalist theory of authorship and consciousness, probably rooted in Hegel and Whitehead. The book consists of essays
originally in *The Times Literary Supplement* and comes equipped with
epigraphs from Hölderlin and Ernest Renan which plumb the terrible depths of glory and hope in the unconsious. Read argues that
images and languages of literature cannot exist in artistic form without individuals who rebel against the cultural forms themselves; long
after the violent state-formed, apocalyptic civilizations have collabo-
rated to produce a culture without mind, traces of emancipatory,
poetic, and visual images continue to exist within the literary mind
which fights against the pathological delusions and illusions of capitalist society. For this reason, when Read reissued *The Sense of Glory*
in 1938 it included his defense of the essayistic compositional style
as the highest form of a Baudelairean or Freudian, culturally engaged
writing suitable for a critically engaged modernism: by using the
results of science, observation, and self-analysis we would avoid any
possibility of being seen to be in collaboration with journalistic,
professional or academic culture.

The expressed thesis of Read's *Collected Essays in Literary Criticism*
(1938) articulates a more unpopular defense of psychoanalytic understanding and the psychoanalytically oriented creative mind and was,
by definition, a challenge to the cultural conservatism of his friend,
T. S. Eliot. In this sense, *The Green Child; A Romance* (1935), which
I discuss later in this essay, written quickly, and in an almost trance-
like state, is a side-by-side counterpart to Read's essayistic, partisan
essays of the thirties. All are grounded in conflict between the artist
and the intellectual. *The Green Child* represents the torment of this
struggle in a fictionalized Blakean-Freudean perhaps even, Lawrentian fable. The conflict in *The Green Child* illustrates the libidinal
depth of Read's search for an aesthetics of self-creation beyond mortality which he pursued through his protean writings in the thirties.
This is the dominating thesis: that art and eros cannot be disentan-
gled and that together they constitute the Kairos of revolutionary

art's capacity to make autonomy and self-repair intelligible for a damaged life in a damaged society.

In the postwar period when Read became something of a celebrity with the American literary establishment—incurring the wrath of Clement Greenberg as well as the irritated response of Barnett Newman, who considered himself an anarchist[6]—he was both lionized and tolerated in America, but not without displaying his own willingness to join the symbolist, Langer-Cassirer and Jungian traditions.

By the fifties any indigenous British surrealism which had survived the thirties was either discredited because of its links to communism, or had been superseded by other movements, even though Read had already abandoned surrealists like E.L.T. Messens who had himself also abandoned Read. Read's demise can partially be explained by noting the antiromantic formalist biases in literary culture, formulated by the epigones of cultural criticism like Frye, Leavis, Eliot, or the leaders of the American new criticism, like Alan Tate or John Crow Ransom had ensured that any contextual or psychological criticism would not be welcome. Tate's editing (in 1963) of a volume of Read's essays notwithstanding,[7] Read's political aesthetics did not fit snugly into any new critical formalist mode. When this reception is seen in the light of the virulent cold war antisocialism and the mood of despairing accommodation of cultural criticism to American capitalism, the now canonical depoliticization of the modernist emancipatory aesthetic that Read championed in the 1930s was already part of a postwar minority culture. From today's vanishing point of Read's reputation, his visionary aesthetic project, formulated so carefully in the thirties, was already in decline, eclipsed in the fifties by new forms of academicism and university patronage, along with the growing influence of Eliot and Leavis as the normative modernist forces in the institutionalization of *textual* explication in the *universities* as the primary mode of reading. The hegemony of abstract expressionism after the war, which became the major American discourse about the avant-garde, mirrored the politics of the end of ideology. The futurist world of pop art mimicked suburban conformism and early conceptual and abstract art flirted in a triumphant manner with the successes of British liberalism and American consumerist democracy: both gleamed with a falsely popular, egalitarian facade.

Read's disillusionment with the early stages of postmodern art was grounded as much in his commitment to the emancipatory ethics of thirties' surrealism, as in his fear that purely autonomous art would end up becoming distanced from the labile, plastic, iconic, and imag-

istic *roots* of art. Art as revolution was a form of thinking *with* art
about the social-historical progress of consciousness toward freedom. For Read, art was always *revealed* as thought in action. This
was a philosophy of the act, and this meant that art was by definition
a process that engaged the irrationality of capitalism: art would have
to communicate the democratic character of its deepest impulses in
order to avoid the cultic formalization circulating among the elite as
postutopian despair. The emergence of a monolithic view of modernism based solely on technical experimentation, which might be
described as a text-centred, but de-authored and depersonalized view
of the creative process, which produced counterfeit and high-kitsch
art, was generally understood as the last gasp of the critical bourgeoisie in the face of the triumph of an alienating industrial culture.

This attentiveness to the flux and concreteness of artistic practice
is reflected in all of Read's socially conscious writings about art and
literature. *A Letter to a Young Painter* (1962), *The Forms of Things
Unknown* (1963), *The Redemption of the Robot* (1966), which reprinted
several of his most demanding anarchist essays on education through
art, and *Art and Alienation* (1967)—all demonstrated that the thirties
had constituted laboratory work on "the forms of things unknown."[8] Read's work in the thirties vanished into the postwar historical ash can, but for him they remained realistic *strategies* in
aesthetic syndicalism and emancipatory, utopian modernism. The
aesthetics of self-creation he self-advertized in the thirties would
continue to show a brave face of social responsibility in the face of
the conformist nature of art-buying and reputation-marketing. Just
as his work in the thirties engaged adversaries and allies alike, his
postwar work engaged Lukács, Sartre, Arendt, Marcuse, and Simone Weil among others, while he still saw himself performing on
the historical stage of "the great refusal": the refusal to accept that
the tragic sense of life *organically* depicted in the way modernity
reified and alienated our innate need for abstraction—thing representations—turned us away from *natural* life forms. Capitalism thrives
on prolonging chaos, and a new naturalism would have to isolate
and analyze the forces which were leading to the construction of a
second nature that would inevitably force the masses into reconciliation with capitalism. The alternatives, that the natural forms of the
mind would become virtually synonymous with religion or fatalistic
redemptive and violent art forms, lead, for Read, to a perverse form
of humanism which became complicit with the vocabulary of the
pseudo-humanist critic who asked the vast majority of mankind to
become guinea pigs for culture. While the artwork might para-
digmatically represent a symbolic and communicable hypermodern

experience, as in Henry Moore's continuing depictions of the shattered torso of an exiled humanism, Read's thirties' anarcho-Freudian
outlook stubbornly maintained that the desensualized and mechanical world of brutal labor can only depict and reproduce horror and
misery. This world could not be reconciled with the idea of a society
without art.

Almost all of Read's work after World War II addressed a fear that
the existing social order had sold out to cold-war capitalism, which
he saw as a preview of a coming society without art, or a society
without the possibility of individual transformation mediated by aesthetic experience. The rational style of his mind subjected his political and aesthetic emotional allegiances to a continuous and rigorous,
almost monastic self-examination. No other critical and pivotal figure of the modern British intelligentsia can be said to have constructed a personal aesthetics of self-creation that used the model of
artistic practice as a social model. This anarcho-rational model of
the mind at its limits would enable cognition to *register* ontologically
grounded representations of psychological forces in the unconscious.
This internal world of the artist constituted a mimesis of self-creation
which was based in a powerful phenomenological revolutionary artistic tendency: the dialectic which contained the dissonant and the
fragmented *coexisted* with a deep need in humans to project an eroti-
cally and compositionally constructed subjectivity. This aspect of
Read's thought is reflected in his struggle to historicize his own
political vision without subjecting art history to a systematic Marxist
or formalist historicism. The following comment in *Poetry and Anarchism* (1938) is a redaction of many of his ideas about the erotic and
sensual basis of consciousness, and was clearly the product of both
anarchism and psychoanalysis formed in the crucible of surrealism's
claims to have a special knowledge of the taboos and sublimations
at the basis of artistic creation:

> What in the attitude of our between-war socialists probably repelled me
> most directly was their incapacity to appreciate the significance of the
> artist's approach. To me it seemed elementary that a belief in Marx
> should be accompanied by a belief in say, Cézanne, and that the develop-
> ment of art since Cézanne should interest the completely revolutionary
> mind as much as the development of social theory since Proudhon. I
> wanted to discuss not only Sorel and Lenin, but also Picasso and Joyce.
> But no one saw the connection. Each isolated on his separate line denied
> the relevance of the force animating the other lines.[9]

Here Read's ideological critique echoes Trotsky, as well as Kropotkin, Stirner, Tolstoy, and Kierkegaard, and reflects his deep aware-

ness of many exiled Hegelian and Marxist art historians and
aestheticians in the thirties, like Carl Einstein, Max Raphael, and
later other radical humanist critics, like Karl Mannheim, Martin
Buber, Arnold Hauser, and Siegfried Giedeon. The social significance and existential reality of this antifascist intellectual community
in exile is never lost on him. In the postwar years he attempted,
perhaps quixotically, to define an aesthetic of anarchism in terms of
a radically contingent attitude toward human nature positioned in
relationship to a social history of art and design. This introduced a
social history of art to England, in what he called a culture of highbrow bad taste. Read's intellectual project in the thirties was nothing
less than a conscious and deliberate attempt to ground artistic practice in a social history of the present in terms that revealed the contin-
gencies of the art practices and their relationship to the social
movements to which he felt a clear sympathy and within which he
could see reflected not only his personal crisis of belief in the efficacy
of art, but his commitment to a new kind of artist and the education
of intelligence away from the class-oriented affectations of British
cultural values: literature and modern art were really laboratories and
studios where nonrational and prerational forms become reflected in
the autonomy of the work itself.

The politics of this pan-revolutionary humanism for which he
sought a vocabulary in the thirties is demonstrated in his hundreds
of commentaries about the radical nature of this project. In order to
function socially, artistic abstraction and dissonance in an age of
brutal and criminal social transformation must stimulate the organic
possibilities of a revolution in perception, which was *already* going
on in the minds of educated and uneducated beholders alike who
had not given up their desire to become free and spontaneous individuals. As a mediator and envoy for this public role of revolutionary art Read serves as both the transmitter of the particular values
of artistic experimentation to the public, who are themselves alienated but not devoid of innate or natural values, and as the representative analyst of working-class connectedness to former craft and naive
cultures. However, these separate and indigenous cultures are in
trouble because of the culture of domination in which they are im-
mersed. The primitive and discursive mythical roots of earlier forms
of social organization have been all but obliterated, and no amount
of utopian news from elsewhere, not Ruskin, not Morris, not even
Marx, could redeem a natural perception of forms from the crisis of
culture into which the masses of peoples had been propelled and
then exiled.

Read was himself almost morbidly aware of the pressures of historical change on his own personality, and in this respect, his analysis of the creative process in *The Green Child,* his single work of fiction, should be understood as being continuous and contiguous with his project of an aesthetic of self-creation that redeemed the perverse social for a personal vision.

The pathos inside *The Green Child* is not only the search for an ideal community of virtue in which a romance and love story carries the burden of disclosing the loss of nature and home. Here Read faces the problem of the loss and reconstruction of both personal and historical memory. Memory is conditioned by a yearning for an ideal world in which an absolute love which cannot be—the surrealist's artistic desire for abstraction that wills elimination of all taboos—reconciles sexual taboos by rescuing an unknown person, the Green Child, the unsexed girl who claims absolute existential rights over the male quester. The male's odyssey *must* free him of all forms of symbolic and unnatural identities. The only source of peace is to purge the will to power, power which is connected to our tendency to indulge ourselves in political abstractions unmediated by art that appears to be innate in the human mind. Only concrete aesthetic experiences can alleviate the misery of an endless search into symbolic systems of knowledge. The anarcho-social aesthetic therefore demands a sensual connection, reciprocity and mutuality as a condition of artistic formation and humanness. Continually aware of the way artists subjected abstractions of space, time, and the conceptual situation of art itself to a continuing critique of contemporary life, artistic activity was for Read a dialogically self-reflexive act which worked against convention and the artificial assimilation of the artist into an authoritarian and violently dehumanizing society. His last works were, as David Thistlewood argues, a critique of painting "that in its post Existentialist manifestations . . . had abandoned the Modernist project" (Thistlewood 1994, 91).[10]

This critique, however, is not just a postwar affectation of pessimism; Read was maintaining a project already underway in the 1930s. It is not difficult to see his deep affinity with the other European aesthetic modernists who formed their dialectical organicism in the period between the war, and who continued the controversies of the thirties, well into the postwar period of modernism. The critiques of Adorno and Benjamin come to mind, and these would have to be compared to Read's, who also saw in the collapse and assimilation of the avant-garde into capitalism's cultural accumulation the failure to provide either a political, cognitive, or aesthetic practice that would sustain the critique that had been fundamental to the origins and continuity of modernism's deep critique of capitalism.[11] If modernism was on the road to becoming an economically driven political theology—a will to power controlled by massive industries of will-formation and will-degradation, in other words a world without individuals or formative institutions—then the gains of modernism would have to be measured by their absorption into an anonymous society which had surrendered its historical memory to a self-absorbed aesthetic attitude without art.

> If the aesthetic attitude as such is now ineffectual, the reason is to be found in our conscious and sceptical attitude to works of art. A deep rift divides the poetic consciousness from the collective instincts of mankind. The poet is an outcast, isolated. As a result he has become introspective and analytically self-destructive. The mass does not resist him—it ignores him. ("The Reconciling Image" 1963, 91)

Read himself writes in his autobiographical memoirs, "The Adamantine Sickle," that

> Actually there was an unfailing continuity in my political interests and political opinions. I would not like to claim that they show an unfailing consistency, but the general principles which I found congenial as a young man are the basic principles of the only political philosophy I find congenial. In calling these principles Anarchism I have forfeited any claim to be taken seriously as a politician and have cut myself off from the main current of socialist activity in England. (Contrary 1963, 392)[12]

The relationship of life to memory and Read's construction of a philosophy of the act can be understood in the mysterious work, The Green Child, his major literary effort written in the thirties. This elusive romance, which fascinated Jung and a younger generation of poets, like Kenneth Rexroth, reveals how his surrealist turn, in both thought, poetry, and action struggled against the forces of sensual derealization, and how an adversarial ideology of "Forward from Liberalism" (e.g., Stephen Spender coming to terms with Stalinism and fascism) would be an emotional swamp for any art and aesthetic self-creation. In order for Read to transform "this life" into "this art"—Merleau-Ponty's representation of Cézanne's experiential life in the immediacy of his paintings—it was necessary to render the psychological image into a political one without losing the essential aesthetic perception that resided in the forms of memory.

2

> Now, Olivero had never forgotten this strange event—in his mind it had the significance of an unresolved symbol, obscurely connected with his departure, and connected, too, with the inevitability of his return.

The Green Child

We shall act
We shall build
A crystal city in the age of peace
Setting out from an island of calm
A limpid source of love.
                    A World Within War

Surrealism was not only an art-historical movement, it was the mimetic simulacrum of the continuing possibility that misrecognition of the erotic core of love inside our morphic forms of creation would destroy the mind and deplete the impulse to combine images with life in order to keep memory alive as an active source of life.

Read's early love affairs with surrealism and with the philosophy of the act are emotionally and formally rendered in his fable, *The Green Child*. The Green Child is a girl, a strange translucently fleshly creature who "comes from a world" from which her Odyssean lover, Oliviero, "has no knowledge." "She had never been able to describe that world to anyone, because there were no earthly words to exchange for her memories" (*The Green Child*, 59). The abstractions in Oliviero's mind must protect him against the erosion of everyday life memories which she hauntingly evokes as he engages on a rescue mission of this tabooed creature. The two characters are then subjected to the mysterious forces of symbolic nomadism. They represent otherworldly peoples whose only baggage is their words and stories—"too many words," Olivero feels, that cannot convey the loss of life found in traditional communal forms that are now wholly imaginary. Read's surreal fable constructs the childhood of memory by fusing the imaginary past and the memory of an *immaculate* love together into a Nadja-like image of extreme happiness. The woman-child is both an image and a body that accompanies the Odyssean hero back to otherworldly, Blakean mythologies where persecution, rape, repression, and ugliness dominate. Surreal memory formation is equated with artistic formation and the search for form passes through dream imagery. Olivero, the Green Child's protector, lover, and intellectual companion, comes alive during the final, deathly phase of his adventures, because he "found it advisable to suppress his knowledge of another world and all his other worldly experience." This anamnestic fall into sensuality allows him to recover his mind, but only "by keeping his knowledge to himself, regarding it as a secret store of dream imagery . . . [can he have] . . . a great advantage over his companions in his discussions" (184). The nonhuman peoples who have created a surreal

community based on geologic principles could not understand the
laws of the natural world, since they "regarded the organic and vital
elements of their bodies as disgusting and deplorable" (175) and
worshipped death. "Their sole desire was to become solid—as solid
and perdurable as the rocks around them" (175). The source of their
misery: deprivation of experience and the loss of nature, *which be-*
comes the loss of the knowledge of eternity embedded in Read's notions of
aesthetic nature. The consequence is the knowledge that the harmony
of artistic creation with the surreal fantasies created in the world by
power-driven individuals is a new form of contingency and necessity. This degradation creates this world of half-creatures who live
with totemistic knowledges and who have no capacity to mourn
the past.

In Kafkaesque parabolic form, without metaphor and without
color or description, Read's fable of human abstraction documents
the derealization of the powers of the imagination. The fable combines rational analysis with dreamlike everyday life sequences in order to create a powerful sense of Read's knowledge of the place of
repression in the construction of abstract art and imagist poetry.
However, this process causes everyday life to disappear like the mi-
rage that it is. The artistic people discovered at the end of Oliviero's
journey do not know any source for their music, geometry, or worship of crystals. They attach no value to change; they have no knowledge of "sensuous anticipation" (*The Green Child,* 189). Their goal
in life: to prepare for death. Oliviero prepares for his death by rigors
of contemplation which ritualize his body through ecstasies "of objective proportions" and anticipation of the "objectivity of death"
(191). Read seems to recognize that the elimination of desire cannot
be allegorized into form without a distancing formal technique,
which in the fable is the awareness that the laws of sight and memory
are somehow entwined in a labyrinthine logic of the repressed body
of memory, where departure and return, recovery and loss occurs.
The stream that flows backward without a source becomes the sign
of the living unconscious of memory and mourning, of grief and
absence and reparation in art. The conflict between Oliviero's memory that was "a long thread, stained with . . . multi-coloured experiences" and which "coiled up in . . . [his] brain", and his encounter
with political tyranny when he turns toward political liberalism in
an obscure Latin-American nation on the verge of revolution Oliviero into an apologist for assassination. In passages which will remind the reader of Rex Warner's *Professor* and *Aerodrome,* or Orwell
or Golding, Read flirts with the seductive power of allegory as he
contemplates the nature of absolute power. However, there is a sub-

stantial difference between Read's fable and Warner's or Orwell's allegories: Read's is an anarchist's deeply personal parable, not a tragic one, nor a liberal one, nor one grounded in Golding's cultural despair that equates children with original sin and politics with animal behaviour.[13] Read's fable is fully nonrepresentational. Read has no faith in a culture without aesthetic experience, and Oliviero discovers that in spite of his liberal pretensions he carries a Jesuitical colonizing frame of mind inside of his Platonic and republican ideals: "Try as I would, I could not solve my personal problem in social terms" (150). All of his ideal reformist plans would shatter the serenity of the indigenous peoples. No matter how civilized his schemes he is obsessed with the presence of the mystery of the green children in his past. How did they appear? Who were they? This failed revolutionary longs

> to know how that mystery had been solved, what had become of them in the course of the years. I began to create an ideal image of them as they had grown up in our alien world: being half-human and half-angel, intermediate between the grossness of earth and the purity of heaven. (*The Green Child*, 151)

The parable interrogates the personal and could be compared to Orwell's *flight* from the personal and the intimate in *Homage to Catalona*.

Oliviero's longing for the past, and his attempt to regain a sense of real experience not governed by power or ideals, reflects the crisis of Read's own spiritual and political odyssey: how to overcome the deathly complicity of art with a history of oppression. How to go back to Norse gods without succumbing to cultic mythology? By creating a parable that describes the failures of revolutions Read changes from a believer in systemic liberalization hopeful of a political revolution to a philosophical anarchist who, like Godwin, Stirner, Tolstoy, Nietzsche, Dostoevsky, and later Gandhi and Simone Weil must live as anonymous figures who are compelled to read history backward: there would be no solution until the personal and the political—that superreal undertaking of self-creation— would find new sources of imaginary representations. Behind this literary fable is Schiller, Marx, and Hegel, and Read's manifestos about surrealism, which are the harbinger of the "art now" movement of new sources of association, complementarity, and contiguity of thought and feeling. A natural tendency of human creativity not yet immune to the powers of appropriating and delineating objects for artistic purposes—his later works on art education for children—are prefigured in this fable.

Behind *The Green Child* lies a Freudian fable about the end of the superego's impossible attempts at philosophical transformation of collective memory into personal history. At the beginning of the fable Oliviero returns to the sources of his intelligence in the foreign land of his childhood, and this shows that Read understood that memory and the construction of the aesthetic self cannot be separated—alienated—from the personal, the subject-in-the-making. The characters in the fable die twice: once, in order to overcome their self-appropriation as rational beings when they dive into the unconscious, and then in order to represent that journey they leave life to confront the powers of objectification. Read understands that surrealism *performs* the ideal: "nothing else than the material world reflected by the human mind, and translated into images. But 'reflection' and 'translation' are not, for us today such simple mechanical processes as perhaps Marx implies. For us the process is infinitely complicated: a passage through a series of distorting mirrors and underground labyrinths" (*Surrealism* 1936, 42).

Read's discomfort with the mystical nature of ideal images is reflected in his statement that "surrealism demands nothing less than such a revaluation of all aesthetic values . . . it has no respect for any academic tradition, least of all for the classical-capitalist tradition of the last four hundred years" whose conventions in reality are the "extensions of the personality" (*Surrealism,* 43–44); however these extensions carry the risk of eliminating the person. The surreal doubleness of the feelingful person requires an awareness of the social powers of relativization. Experience works through the mind, of necessity not the mind of culture-bred artists, but a mind that understands that the more irrational the world the more rational the art object. In this mood, then, in Read's manifesto on surrealism which accompanied the International Surrealist Exhibition in London, in 1936, he rashly announced that it was "his ambition someday to submit Hegel's *Aesthetik* to a detailed examination—to do for the realm of art on the basis of Hegel's dialectic something analogous to what Marx on the same basis did for the realm of economics" (*Surrealism,* 43–44). Read's claim that surrealism, Marx, Hegel re-evaluated the conventions of art would also necessitate a revaluation of the romantic tradition and therefore all intellectual detachment—revealed in the treason of the intellectual clerisy—is in many circles archaic polemics today, even though his position is grounded in knowledge of the traditions of subversive art that he claims to have authority over. His plan is to liberate conventions from the will to power, the abnormal conditions of his times—socialist realism, racial purity, and nationalism are equal menaces—and that requires that the artist ally himself with whatever "promises intellectual liberty." Read's poetry in this period expresses this sentiment in deeply personal terms where "the contradictions of the personality are resolved in the work of art" (*Surrealism*, 90).

Is this personal sentiment only justifying Read's love of the archive and gallery? Read's role in the London reconstruction of the Nazi "Degenerate Art Exhibit" which installed Picasso's *Guernica* might be one answer, albeit one that is too easy to assume surrealism was easy to do. His principled disagreements with the militant communist surrealists shows his independence. But there is one other ready-made truth for understanding the complex question about the fate of emancipatory modernism and its having become a myth adjacent to society.

In Raymond Williams's *Culture and Society*, which has became a kind of bible for contemporary cultural studies' revision of the romantic and communitarian tradition in English modernism, Read is patronized and misrecognized as a follower of Hulme's antiromanticism. This is an error of fact and judgment in the case of both Hulme and romanticism, but in Read's case it is a misrepresentation. Williams's potted critique of romanticism that characterizes Freud and Read as defenders of the artist's "abnormality" is either willfully obtuse or misinformed. Instead of the artist as revolutionary, Williams offers Read as the artist as a liberalistic reformer. Here we have the beginnings of cultural studies shorn of anarchism, surrealism, and the experiential. To be sure, Williams's work that follows *Culture and Society* is serious and substantial. But his version of modernism hides his own antiromantic melancholy. Read had dismissed this antimodernism, which he already had abhorred, in his work of the thirties: what Williams described in *Culture and Society* as a work of "disgusted withdrawal" (*Politics and Letters* 1979, 106). In *Politics and Letters*, Williams returns to Read and *Culture and Society*: his publisher had to shorten the book, and Godwin and the Freud-Read nexus had to go. "I was sorry to let Godwin go. I was so hostile to Read that I was less distressed about that; although I regret it now because it would have been relevant to the sixties, when the whole question of Freud became so important in the discussions of art" (99). However, Freud was equally if not *more* important in the thirties when Read engaged Freud, Freudians, and Jungians along with Wilhelm Worringer and Alois Riegl, as well as Godwin, Marxism, and popular education with surrealism, communism, and Marxism. And while Williams did discuss the Marxian Rex Warner in *Culture and Society* (pp. 288–289), who is a benchmark for the failure of thirties' Marxism, afterward Williams had ample opportunity to return to Read and to the problem of a modernist aesthetic which would have included anarchism and surrealism.

The key question raised by Williams's dismissal of Read and an entire tradition in English modernism is the fate of liberalism. Charles Harrison, the historian of modern art, wrote that it would be hard to overestimate Read's importance, but Harrison gives the standard shrug about Read: "Read's stress on the essentially non-rational or pre-rational nature of the origins of art was an effective prescription for liberalism in response to the eccentricities of modern art" (*English Art and Modernism* 1981, 99). Read's transgressive aesthetics is reduced to liberal, cultural accommodation even though a superficial reading of his essayistic, personal encounters with art, his poetry, and *The Green Child* shows his deep antagonism to any "off to arcadia" natural culture, to the market economy, and to liberal subservience to misery. "Only misery is collective" he wrote, establishing this principle as a basis in the thirties for the debate about the origins and erosion of British modernism into an antiromantic liberalism. Read's thirties' studies of art and literature examined both the accommodating and reactionary tendencies in modernism in order to show the limits of *British* modernism and of the *British* reception of modernism, and his way was to show how modernism assimilated the failures of the various revolutions since the Middle Ages: the revolt against humanism by culturist Anglican populism; the failure of the industrial revolution to provide a standard of living or meaningful work; the slicing off of popular democracy from the French revolution; the Chartist movement's failure to include art and culture; and the 1887 Bloody Sunday uprising in London which petered out into despair; the tyranny of the Russian Revolution and the beheading of the German soviets and the Spanish Revolution by the Communists and Fascists. Only an ethics and aesthetics of modernism could keep the image of the "Green Child" alive as a symbolic nonrepresentational image of nonidentity with England's past and with England's tendency to surrender to the spirit of the times by constructing a cultural theology out of the existing class system.

This was his clear voiced message against liberalism. Read felt that the thirties were the opening into another world—toward a tainted "crystal city" of revolutionary, but fragmented hope. In the thirties he foresaw the future in the self-reproduction of capital, in its ability to maintain the empire and an effete domestic culture without either a strong state apparatus or a nationalized gentry. He knew that a class-controlled society was being governed by a culture bearing class that would always resist finding its own image in either literature or painting. The success of British capitalism until the 1960s resided in its ability to fuse aristocratic privilege and the educated bourgeoisie into new institutions of culture, capital and welfare. His is a *semantic-idealistic model* of art, derived from the traditions of the educated yeoman. For all its failings in the eyes of the current postmodern establishment, whose arguments I cannot go into here, its identity must be recognized. It is not liberalistic but is expressive of a cry of pain against the erosion of sociality, being, habituation, and attention to detail—all of which are loosened by capitalism and in danger of being lost forever. Like his central character in *The Green Child* who settles his account with both a narcissism of loving art too much, and a longing for the historical reconstruction of memory, Read wanted to repair the damages caused by the absent reality of ideal forms by dissolving these forms into the presence of the now, into a loose network of pragmatic associations which are governed by deep relationships which would shine through the ruins of forms. Read's controlled use of phantasmagoria and abstraction in his constructed imaginary world in the thirties combined in his love poems and political poems, like "Herschel Grynspan," the later expressing solidarity with "this beautiful assassin," "your friend" who delivered "love" by shooting Ernst Von Rath in Paris on 7 November 1938.

Read seemed to have a continuing premonition that he would vanish, and with him the emancipatory modernism of the period between the wars, a "world within war" he wrote in a poem of that name. We can sum up this aspect of his own self-war with his self-awareness in his Paul Klee-like fable poem "Picaresque" where fragmented bodies, limbs, and bourgeois picnickers, "are tented above the impious pools of memory": the nomadic figure "cannot disentangle the genesis of any scope" and in turn, "HIS limbs dangle like a marionette's over a mauve sea."

Notes

This essay is dedicated to Wayne Burns and Alex Comfort; both in different ways enabled me to think about Read in the early 1960s after I had discovered his work in the 1950s.—(J.Z.)

1. The recent literature on modernism would fill a small warehouse. Among the most recent that fail to mention Read are Raymond Williams, *What I Came to Say* (London: Hutchinson, 1989) and *The Politics of Modernism* (London: Verso, 1989); Paul Woods et al. *Modernism in Dispute* (London and New Haven, Conn.: Yale University Press, 1991); and John Carey, *The Intellectuals and the Masses* (Lon-

don: Faber and Faber, 1992). Carey's is symptomatic; he describes the tradition of class-based elitism inside of British modernism, but his omission of Read is inexcusable not only because Read can't be placed within the tradition Carey creates, but because Read represents another tradition entirely which Carey seems oblivious to.

2. See Tom Steele, *Alfred Orage and The Leeds Arts Club, 1893–23* (Aldershot: Scholar Press, 1990).

3. David Thistlewood's many essays on Read's aesthetics are unparalleled in working out Read's development of an aesthetic. See in particular chapters 2, 3, and 4 of Thistlewood, *Herbert Read, Formlessness and Form: An Introduction to His Aesthetics* (London: Routledge & Kegan Paul, 1984). James King's study of Read's life and development does not really address the question of his aesthetics: James King, *The Last Modern. A Life of Herbert Read* (London, Weidenfeld and Nicholson, 1990). King sees Read's aesthetics, as do many, for its synthesis of romanticism and classicism. My own view is that this is deeply limited and reduces a complex and evolving aesthetic attitude to simple contexts of influence or affinity. In essence this shows the inability of criticism to find the terms of British modernism. Read's several essays on D. H. Lawrence show why he goes outside of the polarity romantic/classic.

4. The nature of Read's anarchism as it compares to others in the thirties or in the history of anarchism would require more comment than I can give here. David Goodway has recently, and correctly written that "Read's anarchism was not peripheral to his other, varied activities. Rather it was—knighthood and all—at the core of how he viewed the world in general" (Goodway, Introduction to *Herbert Read, A One-Man Manifesto and Other Writings for Freedom Press* (London: Freedom Press, 1994). Goodway, however, believes that Read was not able "to extend his professional concern with the visual arts into a generalised theory of human emancipation" (15). George Woodcock believes that Read's anarchism doesn't stand up to others, like Nicholas Walter or Paul Goodman's (personal communication) and Woodcock's now canonized views on anarchism do not see how Read's visual modernism is connected to his anarchism; Woodcock's views on art and anarchism, and anarchism itself, would have to be assessed along with his view of Read's limitations. Woodcock's views on Read are in *Herbert Read: The Stream and the Source* (London: Faber and Faber, 1972), and in "Herbert Read: The Philosopher of Freedom," in *Anarchism and Anarchists, Essays by George Woodcock* (Kingston, Ontario: Quarry Press, 1992). Another of Woodcock's low-keyed, cool assessments of Read is "Herbert Read, Contradictions and Consistencies," in *Drunken Boat, Art, Rebellion, Anarchy,* ed. Autonomedia Collective (New York and Seattle: Autonomedia/Left Bank Books, 1994). My own view is that Read's anarchism contains the seeds of a Stirnerite *parasitic anarchism,* a term Wayne Burns uses in his "The Vanishing Individual: A Voice from the Dustheap of History, Or How to Be Happy Without Being Hopeful," in *Recovering Literature,* Special Issue, 21 (1995).

5. Most commentators interpret Read's acceptance of the knighthood as selling out of his antistate, anarchist ideals. His acceptance is, indeed, odd considering his pacifism during the war and his antibomb militancy and his work with the Freedom Defense Committee which defended deserters and those whose civil rights were violated by the state. Woodcock finds his life to have been "curiously bourgeois" (Woodcock, *Stream and the Source,* 262). His accepting the knighthood was perhaps a failure of nerve, but Read did not read BBC propaganda during the war, which to me is a larger failure of responsibility to humanity.

6. See Clement Greenberg, *The Collected Essays and Criticism,* ed. John O'Brian (Chicago and London: University of Chicago Press, 1993); in vol. 1 (1939–44) there

are comments generally supportive of Read on modern poetry and surrealism; vol. 2 (1945–49) is very critical of Read on naturalism and abstraction; and in vol. 3 (1950–56) Greenberg finds him incoherent, not "incompetent" as Wyndham Lewis claims, but his aesthetic is "unthought out." Barnett Newman's comments are more cunning than Greenberg's, but not supportive of Read: *Barnett Newman, Selected Writings and Interviews* (Berkeley: University of California Press, 1992).

7. Alan Tate wrote the introduction to a selection of essays chosen by Read. The introduction is very complimentary, but does not see the continuity of Read's thirties' politics of art within Read's poetic development. Tate makes Read into a wholly Jungian symbolist, misinterprets Freud, and assumes that Read's anarchism is like the American new agrarian movement, which Tate claims is also a form of anarchism. See *Herbert Read, Selected Writings* (New York: Horizon Press, 1964).

8. For a recent provocative argument that reflects some of the same concerns of Read's, namely how to defend modernism against the avant-garde's mythologising of art as everyday praxis, see *Boris Groys, The Total Art of Stalinism, Avant-Garde, Aesthetic Dictatorship,and Beyond,* trans., Charles Rougle (Princeton: Princeton University Press, 1992), or the many works of Peter Bürger on the ambiguities of the avant-garde and radical modernism. Read's works in the sixties that reflect his struggle with the ethical basis of avant garde art are: *A Letter to a Young Painter* (London, Thames and Hudson, 1962); *The Forms of Things Unknown, An Essay on the Impact of the Technological Revolution on the Creative Arts* [subtitled on the frontispiece, *Essays towards an Aesthetic Philosophy*] (Cleveland and New York, The World Publishing Company, 1963), and *The Redemption of the Robot, My Encounter with Education through Art,* (New York: A Trident Press Book, 1966) and *Art and Alienation: The Role of the Artist in Society* (New York: Horizon Press, 1967). Epigraphs in the latter book are from Wordsworth and Marx. The young painter referred to in *Letters to a Painter* is the artist, Ruth Francken.

9. "Essential Communism," in Herbert Read, *Anarchy and Order* (Boston: Beacon, 1971; Faber and Faber, 1954); the essay "Essential Communism" was first published in Herbert Read, *Poetry and Anarchism* (1938).

10. David Thistlewood, "Herbert Read's Paradigm: A British Vision of Modernism," in *A British Vision of World Art,* ed. by Benedict Read and David Thistlewood, (Leeds: Leeds City Art Galleries, 1994), p. 91.

11. I argue a case for the continuity and difference in Read's work with Adorno, Benjamin, Marcuse, and Hauser in an essay in progress.

12. *The Contemporary Experience* (New York: Horizon Press, 1963), pg. 392.

13. Both Woodcock and Goodway cite Read's letter to Woodcock about Read's admiration for Orwell, but overestimate the letter's praise of Orwell. In my understanding of Read there can be no affinity between the two figures. Read's comment is of a sick and dying man who was simply accepting his own demise and Orwell's as well. See the letter reprinted in part in Goodway's *Herbert Read, A One-Man Manifesto,* 22. One also has to bear in mind to whom Read was writing, Woodcock who was determined to redeem Orwell as a savior for our times. This could not have failed to impress Read, but I am not convinced that Read saw Orwell as a great man or as a great writer. In addition, most commentators on Read's romance assume it is Jungian inspired. It is *both* Jungian and Freudian. In essence *The Green Child* is a self-criticism and a coming-to-terms with his own tormented, libidinous idealism.

Works Cited

King, James. 1990. *The Last Modern, A Life of Herbert Read.* London: Weidenfeld and Nicholson.

Read, Herbert. 1971. *Anarchy and Order*. Boston: Beacon Press.

———. 1963. *The Forms of Things Unknown*. Cleveland: Meridan Press.

———. 1963. *The Contrary Experience*. New York: Horizon Press.

———. 1936. *Surrealism*. Edited by Herbert Read. London: Faber and Faber.

Williams, Raymond. 1979. *Politics and Letters*. London: New Left Books.

Harrison, Charles. 1981. *English Art and Modernism*. London: Allan Lane.

Steele, Tom. 1990. *Alfred Orage and The Leeds Arts Club, 1893-1923*. Aldershot: Scholar Press.

A Bibliography of Works by and about Herbert Read

Writings on Herbert Read in Book Form

Barker, R. 1987. "A Critical Study of Herbert Read's The Green Child in the Light of Its Cultural Milieu." Ph.D. diss., University of London.

Berry, Francis. 1953, 1961. *Herbert Read. Writers and Their Work*, no. 45. London: Longmans Green, British Council.

Goodway, David. 1994 Introduction to *Herbert Read, A One-Man Manifesto and Other Writings from Freedom Press*. London: Freedom Press.

Hargreaves, Geoffrey. 1973. "Herbert Read as Poet." Ph.D. diss., University of Victoria.

Hortmann, Wilhelm. 1976. *Wenn die Kunst Stirbt*. Duisberg: Walter Braun Verlag.

Keel, John Siegfried. 1960. "The Writings of Herbert Read and Their Curricular Implications." Ph.D. diss., University of Wisconsin.

King, James. 1990. *The Last Modern, A Life of Herbert Read*. London, Weidenfeld and Nicholson.

Read, Ben, and David Thistlewood, eds. 1993. *Herbert Read A British Vision of World Art*. Leeds: Leeds City Galleries.

Skelton, Robin, ed. 1970 *Herbert Read: A Memorial Symposium*. London: Methuen.

Thistlewood, David. 1984. *Herbert Read: Formlessness and Form: An Introduction to His Aesthetics*. London: Routledge & Kegan Paul.

Treece, Henry. 1944. *Herbert Read: An Introduction to His Work by Various Hands*. London: Faber & Faber.

Woodcock, George. 1972. *Herbert Read: The Stream and the Source*. London: Faber and Faber.

1975. *A Tribute to Herbert Read 1893–1968*. Bradford: Art Galleries and Museums.

1984. *Homage to Herbert Read*. Canterbury College of Art.

Herbert Read's Published Works in the 1930s

The standard checklist of Herbert Read's publications by Salma M. Ghanem cites over 400 entries in the 1930s out of a total of 1,165 entries. This is not a complete list. The list cites publications from 1914 until 1962. This means that in the 1930s Read produced about one-third of his published works.

The Major Books That Should Be Associated with Herbert Read's Activities in the 1930s

————. 1926. *Collected Poems 1913–25*. London: Faber and Gwyer.

————. 1926. *Reason and Romanticism*. London: Faber and Gywer.

————. 1927. *Form in Gothic*. Edited by William Worringer, and translated by Herbert Read. London: G. P. Putnam's.

————. 1929. *The Sense of Glory; Essays in Criticism*. Cambridge: Cambridge University Press.

————. 1930. *Julien Benda and the New Humanism*. Seattle: University of Washington Bookstore.

————. 1930. *Wordsworth*. London: Jonathan Cape.

————. 1931. *The Meaning of Art*. London: Faber and Faber.

————. 1932. *Form in Modern Poetry:* London: Sheen and Ward.

————. 1933. *Art Now: An Introduction to the Theory of Modern Painting and Sculpture*. London: Faber and Faber.

————. 1934. *Art and Industry, the Principles of Industrial Design*. London: Faber and Faber.

————. 1934. *Henry Moore, Sculptor, an Appreciation*. London: Zwemmer.

————. 1934. *Unit One: The Modern Movement in English Architecture, Painting and Sculpture*. Edited by Herbert Read. London, Toronto, Melbourne, and Sydney: Casell and Co.

————. 1935. *Essential Communism*. London: Stanley Nott Ltd.

————. 1935. *The Green Child; a Romance*. London: Heinemann.

————. 1935. *Poems, 1914–1935*. London: Faber and Faber.

————. 1936. *Surrealism*. Edited by Herbert Read. London: Faber and Faber.

————. 1937. *Art and Society*. London: Heinemann.

————. 1938. *Collected Essays in Literary Criticism*. London: Faber and Faber.

————. 1938. *Poetry and Anarchism*. London: Faber and Faber.

————. 1940. *Annals of Innocence and Experience*. London: Faber and Faber.

————. 1940. *The Philosophy of Anarchism*. London: Freedom Press.

————. 1940. *Thirty-five Poems*. London: Faber and Faber.

————. 1940. *English Master Painters*. Edited by Herbert Read, London: Kegan Paul.

————. 1941. *To Hell with Culture; Democratic Values Are New Values*. London: Kegan Paul, Trench, Trubner.

2

David Jones's Thirties

JENNIFER FAIRLEY

A Brief Biographical Sketch of David Jones (1895–1974)

DAVID JONES WAS BORN AT BROCKLEY IN KENT ON I NOVEMBER 1895. An exceptionally talented artist, he studied at the Camberwell Art School under A. S. Hartrick, from the age of fourteen until the outbreak of war in 1914. In January 1915 he enlisted as a private with the Royal Welch Fusiliers and served on the Western Front until 1918. After the war a government grant enabled him to study at the Westminster School of Art until 1921.

Jones was received into the Roman Catholic Church in 1921. That same year he met Eric Gill and in 1924 he became a postulant of the Guild of St. Joseph and St. Dominic, living and working with Gill's Ditchling community until August of that year. Between 1924 and 1934 Jones spent some time with the Gills in Wales and in England. During this time he learned the art of wood engraving, designing illustrations for the Golden Cockerel Press. In 1928, the year he started to write *In Parenthesis,* he was elected a member of the Seven and Five Society of artists and sculptors. He stopped painting for a while after a nervous breakdown in 1932.

In Parenthesis was published in 1937 with support from T. S. Eliot, winning the Hawthornden Prize in 1938. Between 1939 and 1945 Jones wrote the first drafts of *The Kensington Mass* and material for *The Anathemata* (1952) and *The Sleeping Lord, and Other Fragments* (1974).

Jones was awarded an Honorary D.Litt from the University of Wales, Aberystwyth, in 1960, and in 1961 was made a Fellow of the Royal Society of Literature, and of the Royal Water Color Society. A fractured hip in 1970 resulted in his spending the remainder of his life in the Calvary Nursing Home, Harrow-on-the-Hill. In June 1974 Jones was made a Companion of Honor in the Queen's Birthday Honors List. He died on 28 October 1974, a few days before his seventy-ninth birthday.

* * * * *

"In the 1930s there was, I think, a feeling that liaison with the whole past of man-the-artist was still possible however 'contemporary' the images employed" (Jones "Notes on the 1930s" in *The Dying Gaul and Other Writings* 1978, 48). So writes David Jones in a 1960s retrospective of the thirties in which he speaks of his own position at that time as being "peripheral," "complex," or "ambiguous" in relation to the contemporary major movements. A sense of periphery and isolation was apparent to a certain extent in much of Jones's postwar life; as a member of Eric Gill's Catholic artistic community for a time during the 1920s and 1930s, and later in a succession of hotel rooms, or "dug-outs." His habit of surrounding himself with his belongings created a curious state of continuity with his own past, alongside a sense of dislocation from the outside world. A similar air of continuity and fragmentation exists in his art and in his writings, in which he uses mythical archetypes to explore, and to attempt to anchor, twentieth-century states of being.

Jones, although not associated with the Auden group, was nevertheless aligned with other thirties artists. Born in 1895, he was a modernist writer contemporary with T. S. Eliot, Virginia Woolf, and James Joyce, although the last of these to publish. He was converted to Catholicism in 1921; a factor which had a profound effect on his poetry, prose, and painting. A survivor of the First World War, he was among writers such as Robert Graves and Wyndham Lewis who delayed the writing of their war experiences. Jones was also one of a number of writers during the thirties exploring various facets of the Arthurian myth.

In "Notes on the 1930s," Jones details his chief concern; the tension which he perceives between man as artist and the contemporary world in which he lives, largely as a result of a "civilisational change" of unprecedented proportions. By this, he means the advances in science and technology which he and others felt to be destroying traditional ways of life and culture. At the root of Jones's concerns was that his defined role as an artist, "making things that are 'significant', that . . . can be justified only as signs of something other" (*The Dying Gaul*, 47), was incompatible with the strictly utile nature of modern technology, "devices that serve a definable purpose and

[which] are in no sense made as signa of something other than themselves" (*The Dying Gaul*, 45).

Jones's poetry and art cluster around mythical centers. Contemporary technology, for Jones, denotes the purely practical or "utile":
he speaks of the "contrivances of our technology which have as their
end pure utility" (*The Dying Gaul*, 47). As these "contrivances"
contain no apparent element of sign, sacrament, or humanity, they
cannot be appropriated into the poetic tradition of myth-making in
which he works, except to symbolize or mythologize utility. "A, a,
a, Domine Deus," begun around 1938, demonstrates clearly Jones's
unease with the modern world which he feels denies the poet the
materials of tradition. Spender's pylons "have no secret"; Jones, too,
can find no adequate symbolism within the utile constructions:

> I said, Ah! What shall I write?
> .   .   .   .
> I have journeyed among the dead forms
> causation projects from pillar to pylon.
> (*The Sleeping Lord and Other Fragments* 1974, 9)

Jones, in "Domine Deus," makes a work of art from his artistic
concerns. He attempts to bring modern technology, the "unfamiliar," within an existing cultural tradition, articulating his search:

> I have been on my guard
>   not to condemn the unfamiliar.
> For it is easy to miss Him
>   at the turn of a civilisation.
> (*The Sleeping Lord* 9)

Jones constructs a work of poetry using the modernity of contemporary technology, but seems unable to construct a liaison with anything preceding that technology.

For Jones, the patternings and order made possible through
mythical archetypes formed an essential element of his work. Myth
can be said to offer the poet, "a complete and ordered cosmos, an
irreducible system of coherent belief upon which he can construct
an ordered and meaningful poetry" (Moorman 1960, 2). Jones, like
Eliot's version of Joyce, found some aspect of order in preexisting
mythical patternings. Jones, however, determined to search for patterns of meanings within the modern world of technology, to attempt to draw it within the past. It seems, though, that his
retrospective view of the thirties as a time when liaison with the
past was still possible, is evident only in his essays. The search which

he details in the thirties' section of "Domine Deus" does not appear to come to fruition.

Despite his fears for the future of man-the-artist, Jones speaks of the 1930s as a time of relative optimism. This air of optimism, however, is confined largely to his observations on the effect of the works of anthropology, mythology, psychology, and archaeology, on the writers of the 1920s and 1930s. Jones cites Joyce as a "quintessentially incarnational" writer using specific locality "to express a universal concept" (*The Dying Gaul* 46). At a time of fears for the survival of "rooted cultures of all sorts" (*The Dying Gaul* 46), Jones believes the artist to be an essential figure, no less than the bards of ancient tribes, as a '"rememberer" and continuator of the tradition . . . of tribal organism' (*The Dying Gaul* 47). This concept gives the artist an aura of urgency and loads the making of a work of art with a great weight. The associated need for social and cultural responsibility is apparent in the quest structures which inform *In Parenthesis*, (1937) Jones's major thirties writing, based around his experiences of the First World War.

Jones's views on the contemporary political situation are discussed in his December 1938 review of René Hague's translation of *The Song of Roland*. Jones uses the review, "The Roland Epic and Ourselves" to explore "a few ideas which it evokes" about the current situation. These ideas, extraordinary in their fusion of political naïveté, and vision, usefully demonstrate Jones's apocalyptic interpretation of contemporary history. Jones's discussion of the work utilizes the language of war and propaganda to reflect upon hostilities both present and past, which render the individual "poor old Jerry" into a collective and monstrous pack of "black heathens." This method of conflating chauvinistic clichés highlights the eternal hypocrisy and the arbitrary nature of war propaganda. Jones had passed through the chauvinistic stage early in the First World War and his dedication to *In Parenthesis* includes, "the enemy front-fighters who shared our pains against whom we found ourselves by misadventure" (*In Parenthesis,* xvii). Jones's reminder of a collective hatred informed by fear and ignorance is timely.

More disturbing is Jones's assimilation of dictators such as Mussolini and Hitler into the realms of heroic romance as resurgent "cult-heroes," a "wild unicorn" able to be tamed only by "a mistress with vision"(*The Dying Gaul* 99). Jones's complex arguments in the review are centered around *The Song of Roland,* a medieval text dealing with an apocalyptic ending, losses, and mass destruction; a text which certainly recognizes the fractures and fissures in the heroic code. The absorption of contemporary political conflict into recur-

rent patterns of myth and history, however, effectively dilutes what
are quietly passionate pleas from a survivor of three years of World
War I, for unity and avoidance of war. The current political dilemma—confrontation or appeasement—is couched in the language
of romance. Jones, in his attempts to put together again "our tum-
bled European Humpty Dumpty," presents the dilemma in a fusion
of romance, tragedy, and ancient history, thereby dissipating the
immediacy of the problem.

> Always pressing upon the ordered scheme from without (miscalculated
> by the tired elements within—the worst enemy), the unicorns (as Penda)
> not to be bought off, must be reckoned with, understood, baptized,
> assimilated, or left to run, misjudged, "forbidden water"—no truck
> with, or (which cannot be) an attempted extermination. If not the for-
> mer, then the latter; if the latter, then, in the end, the Duce's "drama":
>   O Balan my brother, thou hast slain me and I thee,
>   wherefore all the wide world shall speak of us both. (*The Dying
> Gaul* 102)

The fraternal nature of Europe's tribal origins are highlighted in the
quoted passage by the Malorian reference to the two brothers Balin
and Balan who, mutually unrecognized, killed each other. Themes of
political and social disorder are integral to the tale; the great tragedy
described in Malory is not confined to the individuals but reverber-
ates throughout the entire nation, the "Dolorous Stroke" laying
waste the whole land. The theme of conflict arising from noncognition is intrinsic to Jones's vision of human history. Ironically, the
elements of profound tragedy inherent in many of Jones's allusions
remained unrecognized by his audience.

It seems that, for Jones, the continuing condition of war provides
the necessary qualities for connecting past and present. Written during the last two years of the 1920s and the first half of the 1930s, *In
Parenthesis* deals with a tightly focused period of time between 1915
and 1916. Jones takes issues contemporary to that period, but in his
1937 preface, speaks of a significant change that took place during
1916, and that, "Even while we watch the boatman mending his
sail, the petroleum is hurting the sea" (*In Parenthesis,* ix). This sense
of a vital break with traditional ways of life and communities is
apparent in René Hague's definition of *In Parenthesis* as "a poetic
transmutation of personal experience into a memorial to, and a la-
ment for, the ancient unity of this island of Britain" (Hague, 1975
20).

Consistent with the period in which it was composed, the title *In
Parenthesis* denotes an intermediary or liminal stage: "I have written

it in a kind of space between—I don't know between quite what—but as you turn aside to do something" (*In Parenthesis,* xv). The form of the text, described by its author as "a shape in words," exhibits a similar liminal state, frequently shifting between prose and poetry, defying strict generic categorization.

A state of liminality permeates *In Parenthesis* which effectively becomes a quest for a sense of place, both physically for the men involved, and culturally and historically in terms of the experience. Joseph Campbell, in his thesis on the hero myth, ascribes the hero's function as a guide across "those difficult thresholds of transformation that demand a change in the patterns" both of conscious and of unconscious life (Campbell 1949, 10). The prologue to *In Parenthesis* places the text upon a physical and mental threshold, with an extract taken from the Branwen branch of the *Mabinogion,* where the door is opened, imparting awareness on the men "of all the friends and companions they had lost and of all the misery that had befallen them . . . and because of their perturbation they could not rest" (*In Parenthesis,* xix). This sense of sorrowful unease, commensurate with the Catholic state of purgatory, denotes a transitional period; it attributes to the text a sense of continuum, echoed in the lack of closure at the conclusion—there is no neat ending to the experience. Unlike Robert Graves's *Goodbye to All That,* the ghosts are not exorcised through the act of writing; the unease percolates through to, and beyond, the time of composition.

In an attempt to place or replace its characters within a cultural and national tradition, within the "familiar," *In Parenthesis* is informed by a series of quest structures appropriated from Christian archetypes, medieval literature, from their modern interpretation by Jessie Weston, and from Lewis Carroll's parody of the quest, *The Hunting of the Snark.* The eclectic nature of the allusions "conceal" a deeper thematic unity; mirroring Jones's perception of Europe in the 1930s.

During the 1920s, Jessie Weston had created bases for the Grail myth to be appropriated as a contemporary image. Jones had read *From Ritual to Romance* in 1929, and subsequently used the secular Grail myth, with its close Christian parallels, to signal regeneration within the context of a spiritually derelict present.[1] For Jones, grounded in the Thomist theory of "working from the known to the unknown," the Grail provided the necessary pattern of death and rebirth, with sufficient temporal and cultural patterns to sustain its potency.

Weston identified the ancient Grail symbols, the Cup and the Lance, with her theory of Vegetation rites, suggesting that the hero who asked the question concerning the nature of the maimed Grail

King, "had won the sacred kingship not by valour alone, but by entering into conscious awareness of the instinctive process of renewal" (Prudence Jones 1990, 142). *In Parenthesis*, contextualized within the cultural wasteland of the 1930s, "where waste-land meets environs and punctured bins ooze canned-meats discarded" (*In Parenthesis*, 75), signals a continuing need for physical and spiritual renewal through the development of a conscious awareness of a culture in danger of dying.

The elements of noncognition of the sacramental described in Jones's essays are explored in *In Parenthesis* through quest rituals, interpreted by Weston as a search for the meaning of physical renewal and spiritual life. Weston's offering of the Grail as an archetypal storehouse of British cultural origins is appropriated by Jones as a continuing valid myth central to the British Isles; a unifying device between past and present, and between the heterogeneous groups of men from London and Wales, who "bore in their bodies the genuine tradition of the Island of Britain, from Bendigeid Vran to Jingle and Marie Lloyd" (*In Parenthesis*, x). Cultural tradition goes largely unrecognized, however; only Aneirin Lewis "had somewhere in his Welsh depths a remembrance of the nature of man" (*In Parenthesis*, 2). This process describes the order that Jones is seeking to impart upon *In Parenthesis* as a whole.

In an attempt to aid cognition, Dai Greatcoat, a figure cloaked in mystery, makes a speech couched in mysterious terms, which can be equated with the legendary boast of Taliessin. Dai's boast, or riddle, articulates the condition of human conflict evident since ancient history, emphasizing its continuity, concluding with an exhortation to his listeners:

> You ought to ask: Why,
> what is this,
> what's the meaning of this.
> Because you don't ask,
> although the spear-shaft
> drips,
> there's neither steading—not a roof-tree.
>
> (*In Parenthesis*, 84)

In his adaptation of the Taliessin speech, Jones has given answers. Without their relevant questions, however, they are of no use. Jones's direct reference here is to the Welsh *Percivale* story where Peredur is blamed for the devastation: "thou didst not enquire their meaning nor their cause" (*In Parenthesis* 210 n.M). In his essay, "Art in Relation to War," Jones proposes, "if all the world asked the question perhaps there might be some fructification—or some 'sea-change'" (*The Dying Gaul* 123). The speech of Dai suggests a similar proposal to restore meaning by reawakening cultural awareness.

Written at the beginning of the 1940s, the essay "Art in Relation to War" explores problems unresolved by Jones during the 1930s. Proposing that all our artistic and cultural tradition "is of war, and the hero at his tasks" (*The Dying Gaul* 126), Jones believes that the nature of modern life and warfare makes "technical and utilitarian demands" which are reducing civilization to a formless mass. Jones's task is to recover the cultural tradition through a portrayal of modern warfare which appropriates the symbolism of an earlier tradition, and draws attention to its erosion.

The overall effect achieved in *In Parenthesis* is of a generalized wasteland resulting from the mechanized and industrial way of life; already an accepted element of the 1930s. The mechanics of warfare have destroyed the natural aspects of the woods; removing by a "great fixed gulf" the refuge to which men have traditionally come, "both to their joys and their undoing" (*In Parenthesis* 66). Now, instead, the army draughtsman "keeps date with the genius of the place" by marking on a blueprint, "the significance of that grove as one of his strong points" (*In Parenthesis* 66).

In his essay on "The Myth of Arthur," Jones notes, "Arthur's power dissolves with the disappearing, in dark water, of Excalibur" (*Epoch and Artist* 1959, 239). The loss of power is suggested metaphorically in part 3 of *In Parenthesis* where the sword is referred to merely as part of the description of the landscape: "a circular calm water graced the deep of a Johnson hole; corkscrew-picket-iron half submerged, as dark excalibur, by perverse incantation twisted' (*In Parenthesis,* 50). The old symbols of power still exist, it seems, though devoid of power in the wasteland of modern warfare, perhaps because they are not recognized in the cultural hiatus. Jones creates a feeling of helplessness, with no discernible way forward. Nothing, except cognition, exists which will make sense of the chaos. Yet there is no recognized tradition in this wasteland for the "common run," by which to measure the future, "you have no mensuration gear to plot meandering fortune-graph" (*In Parenthesis* 159).

The quest of the author of *In Parenthesis* can be seen in terms of describing the necessary process of recognition. Although the text concentrates on the liminal experience of the Fifty-fifth Battalion "B" Company, the three stages of the rites of passage are described: the separation, initiation, and (potential) return of the hero. The detachment of the men from their country and from their normal lives is portrayed in terms of rebirth into "this new world" (*In Parenthesis,* 9), with the childlike frailty of the soldiers evoking "almost motherly concern" from the officers. A series of initiations are described, equating both with the general hero myth, but also with the two stages of the Grail quest proposed by Weston; the first being an initiation into the mysteries of "generation," of physical life, the second into the spiritual life.

There is an element of symbolic rebirth for the men "confined in small dug concavities, wombed of earth, their rubber-sheets for caul" (*In Parenthesis* 75–76), and a heavily ironic element of regeneration for the wounded, appropriating images from Eliot's *Waste Land:*

> you musn't spill the precious fragments, for perhaps these
> raw bones live.
>   They can cover him again with skin—in their candid coats,
> in the clinical shrines and parade the miraculi.
>
> (*In Parenthesis* 175)

Consistent with the failure of the majority of Malory's Grail questors, the ultimate end of the men is physical death. Any element of rebirth is portrayed with reference to vegetative cycles—John Barleycorn, symbol of death and rebirth in the English folk tradition, is represented by John Ball, who is "cut down at knee" by a bullet, but who lives to incorporate the dead in a metaphoric rebirth within his tale of myth. The essential return phase of the quest occurs "when the questor goes back home with whatever boon he has uncovered to share it with his people" (Prudence Jones, 83). John Ball, the central protagonist and sole survivor, however, is, like Malory's Bors and like the reader, left to decode his own experience.

In Parenthesis concludes with a concealment: "Oeth and Annoeth's hosts they were . . . " (*In Parenthesis,* 187), the mythical heroes whose whereabouts are secret, hidden. The quest is concluded by signaling the need for a further quest. Within the given structures, an end always precedes another beginning. Jones's use of archetypal structures, however, signals a redemptive element within the conclusion. The lack of closure within the text is analogous to the role of the hero in Malorian referents, as "the once and future king."

In Parenthesis is a work which seeks, in its portrayal of liminality, to transcend that state. It aims to place its characters and their experiences within an existing tradition, within the continuity of art and war. Jones's self-professed and committed role as a writer and painter is to highlight the essentially sacramental nature of the arts, to provide a valid means by which the sign world can be carried forward into the future. One threshold may be crossed, but it seems only to lead to others. The qualified sense of optimism apparent in Jones's thirties' writing is perhaps best illustrated by his reaction to the statue of the Dying Gaul which, he says, left him with a sense of a "continuity of struggle and a continuity of loss" (*The Dying Gaul* 26). The redeeming element of this rather somber view of humanity, however, is voiced by Jones in the words of Joyce, "Bedad he revives! See how he raises!" (*The Dying Gaul* 58). It is this sense of redemption which, ultimately, informs the subtext of Jones's work, both in the thirties and beyond.

Notes

1. In a letter dated "Holy Saturday 1932," Jones speaks of managing to "get out to part of the vegetation rites of the Redeemed this morning," in Jones, *Dai Greatcoat: A Self-Portrait of David Jones in His Letters,* ed. René Hague (London: Faber and Faber, 1980), 50.

Works Cited

Campbell, Joseph. 1949. *The Hero With a Thousand Faces*. Vol. 17. Bollingen Series Princeton, N.J.: Princeton University Press.

Hague, René. 1975. *David Jones*. Cardiff: University of Wales Press.

———. 1980. *Dai Greatcoat: A Self-Portrait of David Jones in his Letters*. Edited by René Hague. London: Faber and Faber.

Jones, David. 1937. *In Parenthesis*. Faber and Faber.

———. 1959. The Myth of Arthur in *Epoch and Artist*. London: Faber and Faber.

———. 1974. *The Sleeping Lord and Other Fragments*. London: Faber and Faber.

———. 1978. "Notes on the 1930s." and "The Roland Epic as Ourselves" In *The Dying Gaul and Other Writings*. Edited by Harman Grisewood. London: Faber and Faber.

Jones, Prudence. 1990. "The Grail Quest as Initiation." In *The Household of the Grail*. Wellingborough: The Aquarian Press.

Moorman, Charles. 1960. *Arthurian Triptych: Mythic Materials in Charles Williams, C.S. Lewis, and T.S. Eliot*. Berkeley: University of California Press.

Weston, Jessie, L. 1920. *From Ritual to Romance*. New York: Macmillan Co.

A Bibliography of Works by and about David Jones

Primary

———. 1937. *In Parenthesis*. London: Faber and Faber.

———. 1952. *The Anathemata*. London: Faber and Faber.

———. 1959. *Epoch and Artist*. London: Faber and Faber.

———. 1974. *The Sleeping Lord and Other Fragments*. London: Faber and Faber.

————. 1975. *The Kensington Mass*. London: Agenda Editions.

————. 1976. *Letters to Vernon Watkins*. Edited by Ruth Pryor. Cardiff: University of Wales Press.

————. 1978. *The Dying Gaul and Other Writings*. Edited by Harman Grisewood. London: Faber and Faber.

————. 1979. *Letters to William Hayward*. Edited by Colin Wilcockson. London: Agenda Editions.

————. 1980. *The Roman Quarry and Other Sequences*. Edited by Harman Grisewood and René Hague. London: Agenda Editions.

————. 1981. *Dai Greatcoat: A Self-Portrait of David Jones in His Letters*. Edited by René Hague. London: Faber and Faber.

————. 1980. *Letters to a Friend*. Edited by A. T. Davies. Swansea: Triskele.

Secondary

Blamires, David. 1971. *David Jones Artist and Writer*. Manchester: Manchester University Press.

Blissett, William. 1981. *The Long Conversation: A Memoir of David Jones*. Oxford, Oxford University Press.

Corcoran, Neil. 1982. *The Song of Deeds: A Study of The Anathemata of David Jones*. Cardiff: University of Wales Press.

Dilworth, Thomas. 1988. *The Shape of Meaning in the Poetry of David Jones*. Toronto: University of Toronto Press.

Gray, Nicolete. 1981. *The Painted Inscriptions of David Jones*. London: Gordon Fraser.

————. 1989. *The Paintings of David Jones*. London: John Taylor/Lund Humphries.

Hague, René. 1975. *David Jones*. Cardiff: University of Wales Press.

————. 1977. *A Commentary on The Anathemata of David Jones*. Wellingborough: Christopher Skelton.

Hooker, Jeremy. 1975. *David Jones: An Exploratory Study of the Writings*. London: Enitharmon Press.

Hughes, Colin. 1979. *David Jones, The Man Who Was on the Field: In Parenthesis as Straight Reporting*. Manchester: David Jones Society.

Mathias, Roland, ed. 1976. *David Jones: Eight Essays on His Work as Writer and Artist*. Llandysul: Gomer Press.

Matthias, John, ed. 1989. *David Jones: Man and Poet*. Orono: The National Poetry Foundation.

Miles, Jonathan. *Backgrounds to David Jones: A Study in Sources and Drafts*. Cardiff: University of Wales Press.

————. 1992. *Eric Gill and David Jones at Capel-y-Ffin*. Bridgend: Seren Books.

Pacey, Philip. 1982. *David Jones and Other Wonder Voyages*. Bridgend: Poetry Wales Press.

Pagnoulle, Christine. 1987. *David Jones: A Commentary on some Poetic Fragments*. Cardiff: University of Wales Press.

Raine, Kathleen. 1978. *David Jones and Actually Loved and Known*. Ipswich: Golgonooza Press.

Summerfield, Henry. 1979. *An Introductory Guide to The Anathemata and The Sleeping Lord Sequence of David Jones*. Victoria: Sono Nis Press.

Ward, Elizabeth. 1983. *David Jones Myth-Maker*. Manchester: Manchester University Press.

3
R. H. Mottram: The Great War and *Europa's Beast*

STEVEN TROUT

A Brief Biographical Sketch of R. H. Mottram (1883–1971)

Born in Norwich, Ralph Hale Mottram worked as chief clerk for Gurney's Bank, the Norwich firm which had employed his family for generations, before becoming a professional writer in 1927. A friend of John Galsworthy, whose influence can be detected throughout Mottram's fiction, he first achieved critical notoriety and commercial success with *The Spanish Farm Trilogy* (1924–26), a realistic study of several English and Flemish characters set in Flanders and covering the years from 1914 to 1918. The first volume won the Hawthornden Prize in 1924. The Great War, which Mottram witnessed as a junior officer, also inspired many of his later works, including *Ten Years Ago: Armistice, and Other Memories* (1928), *Through the Menin Gate* (1932), and *Journey to the Western Front Twenty Years After* (1936). In addition, the conflict plays an important role in Mottram's novel *Europa's Beast* (1930), a work that, like Ford Madox Ford's *Last Post* (1928) or Virginia Woolf's *Mrs. Dalloway* (1925), offers a disparaging assessment of English culture in the 1920s. The rest of Mottram's enormous output, consisting of more than sixty volumes, includes travel guides, banking histories, Christmas books, biographies, poetry, dozens of novels (most of them set in his native East Anglia), and several volumes of autobiography. A nostalgia for late nineteenth-century England infuses much of this material, thus separating Mottram from other writers of his generation, such as Richard Aldington or Henry Williamson, who lashed out against alleged Victorian hypocrisies and the imperialistic values that led to the Great War. Mottram rejected the avant-garde as well.

51

He remained, like Galsworthy, unadventurous in terms of narrative technique, and eschewed the literary experimentation of Joyce and Woolf. A Fellow of the Royal Society of Literature, Mottram was granted, toward the end of his long and prolific career, an honorary Doctor of Letters by the University of East Anglia. *The Spanish Farm Trilogy,* a classic text in the literature of the Great War, remains his best-known work.

* * * * *

Few conflicts have fostered more literary obsessions than the Great War. Siegfried Sassoon, who might never have become a serious writer without the First World War, subjected the immeasurable impact of the conflict on his life to an intense autobiographical scrutiny sustained throughout the 1920s and 1930s. Likewise, Henry Williamson returned to the war throughout his prolific career, ultimately making it the focus of his gargantuan cycle of fifteen novels, *A Chronicle of Ancient Sunlight* (1937–67). The Great War, as a subject, also made careers and reputations—especially Erich Maria Remarque's, R. C. Sherriff's, Vera Brittain's, and, to some extent, Robert Graves's. Few cases of either obsession or sudden notoriety were as spectacular, however, as that of R. H. Mottram, whose novel of wartime Flanders, *The Spanish Farm* (1924), established him, virtually overnight, as an influential literary commentator on the Great War.

Mottram's first three novels, collected as *The Spanish Farm Trilogy* in 1927, comprise a still-unsurpassed fictional mosaic of the region in Belgium and northern France where nearly a million British soldiers lost their lives. Focusing on the interaction between a Flemish farming family, whose home, an ancient Spanish stronghold, the British army uses as a rear-area billet, and an assortment of English characters, the trilogy provides what Michael Garrety has aptly called "a primer of the Western Front" (Garrety 1978, 17). By examining the lives of the Flemish peasantry (who are either maligned or ignored in most First World War novels or memoirs), and by analyzing their culture beside that of the men comprising the British army, Mottram achieves a sense of breadth, of near-epic scale, lacking in most fiction about the Great War. In a genre dominated by the quest, by passages or "progresses" through alien, bewildering territory— think of Siegfried Sassoon's *Sherston's Progress* or Henry Williamson's *The Patriot's Progress*—the trilogy presents the Great War not as modern chaos, terrifyingly incomprehensible to the individual

observer, but as an historical event as accessible to the realistic novelist as Napoleon's Russian campaign had been to Tolstoy.

In spite of the considerable acclaim won by *The Spanish Farm
Trilogy,* which triumphed at a time when publishers typically rejected war-related manuscripts on sight, Mottram's subsequent
work, a vast array, remains almost completely forgotten.[1] Although
he produced a formidable oeuvre, more than sixty books, the her-
alded author of *The Spanish Farm* never recaptured his early success—and not without reason. His choice of subjects, often
infelicitous, explains some of this neglect. A former bank clerk,
whose father, grandfather, and great-grandfather succeeded one another as manager of Gurney's Bank in Norwich, Mottram retained
an interest in finance throughout his life, and wrote several books
on the history of English banking and speculation. Less pecuniary
works from Mottram's five decades of writing—he published, on
average, at least a book a year—include a guide to waterways in East
Anglia, volumes of poetry, a biography of John Galsworthy, whom
Mottram (like Conrad) credited with giving him his start in writing,
and a biography of Mottram's father, entitled *Portrait of an Unknown
Victorian* (1936). In novels such as *Our Mister Dormer* (1927), a fictionalized account of his family's century of service to Gurney's
Bank, or *The Bouroughmonger* (1929), set at the time of the First
Reform Bill, Mottram tried his hand at historical fiction.

Though competently written, none of this material is terribly interesting. Mottram was at his best when exploring the subject that
served him so well at the beginning of his career—the Great War.
And, despite his numerous forays into other areas, he returned to
the conflict with obsessive regularity: in fact, one of his final works
was an essay, entitled "Stand To!," included in George Panichas's
fifty-year retrospect on the Great War, *Promise of Greatness: The War
of 1914–1918* (1968). In the 1930s, Mottram stood equal in renown
with Robert Graves, Edmund Blunden, Siegfried Sassoon, and
Henry Williamson as a participant in the ongoing literary debate
over the conduct of the war and the accuracy of the official history.
In publishing ventures related to the conflict, he was ubiquitous—
supplying, for example, a preface for Ernst Jünger's *Storm of Steel*
(1929), appearing in collections of stories about the Great War, and
reporting on the Menin Gate inauguration, held in 1927, for an
English periodical. Mottram also continued to write about the Great
War, and its aftermath, in a series of novels, collections of short
stories, and autobiographical works that spans most of the 1930s:
Armistice and Other Memories (1928), *Europa's Beast* (1930), *Through*

the Menin Gate (1932), and Journey to the Western Front Twenty Years After (1936).

These war-related works of the 1930s—vital documents from a decade marked, in England, by frenetic cultural mythification of the Great War—deserve, I think, greater critical attention. An elegant example of a now-forgotten genre, the Western Front travel narrative, Journey to the Western Front Twenty Years After, for example, poignantly captures the mixture of horror and nostalgia with which survivors of the Great War looked back on their experiences. It could stand reprinting. Likewise, "A Personal Record," Mottram's war memoir included in the collection of stories and autobiographical essays, Through the Menin Gate, is a superlative account, perhaps lacking the individuality of Edmund Blunden's Undertones of War (1928) or Roberts Graves's Good-bye to All That (1929), but richly detailed and vivid.

In terms of fiction, Mottram's novel Europa's Beast, the focus of this discussion, represents a fascinating, if uneven, effort to create a comprehensive mythical interpretation of the Great War. And it is through this novel that we see Mottram's connection with many other writers of the 1930s, their shared preoccupation with the disorienting contrasts between England after the war and the England of 1914, described as "pre-history" in Richard Aldington's Death of a Hero (1929, 199). Of course, the late 1920s and early 1930s marked a watershed in the mythification of the Great War; for example, the sudden outpouring in 1929 and 1930 of "war books"—novels and memoirs detailing combat experience—helped to establish in cultural memory what Samuel Hynes has called the "Myth of the War," a montage of suicidal attacks, bumbling generals, shell shock, and depravity. Other novels published during the interwar decades assessed the Great War as a cultural debacle, as the dividing line between an age of stability and reason and one of chaos and irrationality—or, worse, of emptiness. In F. Scott Fitzgerald's Tender Is the Night (1933), an American example, Dick Diver broods over the Somme battlefield: "All my beautiful lovely safe world," he comments, "blew itself up here" (Fitzgerald, 68). Ford Madox Ford's Parade's End (1924–28) and H. M. Tomlinson's All Our Yesterdays (1930) work from the same conceit, examining England before, during, and after the cataclysm.

Likewise, Mottram's Europa's Beast gloomily eulogizes, by painting a gray portrait of the 1920s, the England irretrievably lost in 1914. Set in an East Anglican cathedral city ("Easthampton" modeled after Norwich) several years after the armistice, the novel picks up the story of Geoffrey Skene, one of the major English characters in *The Spanish Farm Trilogy,* tracing his romantic involvement with a much younger, married woman, Olive Blythway, whose husband has been left unbalanced by a wartime head wound. The novel moves back and forth, in alternating chapters, between Olive's unhappy marriage and Skene's own vague sense of discontent until, ultimately, the lovers are united.

In many respects, *Europa's Beast* closely resembles D. H. Lawrence's *Lady Chatterley's Lover* (1928), yet another delineation of the postwar period, or the "tragic age" as Lawrence described it (Lawrence 1983, 1). (In turn, Mottram's novel perhaps influenced Christopher Isherwood's rendering of the 1920s, in *The Memorial,* published two years later.) Like Constance Chatterley, Mottram's heroine endures marriage to a crippled symbol of the technological reshaping of England, a reshaping introduced, according to Mottram, by the ultramechanized Great War. While Lawrence cruelly symbolizes Clifford Chatterley's inadequacies through his motorized wheelchair, Olive's husband, Ray Blythway, is literally part machine: a silver plate, which occasionally requires adjustment, covers part of his skull. His wound causes him to act like a contraption rather than a man, as if, as his increasingly dissatisfied wife observes, he were "wound up" or "automatic" (*Europa's Beast,* 199). Moreover, Ray is both victim and lover of gadgetry. Nearly blown up during the war by a torpedo (he ultimately dies in a plane crash), Ray is obsessed with machinery and speed; he works at a local car dealership, selling ever faster and sleeker sports cars, while flying in aviation competitions in his spare time. His no less mechanical lovemaking horrifies his wife, who, when she discovers that her robotic marriage will further be complicated by a child, falls into a severe depression that results in a miscarriage.

Geoffrey Skene emerges as Mellors in the novel's Lawrentian triangle. No longer the somewhat one-dimensional character of *The Spanish Farm Trilogy,* Skene becomes in *Europa's Beast* a representative, like Ford Madox Ford's Christopher Tietjens (or, later, Evelyn Waugh's Guy Crouchback), of values and traditions fast disappearing in modern England. While Ray promotes sports cars, Skene designs houses, working to remedy the postwar housing shortage with structures that combine modern utility with aesthetic beauty. As an architect, he aspires to a permanence and immobility that Ray has rejected, and that the Great War has seemingly destroyed. Mottram also contrasts Skene's comparatively stable and static social background as a member of Easthampton's "old Middle class" with Olive's vulgar father, a bounder and war profiteer, and with Ray's parents, aristocrats fallen on hard times. Thus, although Skene's professional activity masks, as we will see, his profound inner despair, his occupation and social background place him in symbolic opposition to the forces transforming postwar England.

Caught between these two men is Olive Blythway, whom Clark Thayer describes as "a young woman who seems to have stepped from an Evelyn Waugh novel leaving all the comedy behind" (Thayer 1985, 177). Admittedly, when compared with Madeline Vanderlynden, one of Mottram's great achievements, Olive seems a tepid creation. Yet her lack of dimension derives partly from one of Mottram's themes—the corrosive materialism of modern England. As an adolescent, Olive dreams of becoming one of the "prominent young hostesses" featured on the pages of *Onlooker, Gossip,* and other high-society tabloids (*Europa's Beast,* 34). Even her decision to serve as a nurse during the war derives from this ambition: attached to a prestigious London hospital, she looks forward to being presented at court, and is pleased that she can select the colors for her uniform, becoming a "perfectly-turned-out angel, hovering, skillful and noiseless, by the bedside of suffering"(41). Marriage to Lord Blythway's son, whom she attends in the ward for head-wound patients, seems the logical next step.

Yet beneath Olive's crass pursuit of social notoriety, a pursuit ultimately frustrated by her discovery that the Blythways have little money, runs an unconscious dissatisfaction with the values she has chosen. A recurring erotic fantasy, inspired by Cagliari's painting *The Rape of Europa,* haunts her each night as she lies half-awake (having consigned Ray to another bedroom): she imagines herself as a naked beauty, a sacrifice, "reclining, with the admiring assistance of other beauties, on the back of a great white bull," an appropriately Lawrentian image of the intuitive, sexual life that Olive has denied (*Europa's Beast,* 203). Olive also betrays her hidden longing for an earthier, more passionate existence through her affection for her grandmother, an epileptic gypsy with the "startling eyes of an owl," who, in one of the novel's clumsiest scenes, prophesies Ray's death in a flying accident (104).

Rather surprisingly—given his initial characterization as the somewhat stuffy, tradition-bound vanguard of Easthampton's old middle class—Skene turns out to be the white bull of Olive's fantasy, Europa's ravisher. Enlisted by a local philanthropist to work together on a charity project, an exhibition devoted to local history (Mottram contrasts Skene's contribution to the display, some paintings of old Easthampton, with Ray's, a pair of prints depicting the local Aerodrome), the two quickly fall in love. And, in a sudden, passionate break from convention, Skene embraces Olive as she stands like a "sacrifice"—that is, Europa—holding up one of his lovingly rendered paintings of eighteenth- and nineteenth-century buildings (*Europa's Beast*, 179). Paradoxically, Mottram joins the couple's illicit, unconventional passion to their shared—in Olive's case, just awakening—sense of the comparative virility and sanity of the premodern world, the time before "Nietzsche, Freud, jazz, cocktails, and the 'emancipated'" (133). Lawrentian passion is wedded to a nostalgia for the pre-1914 age.

The interplay between these representatives of two very different generations—if Olive has stepped from an Evelyn Waugh novel then Skene resembles, at least superficially, a hero out of Kipling, self-sacrificing and devoted to his craft—is perhaps the most fascinating feature of a novel that constantly, if indirectly, juxtaposes Edwardian with postwar England. As Mottram suggests by setting the first encounter between Geoffrey and Olive on Armistice Day, at a cathedral mass for the fallen, the shadow of the Great War hangs over both generations. The middle-aged Skene has witnessed "the old easy settled life" (*Europa's Beast*, 137) of the years before 1914 upset by a conflict that "disastrously failed to justify the spirit in which so many of his sort had entered it" (6). The younger Olive, on the other hand, is a child of the war, her social climbing and interest in Ray's flying and sports cars, unsuccessful attempts to fill the void—cultural, moral, and spiritual—left by four years of slaughter. She reflects perfectly the frivolity and restlessness, the succession of fads and the fascination with exploration and flight, documented in Robert Graves and Alan Hodge's social history of the interwar decades, *The Long Week-End* (1940).

For most of the novel, Skene remains the more believable character of the two—Olive, scarcely more than a collection of contradictory impulses that Mottram, like Lawrence, diagnoses as symptomatic of a diseased, neurotic society. Skene's more subtle psychological malady, his sense of having returned from the Western Front incomplete or hollow, movingly reflects the plight of many First World War veterans: "Under his ordinary office demeanor . . . there was a void that sometimes made him seem like an empty shell with his clothes on, his name known, but nothing of him really present" (*Europa's Beast*, 13). Skene's apparent devotion to his work, his diligence while "Beneath the Yoke" (the title of the third chapter), is, we come to realize, little more than an unsuccessful attempt to fill this inner vacuum. Other passages in *Europa's Beast* expose, perhaps unintentionally, the lure of fascism for ex-soldiers like Skene who have had their faith in democracy undermined by the bloodbath in France. When Skene confronts Olive's father, the narrator introduces

a humorous but nevertheless significant image of violence. "Skene
. . . thrust his hands into his pockets. What else could he do? The
trenching-tool handle that he used to have ready for such occasions,
years before, was no longer at his side" (213). This quick fantasy—
bludgeoning the war profiteer—momentarily shifts the narrative
into the dichotomized world of Siegfried Sassoon's wartime poetry,
with its visions of frontline soldiers exacting vengeance on the home
front (visions partly realized in the street fights of Weimar Germany). Even the thoroughly civilized Skene betrays, at least for an
instant, the impulses of a storm trooper or Blackshirt.

As Michael Garrety has pointed out, Mottram suggests the threat
of postwar fascism or of mob rule in *The Spanish Farm Trilogy*
through the image of the headless man that haunts Captain Dormer
in the final volume. After seeing a decapitated corpse, Dormer imagines the entire army as a headless—thus irrational—force, its potential for anarchy waiting to be unleashed. Yet in *Europa's Beast,* Skene
realizes that the terrible vengeance of the war generation has not
come to pass; instead, the survivors have simply been caught up in
the business world of "getting and spending," and in the prolifera-
tion of technology, as symbolized by the ubiquitous automobile. In
this regard, ex-quartermaster-sergeant Haliday, a minor character
who slips in and out of the narrative, acts as Skene's foil. When the
two men meet after the Armistice Day ceremony and buy one another a drink, Skene, "who seldom found anyone to accompany or
invite him" to a pub, vaguely yearns for the male comradeship of
wartime: "Before Skene's mental vision, the counter and the beer-
handles, settles and small tables of the solid old lounge faded. He
was back in a starved-looking Picard village, trying to find shelter
for his men" (*Europa's Beast,* 9). But Haliday quickly interrupts
Skene's nostalgic reverie with a salesman's pitch: like Ray Blythway,
he sells motorcars. Mottram concludes this poignant scene by having
Skene, who quickly flees, overhear the unruffled Haliday immediately introduce himself to another prospective customer.

Mottram's account of Ray's ultimate betrayal by the machinery
that he adores also juxtaposes images of wartime France with those
of postwar East Anglia, although this time in the interests of a different theme. For example, when it is announced that Ray's crashed
plane is too mangled for an inquest, Skene muses, "What on earth
could they hold an inquest on? A few shreds of fusilage and some
bent metal! He remembered the sandbag burials in front of Thiep-
val" (*Europa's Beast,* 316). By paralleling the gruesome effects of
modern weapons with the wreckage of Ray's aircraft, Mottram suggests a sinister continuity between the refinement of lethal machinery

during the Great War and the speed craze of the 1920s and 1930s. Such imagery reinforces the interpretation of early twentieth-century history presented in *Europa's Beast*—namely, that accelerated technological change, a phenomenon which Mottram depicts as an outgrowth of the Great War, has acted as a dehumanizing force in postwar society.

Nearly twenty years younger than Skene and largely ignorant of the stabler and more confident time before the war, Olive senses the emptiness of modern England only, as we have seen, unconsciously—through the dreams and visions that she has inherited from her grandmother. She is, as Skene observes, "younger even in mind than in age, dating absolutely from that fatal second decade of the century" (*Europa's Beast,* 168). And, when the two meet for the first time on Armistice Day, Skene quickly perceives Olive as "The Victim" (28), a symbol of her entire generation, a generation that "instead of being decadents . . . were simply children [who] had everything before them and nothing behind them"(169). Of course, Skene's dilemma might be described as the reverse: hopelessly out of step with postwar England, he feels that he has left the best of himself back in France. His world ended in 1914, when Olive's was born.

Thus, as the novel proceeds, we realize that Mottram is concerned with telling more than a mere love story. The relationship between these two characters involves a reciprocal process of regeneration, a casting off of the psychological and spiritual blight left behind by the Great War. Olive provides Skene with the promise of a future, disrupting (by encouraging him to pursue a career in painting) his dependence on office routine as an antidote for his feeling of emptiness, just as Skene rescues Olive from the spiritual vacuity of the "lost generation," saving her, in effect, from becoming a character like Brett Ashley in Ernest Hemingway's *The Sun Also Rises* (1926). By the end of *Europa's Beast,* Skene has discovered "how much latent starvation can lie hidden below the prosaic surface of an ordinary professional existence" (*Europa's Beast,* 208), while Olive has shed the neuroses of her modern environment: "once freed from the superficial, half-educated atmosphere of post-War, how deep and strong were her emotions, how true her instincts" (354)! She is no longer a "sort of spiritual orphan" (176).

In *The Spanish Farm Trilogy,* Mottram contrasts two cultural responses to the Great War—the response of the Flemish peasantry, who inhabit a border region traditionally plagued with conflict, and that of the soldiers in the British New Armies, the innocent representatives of a nation completely unaccustomed to full-scale, industrial warfare. Through its dual focus (the first two volumes essentially describe the same events, but from different national perspectives), the trilogy vacillates between the Flemish characters' stoic acceptance of the Great War as part of history, as merely another conflict in an inevitable succession of disasters, and the English characters' overwhelming sense of disorientation and disillusionment. As we have seen, Mottram continues to examine the historical significance of the Great War in *Europa's Beast*—this time through the perspectives of two generations, rather than two countries—addressing questions that absorbed him throughout his career: Did the Great War in fact mark the end of a brighter period in history? Had four years of unprecedented devastation and loss of life strengthened the English national character or left it debilitated, spiritually empty? What were the defining characteristics of postwar society?

Mottram was not alone in considering these issues. In fact, virtually every writer who turned to the Great War as a subject during the 1920s or 1930s sought to tie the conflict into a clear pattern of historical causality, to fashion myths that explained not only how the unthinkable had occurred, but why such unsettling contrasts seemed to exist between England before and after the war. In *Death of a Hero* (1929), for example, Richard Aldington portrayed the Great War in terms of Freudian sublimation, as a violent bloodletting born of Victorian sexual frustration. Henry Williamson, on the other hand, defined war in *The Patriot's Progress* (1930) as the ultimate product of industrial societies—for innocuous unknown citizens such as John Bullock, the transition from office routine to trench routine comes easily and inevitably. In *Good-bye to All That*, Robert Graves endures years of warfare against the bloods at Charterhouse School, before finding himself on the battleground in France. All these writers focused on perceived flaws in prewar society—whether in terms of, respectively, sexual attitudes, class structure, or the public school system—that opened the way for catastrophe in 1914.

In contrast, Mottram's interpretation of the debacle of 1914–18 was closer to H. M. Tomlinson's in *All Our Yesterdays* (1930), a novel that, while punctuated by reminders of the naval arms race with Germany (the narrative opens with the launching of a new Dreadnought) and the waning of the British Empire, wistfully portrays prewar England as a vigorous and confident power. Certainly Mottram never indulged in the withering criticism of Victorian England made fashionable by Lytton Strachey, in *Eminent Victorians* (1918), and later refined by—among others—Aldington and Graves. Accepting of class distinctions, and proud of his family's century-old association with Gurney's, Mottram celebrated the nineteenth century as a period of comparative progress and enlightenment, though conceding that he had been spared, while growing up in East Anglia, from witnessing directly many of the social problems that had attended Victorian successes. In his autobiography, *Another Window Seat* (1957), he contrasted his fond memories of his childhood in the 1880s and 1890s with the cynical portraits of late nineteenth-century England offered in Aldington's *Death of a Hero* or in Graves's *Goodbye to All That:*

> the main facts of the sort [my family] were run thus: My father was the chief clerk of an old private bank in the provinces. He was a dissenter of the mild left-wing type called "Unitarian", a Victorian Liberal. When his first wife died, leaving him three daughters, he soon married again, a much younger woman who had two sons. I was the elder. The story therefore (so runs much modern theory) must be one of sordid financial domination of slave-manned industry, bigoted religion, repressions, family dissension and final decay.
>
> But it isn't. The story I have to tell is the very opposite. (*Another Window Seat,* 10)

Although Clark Thayer perhaps overstates in claiming that Mottram "saw his prewar childhood as having taken place in a Golden Age," a poignant sense of nostalgia and loss pervades virtually everything that Mottram wrote (Thayer 1985, 177). His variation on the myth of the lost prewar idyll is all the more effective because of its subdued and elegiac tone.

Ultimately, however, what most impresses one when looking at *The Spanish Farm Trilogy* and *Europa's Beast* collectively is the depth and variety of Mottram's fictional treatment of the Great War and its aftermath. Though far from creating a modern *War and Peace* (something that critics during the 1920s and 1930s hoped for, but never received), Mottram covered a far broader canvas than most First-World-War writers, examining, again and again, how different nationalities and generations defined the historical and cultural significance of the war. While most of the works in Mottram's eclectic output have been justly forgotten—they linger only in university research libraries, occupying an impressive number of shelves, never checked out—*Europa's Beast* deserves a better fate: to be read, together with *The Spanish Farm Trilogy,* as a profound and in many ways unique portrait of the Great War and of its impact on twentieth-century England.

Note

1. Criticism on Mottram's work after 1927 is virtually nonexistent. Nor has an entire article yet been focused on *The Spanish Farm Trilogy.* I have listed several

general studies of First-World-War literature, those that devote at least a section to the trilogy, in the bibliography. Mottram's volumes of autobiography, including *Autobiography with a Difference* (London: Hale, 1938), *Another Window Seat* (London: Hutchinson, 1957), and *The Twentieth Century: A Personal Record* (London: Hutchinson, 1969), still provide the fullest account of his life.

Works Cited

Aldington, Richard. 1929, 1984. *Death of a Hero*. London: Hogarth.

Fitzgerald, F. Scott. 1933. *Tender Is the Night*. New York: Charles Scribner's Sons.

Garrety, Michael. 1978. "Love and War: R.H. Mottram, *The Spanish Farm Trilogy* and Ernest Hemingway, *A Farewell to Arms*." Klein, Holger Michael, ed. *In The First World War in Fiction: A Collection of Critical Essays*. London: Macmillan.

Graves, Robert, and Alan Hodge. 1940, 1963. *The Long Week-End*. New York: W. W. Norton & Company.

Hynes, Samuel. 1990. *A War Imagined: The First World War and English Culture*. London: Bodley Head.

Lawrence, D. H. 1928, 1983. *Lady Chatterley's Lover*. New York: Greenwich.

Mottram, R. H. 1930. *Europa's Beast*. London: Chatto & Windus.

———. 1957. *Another Window Seat*. London: Hutchinson.

Panichas, George, ed. 1968. *Promise of Greatness: The War of 1914–1918*. New York: Day.

Thayer, Clark. 1985. "R.H. Mottram." In *Modern British Novelists,*

1890–1929: Modernists. Edited by Thomas F. Staley. Vol. 36 of *Dictionary of Literary Biography*. Detroit: Gale.

A Bibliography of Works by and about R. H. Mottram

Primary

———. 1930. *Europa's Beast*. London: Chatto & Windus.

———. 1930. *Miniature Banking Histories*. London: Chatto & Windus.

———. 1930. *The New Providence*. London: Chatto & Windus.

———. 1930. *The Old Man of the Stones*. London: Lindsey.

———. 1930. *Poems, New and Old*. London: Duckworth.

———. 1931. *Castle Island*. London: Chatto & Windus.

———. 1931. *The Headless Hound, and Other Stories*. London: Chatto & Windus.

———. 1931. *John Crome of Norwich*. London: Lane.

———. 1931. *The Lost Christmas Presents*. London: Lindsey.

———. 1932. *Home for the Holidays*. London: Chatto & Windus.

———. 1932. *Dazzle*. London: Ward, Lock.

———. 1932. *Through the Menin Gate*. London: Chatto & Windus.

———. 1933. *East Anglia: England's Eastern Province*. London: Chapman & Hall.

———. 1933. *A Good Old Fashioned Christmas*. London: Lindsey.

———. 1933. *The Lame Dog*. London: Chatto & Windus.

————. 1934. *Bumphrey's*. London: Murray.

————. 1934. *Strawberry Time and The Banquet*. London: Golden Cockerel.

————. 1934. *The Banquet, With Other Stories*. London: Chatto & Windus.

————. 1935. *Early Morning*. London: Hutchinson.

————. 1935. *Flower Pot End*. London: Murray.

————. 1936. *Journey to the Western Front Twenty Years After*. London: Bell.

————. 1936. *Portrait of an Unknown Victorian*. London: Bell.

————. 1936. *The Westminster Bank, 1836–1936*. London: Westminster Bank.

————. 1936. *The Norwich Players*. Norwich: Soman.

————. 1936. *Noah*. London: Rich & Cowan.

————. 1937. *Old England: Illustrated by English Paintings of the 18th and Early 19th Century*. London: Studio.

————. 1937. *Success to the Mayer*. London: Hale.

————. 1937. *Time to Be Going*. London: Hutchinson.

————. 1938. *Autobiography with a Difference*. London: Hale.

————. 1938. *There Was a Jolly Miller*. London: Hutchinson.

————. 1938. *Miss Lavington*. London: Hutchinson.

————. 1939. *Trader's Dream: The Romance of the East India Company*. London: Hutchinson.

————. 1939. *You Can't Have It Back!* London: Hutchinson.

Secondary

Bergonzi, Bernard. 1965. *Heroes' Twilight: A Study of the Literature of the Great War*. London: Constable.

Garrety, Michael. 1978. "Love and War: R.H. Mottram, *The Spanish Farm Trilogy* and Ernest Hemingway, *A Farewell to Arms*." In *The First World War in Fiction: A Collection of Critical Essays*. Edited by Holgar Michael Klein. London: Macmillan.

Onions, John. 1990. *English Fiction and Drama of the Great War, 1918-39*. New York: St. Martin's Press.

Thayer, Clark. 1985. "R.H. Mottram." In *Modern British Novelists, 1890-1929: Modernists*. Edited by Thomas F. Staley. Vol. 36 of *Dictionary of Literary Biography*. Detroit: Gale, 172–77.

4

Irene Rathbone: The Great War and Its Aftermath

CAROLINE ZILBOORG

A Brief Biographical Sketch of Irene Rathbone (1892–1979)

THE OLDEST OF THREE CHILDREN, IRENE RATHBONE GREW UP IN A middle-class family in the countryside near Liverpool (the social reformer Eleanor Rathbone was a cousin). She was educated at a local day school, then at a boarding school on England's southern coast. After graduation in 1910, Rathbone took an apartment in London with a female cousin. During the next few years she became interested in women's suffrage and acting, appearing in a Noel Coward play and in the productions of her cousin Frank Benson's Shakespeare Company, in which another cousin, Basil Rathbone, also spent his apprentice years.

With the advent of war, Rathbone turned her attention to other work: she initially volunteered in YMCA canteens in northern France, then trained as a practical nurse and served as a member of the Voluntary Aid Detachment in military hospitals in London. After the armistice, she moved to Chelsea with female roommates: her youngest brother Benson died of pneumonia with the Army of Occupation in Germany in 1919; her fiancé, Mansfield Priestley Evens, with whom she began a relationship in 1915, was killed in 1920 in a village uprising while serving with the English military government in Iraq.

In the 1920s Rathbone divided her time between the stage and office work in London. She twice visited her surviving brother Reginald, who was serving with military intelligence in China. She began an important friendship with Richard Aldington in the early 1930s and developed a group of literary friends which included Storm

Jameson, the journalist Louise Morgan Theis, and Nancy Cunard. As the unmarried daughter, she took on the care of her parents, sacrificing a more lively and literary life for long periods in Chipping Campden, where her family had settled. After their deaths in 1964, she returned to London, but her friendships had become predominantly epistolary and her life remained circumscribed.

* * * * *

Rathbone explores in her novels complex relationships among class, gender, and war, themes informed by her coming of age in an England still defined by Victorian values. Deeply influenced by her own experience of the Great War, Rathbone like many of her contemporaries only found her voice in the 1930s. Her treatment of these issues in two important novels, *We That Were Young* and *They Call It Peace,* reveals a feminist consciousness quite different from the sensibility that we find in much of literature written by men when treating the subject of the First World War and even different from that we often find in the literature by women. Unlike Vera Brittain, for example, Rathbone seldom romanticizes either the fighting in the trenches or the atmosphere surrounding those who waited at home. Her own experiences at the front as well as those of her female contemporaries in factories and hospitals inform her work, but her writing is particularly shaped by postwar experiences (her own and that of her nation in which the phrase "a world fit for heroes" became increasingly ironic). Thus, Rathbone's sensibility crystallizes in the 1930s when economic and political conditions reflect macrocosmically the more personal dislocation, alienation, and loss which her characters suffer. The author's range of characters (male but especially female) and situations (individual as well as social, i.e., the rise of communism, fascism, and the social credit movement) give her work a scope and ideological resonance rare in women's writing. Rathbone struggled from the perspective of the thirties to understand the contexts of the war and its aftermath by portraying the effects of a horror that shaped her and her generation.

The autobiographical impulse is strong in all of Rathbone's fiction, and throughout her life she developed strategies to veil and unveil her own experiences, to make clear her particular understanding of what happened to her and to her nation in 1914–18. Her early years did not prepare her for the Great War, and a growing resentment of the social forces responsible for that lack of preparation colors her tone and themes. She later reflected:

I never had a classical education. Never much of any sort after the age
of 17. . . . I needed to go to Oxford—my rather cloudy brain needed
precisely the discipline of Oxford—but I was an "only girl," my parents
wanted me at home, they were in *those* days fairly well off, and their
idea was to dress me + send me to dances + keep me at their side.
Crash into this comfortable life came W.W.I. I "did" that war, + never
thereafter came home again.[1]

Rathbone kept a journal of her war experiences, but it was not
until the early thirties that she turned to this source for her fiction.
The intervening years were a period of harrowing inner loneliness
and increasing awareness of loss. She was an active woman who had
several female friends and male companions, but she was at some
deep level alone. The conclusion of *We That Were Young* suggests
the alienation and profound impotence the author felt as a result of
the war: Joan Seddon, the protagonist and Rathbone's persona, does
not agree

> with people who said that sorrow "softened" or "sweetened" one. She
> felt far less sweet now that [her brother] had gone; and she knew that
> as the years went by, unless she could remember him constantly, she
> would harden. With him she had lost a brother, a son and half herself.
> That channel in which a particular set of her emotions had flowed was
> dammed. There was no outlet for them now; they flowed back, ob-
> jectless. (*We That Were Young*, 430)

We That Were Young becomes increasingly a novel about war's
aftermath, about the results of a war whose actual battlefields were
outside the author's and her female characters' direct experience. If
the war was the trenches, bombs in France, combat itself, then
women participated in it in two ways: through alter egos, their
brothers and lovers; and through repercussions which those who
died avoided. These repercussions for Rathbone included a wide
range of experiences: emotionally as well as physically, women were
deprived of male others through whom they might have been expected to live their lives, through whom in fact several women in
the book, notably Joan through her brother Jimmie, are already
living their lives as the novel opens. These "brothers" (actual or
spiritual) are at once specific relatives and the men of her generation.
While Rathbone writes early in the novel that "every separate soldier's view of the state of things 'out there' was coloured by his
individual experience. No general conclusion could be reached" (*We
That Were Young*, 37), she also insists on the collective "we" of her
title. Her method is to follow a panoply of characters, all of them

Joan's friends and acquaintances, through the war years in dated sections of unequal length from "1915" through "1919:1920" to "1928." The individual stories interweave and are connected to Joan first by her participation in them (her brother's youth, enlistment, and leaves; Colin's courtship of her and his leaves; the lives of her female friends in YMCA canteens, VAD dormitories, and hospital wards; London parties and visits to relatives in the country). The novel's characters and situations are also connected to Joan through letters, the relayed information experienced at one remove which has traditionally been the stuff of women's experience and writing and the root of the novel as a modern form. Through correspondence Joan learns of Colin and other men's lives in the trenches; of her brother and fiancé's deaths; of the ongoing lives of women friends in France while she is still at home and later of their lives at home when she is in France or experiencing the grueling labor of wartime nursing in London. The book is thus based on a series of meetings and separations, structured through periods characterized by different kinds of work (Red Cross volunteering, hospital drudgery and horror, factory shifts, and accidents) and various "leaves" (holidays from prep school and Oxford, military leaves from training and the front, and sick leaves for those injured physically or psychologically in battle or infected while nursing).

In other words, the novel is a series of disruptions, of discontinuities. The result is a view of war at once realistic and symbolic. The war is both responsible for the destruction of everything Joan's generation knew as familiar (male and female roles, especially sisterhood, friendship, courtship, sexual mores, marriage and motherhood) and the definition of modern identity. At the book's conclusion, Joan responds to the past, to the war as a global disaster and to "her own personal war," in the context of an Armistice Day remembrance ceremony which is "at the same time beautiful, futile, and a reproach. . . . As though one wanted to remember in that fashion; as though one wanted to forget"(We That Were Young, 463). When a younger woman comments "'How you must have cursed the war,'" Joan responds with the mixture of bitterness and nostalgia, passion and alienation which are for Rathbone the war's emotional legacy:

> "We did—we did. But looking back, now, I think we loved it too. Oh, it's so difficult to explain. . . . So difficult to put one's present emotions back into that period. At the time . . . the war was so ordinary—it was just our life. Yes, we hated it, and loved it, both. Loved it because we gave so much to it, and because it was bound up with our young-

ness. . . . It was *our* war . . . it seems, now, to have a sort of ghastly glamour. . . . Our hearts are there—unwillingly—for always. It was our war." (*We That Were Young*, 465)

While *We That Were Young* is dedicated to the author's dead brother (diminutively "To Bobbin"), her second "war novel," *They Call It Peace*, published four years later, is a work of a more developed sensibility and dedicated to Richard Aldington, whose *Death of a Hero* (1929) probably influenced both books but whose personal acquaintance more noticeably shaped the later novel.

Like its predecessor, *They Call It Peace* is a series of overlapping stories which proceed from a rural prewar idyll in the opening section ("1914: And After") to the present (1934), a prewar nightmare. The Great War itself essentially becomes a gap in the text, the constant reference point as the ideological ferment of the thirties provides the lens through which Rathbone understands the public and personal experience that war was for her generation. In *We That Were Young*, the focus is on English experience: the author is by no means chauvinistic or even nationalistic; she shares, for instance, Joan Seddon's awareness that young Germans lay wounded in Germany just as her English (and Irish and Scottish and Australian) patients lay in graphic pain in London hospitals. But this earlier novel is emphatically a portrait of English experience in a particular time and place, while *They Call It Peace* presents its English characters as representative—of their nation, but also of their gender, class, and age throughout the Western world. Just as after *Death of a Hero* Aldington never again felt that he had to write out in a novel the full experience of war (the writing of it once was painful and cathartic enough), Rathbone too avoids recapitulation in *They Call It Peace*, as if we are, in a way, to read *We That Were Young* into the gaps of the later book. Thus the idyll of Part 1 concludes with a brief ten-page reprise of the earlier novel, but presents a pastiche of French, German, and English experience and emphasizes characters of different social classes, some of whom Rathbone has introduced earlier in this novel, others of whom are and remain anonymous, mere names. Here the language fragments and the images superimpose one upon another, like a Russian formalist film, as Rathbone moves among various levels of consciousness and in and out of the minds of her characters. Jane Marcus emphasizes in her afterward to the Feminist Press' edition of *They Call It Peace* the periodic linguistic discordance of this novel, a technical and theoretical advance over the earlier techniques of *We That Were Young*. Marcus writes that by 1936

Rathbone had learned to disrupt her language as well as her subject, to "break the sentence," as well as breaking "the sequence" to use Virginia Woolf's description of women's fiction . . . *They Call It Peace* is experimental and modernist . . . (*They Call It Peace*, 471)

The text's appearance upon the page wrenches the reader from any easy assimilation of the material: ellipses punctuate onomatopoeic language; incomplete sentences, bits of conversation, exclamation marks, capital letters and varying degrees of small and italicized print pepper the sequence like bullets; snippets of songs and newspaper headlines in three modern languages as well as the schoolboy's Latin intersperse with slang, swear words, prayer, and excerpts from telegrams. Emotionally, the section ranges from lovers' parting to battlefield deaths. This sequence haunts all that follows in the novel just as the war wounds everyone who survives it, but its nearly complete absence from the rest of the text is what must be explained, what ultimately the characters struggle to understand and accept, what the author herself presents as a political and particularly economic collusion among powerful forces which only communal response has any hope of countering.

Rathbone's increasing political involvement in the 1930s also makes *They Call It Peace* a more coherent and pointed work than the earlier war novel, evincing greater control of her disparate material and unrelenting purpose. In fact, this novel becomes at times a political treatise, a diatribe in which an intruding author punctures the narrative to preach economic reform and Douglas's social credit system. The following quotations are representative of these passages which often open or conclude the novel's four chronological parts:

In the summer of 1931 another monster, hatched from among the addled eggs of Orthodox Finance, waddled over the world; and this was known as The Crisis. Closely resembling its brother The Slump, it was even more destructive—had redder eyes, fouler breath. And wherever it squatted it brought paralysis or hysteria. . . . (*They Call It Peace*, 383)

Gold! . . . the fantastic futility of it! Why should a pound be tied to it? Or a franc? Or a dollar? What in heaven or hell is the use of it? . . . (386)

. . . The suggestion conveyed by this "economic interdependence" stuff was that no one country, or group, or community could hope to escape the general world depression. Whereas, of course, the only salvation for this country (or any other) was to *break away* from its abject dependence on a system which was bringing it to economic, social, and cultural ruin. (388)

Rathbone's emphasis here on the massive, global nature of the problem she analyzes suggests a raised consciousness of the implications
of her material, a theoretical awareness that underlies her presentation of myriad individual characters and experiences. Her politics
achieve their most vehement expression in this novel, but it is worth
emphasizing that they persisted in nature and stridency throughout
her life and work; as late as 1948 Rathbone wrote to John Masefield that

> Our rulers *want* us to stew in darkness, have no books, sink into an
> apathetic culture. Certainly the American bosses of our rulers want us
> to. *They* control our paper—our food—our money—overall. England
> has been sold. There is one, only one, remedy: Social Credit. (Postcard,
> 25 January 1948)[2]

My volume of *They Call It Peace,* acquired three years ago from
a secondhand bookseller in England, is signed by the author. Under
her name in parentheses she has written "inscribed during a second
false 'peace'—Dec. 1947." Like Aldington, who typically referred
to the period between the two world wars as "the long armistice,"
Rathbone was seared by her experience of the war and by the understanding of it which she arrived at only in the thirties. *They Call It
Peace,* informed throughout by the unrelenting irony of modernism,
impels itself through over 600 pages to "Remembrance Day," 1934.
Nellie Goodbody, whose husband died in 1918 of wounds received
in France, brings flowers to the Cenotaph both for him and for her
brother who also served in the trenches but who survived only to
kill himself a decade later, despondent because of his ineffectiveness
as a writer and his inability to find work or to love his wife, who
prostitutes herself on his behalf. Nellie justifies the two wreaths:
"For it was really, when you looked at it all round, as though poor
Ed *had* died in the war" (*They Call It Peace,* 613). Inexorably, the
novel rushes to its conclusion: Lorna's husband, Geoffrey Spenser,
who has himself been almost an absence throughout the work, neither passionate lover to his wife nor dead soldier in the field, appears
amid fragmented text:

> Captain Spenser halted his handful—re-formed them. They could hardly
> stand. From haggard eyes under his tin hat he looked into their eyes—
> the eyes of his dirty, but still disciplined, weary, shadowy, age-old men.
> And they looked back.
> "Dismiss!" he whispered. (*They Call It Peace,* 614–15)

This is our last image here of the war as human battle: iterative, depersonalizing, exhausting, ritualistic, valiant, and pathetic. Rathbone follows this passage with images from a hospital ("Exposed red gaps of flesh all down the ward. Yellow, oily green. . . ."), then chronologically with subsequent images of depression poverty and former soldiers without pensions or work, forced to sell their medals and do without milk or meat (*They Call It Peace,* 615). The novel concludes with a return to the present and a cinematic focus on the green and white wreath placed at the foot of the cenotaph by a parade of social credit supporters with the label which is Rathbone's bitter final comment on the war: "In memory of those who died in vain" (617).

The novel is ultimately grim; most of the characters fail to find happiness even in personal or immediate terms. In addition to Ed Kendall's death, we have a host of others, literal and spiritual, presented as individual and social failures. Dorothy Killick, the secretary in her thirties, is finally enabled to marry, but only because of her alcoholic sister's suicide; the ex-soldier Bill Burley's artistic son dies of tuberculosis, his wife during childbirth, his infant son of malnutrition; Lorna Spenser remarries for economic reasons, not without some affection, but without passion—for the sake of her fatherless son. Lorna's brother Paul, who has married a shallow and conniving woman, is unable finally to leave her despite his love for the actress Joan Tressider—he lacks courage, inner fiber because, Rathbone suggests, of his psychological response to the war. Lorna's other brother David, too young for the war, who after a long commitment to communism joins the Social Credit movement and becomes its spokesperson in the last sections of the novel, is also in love with Joan, but his desires are unrequited. Near the end of the book, Lorna talks with him about the future and asks him if he can secure poison so that, in the Armageddon that they anticipate will follow in the inevitable next war, she and young Geoff can kill themselves; David agrees.

Paul and Joan, unable to realize their love which is at the erotic center of this expansive novel, serve as a poignant counterpart to Colin and Joan Seddon of *We That Were Young.* Joan Tressider is the character who comes closest to serving as a persona for the author as a living and sexual woman beyond the political voice I have just suggested. Lorna has much of our sympathies, but she seems a fantasized projection—the woman Rathbone would like to be, whose reason for suffering is a passionate marriage to an officer killed in the war who at least left her a child. Lorna is a thoroughly admirable widow and mother, deeply generous to others and without inner flaw: she has our full sympathy because of her personal strength in the face of what has happened to her.

Joan has not herself endured the war as Paul and Lorna have, for she is younger. Through Paul, however, she suffers war's consequences. Paul is condemned despite Rathbone's portrait of him as a gifted writer and passionate lover because he lacks the courage of his convictions; he is weak. Paul is ultimately a faintly veiled embodiment of Rathbone's understanding of Aldington. Beyond superficial incidentals,[3] Paul like Aldington espouses the only philosophy Rathbone suggests capable of countering not merely social credit economics but any political solution to the world's problems: a strategic retreat, an insistence on the personal, the individual, the transcendental (which is in no way T. S. Eliot's spiritual Christianity as an alternative to Poundian economics, but something altogether more worldly and emotive). Paul contends that he is emphatically not interested in politics but in "'Letters. Beauty. Peace. Especially the last!'"(*They Call It Peace,* 480) Joan feels convinced when she is with him that "We can make our own world" (323) echoing Aldington's contention, voiced most fully in his long poem "The Crystal World" (1937), that lovers can only survive in a space apart. David tries (and fails) to argue politics with Paul (when at some level the real issue may be each man's right to love Joan, although David at this point in the novel has admitted his feelings to no one, perhaps not even to himself). In other words, David tries to argue politics when the real issue may be love. He taunts Paul, who has little patience for David's crusading, "'Do *you* think Life for Life's sake is enough?'" Paul responds: "'Of course'" (*They Call It Peace,* 507).[4]

Beyond the disappointment, even antagonism toward Paul that the reader may feel when he fails to live his life on his own terms, there is this duality at the novel's core: politics or transcendence; communal action or individual solution; social causes or art; economics or erotic fulfillment. Rathbone struggles throughout her work both to pose these oppositions and to explore the possibility of choosing the one over the other; that is, she struggles to offer her characters (and by extension her readers and herself) a choice—but there is sadly from the perspective of the thirties no choice, for the world wins out. Paul may leave Joan because he is psychologically wounded by the war, but Rathbone stresses that it is an inner weakness of character which ultimately betrays him. In the larger scope of the novel, Joan and Paul are merely two people among many; however much their love and its failure may be the personal center of the work for its author, Rathbone courageously contends in this book, even against what she might like to feel (hope for a personal relationship, anger at a lover who has left her), that either there will be a political solution to individual problems or no solution at all.

The personal and the political vie with one another in Rathbone's work, but despite their similarities of subject and theme, the continuity between *We That Were Young* and *They Call It Peace* is delusive, for there are two intervening books of quite a different sort. Rathbone published *The Gold Rim* in 1933 and *October* in 1934. Neither is a "war" novel, and Patricia Utechin describes *The Gold Rim* as her aunt's "first 'proper' novel" in that it is not transparently autobiographical nor based on letters or a journal, adding that the novel "has, as always, an 'Irene' figure, the older spinster woman, scholarly (or artistic), with a love relationship in the past ('killed in the war')—and longed for but, realistically, recognised to be unlikely in the present/future" (letter to Zilboorg 18 November 1993). *October,* however, is definitely the stronger of the two books and the more interesting on several accounts.

Unlike her "war" novels, *October* has a smaller cast of characters (essentially six—three pairs of lovers), a more intimate focus (the narrative is almost exclusively from Rose's point of view), a more confined geography (primarily Berkshire and London) and chronological scope (one month in the autumn). Rathbone plays out a series of disconcerting similarities as characters echo each other and as the fiction resonates against her own experiences. *October* gains more than perhaps any of her other novels by being read in the context of biography. The diaries on which Rathbone based *We That Were Young* (now housed at the Imperial War Museum in London) reveal how close to autobiography that book often is; in *October,* however, Rathbone is clearly writing fiction (most obviously, Rose is married with two children), but she has transformed and encoded autobiographical material so that she can comment on it in ways not available to her earlier; by 1934, she had developed complex aesthetic strategies for examining her identity as a woman, her position as a female in England's postwar society.

Rose is an artist who has written one really good novel but now, with Martin her architect-craftsman husband and two children, she does not write but gardens and attends to the neighborly round. Henri is a career soldier with whom Rose has had a brief affair in Provence four years earlier. He has been shaped by his experiences in war, but feels finally that the English were more hurt by it than the French who are more used to invasions, more prepared. Henri loves Rose in return, but after a year of corresponding, their relationship seems hopeless: he stops writing and eventually she, rejected, stops as well. When they later meet again in England, where he has come to seek her out, she accepts his rationale: he was on desert duty in Africa, could offer no life for a lover or wife, and felt the affair was too painful to continue. Thus England and France, Berkshire and Provence, domestic peace and military adventuring, marriage and passion are juxtaposed and embody the alternatives that face the characters. When at the end of the novel Rose painfully (for her, for the sympathetic reader) rejects Henri's renewed love, she refuses him the promised night of passion in London as well as a holiday with him in France.

This dual rejection and the lovers' painful lot with its apparently impossible resolution reveal in personal terms the aftermath of war which Rathbone later explores more diffusely in a much larger social context. In *October* in 1934, it is Rathbone's affair with Richard Addington in the south of France which recapitualtes the war for her and which inspires this most personal of her novels.

Although Rathbone was aware of Aldington's extremely popular *Death of a Hero* from the time of its publication in 1929, she did not actually meet him until two years later. His novel must thus to a degree have influenced *We That Were Young,* but probably only in a general way: the time was ripe for war novels, and Aldington's book reflected the bitterness and anguish created by the experience of war while demonstrating the readiness of the public to respond. For his part, Aldington reveals his view of Rathbone's autobiographical book at least as early as September of 1932 when at the end of a review of Neil Bell's *Life and Andrew Otway* he wrote,

> I cannot help contrast the falsity of this book with the honesty and deep feeling of a woman's novel, of which I received an advance copy, and which I intended to review this week. . . . It seems to me extraordinary that such a novel should have been rejected by several publishers. . . . It is written from an intense personal experience and with a wonderful sympathy for the lives and suffeerings of others. In reading it I felt it was not the kind of book an author lashes himself up to write but a book which wrote itself, something which simply had to be expressed.

Aldington is clearly working from firsthand knowledge when he notes that the book is based on "an intense personal experience." He concluded: "It is a frank and honest book and expresses in its own way the strange and lamentable tragedy of modern England; and that, I suppose, is the reason it is not wanted, while the bookshops are laden with falsehood and flattery" (Aldington, "Vogue" np). Eventually, *We That Were Young* was published by Chatto and Windus, Aldington's own publisher, whom he may well have influenced in this matter, for, by 1932, Aldington and Rathbone had begun an affair.

In *Was There a Summer,* Rathbone's long narrative poem written in the spring of 1937 but not published till 1943, the female speaker declares that before meeting the male character she "had loved him for a year" through his work and that their relationship had begun and continued for some time only through letters (5). Patricia Utechin has suggested that Rathbone may have initiated the friendship by writing to Aldington in response to *Death of a Hero* in 1929, and her correspondence supports the sequence of events indicated in her poem: by the autumn of 1931, she wrote her editor that "It was nice meeting Richard Aldington in the S. of France from which I have just returned" (Rathbone to Raymond 21 September 1931). During this holiday in Provence, Rathbone realized her love for Aldington and subsequently based the poem on her experience there.

The center of Rathbone's poem is a vivid narrative of her meeting Aldington in Le Lavandou in August of 1931. Rathbone details her apprehensive arrival in Provence where she wonders if she and Aldington have understood each other, if she, a "sub-acid realist" is ready for a romantic encounter "on the top of an old grief for a young love dead" (*Summer* 14). She finds Aldington surprisingly attractive, and she reflects that writers' bodies should be as taut and resilient as their verse. Rathbone describes their relationship through poignant snippets of conversation and vignettes of dining together, sea bathing, and love making. Their passion is particularly trenchant in the contexts that Rathbone creates which echo the antagonistic world found in novels both were writing in the 1930s.

Although Aldington asked Rathbone to stay "'longer,'" she notes "It was death in life to say no,/But unless I stayed for always/ (And that was not asked) 'Longer' was impossible." Aldington did not after all come to visit her in England, and Rathbone never again went to Provence. Both the pleasure and the pain of the experience persist in the present of the poem: "I have been blind with pain/But then/Blind almost with bliss too (*Summer* 39, 43). The speaker is deeply hurt, but cherishes the memory and does not regret the affair.

In the context of *Was There a Summer?*, *October* assumes new significance. For example, Rose's friend Jenny is a sweet, modern, shallow but sophisticated young woman who has had an affair in Paris with Gilbert a few years before the novel opens, an affair which echoes Rose's relationship with Henri but also Rathbone's with Aldington, a relationship which becomes archetypal for the author, even emblematic in her repeated exploration of it. Jenny and Gilbert finally parted painfully in the Jardin Luxembourg; she still is in love with him, but he does not write. In perceiving Rose's love for Henri and his for her, Jenny resolves her passion for Gilbert and goes on to an engagement with Mark. She is the writer of popular sentimental novels and admires Rose for what she has written, encouraging her to return to writing. There is something of a sisterhood here, also a mother-daughter relationship, but Jenny's youth and superficiality allow her choices not available to more serious artists or to women of the war generation whose emotional life is deep and complex in part as a result of the experience of war and in part as a result of thwarted love or, more explicitly, as a result of rejection by men.

This is also a novel about work and about the value of art as work and work as sensual experience necessary for the soul. It is as well a novel about England and France, the settled and the passionate, the married and the sexual. As in *Was There a Summer?* Rathbone juxtaposes the two countries, thereby suggesting the alternatives that face the characters. References to Provence, for example, imply sultry passion, and Henri is throughout associated with the south, while Rose is associated with Berkshire and her dying garden. The novel is, in fact, finally literally and symbolically circumscribed by its setting, taking us emotionally and thematically from the warm end-of-summer to the unavoidable beginning-of-winter.

In 1946, with the Second World War finally over, Aldington returned to France from America, where he spent these years with his second wife and only child. Rathbone, too, began again to visit the country for which she had a life-long affection. The two writers met, probably by accident, in Paris. Rathbone reflected on the experience in a letter to Nancy Cunard:

> If by chance you meet in Paris *Richard A.*, be prepared for his taking a very queer line. He contradicts everything one says about France's sufferings + Resistance. He does it gently but quite decidedly. . . . His indifference to the English war effort, + to anything his old friends have been through, is perhaps natural (part feigned, part real). . . .[5]

Rathbone should not perhaps have been so shocked (Aldington throughout his life made every effort to disengage himself from the political), but it is not surprising that Rathbone on meeting her former lover should seem to have talked mostly of political matters; for her, the personal and the political were increasingly inseparable. In 1939, she had written to her friend Storm Jameson about addressing the seventeenth International PEN Conference, then upcoming in Stockholm: "If you want to go more political, I'm with you. Politics have become ethics."[6] In the same letter to Cunard in which she mentions having met Aldington, Rathbone reflected characteristically on Jameson's situation, stressing her personal life but quickly moving to larger issues:

> Too much is demanded of that woman. Too much. She is ill. Can only just manage her writing. And people batten on her + pile their mountainous troubles on her. Families are the b. [bloody] limit. Artists ought to have more. But then do they slightly shrivel as human beings? Anyhow, demands on them are disproportionate (I talk of female artists).

Rathbone's affair with Aldington would invariably in her life as in her work outweigh any of his other behavior and would continue to obscure finally his attitudes toward political matters. He and his fictional counterparts in *They Call It Peace* and in her other writing would remain a challenge for her since they finally transcended her own politics as the personal came full circle: her experiences lead her quickly to a larger understanding of the psychology and especially the ideology behind them, but the intensity of her own response to particular experience forced her ultimately to respond in personal terms not only in her life (she cancels much of what she writes about Aldington's politics by adding in her correspondence with Cunard, "I loved him once" [27 November 1946]) but in her art (her increasingly long novels are always love stories with political subplots, attempts to reconcile the strange bedfellows of political analysis and romance).

Finally, Rathbone's life and work are characterized by a frustration with women's traditional lot and by a clarity of vision which allows her to explore women's individual struggles as well as the dynamics of the larger social and political issues they raise. Her writing consistently reveals her sensitivity to the physical world and a developed feminist sensibility at a time when most women were circumscribed by family, home, and class. For Rathbone, the Great War shattered forever any peaceful acceptance of such givens. Her affair with Richard Aldington promised her more than he or the relationship could ever have delivered in terms of self-realization or a stay against the impinging realities which limited her experience and possibilities. Rathbone understood this failure, this masculine betrayal which was not so much an act committed by an individual (e.g., Aldington or the male characters in her fiction) as a larger betrayal by a generation of men, by war, by economics, by patriarchy itself. But Rathbone never fully accepted her situation. She would have liked to have married, to have created with a partner her own family. To Louise Theis Rathbone wrote, "you do hit the mark when you say I have been 'flying on one wing' all my life. . . ." Shifting the focus to Theis's own situation, Rathbone offered an analysis of her friend's life which could well apply to her own:

> Your friends, you say, have taken the place of your personal life: the pursuit of certain arts or academic subjects. You are, I guess, by temperament a scholar. . . . You were frustrated. I am deeply sorry to learn that the special young man you wanted to marry died. That fact (+ your mother) did much—did all?—to block the path you should have danced along. But you did marry, + more than once; and had children. I envy you the full normal female experience. Don't repine. Think of that experience, + of the hoards of people who love you + have been helped by you. In another life you may find yourself in the "groves of Academe". . . . Or else among asphodels . . . with your dead young man. But once one begins thinking of the people one will *meet* on the other side (assuming for a moment we believe in another side), one gets confused, because there will be so many of them! So many *young* especially; those killed on the Somme . . . (23 February 1961)

Reflecting on Cunard's vehemence, Rathbone in a letter to Theis described herself in contrast with a statement that reveals more than good manners or beneficent generosity or magnanimity of spirit: "certainly [Nancy] can hate. So can I, but not individual people. I hate the Banking fraternity, I hate Nazis, I hate all power-mongers who inflict misery on the humble. But then I don't know them personally" (17 August 1960).

But Rathbone had known Richard Aldington "personally," and she was deeply moved when she read in the *Times* of his death on 27 July 1962. She wrote to Cunard: "For years + years, as you know, R. + I had not met, not written. Therefore my sorrow may be considered foolish. But I can't somehow bear him not to be in this world" (6 August 1962). After visiting Cunard in southwestern France in September of 1964, Rathbone traveled north to the tiny village of Sury-en-Vaux to place flowers on Aldington's grave. She then continued on to Paris where she met Aldington's friend Alister Kershaw who recalled that "It was very clear that she had never wavered in her love for Richard" (letter to Zilboorg 13 January 1994). Rathbone herself reflected further on Aldington in her late letters to Cunard. Having returned to London in the autumn of 1964, she wrote, ". . . my mind has been travelling backwards over R.A.—to his faults as well as his virtues—. . . . Please don't think (as well you might!) that that man constantly occupies my thoughts. . . . But just lately he has cropped up. . . ." To refresh her memory, Rathbone asked Cunard about her publication of Aldington's work in the twenties, but then concluded parenthetically: "(With regard to the long-ago private relationship between R. + me, that's another thing altogether, + about which NO reminders are required)" (1 November 1964). Rathbone would continue to think about Aldington in part because of the personal intensity of what in the early 1930s had been their "private relationship" but also because the devastation of young men during the Battle of the Somme was as present and painful a reality to her at the end of her life as in 1916 when she nursed the wounded survivors or in 1932 when she wrote the first of her war novels or in 1961 when she recalled them for Louise Theis. The flowers she put on the black slab of Aldington's grave in France, like those her fictional Nellie Goodbody placed at the Cenotaph in 1934, were at once a personal tribute and a symbolic acknowledgment of the tragedy that defined her as both woman and writer.

Notes

*Biographical information comes from four sources: Lynn Knight's introduction to the recent edition of Irene Rathbone's *We That Were Young* (1932); the papers of Brig. R. B. Rathbone at the Imperial War Museum; Rathbone's unpublished letters to Louise Morgan Theis at The Beinecke Rare Book and Manuscript Library at Yale; and personal correspondence and interviews with Rathbone's niece and literary executor, Patricia Utechin.

1. Unpublished letter from Irene Rathbone to Louise Morgan Theis, 13 February 1957, The Beinecke Rare Book and Manuscript Library, Yale University. This and all other letters from Rathbone to Theis are quoted by permission of The Beinecke Library and of Rathbone's literary executor, Patricia Utechin.

2. Rathbone's correspondence with Masefield is quoted by permission of The Harry Ranson Humanities Research Center at the University of Texas at Austin and Patricia Utechin.

3. The parallels are numerous: most obviously, perhaps, Aldington was involved with Brigit Patmore and still married to H. D. throughout the period of his affair with Rathbone; although he and H. D. did not live together after 1919, they did not divorce until 1938 in large measure in order to protect H. D.'s daughter by Cecil Gray, a daughter Aldington always claimed publically as his own. Paul is similarly bound to an unsympathetic wife by paternal obligations to their daughter Phyllis (whose name can be understood as echoing that of H. D.'s daughter, Perdita, just as Paul's surname, "Berington," suggests "Aldington"). Paul, like Aldington, suffers from shell shock, calling himself "a fool" for his response to a war he would like to forget but cannot (*They Call It Peace*, 71), just as Aldington assumes the identity of the fool in his long poem about his fragmented postwar self, *A Fool i'the Forest* (1924). Paul and Aldington share an attractive physical presence: they are tall and dashing, and tend to draw women's attentions. But above all, both Aldington and Paul are writers, initially avant-garde poets who turn in the late 1920s to fiction. Joan's description of Paul's novels might well be Rathbone's of Aldington's:

"you're a far harder and angrier person in your books than you are in life. . . . Perhaps writers have to be like that—unblent. . . . And then about women. . . . In life I should have said you—quite liked them. In your books they go on to the ash heap, along with all old men who misgovern the country, all business profiteers, and all self-advertising second-rate artists. . . . You've conventionalized 'Woman' to suit your own angriness with the world" (*They Call It Peace*, 192–93).

4. Four years after the publication of this novel, Aldington was to begin his memoirs in the United States and to title his book *Life for Life's Sake*, a choice particularly ironic in the context of Rathbone's novel, but a title which underscores the nature of their differences as I examine them here.

5. Unpublished letter to Nancy Cunard, 14 November 1946; this and all other letters from Rathbone to Cunard are quoted by permission of the Harry Ransom Humanities Research Center and Patricia Utechin.

6. Unpublished letter to Storm Jameson, dated merely June 1939, quoted by permission of the Harry Ransom Humanities Research Center and Patricia Utechin.

Works Cited

Aldington, Richard. 1929. *Death of a Hero*. London: Chatto.

————. 1968. *Life for Life's Sake: A Book of Reminiscences*. London: Cassel. The Vogue of the Padded Novel: "Size for the Sake of Size Is Detestable"', *The Sunday Referee*, 11 September 1932, n.p.

Rathbone, Irene. 1988. *We That Were Young*. London: Chatto and Windus, 1932. Reprint, London: Virago Press, 1988 and New York: The Feminist Press, 1989.

————. 1936. *They Call It Peace*. London: J. M. Dent and Sons.

————. 1943. *Was There a Summer?* London: Constable.

A Bibliography of Works by and about Irene Rathbone

Primary

————. 1929. *Susan Goes East*. London: John Lane, The Bodley Head.

————. *We That Were Young*. London: Chatto and Windus, 1932. Reprint, London: Virago Press, 1988 and New York: The Feminist Press, 1989.

————. 1933. *The Gold Rim*. London: J. M. Dent and Sons.

————. 1934. *October,* London: J. M. Dent and Sons.

————. 1936. *They Call It Peace*. London: J. M. Dent and Sons.

————. 1939. *When Days Were Years*. London: Faber and Faber.

————. 1943. *Was There a Summer?* (written in 1937). London: Constable.

————. 1952. *The Seeds of Time*. London: Faber and Faber.

Secondary

While all of Rathbone's books were widely reviewed by the English press, her work has elicited very little scholarly attention. Lynn Knight's introduction to *We That Were Young* (i–xxviii) is the first substantial critical essay and provides a useful survey of Rathbone's life and work with particular attention to this novel; Knight's introduction is reprinted in the Feminist Press edition (ix–xxv) which also includes a perceptive afterward by Jane Marcus, "The Nurse's Text: Acting Out an Anaesthetic Aesthetic" (467–98), in which Marcus examines *We That Were Young* in the context of other women's war novels, among them *They Call It Peace* and *Not So Quiet . . .* by Evadne Price (Helen Zenna Smith).

5

Elizabeth Bowen: Unconscious Undertows: Queer Perspectives on *Friends and Relations*

RENÉE C. HOOGLAND

A Brief Biographical Sketch of Elizabeth Bowen (1899–1972)

BORN IN DUBLIN IN 1899, ELIZABETH DOROTHEA COLE BOWEN WAS the last in a long line of Anglo-Irish writers. Though not in the strict sense a nationality, the Anglo-Irish were a distinct cultural group who produced their own national myths and characteristics. These went to the making of Bowen's character as much as they found their way into her fiction. But the author also clearly belongs to the English literary tradition. Due to her father's mental illness and her mother's premature death, she spent part of her youth shuttling about the two countries, and was to live most of her life in self-imposed exile from her native Ireland.

Bowen's stories first began to appear in *The Saturday Westminster* in the late 1910s. She was to keep up a prolific output throughout the almost fifty years that spanned her writing career. Her remarkable oeuvre consists of ten novels, almost eighty short stories, and a considerable body of critical and other nonfictional work. Not only was Bowen's work well-read and greatly admired during her lifetime, she herself also cut an impressive figure in the literary and artistic circles of Oxford and London in the 1920s and 1930s.

With her second novel, *The Last September* (1929), Bowen perfected what became an inimitable descriptive style: while appearing both highly wrought and elusive, her prose is simultaneously sharply edged, satirical, and extremely witty. Having established her international reputation with *Friends and Relations* (1931) and *To the North*

82

(1932), she published her probably best-known work, *The Death of the Heart* in 1938.

Despite the success of her war novel, *The Heat of the Day* (1949), Bowen's influence began to decline in the postwar years. She started lecturing for the British Council, and, especially after the death of her husband Alan Cameron in 1952, spent a great deal of time teaching and traveling, mostly in the United States. In these final years, Bowen wrote two more novels, *The Little Girls* (1964), and *Eva Trout* (1969). Although far less well received than any of her previous work, these represent radical departures from her earlier style and narrative method, revealing the abiding strength of the author's creative and critical imagination. Bowen was working on a new novel when she died on 22 February 1972.

* * * * *

> The writer, like a swimmer caught by an undertow, is borne in an unexpected direction. He is carried to a subject which has awaited him—a subject sometimes no part of his conscious plan. Reality, the reality of sensation, has accumulated where it was least sought. To write is to be captured—captured by some experience to which one may have hardly given a thought.
> —Elizabeth Bowen, preface to *The Last September*

When *Friends and Relations* was published, Elizabeth Bowen had already gained a small circle of admirers as the author of two earlier novels and three volumes of short stories. Keeping up a prolific output throughout her life, and with her last novel, *Eva Trout* appearing in 1969, Bowen could well be said to "belong" to any decade covered by the almost fifty years of her writing career. Her later work has elsewhere given me occasion to situate this "excentric" author in a postmodern context. There are nonetheless good reasons for including a chapter on Bowen in a study of "neglected writers of the thirties."

Bowen was, in the words of her biographer Victoria Glendinning "heir, in literary and aesthetic terms, to Bloomsbury" (Glendinning 1985, 75). Although her early novels and short stories had been fairly well-received, it was only in the 1930s that she acquired the prominence that a decade earlier had been achieved by such figureheads as Virginia Woolf, Ernest Hemingway, and Aldous Huxley. In the early thirties, Bowen's short stories started to appear regularly in *The Listener,* while in 1935, she began writing book reviews on a regular basis for the *New Statesman and Nation.* In 1936, by then an established novelist, Bowen wrote her first major essay for *The*

Spectator. She gained further recognition as the editor of *The Faber Book of Modern Short Stories,* which came out the same year her essay on Jane Austen appeared in Derek Verschoyle's *English Novelists: A Survey of the Novel by Twenty Contemporary Novelists.* The novels for which this "neglected writer" is, in some circles, still known today, were also written during this decade: *The House in Paris* met with wide critical acclaim in 1935, to be followed three years later by *The Death of the Heart.*[1]

If only because these somewhat arbitrarily demarcated years would turn out to be the most productive of her life, Bowen clearly earns her place within the 1930s gallery of other than "Auden-generation" writers. Still, she also belongs to another assorted group of "forgotten" writers, whose shared existence in the shadowy regions of twentieth-century English literature is largely due to their gender, and to the critical neglect they have suffered on this account. Indeed, I would suggest, it is primarily her status as a "woman writer" that has landed Bowen, like so many female authors before and since, with a marginal place on the literary map. Starting with Jocelyn Brooke's short pamphlet of 1952, whose concluding note of praise highlights "Miss Bowen's" prudence in not "overstep[ping] the bounds" that come naturally with her sex, subsequent literary historians have, whether explicitly or implicitly, insisted on discussing her accomplishment in markedly gendered terms.[2] Where Brooke, in those blissful prefeminist days, could still confidently identify the mere fact of her "femininity" as the underlying cause of a "self-imposed restriction" he attributes to Bowen's writing practice, later critics have gone some way to redress this gender-biased view on her achievement. The author's place in literary history generally, however, has continued to be defined in terms of restriction, alternately being traced to Bowen's class position or to her gender-identity—or, indeed, to both.[3] Even fairly recent accounts of twentieth-century literary history prolong the impression that she was a class-conscious if not snobbish writer of sensibility, whose work, due to the mutually reinforcing constraints of both her class and her sex, is narrow in scope, romantic, and technically conventional.

Both here and in my earlier work on Bowen, it has been my purpose to explore those features that have persistently been considered to "weaken" her fiction, to explore the very idiosyncrasies that have led to her marginalization in both masculist and feminist practices of literary historiography.[4] What has frequently been denounced as a particularly delimiting aspect of Bowen's narrative methods, that is, the conspicuous partiality of, in Douglas Hewitt's words, the "rather unusual points of view" shaping her texts, I have come to regard not so much as a flaw marking even the best of her work but, instead, as a deliberate refusal to aspire to—as literary convention would have it—a "general," even "universal" perspective (Hewitt, 1988, 192). It is, I would argue, precisely the presumed narrowness of Bowen's narrative scope—whether seen in terms of gender or class—that testify to an acute awareness of herself as a speaking/writing subject, a conscious recognition of the specific determinations of both her social and gender positions. Signaling the spuriousness of any individual's claim to what, even in our own "multicultural" times, still commonly passes for a "general" point of view, it is this "unusual" degree of self-awareness that informs the radical, if not subversive potential of this neglected author's work.[5] In what follows, I will explore the narrative implications of Bowen's sharp insight into the necessarily "situated" nature of her own, and, for that matter, any writer's, angle of vision.

* * * * *

Friends and Relations, Bowen's third novel, is an evasive text. Its style is dense and elaborate, the narrative tone of voice amused yet noncommittal, while the text as a whole is qualified by a sustained sense of negativity which is only occasionally relieved by vivid patches of social comedy. The mere hundred and fifty-odd pages of this shortest of Bowen's novels fall into three parts, all more or less equal in length. To discuss *Friends and Relations* in terms of plot development would be beside the point, for the text contains little or no plot to speak of. The whole of its dramatic impact derives from what is, as one of the characters correctly observes, no more than a "large non-occurrence" (*Friends and Relations,* 151). Since it is obviously not the narrative events themselves—such as they are— that are central to the novel's signifying operations, it appears all the more appropriate to concentrate on the ways in which the text takes shape and acquires meaning through the complexities in narrative perspective, especially since the mediating look of the authorial narrator is supplemented with several other focalizing instances.[6]

The novel opens in the Malvern hills near Cheltenham, somewhere in the 1920s. At Corunna Lodge, the rural abode of a retired army officer and his wife, we meet the story's heroines, Laurel and Janet Studdart. At once evoking and inverting a tradition that goes back as far as the English novel proper, the narrative begins where romantic fiction usually ends: under the "inauspicious mutter" of steadily falling rain, the stage is being set for the elder daughter's wedding to handsome Edward Tilney. Nervously giving "instructions" and looking after "arrangements," the Studdarts reveal their preoccupation with social decorum, their anxiety to abide by the rules of country propriety. The comic depiction of the theatricalities involved in this most admirable of social occasions initiates a line of narrative critique which is throughout sustained. While providing the perfect scene for an exposure of the moral inertia reigning within this pleasant middle-class family, the wedding also yields the germs of, what Bowen has called, the "internal combustion" on which the movement of plot depends ("Notes on Writing a Novel 1975, 177).

That things are not all as happy as they may seem, becomes clear when the text obliquely discloses Janet's secret desire for her sister's high-strung young husband, whose "dazzling courtship of the entire family" in the preceding months had not for some time "particularized in the direction of Laurel" (Friends and Relations, 16). An apparent contrast is set up between the two sisters, suggesting that Edward's emotional balance eventually tipped in favor of Laurel's fairness, charm, and "irregular prettiness," at the expense of her younger sister: Janet is said to have "little charm," appearing "even forbidding" (14, 15). The more elusive character of the two, this dark "heavy-lidded and rather somber Diana," being prematurely ousted from the romantic plot, figures as an object of pity among the assembled wedding guests. However, as one of them sensibly reflects: "Girls could not all expect to marry" (13). Fortunately, Janet has "many interests," and is presently occupied with supervising her Wolf Cubs, having given up on her appointed task of coping with the bridegroom's mother, Lady Elfrida.

While the attractive bridal pair ostensibly draw all our attention, it is Lady Elfrida—"always a little too gracefully [playing] a losing game"—who stands at the uneasy center of the scene. "Being a divorcée" (a circumstance which, the narrator adds, "should but does not subdue"), this figure "in claret-coloured georgette" forms a potential threat to the ritual establishment of the Studdart/Tilney connection here being enacted (Friends and Relations, 10). Having left Edward's father some twenty years ago for onetime explorer and big-game hunter Considine Meggatt, Elfrida had not only failed to do the proper thing, that is, marry her "corespondent," but also abandoned her child to the care of assorted relatives, while herself making her way to Paris. A brief return to England, when Edward was "at the most sensitive age," had not prevented her from working in a hospital in the south of France during the war, after which she had come back to take up residence in London's Trevor Square. Such sexual, social, and moral independence in a woman obviously sits uncomfortably with the codes and conventions by which the family-structure sustains itself. The Studdarts, not knowing "whether to condemn her as a lady or as a woman," consider their extravagant new relative a distressing social liability (17).

Having personally little stake in middle-class pretension, Lady Elfrida immediately grasps Janet's barely concealed feelings for her son. Although she does not subscribe to the Studdarts' ambition to keep up the "happy tradition" of girls marrying "out of [their] 'teens," Elfrida would have preferred to see Edward's difficult character being entrusted to the capable hands of the younger of the Studdart sisters. Perceiving the young bride's motherly concern with her son's "surviving childish gravity," she correctly anticipates Laurel's future indulgence of Edward's egotism (*Friends and Relations,* 15). A disreputable mother herself, she knows what ravaging effects such complicity with established gender convention may have, especially on members of her sex who choose not to comply with the rules. It is, after all, precisely such accommodating girls as her lovely daughter-in-law who unwittingly uphold the double standard by which Lady Elfrida herself cannot but be regarded as déclassé. The sight of Laurel's soothing response to Edward's "perversity" and "impassibility," hence evokes in her, in "less than [a] moment of consternation," the feeling that "her own life was ruined, ruined—" (14). A generally unrepentant individual who has paid for her independence with a life of few friends, near solitude, Lady Elfrida at once takes a liking to Janet, possibly because she could be said to be also "in the wrong." When the latter, no more than six weeks later, announces her engagement to Considine's nephew Rodney Meggatt, the news hence cannot but strike Lady Elfrida as a "personal disappointment" (18).

As my reading of the novel's opening scene so far suggests, *Friends and Relations'* thematic focus falls unequivocally on the operation of patriarchal gender ideology in society generally, and within the confines of the traditional middle-class family in particular. It may at first seem farfetched to read such an outspoken critique of established gender-relations in a novel whose drama is so emphatically "underplayed," and whose finely attuned texture creates a highly wrought atmosphere of overall indirection. We should bear in mind, however, that, at the time of its writing, the "Woman Question" had come to figure centrally on the English social stage. By the end of the 1920s, the heyday of the first feminist wave, with its heated parliamentary debates and public outrage over suffragette militancy, had long been over. But the radical changes of the fin-de-siècle, and the subsequent decline of the Victorian family and its values, had given rise to a general sense of despair: in retrospect, the crumbling of the Old Order to many seemed to have coincided with the emergence of the early women's liberation movement. Moreover, in the aftermath of the Great War (to which women from all walks of life had actively contributed), many middle-class women refused to reassume their former roles as Angels in the House. This furthered in the public mind the connection between the gloomy, even apocalyptic visions on the future of civilization—articulated by, for example, T. S. Eliot's "Waste Land" (1922)—and the changes that had irreversibly altered relations between the sexes, both in society at large and in the middle-class family home.[7] The text unmistakably alludes to these larger sociohistorical questions when we learn that Rodney has been raised on his uncle's "cheerful ruthless generalizations as to *the Sex*" [emphasis added]. While underlining the lingering centrality of the Woman Question in public discourse, these remarks also serve to inscribe both Rodney's and Janet's exceptional positions within the fiction of heterosexual romance. The former's attraction to the latter, rather than springing from his future wife's conventional feminine charm, stems from her "rather masculine unawareness of 'situation.'" For, as the narrator informs us: "The Sex did not interest [Rodney]" (*Friends and Relations,* 37).

Perhaps the most significant fact about the wedding scene, however, at least within the context of the present discussion, is that the author-narrator's is not the only perspective we gain on this festive occasion. The static character of the entire sequence is punctuated by the vivid mental observations on the part of a precocious, fifteen-year-old girl, Theodora Thirdman. As I have argued elsewhere, the character of the female adolescent functions as an ambivalent yet privileged signifier in Bowen's fiction generally (hoogland 1994, 24–106). If only because of her conspicuously alliterative and highly suggestive name, this particular version of what clearly was one of the author's favorite characters, immediately draws attention to herself.

The "godsend" creature is a disconcerting presence at the wedding for, seeming "awkwardly anxious to make an impression," she unwittingly reminds the assorted company of their own tenuous hold on their social positions. Theodora's striking looks and snide remarks hence result in her being altogether ignored. Explicitly identified as a "third man," at a time when concepts such as the "Third Sex," the "mannish lesbian," and the female "invert," were no longer restricted to professional sexological discourse but widely available among the public at large, Theodora could furthermore be argued to occupy a potentially subversive position with regard to the system of gendered heterosexuality which, receiving its official stamp at occasions like these, forms the prime focus of the narrative critique.

Almost half of the opening scene is filtered through the mind of this "spectacled, large-boned," and unengaging adolescent. Her curious perspective on characters and events is hence not so much secondary to but, in fact, runs parallel to the narrator's organizing look. Through this strategy of double focalization we are given an outsider's view on traditional female lives geared to "romantic love," the constraining effects of which are shown to find their formal seal in its institutional enactment: the joining of man and woman in holy matrimony. Already belying her name by occupying a privileged position on the novel's extradiegetic level, Theodora, we shall see shortly, will also turn out to play a subversive role in the all but dramatic plot enacted on its intradiegetic level. For the moment, our look into the inner landscape of this literal bystander (whose personality is still "too much for her, like a punt-pole") allows us to become aware of Janet's suppressed passion for Edward. Realizing that this "was a day of chagrin, possibly of despair" for the bride's sister, Theodora at once develops an attraction for her—attraction, not love, for due to her "unfortunate age," the girl "could understand, but not yet love" (*Friends and Relations*, 13).

In this first section's remaining chapters, the Studdart sisters and Theodora's story lines run more or less parallel, occasionally intersecting each other. We learn that Janet's engagement is momentarily called off since Edward is being "difficult" about the inconvenient family connection her marriage to Considine's nephew would set up between his disgraceful mother and her onetime corespondent. While the young Studdarts try to face up to what their transference from one man's hands to those of another entails, Theodora seeks refuge from her well-meaning but horribly boring parents (whom she constantly bullies for being so "absolutely *superfluous*" (*Friends and Relations*, 28)), to attend a girls' boarding school in Surrey. Enjoying the "excellence of [a] Swiss education," there is little for her extraordinary brain to gain in terms of formal knowledge. However, the girls at Mellyfield are primarily "interested in their own personalities, which they displayed, discussed and altered." Already having "a good deal of personality" at her disposal, Theodora succeeds in causing a pleasurable disturbance and distinguishes herself by "making a marvellous man" in the school's Saturday night plays (28, 44). When she hears from one of her fellow pupils, Marise Gibson (sister of Edward's best man, Lewis), about the near-collapse of Janet's engagement, she "c[an]not help thinking, 'This may be where I come

in?'" (45). Unfortunately, although the engagement is for one day
suspended, the whole "miserable affair" proves not sufficiently inconvenient to put the future alliance as such on the line. From then
on Edward and Janet are "relations for life." (We later learn that
Janet's acceptance of Rodney was actually inspired by her wish to
be officially related to her brother-in-law: though separate they
would be linked by scandal.) True to character, Lady Elfrida responds to Janet's act of disaffection, that is, giving up her independence and accepting her appointed place in the social order, by
behaving abominably throughout the settlement of "this affair of
extreme delicacy": Edward's mother bluntly refuses to consider her
distressing past in any way capable of rendering the situation awkward (16).

Janet's capitulation to convention represents more than just a—
perhaps all too easy—way out for an otherwise promising individual
woman. By abandoning her "many interests" to become a wife and
mother, and thus blending into the social pattern, Janet willfully
succumbs to the stultifying power of "ordinary" middle-class life.
She therewith does not only give up the "masculine" part of herself,
her claim to subjective agency, but also reinforces the operation of
the family structure in the maintenance of unequal gender-relations
in society at large. In this sense, her failure to live up to her own
potential—the ultimate character flaw in Bowen's ethical framework—is not merely a sign of personal deficiency: it signifies first
and foremost a foregoing of one's social responsibility. As Janet
herself is later to point out, this is, after all, precisely what families
are all about: "It's possible to be so ordinary; it's possible not to say
such a lot" (Friends and Relations, 47, 49).

While foregrounding the novel's overall critique of middle-class
family life, the section's concluding note also indicates that, in spite
of the outward contrast between the Studdart sisters—"interesting"
Janet, with her dark, brooding nature, versus pretty Laurel, excelling
in pleasant superficiality—their characters are inevitably to be similarly moulded by the grid of ordinary (married) life. Though shifting
the blame for the loss of her friend in the wrong direction, Lady
Elfrida hence does hit on an unexpected truth when she regrets Janet's having had a sister at all: "I always feel, with women, the
mould should have been broken, not used again and again" (Friends
and Relations, 38). Since, apparent dissimilarities between them notwithstanding, the "mould" has clearly not been broken within the
Studdart family, it is not the younger sister's illegitimate feelings for
her brother-in-law that, as earlier critics have claimed, form a threat
to the established patterns of friends and relations that the novel

holds up for critical scrutiny. Nor, conversely, does Janet's unlawful desire constitute the "internal combustion" upon which the unfolding of the novel's narrative pattern depends. Rather, as my foregoing comments suggest, it is the *extra*ordinary character of Theodora Thirdman who embodies a disruptive force within the family-romance, and hence, it is she who carries a potential threat to the established patterns of social relations. Situated in a truly excentric position within the play of gendered heterosexuality enacted in the foreground of the narrative scene, she will subsequently move center-stage by assuming the role of interruptive narrative agent, so as to underscore her significance as the text's ideological and underlying emotional core.

* * * * *

The novel's second part, entitled "The Fine Week," takes us ten years ahead in time. Janet and Rodney live a quietly rural life with their daughter Hermione at the Meggatt estate annex fruit farm, Batts Abbey. Laurel and Edward, the latter now a civil servant at Whitehall, share a more sociable existence with their two children in London's Royal Avenue. The scene is Batts, where both the young Tilneys, Lewis Gibson, Colonel Studdart, and Considine have joined the Meggatts to spend this fine week in midsummer. We learn that Lady Elfrida's visits to Janet have thus far never been allowed to coincide with Considine's and those of the Tilney children, since Edward is still being difficult about the scandalous family connection. This time, however, Janet and Rodney, suddenly seeing no reason why Elfrida should not visit at Batts with Considine, decide to break with this long-standing practice of enforced delicacy. The narrator comments:

> Today proved to be one of those weekdays, vacant, utterly without character, when some moral fort of a lifetime is abandoned calmly, almost idly, without the slightest assault from circumstance. So religions are changed, celibacy relinquished, marriages broken up, or there occurs a first large breach with personal honour. (*Friends and Relations*, 69)

While underlining the fundamental instability of seemingly fixed patterns of behavior as well as signaling the transient nature of time-honored moral standards, the relevance of these remarks does not immediately become clear, since it appears as if Lady Elfrida's arrival will occasion little disturbance. Janet's message to Laurel, informing them about the decision, evokes no emotion whatsoever in Edward, while the elder sister replies that she does "not feel so much as though there had been an earthquake, but as though I should never see you, or you would be different" (*Friends and Relations,* 70). While slightly disturbing in itself, Laurel's sense of foreboding will only begin to acquire meaning when, several days later, Theodora Thirdman pays tribute to her Christian name by descending upon the narrative scene in the role of a proper deus ex machina.

By now in her midtwenties, Theodora has grown into a handsome professional woman, sharing a fashionable attic flat in London with her former schoolmate Marise Gibson—the latter being, significantly, a creative writer. Still in love with Janet, Theodora exhibits a "lucid perplexity" as to the ordinariness of this capable housewife's uneventful and orderly life. An orderliness which, in fact, appears not even to be affected by the radical break with established custom occasioned by the elderly couple's unwonted joint presence. The formerly so unsettling power of Lady Elfrida's unorthodox character has obviously diminished, so as to give way to the disruptive potential of the truly "outcast" figure of Theodora Thirdman. Displacing the former from her customary position as agent provocateur, it soon turns out to be the latter who succeeds in upsetting the "delicate rhythm" of the smoothly running family machinery: Theodora's unexpected visit produces a disconcerting effect on the party as a whole.

Lady Elfrida who, despite her unconventional ways, has always been able to rely on the cunning exploitation of her feminine charm, feels "quite hysterical" in the presence of this sexual "dark horse." She tries to subdue the anxiety provoked by the rather daunting "masculine" creature by at once acknowledging and dismissing what she obviously perceives to be the underlying nature of Theodora's oddness: "She had passions for women—awkward, such a tax on behavior, like nausea at meals" (*Friends and Relations,* 82).[8] Although Janet, once having decided to repress her misfired passion for Edward, has made it her life's work to perfect her role as a "positive no-presence" (33), she is also affected by the unexpected visitor. Indulging Theodora in expressing her fondness of her, she inadvertently allows her guest to stir up memories, especially of that "extinct sin" that accounts for the "persistence of an emotional Edward in [her] landscape" (77). The bond connecting Edward (Hermione's godfather), to Theodora (her daughter's godmother) in the "old crater, now so cheerfully verdant" of her inner landscape, soon makes itself felt: Janet finds herself silently repeating to herself, as if she had woken up from a dream, that she "still lived and had to command emotion" (74).

Theodora is aggrieved to perceive such moral and spiritual atrophy in the object of her desire, and blames Edward for it. While she "could have forgiven [him] a childish anguish if this had not perpetuated itself," she cannot forgive him the tenure he has, "this mortmain on Janet's spirit." Since the latter seems permanently sealed behind her life's undintable surface, and despite the fact that the "whole theory of victimization" is disagreeable to her, Theodora decides that it is "time *something* happened" (*Friends and Relations,* 75, 77). She surreptitiously sends off a letter to Laurel. Within twenty-four hours, this mysterious missive brings Edward storming down on Batts, ostensibly to rescue his children from the unhealthy moral climate created by the presence of the corrupt elderly couple. But since almost a week has passed since Lady Elfrida's arrival, Edward's sudden outrage obviously stems from another source than his professed concern for his children's spiritual welfare. In a private interview with Janet, Edward lets on that it is not Lady Elfrida's presence so much as Theodora's hints about the Meggatt's "unreciprocal" love, as well as the letter-writer's own relationship with Janet, that have brought him down in a fury. While innocent enough in themselves ("I brush her hair at nights; I brush well. Never let her cut it"), Theodora's suggestions of female same-sex intimacy have aroused his almost congenital jealousy. Janet astutely remarks: "*You* can't bear anything to be going on that you're not in. You behave like someone who's missed a train" (94). Edward's feverish thoughts reach the point where "dread and desire ran round the circle to meet," but when he becomes aware of the "cold, mounting excitement under [Janet's] manner," he backs out by asserting that *he* never wanted them to fall in love (95).

The barely acknowledged emotional turmoil in its mistress produces a crisis which, remaining unresolved, continues to spread in ripples through the house. While Theodora and Hermione are joined in their manifest enjoyment of the commotion, Rodney is solely conscious of a sudden cleft between him and his wife, whose silent rebuff he accepts without resentment. Over tea, Edward reconsiders his relationship with Janet, weighing the balance between her and Laurel. The latter's solicitude, reaching him "almost before he suffered, fostering sensibility" is something he clearly cannot do without: "Life after all," he realizes, "is an affair of charm, not an affair of passion" (*Friends and Relations,* 99). Lady Elfrida, confronted with her son's "miserabl[e] hardness," suffers a solitary moment of guilt. At once "impatient for herself and her sex," she subsequently disassociates herself from the whole affair, implying that "it's impossible to be anything but indifferent" (102). The Tilneys' hasty departure on the evening train leaves the party not merely diminished but in disarray: to underscore that the fine week has irrevocably come to an end, a "film [is] coming over the sky," the landscape emitting an "after-glow from a week, a season, a finished eternity, more than a day" (103).

A long conversation between Janet and Lady Elfrida later that night concludes the novel's second section. Under her friend's close observation, Janet is forced to look back on the past to gain a view on her present predicament. "With passive docility," she explains that, having falling in love with Edward, after what had been a "false dawn" to her, she had felt at a loss: "No one explained the part to me. So I stood there with no words to say and nothing to do with my hands" (*Friends and Relations*, 106). When Rodney came round, offering her a place in the network of friends and relations, she allowed him to give her life's directions. (This "strange desire to be related" strikes Lady Elfrida as rather frightening, a "dark power" that she herself, "loved as she loved: to extinction," has never "exercised" (107). In "len[ding] herself to retrospect," Janet comes to an understanding of the fragility of the family structure in which she believed to have found firm foothold. The narrative line of critique here unfolds itself in a complex pattern of imagery.

Through Janet's mind's eye, we witness the emergence of a tree, a "fatal apple-tree in a stained-glass window" which, rooted in that "old branching sin," hides in its shadows Considine and Elfrida, "related only in balance for the design." While the narrator/focalizer merges with the character's consciousness, the tree of carnal knowledge/sin gradually turns into the tree of Jesse—"that springing— not, you would think, without pain somewhere, from a human side." Janet must face up to the fact that one "vital incision" would be enough to bring all those "perplexed similar faces" come dangling down, to be scattered about like July apples, having "no more part in each other at all." The narrator's asides simultaneously reveal that it is Lady Elfrida who has suffered the pain for the flowering of this illusory structure: now so "impatient of all this burden," she has paid for her independence by being forever in the wrong: "Never to be in the right—it's the only possible ruin, I daresay, if one's nothing besides a woman" (*Friends and Relations*, 104, 107).

When the topic of love enters the conversation, Lady Elfrida's intent look burns itself out on Janet's downcast eyes. "Nature as well as circumstance" having made this "shady" Lady conceive of love as a "very high kind of overruling disorder," she had hoped much of "any break with the amenities." Faced with Janet's distance even from love, she is forced to acknowledge that nothing is going to happen after all: her friend's apparent detachment merely "made her enigmatic when indeed she was not enigmatic at all but a plain woman" (*Friends and Relations*, 109). Janet, ready for "the call, any call," subsequently makes her escape by attending to Hermione's night fears. Having duly comforted her little girl, she can "presently . . . creep away" (110).

* * * * *

Despite her desperate efforts, the opening of the novel's final section, "Wednesday," reveals that Janet has not quite succeeded in dispelling her feelings. She embarks on a trip to London, intent on resolving her own uneasiness by talking to Laurel. Finding her sister missing from Royal Avenue, she has lunch with Edward instead. An "extraordinary intimacy" at first seems to succeed in breaking the mold of their natural brother-and-sister behavior. Edward, however, having always shied away from the "inconvenient cruelty of passion," finds Janet's "penetrating non-comprehension" to be the "enemy of his spirit" (*Friends and Relations*, 119). Later that night, he does suggest that they might "comfort each other," but his moral and emotional immaturity renders him incapable of rising to the occasion of Janet's "passionate fatality" (128). Hence, while Janet returns in the middle of the night to Batts Abbey, Edward next morning seeks refuge in the "miniature happiness" offered by his wife's ever-comforting arms (105).

What could have been a devastating family tragedy thus amounts to what is, as I have mentioned before, no more than a "large nonoccurrence." Indeed, the destructive potential of the script of passion, its power to shatter "all the dear conventions," seems to have had reality only in the minds of those who, falling outside the family scenario, would have had no role to play within it: eternal bystander Lewis Gibson and "queer Theodora" (*Friends and Relations*, 155), (Lady Elfrida being, "at this inadmissable crisis . . . elsewhere, the Irish side of the Channel, innocently abroad" (129). When, for a moment, it does seem as if Edward and Janet have in fact run away together, these unlike onlookers meet on their common grounds in the margins of the dominant social plot. Lewis's apparent consternation soon turns out to be basically a rather selfish chagrin. Feeling ousted from his position as friend of the family, he reproachfully observes: "They've got their cue, but they're leaving all of us none" (145). "Dramatic in her sincere misery," Theodora is in effect the only one to break with the bland civilities of "happy custom" by unrestrainedly expressing her feelings. At once furious, jealous, and truly unhappy, she bursts out to Lewis: "I can't stand this; I love her! I tell you, idiot, I love her beyond propriety—" (146). "Land-bound" Lewis, seriously taken aback by such unwonted emotional energy, is capable of no more than icily admitting that "Yes, it is most upsetting" (146).

* * * * *

Bringing the story line full circle, the novel's closing pages take us back to Corunna Lodge. The narrative summary of the Studdart daughters' yearly visits to their parental home, the "family recon-struct[ing] itself with talk and laughter," may at first seem to convey a sense of happy restoration. The poignant irony, however, which qualifies the narrator's depiction of Cheltenham civilization ruth-lessly exposes the moral complacency of its inhabitants. Mrs. Stud-dart's anxious yet discriminating thoughts about her daughters' characters furthermore underline the destructive effects of the near immutable, ideologically enforced social patterns in which their lives are inescapably inscribed.

The main beneficiaries of the restoration of order, the reassertion of the power of the family, are evidently the nominal heroes of the novel's first section: Edward and Rodney. While the former can go on indulging himself in his wife's maternal forgiveness, passively acquiescent Rodney is content just to have Janet back, even if she "had explained nothing, accounted for nothing" (*Friends and Rela-tions*, 135). In contrast, an irreparable cleft has been wrought between the Studdart sisters, although the "catastrophe [had been] very quiet" (129). Laurel's ingenuous love for Edward has also been sorely af-fected: the root of suspicion having irrevocably implanted itself, she foresees a "hundred solitary woman's wakings, beside but without him" (153). The benefits reaped from family stability are clearly unequally differentiated along gendered lines. Even so, whereas Lau-rel is obviously to a certain extent victimized by the social system's gendered operations, she is also shown consciously to reassume a position of complicity within it. Like Janet, who seems to have made it her life's purpose not to think, to entomb herself in "thought that was no thought," Laurel is equally set on leaving things unsaid. Realizing that it is only by "keep[ing] still, not rocking their boat" that she and Edward will be able to continue "along the smooth stream," she willfully seeks oblivion, telling herself that she remem-bers nothing (153). If Laurel's shying away from herself is denounced in mildly critical terms, Janet's deliberate withdrawal is brought to the fore with unmistakable irony: the day after her nocturnal nonadventures in London, she wakes up to take charge of the annual meeting of the Mothers' Union taking place on her lawn.

It would appear that it is only queer Theodora who can stand up to the moral scrutiny that determines the novel's narrative vision. Though eventually all but fading into the background, the moral value of her character is not only inscribed on the novel's intradiegetic level, but also borne in on the reader through the strategies of focalization that structure the text's extradiegetic operations. The fact that this sexual "dark horse" is the only truly "sensationalist" character attests to her function as the focal point within the narrative's overall moral framework. For, as Bowen points out in one of her autobiographical sketches, it is such sensationalists that form the privileged signifiers in the typical "Bowen terrain:"

> Bowen characters are in transit *consciously*. Sensationalists, they are able to re-experience what they do, or equally, what is done to them, every day. They tend to behold afresh and react accordingly. ("Notes on Writing a Novel," 1975, 177)

That a professional, independent young woman should perform this pivotal function in *Friends and Relations* is, in view of Bowen's own experiences in "so-called real life," not so surprising. Theodora is, however, more than the odd one out within the prevailing system of gender relations. She is also clearly a sexual "deviant" within the pervasively heterocentrist sociohistorical order against which the narrative is set. That it should fall on a lesbian character to become the principal conveyor of the text's moral meanings may be partly accounted for by the novel's critical focus on the seat of (reproductive) heterosexuality, the traditional nuclear family. It may also have to do with the fact that even a highly self-conscious writer such as Bowen will, "like a swimmer caught by an undertow," inevitably be "borne in an unexpected direction . . . captured by some experience to which one may have hardly given a thought." And it is this, I would suggest, that renders Bowen such an outstanding novelist. More than any other of the features contributing to her remarkable achievement, it is such willingness to be lured by the unknown and the unexpected, to embrace experience in all of its destabilizing aspects, that makes her elusive, sometimes highly disconcerting narratives so challenging: in moral as well as literary terms.

Notes

1. The Second World War and its dislocations caused a break in Bowen's novelistic career, creating a lapse which was to last almost eleven years. Whereas she

continued publishing throughout the 1940s, it was not until 1949 that she was able to finish the novel dealing with this bewildering historical period, *The Heat of the Day*. In the 1950s and 1960s, Bowen's earlier fame and influence steadily went on the decline. Although she still enjoyed a distinct celebrity, her later novels were critically less well received, and still less appreciated by her original fans. In some respects showing a radical departure from her accustomed style and manner, the author's last two extensive narrative texts disappointed many by deviating markedly from what had come to be expected of the "typical" Bowen novel.

2. An inevitability that necessitated her to "deliberately confine herself . . . to the themes which she feels to be safely within her range as a woman novelist," Brooke gives the impression that it is in effect her sex that he admires most about "Miss Bowen," or rather, the way she handled the "limitations and specific advantages of her femininity." In his view, the author distinguished herself favorably from "many women novelists" who have "too boldly . . . ignored the limitations which (whether they like it or not) are implied by the mere fact of being female." Jocelyn Brooke, *Elizabeth Bowen* (London: Longmans, 1952; for the British Council and the National Book League), 30.

3. Douglas Hewitt numbers Bowen among those "novelists who established themselves in the late 1920s and 1930s," such "minor" figures as Ivy Compton-Burnett, Henry Green, and Evelyn Waugh, who are suggested to have "chosen deliberately smaller subjects and to have turned their backs on technical innovation." Literally echoing Brooke, he remarks upon the "self-imposed restrictions" these writers set themselves, the origins of which he locates not so much in the issue of gender as in that of class (Hewitt 1988, 198). Describing Bowen's narratives as "limited" in "social and emotional range," Hewitt's implicit gender-bias makes itself felt when he, without further ado, classifies her as a traditional novelist who published "a number of delicate small-scale post-Jamesian studies, mostly of children and adolescent girls." Hewitt, *English Fiction of the Early Modern Period* (London: Longman, 1988), 196–97.

Even an explicitly feminist critic such as Rosalind Miles, whose purpose it is to counter the "extraordinary process of denial and annihilation" that persists in negating the "supremacy of the role of women writers in the evolution of the modern novel," reinforces rather than redresses standard practices of sexual stereotyping when briefly discussing Bowen. Isolating hers as a "classic case" among forgotten "women writers whose reputations in their own day were not merely respectable but towering," Miles repeats precisely the kind of constraining gestures which she purports to denounce, albeit in terms of class rather than sex. Reducing Bowen's "gift" to the "evocation of class romance," Miles rejects what she misreads as "unexamined social assumptions" which, and here sex obliquely reenters the discussion, also underlie the work of Rosamond Lehmann, "though [the latter's] subject-matter and technique are not otherwise comparable with those of Elizabeth Bowen." Miles, *The Female Form: Women Writers and the Conquest of the Novel* (London: Routledge & Kegan Paul, 1987), 30. Unfortunately, the differences between these two authors, whose names often appear associated, remain unspecified.

4. *Masculism* is a term developed within feminist criticism, used to designate "old-fashioned humanism, which considers the study of woman to be a special interest and defines women in terms of man." Gayatri Chakravorty Spivak, "Explanation and Culture: Marginalia," in *In Other Worlds: Essays in Cultural Politics* (New York: Routledge & Kegan Paul, 1988), 283 n. 9.

5. While I am not the only nor the first to have sought to bring Bowen back into the limelight, few critics have done so by approaching her work from a feminist

perspective. To my knowledge, the only other explicitly feminist reading of Bowen's novels is Phyllis Lassner's *Elizabeth Bowen* (London: Macmillan, 1990), a brief and somewhat superficial study which appeared in Macmillan's Women Writers Series. Although Hermione Lee pays considerable attention to the operations of sexual difference in the author's texts, she does not herself assume a feminist critical stance. Cf. Lee, *Elizabeth Bowen: An Estimation* (Totowa, N.J.: Barnes & Noble Books; London: Vision Press, 1981).

6. The narratological term *focalization,* originally introduced by Gérard Genette, refers to the relation between the angle of vision through which narrative events are mediated—including its cognitive, emotive, and ideological orientation—and the events themselves. The term is preferable to more traditional ones, such as *perspective* or *point of view*, in that it enables the theoretical necessity of distinguishing between speaking and seeing, narration and focalizing. Cf. Mieke Bal, *Narratologie: Essais sur la signification narrative dans quatre romans modernes* (Paris: Klinksieck, 1977); and Shlomith Rimmon-Kenan, *Narrative Fiction: Contemporary Poetics* (London: Methuen, 1983).

7. Women in England had to wait till after World War I to finally gain the right to vote. In 1918, general suffrage was granted to all men of twenty-one and older, while women had to grow to the mature age of thirty to warrant the same privilege. It was only in 1928 that the required age for female voters was also lowered to twenty-one. Bowen, having earned her own living since she was in her early twenties, hence acquired this formal token of full citizenship at the age of twenty-nine.

8. In her reading of this passage, Lee, failing to take into account the shifts in focalization, assumes these thoughts to be the author-narrator's rather than Lady Elfrida's. Missing the irony implicitly shed on the focalizing character, she uncritically falls in with these thoughts' anxious momentum, and reveals her own unacknowledged lesbophobia by asserting that Theodora has grown into a "ghoulish lesbian." Lee, *Elizabeth Bowen*, 65.

Works Cited

Bowen, Elizabeth. *Friends and Relations*. London: Constable, 1931. Reprint, Harmondsworth, Middlesex: Penguin Books, 1982.

———. 1975."Notes on Writing a Novel." In *Pictures and Conversations: Chapters of an Autobiography with Other Collected Writings*. Edited by Spencer Curtis Brown. London: Allen Lane.

Brooke, Jocelyn. 1952. *Elizabeth Bowen*. London: Longman; for the British Council and the National Book League.

Glendinning, Victoria. *Elizabeth Bowen: Portrait of a Writer*. London:Weidenfeld & Nicolson, 1977. Reprint, Harmondsworth, Middlesex: Penguin Books, 1985.

Hewitt, Douglas. 1988. *English Fiction of the Early Modern Period*. London: Longman.

Hoogland, Renée c. 1994. *Elizabeth Bowen: A Reputation in Writing*. New York: New York University Press.

Miles, Rosalind. 1987. *The Female Form: Women Writers and the Conquest of the Novel*. London: Routledge & Kegan Paul.

Spivak, Gayatri Chakravorty. 1988. *In Other Worlds: Essays in Cultural Politics*. New York: Routledge & Kegan Paul.

Verschoyle, Derek. 1936. *The English Novelists: A Survey of the Novel by Twenty Contemporary Novelists*. London: Chatto and Windus.

A Bibliography of Works by and about Elizabeth Bowen

Select Chronological List of Major Works by Elizabeth Bowen

———. *The Last September*. London: Constable, 1929. Reprint London & Harmondsworth, Middlesex: Penguin Books

———. *Friends and Relations*. London: Constable, 1931. Reprint, Harmondsworth, Middlesex: Penguin Books, 1982.

———. *To the North*. London: Victor Gollancz, 1932. Reprint, Harmondsworth, Middlesex: Penguin Books, 1984.

———. *The Cat Jumps and Other Stories*. London: Victor Gollancz, 1934. Reprint, London: Jonathan Cape, 1949.

———. *The House in Paris*. London: Victor Gollancz, 1935. Reprint, Harmondsworth, Middlesex: Penguin Books, 1983.

———. *The Death of the Heart*. London: Victor Gollancz, 1938. Reprint, Harmondsworth, Middlesex: Penguin Books, 1984.

———. *The Heat of the Day*. London: Jonathan Cape, 1949. Reprint, Harmondsworth, Middlesex: Penguin Books, 1983

———. *The Little Girls*. London: Jonathan Cape, 1964. Reprint, Harmondsworth, Middlesex: Penguin Books, 1982

———. *Eva Trout*. London: Jonathan Cape, 1969. Reprint, Harmondsworth, Middlesex, 1982

Select Alphabetical List of Shorter Works by Elizabeth Bowen

"Jane Austen: Artist on Ivory." In *The English Novelists: A Survey of the Novel by Twenty Contemporary Novelists*. Edited by Derek Verschoyle. London: Chatto & Windus, 1936, 97–110. First published in "Saturday Review of Literature" 14 (1936): 3–4, 13–14.

———. 1938. "The 1938 Academy: An Unprofessional View." *Listener* 19:952–53.

"This Freedom." 1936. In Review of *Our Freedom and Its Results*. Edited by Ray Strachey. *New Statesman* 2:678.

———. 1936. "What We Need in Writing." *Spectator* 901–2.

For Further Prefaces, Essays and Reviews Written by Elizabeth Bowen in the 1930s

———. 1950. *Collected Impressions*. London: Longmans.

———. 1986. *The Mulberry Tree: Writings of Elizabeth Bowen*. Edited by Hermione Lee. San Diego: Harcourt Brace Jovanovich.

Select Alphabetical List of Works about Elizabeth Bowen

Austin, Allen. 1975. *Elizabeth Bowen*. Lewisburg: Bucknell University Press.
Bennett, Andrew, and Nicholas Royle. 1994. *Elizabeth Bowen and the Dissolution of the Novel*. London: Macmillan.

Blodgett, Harriet. 1975. *Patterns of Reality: Elizabeth Bowen's Novels*. The Hague and Paris: Mouton.

Brooke, Jocelyn. 1952. *Elizabeth Bowen*. London: Longman.

Glendinning, Victoria. *Elizabeth Bowen: Portrait of a Writer*. London: Weidenfeld & Nicolson, 1977. Reprint, Harmondsworth, Middlesex: Penguin Books, 1985.

Heath, William. 1961. *Elizabeth Bowen: An Introduction to Her Novels*. Madison: University of Wisconsin Press.

hoogland, renée c. 1994. *Elizabeth Bowen: A Reputation in Writing*. New York: New York University Press.

Kenney, Edwin J. 1975. *Elizabeth Bowen*. Lewisburg: Bucknell University Press.

Lassner, Phyllis. 1990. *Elizabeth Bowen*. London: Macmillan.

Lee, Hermione. 1981. *Elizabeth Bowen: An Estimation*. Totowa, N.J.: Barnes and Noble Books. London: Vision Press.

For Detailed Listings of Articles about Bowen Published in Books and Periodicials up to 1977

Sellery, J'nan M. 1977. *Elizabeth Bowen: A Descriptive Bibliography*. Austin: Texas University Press.

6

The Melancholia of Modernity: Anthony Powell's Early Fiction

JOHN BOWEN

A Brief Biographical Sketch of Anthony Powell (1905–   )

ANTHONY POWELL WAS BORN IN LONDON IN 1905, AND EDUCATED AT Eton and Oxford, where he received a degree in history and made friends with, among others, Evelyn Waugh and Henry Green. Moving to London, he worked for the publishers Duckworth for several years before a brief spell as a film scriptwriter. His first novel, *Afternoon Men* appeared in 1931 to be followed by four more novels over the decade, of which *Venusberg* (1932) and *From a View to a Death* (1933) are the most admired. In 1934 he married Lady Violet Pakenham, and they have two sons. He served in the Welch Regiment and in the Intelligence Corps in the Second World War, becoming a major. *A Question of Upbringing*, the first book of his twelve-volume roman-fleuve, *A Dance to the Music of Time* appeared in 1951 and the series was completed by the 1976 *Hearing Secret Harmonies*. At Lady Molley's (1957) won the James Tait Black Prize and *Temporary Kings* (1973) the W. H. Smith Fiction Award. Powell has published two subsequent novels *O, How the Wheel Becomes It!* (1982) and *The Fisher King* (1983), a biography, *John Aubrey and His Friends* (1947), two plays, and a good deal of literary journalism, now collected in *Miscellaneous Verdicts* (1990) and *Under Review* (1991). His biography, *To Keep the Ball Rolling* appeared in four volumes between 1976 and 1982. For several years he was literary editor of *Punch* and he has often written for *The Daily Telegraph*. He has received many decorations and awards, and is a Companion of Honour.

* * * * *

1

Anthony Powell's work has often caused problems for critics. On the one hand he has been described as "one of a small handful of contemporary British novelists who can reasonably be considered major" (Morris 1976, 1103) and "the best comic novelist of his generation" (Seymour-Smith 1973, 288); on the other, widely treated with indifference and neglect. He rates only a passing mention, for example, in David Lodge's *The Modes of Modern Writing* (1977, 25, 47), and Edmund Wilson's (1961, 536) characterization of the novels as "just entertaining enough to read in bed late at night in summer" is hard to recover from. John Holloway captures the bafflement of many critics in his description of Powell's major work *A Dance to the Music of Time* as

> a *tour de force* of a curiously negative kind: a sort of anti-Proust *roman fleuve* of deliberately Proustian dimensions, arrangement and title. In every material respect, Powell seems to intend a memorable effect by means the direct converse of all the things that are taken to secure effect in fiction. The style is unrelievedly flat, it even seems sometimes clumsy; the characters, with few exceptions, are the same, loosely integrated and colourless, the events are trivial or simply tedious, their concatenation loose and shapeless, any overall design, direction, or conviction almost ostentatiously lacking. (Holloway 1983, 104–5)

The "tour de force" of Holloway's description floats free and unsubstantiated, but the sense of Powell's achievement being an essentially negative one is shared by those who rank his work highly. Jocelyn Brooke, for example, having pointed to the difficulties that Powell's work creates, argues that its virtues are "largely negative" (Brooke 1960, 62).

Powell's five novels of the 1930s have been relatively neglected, although two in particular have been highly valued. For Bernard Bergonzi, the first of these, *Afternoon Men* is "one of the few outstanding first novels to appear in England during the twenties and thirties" (Bergonzi 1971, 3). For Frank Kermode, this novel and *From a View to a Death* are "among the best work of the period" and despite what he calls the "extraordinary quality of the post-war work" professes a preference for these early books (Kermode 1962, 127). Despite this high praise, these novels are not usually thought to be fictional landmarks. Valentine Cunningham's survey of the period salutes them in passing but grants them none of the centrality that Bergonzi or Kermode's words would justify. His essentially thematic understanding of the period leaves no place for Powell's

interest in plagiarism, melancholia, or Nietzsche. Powell's apparent
lack of politics in the most highly charged political literary decade
of the century, his apparent passivity in an era of action, leave these
books in the margins of orthodox literary history (Cunningham
1988).

The reason for this is, no doubt, twofold: awkwardness of both
temporal and spatial location. Bad timing, because England, after
sheltering James, Eliot, and Conrad, had complacently turned its
back on modernist innovation by the early thirties; spatially because
as modernism became increasingly international in scope and American in critique, Powell would appear hopelessly arrested in provin-
cial English reaction. Bad timing too in missing both modernism
and the post-; it is only quite recently that the figures who span
the two high tides—Nabokov, Beckett, Borges and, I would add,
Powell—have been given their distinctive place in literary history.[1]
The advantages of this isolation are real, however, for Powell's novels have something of the pristine, unassimilated force that Fredric
Jameson (Jameson 1979) finds in the work of Powell's older contemporary, Wyndham Lewis.

This neglect is nowhere clearer than in criticism of the novels,
which are often described as rather slight comic affairs, to be linked
opportunistically to those of Powell's friends Henry Green and Evelyn Waugh. Readers led to expect Waugh's manic inventiveness meet
Powell's melancholic flatness only to turn aside. But Powell fares
little better with more formal-oriented accounts. David Lodge has
argued that a distinctive mark of thirties fiction in England is that
it is characteristically realistic and metonymic (Lodge 1977, 190–91).
This accurately reflects certain of Powell's qualities, but fails to register what is truly distinctive in the work: a concern with derealized
states, pastiche, surfaces, and cultural eclecticism; the use of "little
narratives" of gossip and anecdote without enigma or suspense; and
the dissolution of unified subjectivities in uncanny returns. These
qualities which link his work both to prenovelistic narrative forms
and to contemporary formal innovation are rendered invisible in the
orthodoxies of both literary history and formal typology. They have
also been presented (absurdly) as essentially moral or allegorical
works, but are best described as on the one hand a kind of "prefigu-
rative postmodern," a postmodernism *avant la lettre,* peculiarly English and the product of the immediate aftermath of high modernist
experiment; on the other as a truly distinctive, hitherto neglected,
variation within modernism itself. We can call it deflationary, effete
or, perhaps best, melancholic (post)modernism.

Part of the difficulty, as Holloway's remarks reveal, is to decide by what criteria to judge the books. Even Powell's admirers, like Kermode and Bergonzi, have preferred the less experimental and innovative of these novels, *Afternoon Men* and *From a View to a Death*. But *Venusberg, Agents and Patients,* and *What's Become of Waring* have a remarkable fictional energy behind their poker faces. In one way they clearly belong to a realist tradition; the novels are set in a recognizable world without divine or supernatural intervention, with realistically motivated individuals. Some critics have allied them to the tradition of stable irony, tact, and wit that leads from Jane Austen, but a reassuringly Austen-like world will suddenly seem mere pasteboard, opening a vertiginous descent into meaninglessness and anomie. Many of Powell's most striking effects are like this; as Jocelyn Stephens puts it "behind the facade of urbanity, lies a void, an abyss of boredom in which all human values are negated" (Brooke 1960, 62). Mountains will appear to be made of cardboard, or a corner of a London street an effect of cinema. Material reality itself seems to fade or quiver, appearing to the narrator or character like a film, a mere simulacrum of reality.

Powell's fictional career began in the early 1930s, at a time when the British and American economies were suffering from the most severe deflation in their history. Powell's dominant idiom is also that of deflation. His novels take typical fictional situations—romance, travel, courtship—and in each plot, each scene, each dialogue, allow tension to fall, meaning to disappear, sense to become obscured. His characters seem fragile in the extreme, lacking all will, intention, or hope, hollow shells of externally observed mannerisms, the space in which different and eclectic impulses flow. Those who show life are either utterly egotistical and selfish or theatrical, the mere agglomeration of external mannerisms. But it would be wrong to present Powell as a moralist, for his narration lacks all emotional affectivity, all moral or other kind of judgment.

Afternoon Men, Powell's first novel, appears in the same year as that high-water mark of modernist innovation in England, Virginia Woolf's *The Waves*. Powell's novel is very different, portraying a bleakly anonymous world of ennui and emptiness. At the margins of a sterile world of inconsequential parties and futile affairs William Atwater, a young man in a museum, listlessly pursues a woman, Susan Nunnery, whose name invokes the melancholy Hamlet's cry to Ophelia and who ends the novel with another man. A friend of his, also crossed in love, attempts suicide by swimming out to sea, but is rescued. The novel ends as it began with a small group of people who do not like each other very much planning to go to another party. It is a novel recognizably of its period, in its brittle sophistication, its overwhelming sense of futility, and its lack of communication between its characters. Wistful and ironic in tone, it lacks all illusions about the fundamental selfishness of the class of people it depicts. There can be few such collections of tightfisted characters in English fiction as those in *Afternoon Men*, which begins with an argument about a bar bill and climaxes with a four-page discussion about whether it is appropriate to tip a fisherman who has rescued your friend from drowning ten shillings or a pound.

David Lodge has argued influentially that there is a reaction in the 1930s against the essentially metaphoric tendency of modernist fiction. In the 1930s writing, he argues, "was characteristically anti-modernist, realistic, readerly and metonymic" (Lodge 1977). These early novels by Powell appear at first to be part of this movement. The prose has few metaphors; synecdotal detail is piled up to evoke the flat banality of a world without significant action or meaning. Discrete units of information are conveyed to the reader through a cumulative prose, juxtaposing moments, people, and things in unlikely combinations.

> His father, a businessman from Ulster, had bought a Cézanne in 1911. That had been the beginning. Then he had divorced his wife. Later he developed religious mania and jumped off a suspension bridge. (*Afternoon Men*, 8)

Metonymy is the hegemonic idiom of the novel, a metonymy that gives little scope for metaphor or imagination to transform or connect the discrete particles of urban existence. When metaphor is used, it is to highlight the flat banality of what surrounds it in both the prose and the world.

> "I'll tell you this, George. I was squiffy after two of them. It's a fact." He said it confidentially, as one might say "the gift of tongues descended on me last night after months of fasting." Atwater ate chips. (*Afternoon Men*, 102–3)

It is a characteristically "baroque" Powell metaphor (the word "baroque" is the answer to Mr. Nunnery's crossword clue "of whimsical design") which is much more highly developed in his later fiction, a willfully arbitrary and flattening use, emphasizing only the futility of attempting significant connections in the world. At one point, the hung-over Atwater attempts to read a volume of art criticism which establishes relations between apparently unrelated objects, "the isomorphic relationship between the orifice of a glass and the hole of a guitar is the result of a unilateral comparison, since the relation exists between two objects, practically identical. . . ."

He knew now it was a mistake to invite Lola back to the flat. (*Afternoon Men*, 35)

The novel is full of such self-reflexive moments, where the radical formal innovation of a decade or two earlier (here the description of a cubist painting) has become frozen in the clichés of art discourse. The art, like the life, remains fragmented and banal; neither relationship nor significance is established. A gap or fissure opens between two inadequate orders of discourse, the elaborated ratiocination of art-criticism and the urgent banalities of desire, and wit from the (suppressed) link between the glass's orifice and the thought of Lola.

The casual impersonality of the narrative voice and the insensitivity displayed by the characters toward each other convey the book's lack of emotional affectivity. No one pursues anything with passion or hope. The novel is forwarded by staccato, fragmented dialogue which trembles on the brink of the absurd, communicating only by failing to; such dialogue both looks across at the talkies and forward to existential despair. The flatly impersonal narrative voice, akin to the aesthetic of the Neue Sachlitkeit or the early Isherwood, occasionally rises to a heavier irony.

"These are very striking, aren't they?" she said, meaning Pringle's pictures.

"Very striking."

"Don't they remind you of somebody?"

"Everybody."(*Afternoon Men*, 95)

Such emptiness permits the virtues associated with it: slickness and wit, a frankness which admits to the worst and an irony that can make it seem funny. Compared to the great modernist achievements of the previous three decades, Powell's novel is of course self-consciously slight. Powell borrows Wauchop's name from Eliot's *Sweeney Agonistes* and a corresponding urban banality, but there is none of Eliot's ambition to invest such actions with mythical weight or ritual significance. An unsympathetic account would see it as a kind of "commercial modernism," borrowing narrative techniques from Hemingway and cinema (the first section is entitled "Montage"), but only enough of modernism to speed the efficiency of its narration, without seriously challenging the ways in which novels are written and read; a modernism of streamlining, rather than of the avant-garde.

But the novel is a good deal more interesting than such an account would allow. As the passage about art-criticism makes clear, it is sharply aware both of avant-garde practice and of its rapid assimilation into the banalities of critical prose.

> Atwater, thinking of friendship, remembered that he was having tea with Barlow that afternoon. He went back to his desk and took up his book again and began to read: "instinctively drawn to the constant renewal of the data of his imagination, he is careful not to take certain products of the use of those data as the basis for new works. The form which he lends to a particular metaphor, or to certain specific or closely or distantly connected volumes, is never given to the elements of a picture a priori, but purely and simply in consequence of the developments required by the composition of a picture. . . ."(*Afternoon Men*, 46–47)

It is a deeply self-conscious book, as all these novels are, which explore in innovative ways what it is to write in the wake of modernism and how space, desire, and representation can be figured in such circumstances. This appears in particular through visual (both painterly and cinematic) questions, and in several different ways. Cinema can work as a metaphor for the passivity of subjectivity and emptiness of mind: Atwater faced with Dr. Crutch's desire to get his hands on the (presumably obscene) images in Room 16, case B, sees before him "a picture, or rather an interminable reel, a lugubrious procession of close-ups, of all the trouble he would have" if he permitted it. It can also figure the derealization of the material world as (in a recurrent trope) the London townscape appears as "curiously grey, like the backcloth of a scene on the films" (*Afternoon Men*, 34). Most interestingly of all, these effects of derealization occur at scenes of desire. To desire an object is to render it unreal in Powell's fiction, to grasp it only as representation; the only objects of desire are unreal or derealized ones. When Susan Nunnery first appears,

> her entrance into the room made her the immediate object of perception. It was the effect of a portrait painted against an imaginary background, an imaginary landscape even, where the values are those of two different pictures and the figure seems to have been superimposed. (*Afternoon Men*, 26)

She is manifested not as an object, nor as image, but in the space or gap between modes of representation. The most significant, indeed the only significant, object of desire in the book exists in the gap or space between codes of signification, as in the gap between colorvalues in a painting or two paintings. This difficulty or problem of representing the desired object appears again at the end of the book in the hesitation of Atwater's non-conclusion that "when she had gone he had known that he was wrong and it was his imaginary picture of her that was real and her own reality the illusion" (*Afternoon Men*, 186). The relation here is not as McEwan suggests "the shattering of illusion by reality" (McEwan 1991, 7) but a precise undecidability between two orders of representation.

This is deeply related to the dominant psychological concerns of the book. If the dominant trope is synecdoche, the dominant psychological position is that of melancholia. There is no contrast in the book between a banal world and a well-stocked mind; both are equally poor and flat. Knowledge is a cabinet of curiosities in a museum or the insane Dr. Crutch's pamphlet on the unification of craniometric and cephalometric calculations. The postmodern is commonly identified with "ecstatic" or "schizoid" states of mind, a kind of manic overcoming of anomie in the labile acceleration of intensities; the modern with anxiety or terror. In Powell we see something much more akin to Freud's "melancholia," the sense of the self as "poor and empty" manifested in "painful dejection, cessation of interest in the outside world, loss of the capacity to love, inhibition of all activity, and a lowering of the self-regarding feelings'" (Frend, 1985, 254, 252). Melancholy will become a great concern of the later Powell, the narrator of whose later novels will write a book on the author of *The Anatomy of Melancholy* and find his types throughout the social world. In *Afternoon Men* what appears to be a romance is in fact nothing of the sort, invoked as it is through its absence: whereas romantic fiction moves through a set of emotionally heightened landscapes and events to the eventual reconciliation, *Afternoon Men* moves through a set of scenes drained of emotion to an eventual dissolution and circularity. The melancholic derealization of Atwater's desire is grotesquely echoed by Dr. Crutch's impossible wish to possess the locked images of the cabinet.

2

Venusberg and *Agents and Patients,* Powell's second and third novels, have been seen as light social comedies, rather slighter than their precursor. But what is significant is how Powell uses this popular form. *Venusberg* is another romance of sorts, albeit a frustrating and frustrated one. As in *Afternoon Men,* the action "goes nowhere," but the circularity is not that of failure but of a "success" that is no success, merely a return to what was before but in a more resigned way. The vestigial pathos of frustrated desire that weakly animated

Afternoon Men is here absent, and Powell with a good deal more confidence creates a world of liminality and pastiche in which the impossible real constantly slips through the meeting of codes and signifying domains, with as much and as little "reality" as the flicker of a projector or the space in the gallery walls.

Most of *Venusberg* is set in an unnamed Baltic country, an eclectic, unreal world without stable identity. In this way, the novel resembles Wyndham Lewis's *Tarr* or Thomas Mann's *The Magic Mountain* in its aristocratic-bohemian and cosmopolitan setting, but it is a decidely downmarket and marginal variant. Its culture is a curious mixture, to say the least: the restaurants are German and Hungarian, the nightclub decorated in French Second Empire style, the dancers Russian, the band the Bristol Mondial Boys. The cabaret dancer appears successively in Spanish costume, as a man, in peasant dress, and as Columbine. Such eclecticism (the "degree zero" of contemporary culture, according to Jean-François Lyotard) applies to the people too: Da Costa despite his name is in fact a British diplomat (Lyotard 1984, 76). Baron Morgan and Count Mackintosh are Balts. Panteleimon (Greek for "perfection" or "consummation") is a Viennese professor of psychology. Lushington, the archetypal English central character, is mistaken for a Pole.

But this eclecticism is only one manifestation of a more important derealization. James Tucker has described Ortrud Mavrin, Lushington's lover, as "a delightfully living character, with a tangible physical presence" (Tucker 1976, 25). This seems wholly to misrepresent the text, which on all occasions questions the reality of the experiences Lushington has and the place he has them in. Frau Mavrin who appears to Lushington like "the leading lady in a German musical comedy" (22) has a particularly uncertain presence. As Count Scherbatcheff says,

> There are times when women seem to me no more than the illusions that the camera throws on the shaking screen. The shadow of life. In the mythology of the Scandinavians they tell of creatures who present to the eye the appearance of flesh and blood and beauty. And yet, going behind them, they are discovered to be flat. They have no substance. They are like pictures hung on an easel that have no thickness. (*Venusberg,* 106)

Again we see the link established between desire and dematerialization, figured through cinema and painting, but it is not simply Ortrud who is derealized in this way but the entire place.

The place was quite unreal, Lushington noticed. Flosshilde said that there would be snow soon. When that came this unreality would be absolute, although as a setpiece the scene would remain unstylised. Because the unreality was something in itself. Not the product of historical association nor even the superimposed up-to-dateness. (*Venusberg*, 38)

Powell insists here on the irreducibility of the effect of the unreal; it is "something in itself." Flatness, unreality, marginality, and eclecticism are all confirmed as the book progresses. When Lushington goes to Da Costa's flat after his absurd and tragic death, the policemen are like "stage policemen out of a knock-about farce"(*Venusberg*, 138). When he leaves "the unreal city"(147) for the last time he sees what he describes as "the final and rather masterly shot of the reel"(147).

A prolepsis in *Venusberg* marks the book's most important innovation. Lushington leaves London at least in part because of his love for Lucy, who in turn loves the indifferent Da Costa. During his trip he meets and falls in love with Ortrud Mavrin, without it seems losing his feelings for Lucy. On the boat out, Mavrin's friend Baroness Puckler predicts his future with cards. As the novel progresses we see that her prophecies, although couched in rather unspecific terms, come true. At the time of the card-reading the Baroness also encourages Lushington to make a wish, which he does and she assures him that it will come true. We do not know the content of the wish, but can surmise that it is to gain Lucy. It too is fulfilled: at the end of the book Da Costa and Frau Mavrin are accidentally shot, leaving Lucy and Lushington free for each other. But there is no real fulfillment. When Lushington returns home, he is taken on a "pilgrimage" by Lucy who is dressed in "a sort of mourning," where she makes him an offer of sorts.

"I suppose I am more or less yours now."
"Yes."
"If you still want me." (*Venusberg*, 155–56)

It is a moment of pure ennui, intention sundered wholly from action. Fulfilment, as in Larkin's "The Less Deceived," is a desolate attic; to articulate a desire is to render it empty and absurd.

The prediction passage is interesting as the first appearance of one of the central concerns and methods of Powell's fiction, which will become a veritable menagerie of table-rappers, mages, and planchettes. Puckler first characterizes Lushington as "Like all your countrymen . . . a prey to melancholy."(*Venusberg*, 25). We have already seen melancholy in *Afternoon Men* as the sign of the loss or impossibility of attaining the loved object and the pattern is here confirmed in the death of Ortrud and in the emptiness of the ending. But it is Puckler's successful intimation of the future that is most striking and distinctively new. Freud in his essay on "The Uncanny," analyzed the use of such "uncanny" effects in fiction which, he argues, force upon their readers "the idea of something fateful and inescapable, when otherwise we should have spoken only of chance" (Freud, 359–60). This is precisely the reader's experience of the death of Ortrud and Da Costa, which seems simultaneously contingency and fate. Freud contends that this effect of "the unfamiliar which is also strangely familiar" often manifests itself in fiction in the presence of humanlike automata, in belief in the omnipotence of thoughts, and in magic. This seems very close to Powell's world, where characters stripped of human motivation, like the automata of Hoffmann's tales, move without will or desire in empty cycles of absurd contingency, punctuated by intimations of a fated determinism which cancels desire in absurdity and loss.

For desire is a central concern of all these novels, seen at its simplest in *Afternoon Men* in the opposition between Lola, whom Atwater sleeps with and Susan Nunnery, the unreal and impossible object of desire. Sexuality, which in Powell's older contemporary Lawrence is the ground and origin of a Being-in-the-world radically opposed to "machine consciousness," becomes in one of Powell's most revealing metaphors the very opposite, as absurd and inauthentic as it is mechanical.

> Slowly, but very deliberately, the brooding edifice of seduction, creaking and incongruous, came into being, a vast Heath Robinson mechanism, dually controlled by them and lumbering down vistas of triteness. With a sort of heavy-footed dexterity the mutually adapted emotions of each of them became synchronised, until the unavoidable anti-climax was at hand. Later they dined at a restaurant quite near the flat. (*Afternoon Men*, 77)

Lushington in *Venusberg* has a single desire—for Lucy—and in articulating it to himself he in some sense causes or feels that he causes the death of Da Costa; the reader is left to consider the feasibility of the omnipotence of thoughts. The alternatives in the typology of male desire that surrounds Lushington are not much better: Count Bobol is interested in prostitutes and leaves when he makes Flosshilde, about to be married to Pope, pregnant; Courtney idealizes women in a moral way; Da Costa is wholly indifferent to them. Undervaluation, overvaluation, and indifference surround Lushington, whose own feelings are never made clear: after he has made love to Frau Mavron, he thinks about Lucy "But he did not think anything definite about her. He merely thought about her." (*Venusberg,* 34).

Unsurprisingly, there is no happy return to a more real or fulfilled world at the end of the book. Lushington returns to an England flat, empty, and drained of affect. The final scene, like the first view of the unnamed Baltic country, is also liminal, on the edge of the Thames with a foreground of sea.

> "From what you say it must all have looked rather like this."
> "Do you remember when we saw the ships through the trees as if they were growing in the field?"
> "Was it like that?"
> "Only less real."
> "How do you mean, real?"
> "I don't know exactly." (*Venusberg,* 155–56)

It is a melancholy moment, and one that most clearly articulates (or rather, fails to) the derealization of fulfilled desire in the story. Freud identifies uncanny effects with a "compulsion to repeat"; here Lushington and Lucy seem compelled to repeat their earlier lack of communication and resolve in a place that is uncannily like the one Lushington has just left behind. It ends with a futile return, much as *Afternoon Men* ended with Atwater and his cronies seemingly condemned to go to a party they know they will not enjoy.

3

The country house has long provided a rest home for English novelists too lazy to imagine other kinds of community, but there can be few bleaker versions of it than *From a View to a Death,* Powell's third novel and one of his most admired. It is a world sunk in torpor, where all sexuality and creativity is repressed or ignored, showing a social class in apparently terminal decline; vacuous, conservative, mean-spirited and philistine. In Powell's hands it is as flat and derealized as his London street scenes or Baltic capital. The Passengers' car is "an exhibit" (*From a View to a Death,* 7) and their pictures "copies of copies" (8–9). Major Fosdick dresses like "the Old Squire in a melodrama" (188) and appears as "a spectre conjured up out of a mist" (18), while Fischbein looks like a bad piece of realistic sculpture" (103) and a "badly-carved gargoyle" (210). The "two-dimensional" (214) Mrs. Brandon speaks in a tissue of plagiarisms, like Jasper Fosdick who falters "between ill-imbibed patter culled from the talkies and the argot of wartime musical comedy"

(68). History is the village pageant set in the Restoration period and costumed eclectically from the cinquecento to the 1850s. Even the sky itself becomes "a canvas background, an Assumption scene or baroque ceiling" (174).

From a View to a Death has a good deal of indifference and casual violence, from which the narrator is not exempt, much of which stems from, or is directed at, Zouch, a bad but successful painter who ingratiates himself with the landed Passenger family, becomes engaged to Mary Passenger and is eventually killed in an accidental fall from a horse. Powell, almost uniquely in these novels, gives him an explicit ideology, albeit one that simply rationalizes his own self-interest. Unsurprisingly, in a world in which act and intent are so profoundly sundered, Powell shows more than a passing interest in the philosophy of the will. Nietzsche's man of will has already appeared in the figure of Hector Barlow in *Afternoon Men,* a bad but successful painter, who enjoys success with women and reads Nietzsche and in Count Bobel, seducer of Flosshilde and "familiar with the works of Nietzsche"(*Venusberg,* 149) in *Venusberg.* But Zouch, who sees himself as a "fair English equivalent of the Teutonic Ubermensch"(*From a View to a Death,* 12) and reminds himself that "Knowledge is Power," is a more developed example. The nature of the conflict in the novel is clear: Zouch whose parents "had never quite succeeded in throwing off wholly the influence of William Morris"(12) is made to feel "like a slum child"(30) by the Passengers, whose daughter he will become engaged to. In depicting a character who sees life "as a sort of quick-lunch counter where you helped yourself and all the snacks were free"(12), Powell offers his sharpest view of social conflict, in which an enervated and reactionary upper class is surrounded by parasites and confronted by diseased cretins, dissimulators, and tuft-hunters.

The flat, eclectic, unreal, and marginal worlds of Powell's novels can be seen as postmodern, but it is important to see them also, as the novels do, as postrevolutionary or threatened by revolution. This is particularly so in *Venusberg* where so many of the central characters are the detritus of 1917 washed up on the farthest shores of European culture. Baroness Puckler, for example, has lost the world in which she was brought up and so "had constructed a neat miniature world from which she had found it possible to exclude some of the more glaring defects of the great capitals."(*Venusberg,* 65) Frau Mavrin's family lost its wealth with the defeat of the Austro-Hungarian empire and Count Scherbatcheff left Russia after the revolution. At the climax of the book Da Costa is shot by Bolsheviks attempting to assassinate the chief of police, in retaliation for his persecution of them(69). Lushington and Frau Mavrin have a romantic assignation among the ruins of the little palace, among the fragments of broken imperial statues, "a place . . . left without meaning" and a future "potential state institution for mental defectives"(91). A peasant "with obscure remembrance of another epoch" touches his cap to them as they encounter a group of soldiers who resemble "the accepted representations of Noah and his children." Akin not to the survivors of the Flood but to their representations, they linger on, derealized, after the deluge.

It is perhaps this that explains the peculiar violence and unreality of the texts. Bernard Bergonzi has described Powell as a "detached but sympathetic observer" (Bergonzi, 1970 3), but the limits to the sympathy are sharply marked. Working-class characters in particular are treated with contempt. Almost without exception they are characterized as cretins, dotards, and thugs. Doormen in particular, who exist on the thresholds of privilege and mark its limits, are most brutalized. In *Afternoon Men* they appear as "two Shakespearean murderers, minor thugs from one of the doubtfully ascribed plays"(*Afternoon Men*, 18), a "senile cretin" (100), and "an ape-faced dotard in uniform"(96). As class marks a limit, so does race, from Verelst in *Afternoon Men* who "was dark and had bags under the eyes and rather a big nose, but the general effect was not bad and he hardly looked like a Jew at all"(*Afternoon Men*, 86) to Hugh Judkins in *What's Become of Waring* who gives "several little intakes of breath like a Jap"(*What's Become of Waring*, 90). Comic, violent, but not in the least carnivalesque, Powell's novels move to, or center on, loss and absence. The pleasure principle that appears to motivate the characters yields constantly to death and repetition: Ortrud, Da Costa, and Count Scherbatcheff die in *Venusberg* as do Zouch and Mrs. Brandon at the end of *From a View to a Death*; *What's Become of Waring* begins with a fake death and ends with four apparently real ones; *Afternoon Men* and *Agents and Patients* conclude (or fail to) with the loss of Susan Nunnery and Blore-Smith's hopes. Fotheringham's monologue on "The Secret of Life" in *Afternoon Men* ends, Beckett-like, in fragmentation and incoherence, while Count Bobel's final advice to Lushington in *Venusberg* is to recommend "an expression—Nitchevo. . . . It means 'nothing' or, more freely, 'what does it matter?'"

Critics have often commented on the peculiar "objectivity" of Powell's fiction and have rightly sought parallels—Hemingway and Wyndham Lewis—among his contemporaries. It may be more useful though to relate his work to that of contemporary sociological thought, in particular the work of Max Weber. For there is a clear parallel between Powell's narrative detachment and Weber's adherence to the virtues of "value-free" narration. Fredric Jameson, in some brilliant pages on the sociologist's work, presents it as an emblematic example and analysis of the central experience of modernity, in which "Life becomes meaningless in direct proportion to people's control of their environment" (Jameson 1986, 7). Repetition, sameness, desolation, and tedium characterize Powell's England; "that misty kingdom of the spleen," in Baudelaire's telling phrase (Benjamin 154).

But it is not simply a thematic matter, for the "paralysed detachment" is also a quality of the narration itself, in which sharp technical control coexists with a willed banality of narrative content. It is a remarkable fictional achievement, refusing the onward thrust of enigma and suspense and the critical attachment of symbolic depth. Powell's ennui resists metaphysical explanation through its particular social location: a world in which Powell's characters—bad painters, minor writers, journalists, art-dealers, and models—know only too acutely what it means for all residually meaningful activities, such as art or desire, to be subject to the law of the commodity. But the alternatives to the numbing banalities of work and the self-deceit of art are no better: Zouch in *From a View to a Death,* "one of the shapeless entities torn out of the abyss of time," attempting an escape from the melancholy exigencies of commodified art, thinks "with jocularity" of his entry into the English ruling class as the occupation of "a reserved place . . . in one of this catacomb's sarcophagi" (*From a View to a Death,* 177).

4

The title of *Agents and Patients* evokes an apparently more familiar thirties landscape of institutions and spies while pointing to the novel's central concern with dominant and subordinate partnerships. Like its predecessors, the novel relates a life of futility and ennui, punctuated by an "adventure" which is simultaneously more and less real than what precedes it, and returns at the end to a state similar to that which began it. Blore-Smith, a young man in London of matchless conformity and dullness, leads a lonely and frustrated life, until he is persuaded by Chipchase and Maltravers, whom he meets by chance, to be psychoanalyzed and to finance a film they are making. After various escapades in which he loses a good deal of money, he returns to the life he has left. The story thus makes thematic—in psychoanalysis and cinema—the concern with subjectivity and image that has permeated the other books. *Venusberg* had a number of characters, including the pseudo-Russian pseudo-aristo-crat man of will Count Bobel, whose identity remained undecidable and enigmatic. Here the whole action of the book is centered on two conmen for whom the celluloid surfaces and the depths of the unconscious are equally unreal.

Early on in the book, echoing the title, the three main characters witness a street entertainment in which one man in chains is threat-ened by another with a sword. The place in which it occurs is as significant as the act itself; it takes place in a square which supplies "a surrealist background to the various performers who paused to do their stuff" (*Agents and Patients,* 11). A wigwam, some stage scenery, the dispersed lumber of urban detritus randomly feature in a space of dissociated performers, observed by desultory groups. It signals the pervasive concern in the book with fields of apparently unrelated activity. As in its precursors the metafictional interests are displaced into questions of visual representation: Blore-Smith characteristically attempts to break out from his world of Medici prints and stifling conformity by buying an execrable modernist work of art.

But it is not pictures but moving pictures which are the dominant concern of the book. The whole novel is deeply cinematic, both in its form and its concerns. Cinema-going indeed appears to be the major social activity of the novel: Blore-Smith prefers London to Oxford because there are more cinemas and takes Susan Maltravers to the cinema before attempting to seduce her; Maltravers works in films; Chipchase, Maltravers, and Blore-Smith spend some time on the set of the Niebelheimnazionalkunstfilmgesellschaft, the German film studio. Like a film script, and Powell's other novels, large swathes of the action are forwarded through dialogue, with almost no attempt to characterize motivation other than the depiction of exterior mannerisms, a kind of behaviorist realism whose effect is to render unreal.

The film that Chipchase and Maltravers claim to be making is to be both a direct transcription of life and an illustration of the most advanced theoretical practice, psychoanalysis.

> I want my film to be a document of behaviour founded to a considerable extent on the findings of psycho-analysis. I take a small group of people. I show certain salient features of themselves. Dreams. Desires. I illustrate their behaviour . . . a great many of the best films are pictures in which professional actors play minor roles or no role at all . . . . My extension of it is to collect a cast of, let us say, intellectuals without previous training and watch them behave intellectually. (*Agents and Patients,* 9)

Cinema and psychoanalysis are Blore-Smith's downfall. Both the production of images and the examination of psychic depths are mere illusions designed to relieve him of his wealth. The film (whose working title is *Oedipus Rex*) is either unmakable or never seriously intended ("With the best will in the world, one can't photograph a passive man subconsciously hating his father"(*Agents and Patients,* 55) says Maltravers at one point); nothing can relate or mediate surface appearances and the depths of the heart. Indeed there are no depths; merely troubling and deceptive surfaces: "In this part of London the light was always of a thin quality and passing through its streets gave the illusion of cinema"(17).

If one reads *Agents and Patients* as a realist text, it is open to all the charges that are usually made against Powell's fiction. The characterization, limited to the reporting of dialogue and external appearance, is superficial; the action trivial; the climax bathetic. For Neil McEwan, the characters are "puppet-like, with little or no inner life" (McEwan 1991, 35). But if one sees it as motivated by very different concerns about the melancholic impossibility of desire and figuration, it looks very different. Blore-Smith is, in a sense, the terminus of the flâneur: inhibited, dejected, lacking self-regard, he is promised a little carnival of cinematic desire and somatic recovery through pseudo-psychoanalysis, but ennui yields only to anxiety, stasis to loss, and inauthenticity to meaninglessness. At the end of the escapades of the book, Chipchase and Maltravers visit Blore-Smith, and insist that he pay them once more. He writes them a check and in exchange they give him an envelope. Inside is a photograph of the two of them standing by an urn. Like the soldiers in Godard's *Carabinières,* he looks for life and experience and returns only with an image. He first discards it, and then places it on the mantelpiece.

In *What's Become of Waring,* Powell's final prewar novel, these concerns come most strongly together. The first to be written in that decentered first-person style that will later mark all the volumes of *A Dance to the Music of Time,* it is the most thoroughly metafictional of the early novels, exploring through writing as well as cinema and painting his characteristic concerns with derealization, melancholia, and the uncanny. The landscape of the novel is a characteristically melancholic one, trapped in an eternal present tense, cinematic and banal.

> This waste land might have been some walled-in space in the suburbs where businessmen practised their golf shots; or the corner of a cinema studio used for shooting wilderness scenes. It had neither memories of the past nor hope for the future. (*What's Become of Waring,* 64)

The characters similarly seem to fade into representation, or into the space between representations. The barracks behind the melancholy Eustace Bromwich are "like the background to a satirical print of which he was the subject"(*What's Become of Waring*, 8); the railway station "appeared neatly arranged as for the opening act of a musical comedy"(137); the narrator, questioned by Bernard Judkins, likens it "to being cross-questioned by a stage-detective"(195); his brother is "like a saint in a stained glass window"(212); going to a wedding is for the enigmatic Bromwich "rather like a visit to the cinema"(25); General Pimley "looked like an immensely distinguished conjuror"(111). The only fact that we are told about a woman the narrator meets at a dance is that she was "strongly reminiscent of Picasso's Femme à la chemise"(121); a page later she is simply "the little Picasso"(122).

Most critics have undervalued the book. For James Tucker it is "a very capable lightweight exercise" which "represents a pause in Powell's progress"(Tucker 1976, 37) and Bernard Bergonzi has argued that it "lacks real inventiveness" (Bergonzi 1971, 9). In fact it is a much more interesting and complex book than this, pursuing Powell's interest in fictionality, uncertainty, and identity in a new direction, one which doubts deeply the possibility of "inventiveness" or "originality" in writing at all. It is striking that almost everyone in the novel is a writer of one sort or another: the narrator works in a publishing office and is in the midst of a stalled study of Stendhal; Minhinnick and Shirley Handsworth both wish to write the pseudonymous Waring's biography; Roberta Payne is a journalist producing a book; Captain Hudson is writing the regimental history and the Waring biography; Captain Pimley has written a book in his youth, now plagiarized by his grandson; Alec Pimley alias Robinson alias Mason alias Waring is the author, or rather plagiarist, of several travel volumes. But almost all this writing, as the novel develops, is seen as lacking originality or truth: Waring is a plagiarist; Roberta Payne's memoirs are fantasy; Eustace Bromwich writes as "Red-handed Mike" and "B. Mussolini"; even the relatively certain Captain Hudson takes his regimental history from someone else's diary and falls for Roberta and "Waring's" fictions.

The story is told not in the studied impersonality of the earlier books, but through a tentative, self-effacing first-person narration akin to that of Nick Jenkins in the later twelve-volume sequence. Other than the most conventional information, the narrator tells us very little about himself. Instead he tells us about others. But their identity too is uncertain.

No one could ever tell when Eustace was giving an imitation and when a confidence. He threw himself with such heart and soul into his impersonations of splenetic generals, White Russians, Cockney privates, and Levantine panders that he actually became them. (*What's Become of Waring*, 10)

Indeed the entire action and characterization of the book is profoundly uncertain: "it was generally supposed" and "no-one could ever agree" are characteristic modes of narration. Eustace Bromwich like Waring, Roberta Payne, and the narrator himself, is a space through which other voices play, lacking consistent public identity and diminishing the coherent self to a set of mannerisms. One of the narrator's very few judgments in the novel is to say that he admires Alec Pimley the successful fraud and plagiarist much more than T. T. Waring the successful and serious author.

At first sight the novel appears open to the charges made by Holloway against the later sequence. The plot (which centers on the revelation that T. T. Waring, a best-selling travel writer, is in fact a plagiarist) appears rather episodic and loosely constructed. The revelation of his true identity occurs two-thirds of the way through and provides no emotional or narrative climax. The plot consists of a set of non-events: Waring's supposed death is not real; Waring himself is not real; Hudson's book is abandoned; the narrator's study of Stendhal is arrested at the second chapter; Judkins and the narrator both abandon publishing at the end. It is only when we see how deeply the concern with writing and its relation to the dissolution and faking of identity runs through the book from the moment on the first page when Eustace Bromwich (in the character of "Red-handed Mike") throws a note to the narrator threatening death that we can see how unified the text is. Even the apparently irrelevant plot-device of the return of a stamp album reinforces the obsessive concern with the transmission of messages in writing. Powell's work has been described as "dogged with the question of literary indebtedness" (Hall 1962, 168) and the associated uncertainties are intense in the book.

In particular the book develops Powell's concern with "uncanny" material into an understanding of authorship itself. The narrator is persuaded to visit a séance at which he encounters (or fails to) the ghostly presence of George Eliot who, insisting on being addressed as "Mimi," speaks through a medium the two enigmatic syllables "teetee" which reveal (or fail to) the (faked) death of the plagiarist Waring, whose entire career has been built on rewriting the works of other authors. It would be hard to think of a bleaker or funnier view of an author's relation to his or her readers: the great nineteenth-century novelist with a new, absurd pseudonym is constrained to produce two bare syllables which only in retrospect can be thought meaningful and then only to reveal what is already common knowledge, and false.

A second séance which ends the book is equally important and enigmatic, although this time the message is more ample. An Indian medium, Lal, gives a detailed account of Pimley the plagiarist's progress; his revelation confirms what the reader (but not his audience) knows and he is interrupted before telling us anything new. The source of his knowledge is unclear: Lal may have been told the story by the younger Pimley sister (who hotly denies it); if not, he has supernatural knowledge. We know almost nothing about Lal and in a novel full of assumed identities we are led to wonder if Lal is not another incarnation of Alec's, wearing like him a distinguishing turban. In a characteristically uncanny way, we are left to hesitate between unlikely and impossible explanations.

The title of the book which comes from Robert Browning's poem "Waring," is simultaneously a question and a statement, and unsurprisingly does not help to resolve these problems of interpretation in its enigmatic tale of a character called Waring who is full of literary or artistic or musical promise, suddenly disappears, is once glimpsed on board ship and never seen again. There are clear parallels between the two stories: Waring in the poem is a writer who produces only fragments, whom the narrator imagines in various places, including at one point, in the only other passage from the poem quoted in the book as a Hindu god. "In Vishnu-land what avatar?" he asks. An avatar is an incarnation or the descent of the deity to Earth in human form, Vishnu the supreme deity and "all-pervader," Vishnu-land India. We remember Alec's kinship to Lal and Captain Pimley's confusion of the narrator with his grandson. Writing, like meaning and identity, is constantly displaced in the book, a profoundly uncanny affair for Powell, akin in Peter Conrad's words to "a ghoulish resurrection of the dead" (Conrad 1985, 692).

Notes

1. See Fredric Jameson, *Postmodernism, or the Cultural Logic of Late Capitalism* (London, 1991), 305. On Nabokov see Richard Rorty, *Contingency, Irony, and Solidarity* (Cambridge, 1989).

Works Cited

Secondary

Benjamin, Walter. 1973. *Charles Baudelaire: A Lyric Poet in the Era of High Capitalism*, Verso.

Bergonzi, Bernard. 1971. *Anthony Powell*. London: Longman.

Brooke, Jocelyn. 1960. "From Wauchop to Widmerpool." *London Magazine*, 7 no. 9.

Conrad, Peter. 1985. *The Everyman History of English Literature*. London: Everyman.

Cunningham, Valentine. 1988. *British Writers of the Thirties*. Oxford: Oxford University Press.

Ellis, G.U. 1939. *Twilight on Parnassus*. Michael Joseph.

Freud, Sigmund. 1984. "Mourning and Melancholia." In *The Pelican Freud Library*. Vol. 11 *On Metapsychology: The Theory of Psychoanalysis*. Harmondsworth: Penguin.

———. "The Uncanny." 1985. In *The Pelican Freud Library*. Vol. 14 *Art and Literature*. Harmondsworth: Penguin.

Hall, James. 1962. "The Uses of Polite Surprise: Anthony Powell." *Essays in Criticism* 12, no. 2.

Holloway, John. 1983. "The Literary Scene." In *The New Pelican Guide to English Literature*. Vol. 8 *The Present*. Edited by Boris Ford. Harmondsworth: Penguin.

Jameson, Fredric. 1979. *Fables of Aggression: The Modernist as Fascist*. California: University of California Press.

———. 1986. "The Vanishing Mediator; or Max Weber as Storyteller." In *The Ideologies of Theory. Essays 1971–1968. Vol. 2, Syntax of History*. London: Routledge.

Kermode, Frank. 1962. *Puzzles and Epiphanies*. London: Routledge.

Lodge, David. 1977. *The Modes of Modern Writing*. London: Edward Arnold.

Lyotard, Jean-François. 1984. *The Postmodern Condition: A Report on Knowledge*. Manchester: Manchester University Press.

Mann, Thomas. 1960. *The Magic Mountain*. Harmondsworth: Penguin.

McEwan, Neil. 1991. *Anthony Powell*. London: Macmillan.

Morris, Robert K. 1976. "Anthony Powell." In *Contemporary Novelists*. Edited by James Vinson. Pittsburgh: University of Pittsburgh Press.

Powell, Anthony. 1931, 1973. *Afternoon Men*. London: Fontana.

———. 1932, 1961. *Venusberg*. Harmondsworth: Penguin.

———. 1933, 1968. *From a View to a Death*. London: Fontana.

———. 1936, 1961. *Agents and Patients*. Harmondsworth: Penguin.

———. 1939, 1969. *What's Become of Waring*. London: Fontana.

———. 1978. *Messengers of Day*. London: Heinemann.

Seymour-Smith, Martin. 1973. *Guide to Modern World Literature*. London: Wolfe.

Tucker, James. 1976. *The Novels of Anthony Powell*. London: Macmillan.

Wilson, Edmund. 1965. *The Bit Between My Teeth*. London: W.H. Allen.

A Bibliography of Works by and about Anthony Powell

Primary

———. 1931, 1973. *Afternoon Men*. London.

———. 1932, 1961. *Venusberg*. Harmondsworth: Penguin.

————. 1933, 1968. *From a View to a Death*. London: Fontana.

————. 1936, 1961. *Agents and Patients*. Harmondsworth: Penguin.

————. 1939, 1969. *What's Become of Waring*. London: Fontana.

Secondary

Bergonzi, Bernard. 1962. *Anthony Powell: Writers and Their Work 144*. London: Longman.

————. 1970. *The Situation of the Novel*. Harmondsworth: Penguin.

Brennan, Neil. 1974. *Anthony Powell*. New York: Twayne.

Ellis, G. U. 1939. *Twilight on Parnassus*. London: Michael Joseph.

McEwan, Neil. 1991. *Anthony Powell*. London: Macmillan. Useful bibliography.

Morris, Robert K. 1968. *The Novels of Anthony Powell*. Pittsburgh: University of Pittsburgh Press.

Russell, John. 1970. *Anthony Powell, A Quintet, Sextet and War*. Indiana: Indiana University Press.

Tucker, James. 1976. *The Novels of Anthony Powell*. London: Macmillan.

Powell's autobiography, *To Keep the Ball Rolling,* especially the first two volumes, *Infants of the Spring*. London, Heinemann, 1976 and *Messengers of Day*. London, Heinemann, 1978 are very revealing of Powell's milieu at this period.

7

H. E. Bates: *The Poacher*

Dean Baldwin

A Brief Biographical Sketch of H. E. Bates (1905–74)

H(ERBERT) E(RNEST) BATES WAS BORN ON 16 MAY 1905 IN RUSHDEN, Northamptonshire, to Albert and Lucy Elizabeth Lucas Bates, the oldest child of a family of three. The most important influence of H. E.'s childhood was that of his maternal grandfather, George William Lucas, who introduced the boy to the Northamptonshire countryside, told him stories of shoemaking and poaching, and worked his small freehold farm just outside Higham Ferrers.

In 1916, Bates won a free place at Kettering Grammar School, where he met English teacher E. E. Kirby, who encouraged Bates to write. Leaving school in 1921, Bates tried journalism for a time, but when Edward Garnett recommended that Jonathan Cape publish Bates's first novel, *The Two Sisters* (1926), his career was launched.

In 1931, Bates married Margorie Cox, and during the 1930s, he supported his growing family mainly by writing short stories and reviews. His novels and stories of rural life gained a considerable reputation with critics, but financial success eluded him until World War II, when, under the pseudonym "Flying Officer X," he published a series of stories about RAF pilots. After the war, his escape thriller *Fair Stood the Wind for France* (1944) and three other war novels became best-sellers, gaining him a wide popular following but damaging his reputation with critics.

His reputation as a popular entertainer has dogged Bates since the 1950s, even though he has produced works of undoubted excellence, including the novels *Love for Lydia* (1952) and *The Distant Horns of Summer* (1967), novellas like "Dulcima" and "The Triple Echo," and many fine short stories. Bates's aloof manner and preference for country living distanced him from London literary life, and though he was made a Commander of the British Empire in 1973, his death the following year was hastened by heavy drinking, motivated in part by disappointment over critical neglect.

His most important legacy is his contribution to the short story and the rural novel, genres often slighted by contemporary critics.

* * * * *

H. E. Bates was a prolific writer from the time of his first publication in 1926 until his death, but no period was more productive in quantity and quality than the 1930s. During this decade, Bates published five novels, seven collections of new stories, three books of essays, and a play. Although the short stories are artistically superior to the novels, the novels—*Charlotte's Row* (1931), *The Fallow Land* (1932), *The Poacher* (1935), *A House of Women* (1936), and *Spella Ho* (1938)—are far more interesting socially and politically. Collectively they paint a unique and arresting portrait of the economic and social changes that transformed the English midlands between 1870 and 1931. During this sixty-year period, the area around Bates's hometown of Rushden, Northamptonshire, witnessed a decline in the traditional agricultural way of life and the arrival of mechanized farming and factory manufacturing.

In his youth, Bates often affected socialist ideas and attitudes, but the collectivist mentality that characterizes much of the political writing and thinking of the 1930s never really captivated him. For Bates, the tragedy of the machine age was the loss of individuality and personal freedom and the rise of a stultifying middle-class respectability. These ideas are first taken up in *Charlotte's Row*, which depicts the imposition of the factory system and its consequent spoliation of the countryside and imprisonment of workers in airless factories under iron discipline. *The Fallow Land* and *The House of Women* are rural novels, detailing the economic difficulties and technological changes agriculture faced between 1890 and 1920. They are also novels of character, not simply of impersonal forces, portraying vividly the personal struggles farmers faced from the recalcitrant land, unpredictable weather, the vagaries of the market, and the challenges of new machinery. *A House of Women* covers 1905–25 and includes, in addition to the themes of *The Fallow Land,* the repressive morality of chapel-driven respectability. *The Poacher* and *Spella Ho* span the years 1870 to 1920 and are set in the same location. The former traces the shift from cottage manufacturing to factory work and the resulting influence of middle-class manners and respectability. The latter covers the same ground from the point of view of Bruno Shadbolt, who raises himself from poverty to wealth by building the businesses and factories that transform the workers' lives and pollute the countryside with factories, sprawling housing estates, and mechanized transportation.

The economic and social phenomena that Bates observed in rural Northamptonshire are clearly reflected in macroeconomic studies of the 1870–1914 period. In general, agriculture declined relative to the gross national product, from 17.4 to 6.7 percent of the total. Concurrently, rural occupations ceased to be representative of the whole, and rural life and traditions began to deteriorate (Ashworth 1960, 68–69).

The relative decline of agriculture and the changes in rural life that resulted from it were accompanied by an equally devastating change—another wave of factory building. Scattered handicraft industries became centralized in one or two locations within a district or came from all over the country to a central location, as boot and shoemaking did in Northampton (Ashworth, 87). Bates documented this shift in his novels as independent shoemakers working from their homes or backyard sheds were rapidly replaced by centralized factories. Gone were the fiercely independent and free-thinking shoemakers of his grandfather's day, men who worked to their own rhythms and frequently threw down their tools to enjoy a dog race, watch a prize fight, or work in the fields at harvesttime. In their place was a race of exploited proletarians, subject to the artificial rhythms of the factory whistle and degrading subservience to machinery. Accompanying these changes were new roads and housing developments, motorized transportation, and the rapid growth in towns and cities. "Gentrification" was the inevitable result in manners and mores.

As just noted, all five of the novels (and some of the stories) Bates wrote during the 1930s deal in some measure with these economic and social trends. Of these, *The Poacher* is the most comprehensive in its treatment of the themes, and as such it can stand as representing Bates's feelings about social and economic issues.

The Poacher opens in 1881 and introduces "Buck" Bishop as a typical independent shoemaker. Buck is an atheist, an ardent supporter of the maverick member of Parliament William Bradlaugh (1833–91), and a successful poacher. There is no mistaking Bates's admiration for Buck and the breed of men he represents.

Nenweald, like all the towns of the Nen valley, was a shoemaking town and Bishop himself was a shoemaker when he chose to work between his poaching and his long hours of idleness in his favourite bars. And he was great in argument, driving home his points by smashing his hammer down on the bench, sending the bright steel tingles and the myriad brass rivets dancing up and down like sparks. And now, refreshed with the argument and the beer, he looked superb, the blood rich in his cheeks, his eye jaunty, the very tilt of his head spirited and happy, the muscles of his great legs taut with arrogant life. (*The Poacher*, 31)

Nor is Buck's appeal simply in his swaggering confidence and sometimes irresponsible independence. At harvesttime, he can work with incredible endurance and energy, scything the hay or grain tirelessly with "serene strength" (*The Poacher*, 67). But poaching is Buck's year-round passion, and he pursues it with relentless determination and practiced skill. Although there is money and food in poaching, its appeal lies in its excitement, closeness to nature, and perhaps above all in its defiance of authority. A new gamekeeper in Buck's territory is a threat but also a challenge, and Buck is determined to beat him. Unfortunately, Buck overreaches himself and is fatally wounded. His death leaves his son Luke "robbed of all spirit" (87) and signals the end of an era. Buck is the last, or all but the last, of his breed. Changes are on the horizon that will force Luke to grope his way through a very different set of problems. A kindly aunt with some money to spare urges Luke to forsake shoemaking and poaching and to study law, but his skills are physical rather than intellectual, and after a period of deep mourning and aimless sloth he returns to his father's old haunts, only to find himself suspected of murdering the gamekeeper who killed Buck. Panicked flight takes him to new territory and into a new identity, that of farm laborer and harness mender for Elijah Thompson, a Methodist lay preacher and prosperous farmer. This phase of Luke's life is transitional and prophetic. In many ways, he is just marking time—getting his strength back after an illness, finding a direction in his life. In other ways, however, he is laying the groundwork for his future without realizing it. Thompson hires him as a farm laborer, and though he eventually proves more valuable as a cobbler and harness-mender, he forms a permanent attachment to the land. Moreover, he meets and falls in love with Lily, Thompson's stepdaughter. To him, she is an exotic figure with the leisure to spend her days reading romantic novels and idly dreaming. "They [Lily and her mother] were symbols of a genteel and leisurely life he had hardly believed could exist" (161–62). In direct contrast to them is Thompson himself, an iron-fisted taskmaster to his workers, and a bible-thumping pillar of rectitude and hypocrisy to his family and parishioners. Through them,

Bates introduces factors that will emerge as major forces in the novel—the combination of middle-class respectability and gentility that will transform Luke's world as dramatically as the imposition of the factory system.

Luke and Lily, drawn together more by physical passion and their common hatred of Thompson than by genuine compatibility, elope and settle in Nenweald. Here Luke rents a piece of land and begins working it, first raising grain but then shifting to more profitable garden crops like lettuce and carrots. Later, he also raises pigs. Unconsciously, Luke is responding to shifts in agriculture generally—away from cereals and toward meat and table vegetables (Ashworth, 55). He is to this extent successful. However, his life has come full circle, and being back in Nenweald he has ceased to grow or change. Chained to the land by its demands, he settles into a life of drudgery, while the world around him changes dramatically.

> Machinery was beginning to come in, factories like tall brick and slate boxes, with thick glass windows, were springing up among the houses, and the town was growing. . . . Already [change] was becoming apparent in the wage disputes, the black-aproned shoemakers arguing at the factory corners in the dinner-hours, the hammer and whine of new machinery, strikes, politicians spouting on the Square in the evenings, echoing the thunder of Bradlaugh. Religion was coming in with the machines; little chapels of corrugated iron and raw brick were springing up, indistinguishable at a distance from the factories and tanning-sheds; and with it all the speculator in property, the temperance reformer, and the rise of a new class, the working-class, as distinct from the labourers and the old shoemakers working by hand, independently.
>
> But working on his piece of land, alone, Luke scarcely noticed it. (*The Poacher*, 179–180)

Luke is increasingly an anachronism, a lone farmer on a small piece of land, hardly distinguishable from the workhorses he periodically hauls to the knacker's. His aunt believes he belongs to the future, but he really belongs to the past. Meanwhile, Luke and Lily grow apart: a quarrel occasioned by his snaring a rabbit indicates literally and symbolically the rift between them. Lily "won't have it," insisting that her child will be "respectable" (*The Poacher*, 197–98).

The year 1892 marks another stage in the road dividing Luke and Lily: the universal compulsory schooling act creates an instant demand for teachers, and Lily becomes one of them. Her status rises, while his falls further. Lily's guests to the house use the front door, something previously reserved only for weddings and funerals. By

1900 Luke has fallen into a rut. His figure is stooped. He withdraws from his wife and family, unwelcome even in his own home because of his crude speech and table manners. Meanwhile, his wife has advanced to headmistress at her school, removing her one step further from Luke both socially and intellectually. Luke's monotonous, routine life on the land mirrors changes taking place in the lives of the shoemakers. Independent shoemakers become caught in the rigid discipline of factory life, depriving them of the spontaneous holidays to follow the hunt, watch a boxing match, or work the harvest.

> The flame of that shifting and independent life was suddenly snuffed out. And in its place came an artificial, fixed, incandescent gas-flame kind of life, a life that burned for a given period and was turned off. It burned behind the thick glass factory windows just as a gas burns behind the mantle-globe, protected, shut away. (*The Poacher,* 216–17)

Bates's attitude here is clear, not only in the general picture he draws but also in the recurring flame imagery. Heat and its attendant images of sun, flame, light, and warmth are almost without exception positive ones for Bates, whether they are depicting the warmth of sexual passion, the heat of a summer's day, or the flame of a farmer's determination in the face of obstacles. Like the workers themselves, this essential flame of life becomes imprisoned, to break free only sporadically during the day or in conflict. Human energy is bottled up, replaced by somnolence; independence is stifled, snuffed out.

Although these changes do not affect Luke or even register in his mind, he cannot escape them altogether. They come to him in the form of a son-in-law, Walter, who enters Luke's life with the energy and foresightedness of youth. He attends night classes, works hard, avoids drink, and takes up music.

Here is the other side of "progress" as Bates sees and understands it—a new way of life that brings comforts, efficiency, and high culture. Try as he might, Bates cannot dismiss the benefits that derive from the changes he deplores, anymore than he can ignore the slovenliness and inefficiency of Luke's habitual ways and attitudes.

Walter introduces Luke to publications on scientific farming, rebuilds the ramshackle sheds on his farmstead, and persuades him to plant fruit trees and milk cows, but these pale in significance to the birth of Walter's son. This grandson not only reawakens Luke's interest in life but also provides a link to the future. The boy is something Luke can nurture and teach, in spite of his parents' aspirations toward respectability, symbolized by the new Methodist chapel where young Edward is the first to be baptized.

Edward (who is modeled on Bates himself, just as Walter is Bates's father and Luke his grandfather Lucas) inherits something from each generation. During the week, the boy attends school, and on Sundays he sits uncomfortably in the Methodist chapel, absorbing the manners and mores of the middle class—"the respectability of holiness," as Bates contemptuously calls it (*The Poacher*, 232). But on Saturdays and school holidays, including the long summers, Edward is with Luke, absorbing country lore as quickly as the Apostles' Creed. But if young Eddie is absorbing something from two generations, Luke remains rooted in the past. Neither Walter's improvements to his farm nor Edward's education can drag him into the new century. It is not simply that he is behind the times; gentility is as much to blame as technology. "And he sensed, vaguely, that he was becoming an outsider, different, a bit common. . . . He was an old toad, a fool. A fart in a colander. No good. Where had he got in thirty years? Nowhere" (237–38).

The defeat of Luke by the combination of technology and gentility is now nearly complete. He savors a brief moment of potential prosperity when his aunt dies and leaves him her property, but he makes it over to Walter for Eddie's education. When war breaks out in 1914 and Edward goes off to school, Luke relishes a brief Indian summer of unrestricted poaching, for the keepers have gone off to war and no one else cares. In 1920, however, the keepers return, and Luke is caught and sent to jail. Shortly after he is released, the owner of the land cancels his lease so that the property can be developed for housing, and Luke can only watch helplessly as his buildings are torn down and his fields are surveyed. As he trudges from the field toward Nenweald, it was "beginning to occur to him fully that he had nowhere to go" (*The Poacher*, 273).

The ending is perhaps more pathetic than tragic, for Luke is not dignified by defeat nor ennobled by suffering. He is simply beaten—the last remnant of a once-vital and rich way of life. He was never as fully integrated into the old ways as his father was, nor could he adapt to the new. What Bates laments through him is the passing of Luke's independence—as a small farmer, as a shoemaker, as a poacher, as a member of a formerly populous class of rural workers whose lives were hard but their own. To his credit, Bates does not romanticize the old ways: Buck Bishop was indifferent to his family, frequently irresponsible, sometimes drunk, and probably unfaithful. But he was his own man, and the rhythms of his life were those of his inner urgings and nature—not those of the factory whistle. And while his manners may have been crude and his morals less than exemplary, he was without the hypocrisies and stultifying Puritanism of middle-class Methodism. Moreover, Bates was aware of the compensations brought by the new ways, for he was a personal beneficiary of the school act that lifted his father out of working-class drudgery into middle-class comfort. What he personally resented more than anything was the repressive sexual morality of his religious heritage. Nearly every Bates heroine is warmly sensual, occasionally even promiscuous.

For all of its reputed radicalism, the 1930s produced no canonical fiction about working-class protagonists. Those who could depict the urban or rural proletariat convincingly—Ralph Bates, Hugh MacDiarmid, Storm Jameson, James Hanley, Winifred Holtby, and Phyllis Bentley, for example—have been relegated to the second or third rank by critics and literary historians (Branson and Heinemann 1971, 265–80). Bates, likewise, has been passed over as a potboiler or rural romantic. He shares with Rhys Davies and others a debt to Thomas Hardy and the early D. H. Lawrence, but his work is best read as an uneasy combination of romanticism and naturalism, of lower middle-class and working-class sympathies. And while he writes tellingly or even movingly of the social and economic changes that transformed the English midlands in the years 1870–1930, he never descends into simple polemics or oversimplifies the issues or the people. The novels he produced during the 1930s, particularly *The Poacher,* deserve a more sympathetic reading than they have generally received.

Works Cited

Ashworth, William. 1960. *An Economic History of England 1870-1939.* London: Methuen.

Bates, H. E. 1935. *The Poacher.* London: Jonathan Cape.

Branson, Noreen, and Margot Heinemann. 1971. *Britain in the 1930's.* New York: Praeger Publishers.

A Bibliography of Works by and About H. E. Bates

Primary

———. 1932. *The Black Boxer.* London: Pharos Editions, Jonathan Cape.

———. 1939. "Carrie and Cleopatra: A Play in Three Acts" (performed at the Torch Theatre, London).

———. *Charlotte's Row.* London: Jonathan Cape, 1931; N.Y.: Jonathan Cape and H. Smith, 1931.

———. *Country Tales*. London: Readers Union, 1938. Reprint, London: Jonathan Cape, 1940.

———. 1935. *Cut and Come Again: 14 Stories*. London: Jonathan Cape.

———. *Down the River*. London: V. Gollancz, 1937; N.Y.: Henry Holt, 1937.

———. 1935. *The Duet*. London: Grayson and Grayson.

———. 1932. *The Fallow Land*. London: Jonathan Cape.

———. 1935. *Flowers and Faces*. Waltham St. Lawrence, Berkshire: Golden Cockerel Press.

———. 1939. *The Flying Goat*. London: Jonathan Cape.

———. 1932. *A German Idyll*. Waltham St. Lawrence, Berkshire: Golden Cockerel Press.

———. 1930. *The Hessian Prisoner*. London: William Jackson.

———. *A House of Women*. London: Jonathan Cape, 1936. Reprint, N.Y.: Henry Holt, 1937.

———. 1933. *The House With the Apricot and Two Other Tales*. London: Golden Cockerel Press.

———. 1931. *Mrs. Esmond's Life*. London: E. Lahr (later retitled *Charlotte Esmond*).

———. 1939. *My Uncle Silas*. London: Jonathan Cape.

———. *The Poacher*. London: Jonathan Cape, 1935; N.Y.: Macmillan Publishing Co., 1935.

———. 1932. *Sally Go Round the Moon*. London: White Owl Press.

———. 1937. *Something Short and Sweet*. London: Jonathan Cape.

———. *Spella Ho*. London: Jonathan Cape, 1938; Boston: Little, Brown and Company, 1938.

———. 1932. *The Story Without an End* and *The Country Doctor*. London: White Owl Press.

———. 1934. *Thirty Tales*. London: Jonathan Cape.

———. 1931. *A Threshing Day*. London: W & G Foyle. (later retitled *A Threshing Day for Esther*).

———. *Through the Woods: The English Woodland, April to April*. London: V. Gollancz, 1936; N.Y.: Macmillan Publishing Co., 1936.

1926. *The Two Sisters*. London: Jonathan Cape, New York: Viking Press.

1944. *Fair Stood the Wind for* France. London: Michael Joseph; Boston: Little Brown and Company.

1952. *Love for Lydia*. London: Michael Joseph; Boston: Little Brown and Company.

1967. *The Distant Horns of Summer*. London: Michael Joseph.

———. 1930. *The Tree*. London. E. Lahr (Blue Moon booklet no. 3).

———. *The Woman Who Had Imagination and Other Stories*. London: Jonathan Cape, 1934; N.Y.: Macmillan Publishing Co., 1934.

Secondary

Alderson, Frederick. 1979. "Bates Country: A Memoir of H. E. Bates (1905–1974)." *London Magazine* (July): 31–42.

Allen, Walter. 1981. *The Short Story in English*. N.Y.: Oxford University Press, 260–64.

Baldwin, Dean. 1984. "Atmosphere in the Stories of H. E. Bates." *Studies in Short Fiction* 21 (Summer): 215–22.

———. 1982. "Uncle Silas: H. E. Bates's Romantic Individualist." *West Virginia University Philological Papers* 28: 132–39.

———. "H. E. Bates." 1983. In *Critical Survey of Long Fiction*. Edited by Frank Magill. Englewood Cliffs, NJ: Salem Press, 178–86.

———. 1983. "H. E. Bates's Festive Comedies." *West Virginia University Philological Papers* 29: 77–83.

———. 1987. H. E. Bates: A Literary Life. Cranbury, N.J.: Associated University Presses.

Beachcroft, T. O. 1968. *The Modest Art*. London: Oxford University Press, 185–88.

Braddock, Joseph. 1926. "H. E. Bates: The Man and the Story Teller." *Books and Bookmen* (May): 7, 9.

———. 1949. "H. E. Bates's War Stories." *Fortnightly Review* (March): 205–6.

British Novelists 1919–1939. Forthcoming. Edited by George Johnson. Detroit: Gale Research/Bruccoli Clark Layman.

British Short Fiction Writers 1919–1945. Forthcoming. Edited by John Rogers. Detroit: Gale Research/Bruccoli Clark Layman.

Cavaliero, Glen. 1977. *The Rural Tradition in the English Novel, 1900-1939*. London: Macmillan, 196–200.

Cunningham, Valentine. "Pastoral Perfick." Review of *The Best of H. E. Bates*. TLS (9 January 1981): 27.

De'Ath, Wilfred. 1973. "The Quiet World of H. E. Bates." *London Illustrated Magazine* (May): 43–44.

"Epics in Miniature." 1963. Review of *Seven by Five* by H. E. Bates. *TLS* (13 September): 688.

Garnett, David. 1980. *Great Friends: Portraits of Seventeen Writers*. N.Y.: Atheneum Publishers, 204–9.

Gindin, James. 1985. "A. E. Coppard and H. E. Bates." In *The English Short Story 1880–1945: A Critical History*. Edited by Joseph M. Flora. Boston: Twayne, 113–41.

"H. E. Bates." In *Short Story Criticism*. Vol. 10. Detroit: Gale Research, 109–40.

"H. E. Bates." Forthcoming. In *Dictionary of Literary Biography: British Short Fiction Writers, 1914–1945*. Columbia, S.C.: Bruccoli Clark Layman.

Urquhart, Fred. 1939. "The Work of H. E. Bates." *Life and Letters Today* December, 289–93.

Vannatta, Dennis. 1983. *H. E. Bates*. Boston: Twayne.

——— ed. 1985. *The English Short Story 1945–1980: A Critical History*. Boston, Twayne, 41–42, 101–2.

8

"No Struggle But the Home": James Hanley's *The Furys*

Patrick Williams

A Brief Biographical Sketch of James Hanley (1901–85)

James Hanley was born in Dublin in 1901, though his family moved to Liverpool when he was very young. Like many of his early fictional characters (including various members of the Fury family), Hanley left home in his teens (in his case before he was fourteen), and joined the merchant navy, despite the not very encouraging model of his father's experiences in that area. During the First World War he served on troopships in the Mediterranean, then, using an assumed name, joined the Canadian army and fought in France with the Thirteenth Battalion. After the war, Hanley returned to Liverpool and his parents' home, and spent the next ten years working on the railways, reading voraciously, writing, and having his writing rejected by a variety of publishers. After his first book was accepted for publication in 1929, Hanley left both Liverpool and the railways, and moved to the Welsh village where he spent much of the remainder of his life, producing a steady, sometimes remarkable, quantity of work, principally novels, but also, particularly in later years, short stories and plays. With the determination and application which characterized his entire career, he continued writing into his eighties. James Hanley died in 1985.

* * * * *

Few twentieth-century writers can have suffered a more contradictory fate than James Hanley: on the one hand, consistently praised by reviewers in lavish, if not extravagant terms; and on the other,

134

consistently ignored by that academic section of the literary establishment whose kind attention guarantees a proper posterity. As Edward Stokes notes in *The Novels of James Hanley,* Hanley has been compared, usually favorably, with (among many others) Beckett, Conrad, Dickens, Faulkner, Hardy, Joyce, Lawrence, Melville, Pinter, Dylan Thomas, Balzac, Maupassant, Zola, Dostoyevsky, Kafka, and Strindberg. At the same time, critics have been unable to find a place for Hanley among the "serious" contemporary writers which such a formidable list of comparisons would seem to demand. Whether this contradictory fate owes anything to the contradictory nature of Hanley's writing is clearly a matter of debate. Without pretending to resolve such issues, the present essay will examine some of the contradictions in one of Hanley's most important novels from a particularly productive decade.

Published in 1935, *The Furys* can be read as simultaneously typical of Hanley's work and as a series of departures from whatever norms he had established in his writing, and its contradictory nature poses a range of questions for the critic. *The Furys* appeared in the middle of a decade which saw important changes both in the forms of Hanley's writing and in its success. In the twenties, in common with other aspiring working-class authors, Hanley had written short stories, but, perhaps as a result of his "difficult" style, had had even less success than many contemporaries in finding a publisher. Consequently, his earliest writings were privately printed. In the thirties, however, apart from the collection *Men in Darkness: Five Stories* in (1931) which could be seen as a continuation of his work of the twenties, his output consisted principally of novels, though it also included a sociological study of working-class Welsh children and an autobiographical "excursion"; while the range of publishers involved in the production of his writings included several respected firms such as Methuen, Chatto and Bodley Head. The growing success could, on the one hand, be attributed to a proper recognition of Hanley's talent, but it could also be seen as significantly linked to the patronage of him by literary and establishment figures such as John Lehmann and Nancy Cunard. While this type of patronage was not uncommon, and Hanley along with other working-class writers was published in magazines such as *Criterion* and *New Writing,* it does nevertheless create the potential for producing further contradictions at the level of class location and affiliation, the tension, as Carole Snee says, "between a working class person who writes in order to explore his world, and a person from the working class who seeks to become an 'Author' with all that that implies of the dominant literary culture" (Snee 1979, 181).

However such contradictions might manifest themselves, a disavowal of working-class origins or of working-class life as the subject matter for his novels was not among them. Throughout a writing career which lasted over half a century, Hanley continued to use the conditions of the working class—at home in the cities, or, most famously, on board ship—as material for his stories. This dual source of narratives—at home or abroad, at rest or in motion, concerned with place or with forms of displacement—is how Walter Benjamin, also writing in the thirties, categorized the two fundamental forms of storytelling. "If one wants to picture theses two groups through their archaic representatives, one is embodied in the resident tiller of the soil, and the other in the trading seaman. Indeed, each sphere of life has, as it were, produced its own tribe of storytellers." Although these may be in some senses analytically and historically separable, as Benjamin goes on to point out, "The actual extension of the realm of storytelling in its full historical breadth is inconceivable without the most intimate interpenetration of these two archaic types" (Benjamin 1973, 84–85). Ken Worpole, in "Expressionism and Working Class Fiction" (Worpole 1983), one of the most useful articles on the subject, extends Benjamin's model to twentieth-century working-class writing.

The Furys is representative of the movement of Hanley's novels in the thirties in bringing together the two loci of narration. Whereas earlier works like Boy or Captain Bottell had concentrated on life on board ship, and later ones like Stoker Bush alternated between ship and shore, The Furys is set entirely on land, though ships remain an important dimension—past, present, and future—of the life of the Fury family. If The Furys is slightly unusual among Hanley's novels of the period in being set entirely on shore, then it is even more so to the extent that it includes some militant working-class action, in the shape of a strike which paralyzes Gelton (Hanley's fictionalized Liverpool) for several weeks. This location on land has a number of consequences in the novel. One is that the book focuses on a family and its problems (indeed, The Furys is the first part of a five-volume family saga, and as such is without parallel in working-class writing, with the exception of Lewis Grassic Gibbon's A Scots Quair, and perhaps Alan Sillitoe's projected but incomplete chronicle of the Seaton family begun in Saturday Night and Sunday Morning). This "return to the family" on Hanley's part might seem no more than a proper return to what many regarded as the appropriate focus for working-class fiction. As Worpole remarks, "Family life, then, was portrayed as the natural cell of the working class community, and the permanent continuity of place and employment were the buttresses needed to ensure that family life continued as it should" (Worpole, 78). While such an image is by no means completely divorced from reality, it was the case, as Worpole acknowledges, that for some sections of the working class stability and continuity were categorically not the norm. For each group, the needs of capitalism for a static or a fluid work force (or even for no work force at all in certain circumstances), rather than any characteristic or dynamic of the community itself, determine whether the lived experience is one of place and continuity or transience and displacement. (These could of course be experienced in different ways, as, for instance, when people aimed for continuity of employment by following the same job from place to place, or, perhaps a more common option, where by choosing to remain in one place people were forced to move from one job to another.)

Although the family is the focus of *The Furys,* it is a fragmented family, divided against itself at every level, where even those members who are still living together are variously alienated from one another. Even Denny Fury, the father and perhaps the most human character, feels this. "Family. His family. Christ! It made him laugh. Bloody fool he was ever leaving the *Cardine.* Yes, he thought, a bunch of strangers. Their father. It made him laugh" (*The Furys,* 50–51). The novel follows a period of crisis in the family (which happens to coincide with the period of the strike). The youngest son Peter returns home unexpectedly from his Catholic college in Ireland, expelled, as we learn later, for immorality. This is a particular blow to his mother, Fanny, who has not only invested all her hopes and aspirations in him, but also rather more money in the shape of college fees than other family members considered reasonable, and it is resentment over the preferential treatment given to Peter which is one of the divisive factors in family relations. The alienation of the family members from one another is a mirror of relations in society at large—in a classically Marxist way, though this is certainly not the perspective Hanley is using. Personal contact appears limited, superficial, or undesired; neighbors are interfering, workmates tedious. Exaggerated, even callous, individualism is counseled and practiced, but then, in one of the novel's many disconcerting shifts, is (seemingly) undermined by the extraordinary and unlooked-for generosity shown by Joe Kilkey, the son-in-law whom Fanny has previously despised and shunned.

Sudden shifts also occur frequently in characters' assessments of one another, which can make reading an unsettling process. To her husband, Fanny can be stubborn domineering, overemotional, unpredictable, even "a devil," "driven by an almost insane ambition," but then suddenly she can be "a brick," worth ten of her sister, and far too good a person to be treated in the way that Peter is currently behaving toward her. Perhaps the most extreme example of such a volte-face occurs in Peter's strange, almost hallucinatory, encounter with the bizarre Professor Titmouse, which ends with Peter's violent rejection of the latter's sexual advances. Thereafter, Peter feels disgusted, nauseated at the memory of this "madman," but in a sentence or two this has changed to "'Poor man!' said Peter, 'he said he was lonely. Poor man!'" (*The Furys,* 250) One effect of such shifts is no doubt to discourage any secure reader position with regard to the character being assessed, and, in addition, to the character doing the assessing. Such a lack of readerly certainty finds a correlate in the world of the novel, where nothing, it seems, can be relied on, and certainly not people. For Fanny, this is powerfully demonstrated by the person she had placed her hopes on, her favorite son Peter, who progressively crushes her, firstly by his departure from the seminary, secondly by the revelation that he was expelled for immoral behavior, and finally by the disclosure, on the last page of the novel, of his affair with his sister-in-law.

Questions of place and displacement may be subject to less disconcerting shifts, but are nevertheless not the site of any stable signification. Place, not surprisingly, connotes roots and security: before the onset of complete senility, old Mr. Mangan, Fanny's father, frequently expresses the desire to return to Ireland; for Denny, in spite of all the upheavals, "There was something splendid about the word 'home', there was something to look forward to. . . ." (*The Furys,* 207). At the same time, it can be stagnation or entrapment. Denny, for example (contradictorily, unsurprisingly) feels stifled on land, and longs to go back to sea. "Once he had been a seaman. Now he felt he was nothing. He was unused to living ashore; a street was only another sort of monstrous stone cage, behind the brick bars of which the human monkeys chattered incessantly" (49). For the Fury family, their years in Hatfields seem to be a period of stagnation and missed opportunities rather than of stability or security. Conversely, displacement can be seen negatively: Mr Mangan forced to leave home by his father during a period of famine; both Fanny and Denny forced to come to England to look for work; the family dispersed and disunited. It can also have its appealing aspects, however, in the freedoms offered by a life in the merchant navy, for instance, which claims so many members of the Fury family.

It is the depiction of, and attitudes toward, work (including the merchant service) and the working class which form the most important area of representation in the novel. The detailed description of work (especially the manual labor of the working class) does not often appear in mainstream literature. In *The Political Unconscious,* Fredric Jameson notes what he calls the "aestheticising strategy" by which the fact of work is transformed in literature into something "derealised," hence more acceptable and consumable. In *Lord Jim,* for instance, which Jameson discusses, labor issues as a distant rhythmic noise from somewhere deep inside the ship. In *The Furys,* a possible parallel would be the work in the bone yard which issues as an all-pervading smell (though it is perhaps difficult to see this breath-stopping stench as "aesthetic"). The novel does, however, contain an important representation of work, when Peter observes the railway gangs at work at night. Apart from showing the actual processes of work, the passage is important because it also emphasizes the difficult conditions of work, its extreme dangers (one man is almost killed as Peter watches), and the fact that such unremitting and unseen work is the basis for the continuation of ordinary daytime existence. It is, however, the last description of work, since the chapter ends with the news that the strike has begun.

If work is rather conspicuous by its absence, it nevertheless functions as a kind of "absent cause," determining the actions, the presence or absences of characters, organizing their lives, and to that extent, arguably ever-present. Paradoxically, its double absence during the strike only seems to make it more obsessively present in people's thoughts and conversations. The strike has been mentioned—if scarcely discussed—prior to its starting. The general attitude in the Fury household appears to be to ignore it until it happens. Here again, we meet the apparently unmotivated swings of opinion mentioned earlier. Denny, for example, rejects the strike. "Strike. Confound the damn strike. It would come now" (*The Furys,* 78), but soon after comes to say "'There's going to be a real strike. No half-hearted affair. They want us to support the miners. Poor bastards! They always do it dirty on the miners'" (106). People such as Fanny's sister Brigid see the strike purely in terms of how it inconveniences them personally, while others like George Postlethwaite feel it is an infringement of their individual rights which far outweighs any potential collective gain. "'Rights! What rights? Seems everybody's gassing about rights. What about other people's rights, Fury? What with all these rights that's been fought for and lost, and fought for and lost again, seems to me there's precious little rights left'" (183). For Fanny, the strike is a series of obstacles which stand in the way of her getting on with what is important to her—the day-to-day struggle to survive, and for many others, the strike is no more than a novel, temporary, and curious backdrop to their daily lives. Even the fact that it lasts for several weeks only serves to make it seem somehow normal, a quasi-fact of life.

The ideological implications of this downgrading of the importance of the strike can perhaps be gauged by contrast with the weight which a strike can carry in literature.

> Indeed, a curious sub-form of realism, the proletarian novel demonstrates what happens when the representational apparatus is confronted by that supreme event, the strike as figure for social revolution, which calls social "being" and the social totality itself into question, thereby undermining that totality's basic preconditions: whence the scandal of this form, which fails where it succeeds and succeeds where it fails, thereby evading categories of literary evaluation inherited from "great realism." (Jameson 1981, 193)

In *The Furys,* however, there is absolutely no question of the strike acting as a figure for revolution or for the undermining of the social totality.

The downgrading of the strike is paralleled by the nature of the representation of political action and political activists. The character apparently most committed to the working-class struggle is Fanny and Denny's eldest son, Desmond, but he is revealed as both self-seeking and contemptuous of the people on whose behalf he is organizing:

> "[I'm] going to walk out of this stinking muck-heap, and on somebody's back too. Doesn't matter whose. . . ."
> "Well," said Peter, "that's honest. Is that why you joined the Labour Party?" "Yes," he said. "Do you think those people are interested in bettering themselves, in improving their conditions? No sir! . . . Let the bastards vegetate, let them lie in their own muck. They're not interested." (*The Furys,* 277)

Other working-class organizers are shown to have similarly insulting attitudes; for Desmond, however, the strike is principally an opportunity for advancement, and one which he is determined not to let slip. Though the ruling class is ultimately the enemy for Desmond, there is no sense of his being motivated by the sort of mean-spirited desire to overthrow them simply because they are the ruling class which is held to characterize working-class leaders (and indeed in later volumes in the Fury saga he seems actively to prefer the idea of joining the rulers rather than beating them). While this is perhaps a change from the standard middle-class explanation of working-class political action as motivated by *ressentiment* (Jameson 1981 Chapter 4), it is scarcely a great improvement.

Although the attitudes of Desmond and his comrades may seem crudely contemptuous, there is no alternative or more positive image of mass action, or of the mass of the people, to be found in the book. Professor Titmouse may be politically very distant from Desmond, but his view of the crowd gathered to protest against earlier police brutality is at least as negative.

> "Come," said the professor. "Stand up and look into the seething abyss. Behold those who have risen from ten thousand stinking mattresses, who have emerged from their rat-holes. Look at them! Bury your nose in that stinking heap." (*The Furys*, 247)

Significantly, both Professor Titmouse and the labor leader who comes to address the mass meeting regard crowds as "headless monsters," and their rapid degeneration from orderly meeting to rampaging mob would seem to bear out that assessment. There remains the suspicion, however, that it is behavior rather than politics which counts: we are told of the mass meeting that "It was not authority that was being questioned by the crowd, but the manners of authority" (*The Furys*, 197)—a question, then, not so much of politics as of *politesse*.

This whole area does appear to have been a continuing problem for Hanley. Worpole comments on an earlier book.

> Socialist politics enter the novel only briefly, represented by the least convincing of any of the characters in *Drift*. The socialists are portrayed as middle and upper class aesthetes who lounge about in each other's flats listening to Beethoven and talking about Tolstoy and modern sculpture. Such a portrait was clearly a deliberate misrepresentation by Hanley. . . . (Worpole, 81)

The upper-class aesthetes may have gone from *The Furys* (leaving Professor Titmouse as a distant, surreal echo), but arguably the misrepresentation of working-class politics in Liverpool remains as strong. The possible explanation for this type of attitude, that the early thirties was a period of disenchantment with working-class politics after the failure of the General Strike, is not available in this case, since activism, and strikes, continued.

If work stops or disappears from view in the novel, if the working-class struggle is accorded little importance, there is still one place where work continues, and that is the home. Revealingly, this is also the only context in which the word struggle actually occurs in the book, used on a number of occasions by Fanny, and as such warrants the inversion of the title of Edward Upward's novel *No*

Home But the Struggle—written in the 1930s but not published until the 1970s—in the title of this essay. This ideological shift to the private sphere is no doubt justified in the text's terms, since, despite Worpole's assertion—"Once again, this family, or 'workers' dynasty' as Soviet critics have come to call this kind of novel, is centered round the whims and wishes of the father, Denny Fury" (Worpole 83)—it is Fanny, not Denny, who is the center of what happens in the family (as well as being the character whose behavior merits the term *whim*). This is not simply a "realist" shift of focus or emphasis as a result of the absence of "proper" work outside the home, but owes more to a revaluing in various ways of the domestic, the female, and the personal in the novel, at the expense of the public, male, and collective dimensions. *The Furys* is a more female-centered text than Hanley's earlier works, with women featuring as central, and generally autonomous, characters. Not that female autonomy is necesarily seen as a good thing: in some ways, the most autonomous (because least constrained by accepted norms of proper behavior for women) is Sheila, Desmond's wife, who refuses both domestic role and domestic location. The fact that she goes for a walk or sits on the seashore alone is at best a puzzle and at worst a scandal for family and neighbors. This appearance of being out of control is most warranted by her sexual behavior: she is willing to start an affair with her young brother-in-law Peter, and there is a suggestion that she may be a part-time prostitute. Significantly, however, the impetus for the affair comes not so much from her as from Peter. Although this maintains an interest in the problems of adolescent sexuality visible in some of Hanley's earlier works, it shifts the emphasis from the adolescent as sexual prey—graphically enacted in *Boy*—to the adolescent as sexual predator. Like his predecesor Joe in *Drift,* Peter has been involved with a prostitute (the reason for his expulsion from the seminary) but his decision to start an affair with his sister-in-law does seem much more predatory. Worpole comments:

> Sexuality is "an abyss of desire" which is likely to consume and devour. It stands in opposition to the declared values of proper family life and therefore can only be found away from the community in the twilight world of those who have rejected (or have been rejected by) the puritan certainties of those working class communities where religion is a much more powerful ingredient of consciousness than are the material exigencies of class. (Worpole, 81)

On the face of it, sex with your sister-in-law might seem anything but "outside the community," but the contradiction may be more apparent than real. Sheila is a Protestant, and in marrying her Desmond has put himself on the margins of, if not completely outside, certain forms of community: he is ostracized by his family; he does not go to church, but he is still part of the working, and politically active, segments of the community, insofar as any sense of community can survive in Hanley's world of fragmented families, antagonistic neighbors, alienated and self-seeking individuals.

The contradictions examined so far at the level of content and ideology are also present at the level of genre and style, as the novel shifts between detailed realism and non-realist modes, including allegory and what we might call hyper-realism. The latter is most strongly present in scenes such as Peter and Professor Titmouse's visit to the gathering in the square, which has a Joycean "Nighttown" feel to it, but also occurs in the daydreams, visions, and strange mental states experienced by a number of characters. This stylistic variation has troubled critics' attempts to locate Hanley: early commentators tended to see him as a realist; Stokes reads him as both realist (of sorts) and naturalist; Worpole argues for him as an expressionist.

Those allegorical elements which critics have noted are most visible in the move away from geographic and historical specificity. For instance, although the strike in *The Furys* is a major one, there is no attempt to locate it historically, and virtually no internal evidence on which to base an informed guess. Consequently, commentators make of it what they will: the Penguin reprint makes the obvious assumption, and decides that it is the General Strike of 1926; Stokes says that it is "the railway strike of 1911" and/or "the 1912 transport strike"; Worpole puts it a decade later: "[Peter] witnesses the large demonstrations of the Liverpool unemployed and their brutal suppression by the police (described at length by George Garrett in *Liverpool 1921–1922* and later by Jim Phelan in *Ten-a-Penny-People*)" (Worpole, 84). The politics of allegory are contradictory: on the one hand, the lack of specificity has historically been claimed as a necessary precaution against adverse reaction, including censorship or suppression of the text; on the other hand, that same lack of specificity has been attacked, by black and Third World critics, for example, as a refusal to engage directly with contemporary political and social problems—an accusation which might with some justice be leveled at Hanley.

There is, however, another reading of allegory which would make its use here appear more appropriate. For Walter Benjamin, modernity is characterized by discontinuity, fragmentation, and shock, and his description of allegory is of a mode particularly suited to the contemporary world and to our experience of it—unlike the non-allegorical narratives of someone like Leskov in "The Storyteller," whose approach is out of touch with the modern. Allegory for Benjamin is a mode of fragments, "the privileged mode of our own life in time, a clumsy deciphering of meaning from moment to moment, the painful attempt to restore a continuity to heterogeneous disconnected instants" (Jameson 1971, 72). These, plus Benjamin's paradoxical notion of progress as catastrophe, typify life under contemporary capitalism as experienced by Hanley's characters. In this, the home, usually seen as a place of safety and certainty, is, no less than the world outside, the site of the crucial struggle to make meaning, to make the connections that matter.

Works Cited

Benjamin, Walter. 1973. "The Storyteller." In *Illuminations*. London: Fontana.

Hanley, James. 1985. *The Furys*. Harmondsworth: Penguin.

Jameson, Fredric, 1981. *The Political Unconscious*. London: Methuen.

————. 1971. *Marxism and Form*. Princeton, N.J.: Princeton University Press.

Stokes, Edward. 1964. *The Novels of James Hanley*. Melbourne: F. W. Cheshire.

Snee, Carole. 1979. "Working Class Literature or Proletarian Writing?" In *Culture and Crisis in Britain in the 30s*. Edited by Clark et al. London: Lawrence and Wishart.

Worpole, Ken. 1983. "Expressionism and Working Class Fiction." *New Left Review*. 130, 1981 Reprinted in *Dockers and Detectives*. 1983. London: Verso.

A Bibliography of Works by and About James Hanley

Publications in the 1930s

Novels

————. 1930. *Drift*. Joiner & Steele.

————. 1931. *Boy*. Boriswood.

————. 1932. *Ebb and Flood*. John Lane, The Bodley Head.

————. 1933. *Captain Bottell*. Boriswood.

————. 1934. *Resurrexit Dominus*. Privately printed.

————. 1935. *The Furys*. Chatto & Windus.

————. 1935. *Stoker Bush*. Chatto & Windus.

————. 1936. *The Secret Journey*. Chatto & Windus.

————. 1938. *The Hollow Sea*. John Lane, The Bodley Head.

Short Stories

————. 1930. "A Passion Before Death." Privately printed.

————. 1931. "The Last Voyage." Joiner & Steele.

———. 1931. *Men in Darkness: Five Stories.* John Lane, The Bodley Head.

———. 1932. "Stoker Haslett." Joiner & Steele.

———. 1932. *Aria and Finale.* Boriswood.

———. 1934. "Quartermaster Clausen." Arlan.

———. 1935. "A Changed Man." *Criterion* 14, no. 56 (April).

———. 1935. "At Bay." Grayson.

———. 1936. "Aunt Anne." *Criterion* 15, no. 60 (April).

———. 1937. "Day's End." *New Writing* 3 (spring).

———. 1937. *Half an Eye.* John Lane, The Bodley Head.

———. 1938. *People Are Curious.* John Lane, The Bodley Head.

———. 1938. "From Five till Six." *Criterion* 17, no. 69 (April).

———. 1938. "Seven Men." *New Writing* 5 (spring).

Nonfiction

———. 1932. *Broken Water* (autobiography). Chatto & Windus.

———. 1937. *Grey Children* (sociological study). Methuen.

———. 1939. *Between the Tides* (documentary narrative). Methuen.

9

C. Day Lewis: Moral Doubling in Nicholas Blake's Detective Fiction of the 1930s

JAMES GINDIN

A Brief Biographical Sketch of C. Day Lewis (1904–72)

NICHOLAS BLAKE IS THE PSEUDONYM FOR THE DETECTIVE FICTION BY Cecil Day Lewis. Day Lewis was born in Ballintubber, Ireland, on 27 April 1904, the only child of a Church of England clergyman. His mother died when he was young, and he was sent to school at Sherborne in Dorset. After receiving a degree in classics at Oxford in 1927, he taught at Cheltenham College in Gloucestershire from 1930. He had begun publishing poetry while still at Oxford and was, during his later years at Cheltenham, becoming increasingly well-known as both a poet and essayist through the widely read *Hope for Poetry* (1933), which articulated the social reforming aims of the young MacSpaunday poets. After the success of his first detective novel, *A Question of Proof* (1935) and a contract for his second, in 1935, he resigned from Cheltenham College.

Continuing to write poetry and detective fiction, as well as to translate Virgil and other Latin poets, Day Lewis joined the British Communist party in mid-1936. He spoke at meetings and did journalistic reports about British Fascists and local militia groups, although he resigned from the party in the summer of 1938 and moved to a cottage in Devon. During the Second World War, he worked as an editor in the Ministry of Information in London.

After the war, he continued to write, translate, and edit, as he received numeros honors and university appointments. He was Professor of Poetry at Oxford (1951–56), delivered the Clark (1946–47) and Sidgwick (1956) lectures at Cambridge, and was Norton Professor of Poetry at Harvard (1964–65). He was long a Fellow and later

146

a Companion of the Royal Society of Literature and a member of the American and Irish academies of Arts and Letters. He was appointed Poet Laureate in 1968.

Day Lewis married Mary King of Oxford in 1928, by whom he had two sons. In 1951 they divorced, and he married Jill Balcon, an actress by whom he had a daughter and a son. He died of cancer on 22 May 1972.

* * * * *

In 1930, just at the height of the "Golden Age" of detective fiction of the "locked room" or the intricate logical puzzle, Anthony Berkeley, the secretary of the Detection Club that formulated rules for the puzzles and the author of numerous detective novels (under his own name and the pseudonyms of Anthony Berkeley Cox and Francis Iles), wrote in the preface to *The Second Shot,* "the detective story is in the process of developing into the novel . . . holding its readers less by mathematical than by psychological ties." Although a number of writers in the 1930s used forms of detective fiction as psychological and social statement, Ngaio Marsh, Margery Allingham, and Dorothy Sayers among them, few represented a new generation's psychological and social points of focus as clearly as did Cecil Day Lewis, poet, translator, and essayist, who wrote his detective fiction under the pseudonym of Nicholas Blake. The *Times Literary Supplement (TLS)* called his first novel, *A Question of Proof* (1935), "highbrow," and the detective reasons and speculates psychologically about suspects to determine the murderer within a world in which most still question the value and propriety of psychology. In Blake's second novel, *Thou Shell of Death* (1936) the series detective, Nigel Strangeways, who resembles W. H. Auden, is introduced as having survived "a brief stay at Oxford, in the course of which he had neglected Demosthenes in favour of Freud."

The same *TLS* review also praises Blake's "perfectly simple and straightforward" style, an attempt, like that of many other young intellectuals of the 1930s, to write of popular subjects and contemporary themes for a wide audience. Mastering new technology is important, as worthy characters must drive cars skillfully, although, by the second novel, new industry can create noisy urban horror as "traffic seems to pulse with greater din and violence through the main arteries, as though the whole city was sprinting desperately down a last lap" and implement "another triumph of savagery over civilised reason." Cricket, although sometimes satirized, signifies as a measure of individual worth (as with Dorothy Sayers's Peter

Wimsey), a mirror of the complexities of class, and, in *A Question of Proof,* the venue for discovery of the murderer. Like other writers of his generation, Blake frequently dramatizes conflicts of class from the point of view of one who sees its inequities, shallowness, and contradictions clearly: the master and the servant, in the army in India, united in scorning the middle-class opportunist who uses his military position to tyrannize others; the rebellious, upper-class woman on drugs attracted to the vulgar vitality of the novelist from the working classes. Class, too, particularly in *Thou Shell of Death,* is geographic, the condescension toward the Irish (central to the plot) or the Scottish (attitudes toward the police) in a novel in which the legacy of the First World War, violated by crime and persisting in the society of the mid-1930s, was to yield a more unified and socially democratic Britain.[1]

The *TLS* review of Blake's first detective novel connected "highbrow" not with class but with the copious use of literary references and quotations. The quotations are not simply decoration or gestures to lure the initiated. Rather, they are central to the motives of the characters and to the discovery of the murderer—even without the theatrical and academic settings that justified uses of Shakespeare in other 1930s fiction like that of Ngaio Marsh and J.I.M. Stewart (writing as Michael Innes). Blake's *Thou Shell of Death* is full of Shakespeare, even from a passing tramp who gives Strangeways helpful information. Understanding, however, requires a deeper knowledge of the darker, more gory textures of Jacobean tragedy, and quotation moves through the territory of Webster to Tourneur's *Revenger's Tragedy* to illustrate the motive of long-delayed revenge that has propelled the heroic flyer to stage his own suicide to look like murder and, thus, to implicate and destroy his two enemies from the past. As in the quotation, death is the "shell" that must be broken or penetrated to find the horrors, crimes, and flagrant injustices it covers. Specifically, in this novel, an excursion to Ireland that reveals what happened over twenty years earlier and another account from the First World War are necessary to uncover the cruel destructions the flyer has justifiably avenged. One criminal caused the death of the young woman in Ireland the flyer loved; the other was responsible for the death of her brother, the flyer's closest friend, in the war. The flyer needed the distance of twenty years of heroic success and social position to accomplish his revenge, as the detective needs knowledge of the distance to understand the motives for the crimes.

The fact that the initial victims were brother and sister is significant in Blake's fictional world. The sibling closeness, two sides of the same identity, in various psychological and moral combinations, always intensifies the emotions and effect of Blake's fiction. In the same novel, two suspects are also brother and sister. The brother is guilty, the original and casual betrayer of the Irish girl; the sister, the moral opposite, is an explorer who has been the flyer's mistress. Yet she will lie to protect her brother, while he, when the plot turns to expose him, tries to throw blame on his sister. These different combinations of sibling closeness and loyalty, identity and distance, provide much of the emotional commitment of the novel. The siblings, the varieties of close relationship and the intricacies of such proximate identity, are also part of the fabric of the literary past, for the references to Jacobean drama (like the Webster) often depend on the contrasts and identities of siblings. Looked at from the points of view of both mistaken identity and the psychological insight that frequently locates an alter ego within a character, the old literary machinery of doubling, in both character and plot, is naturally adaptable to detective fiction.

Blake, more than almost any other detective novelist of the 1930s, uses doubling, in one form or another, in almost all his fiction. The doubling carries moral or religious significance, for, even in the first novel, Nigel explains the killer as motivated by hate, "just as in the celebrated Cain-Abel case." In much of the detective fiction of the 1930s, the emphasis on good and evil, the moral shape, is within the ambience of the decade's moral seriousness, its difference from and response to what most writers saw as the flippancy of the 1920s or the intellectual distance of the form of the "locked room," the emphasis on the clever "how" of crime rather than on its moral and social irresponsibility. Margery Allingham, for example, in *Black Plumes* (published in 1940, though written and set a few years earlier) records style and decor the 1920s used as "outrageously expensive, comparatively exclusive, and . . . pleasant without being in any way good." The character most helpful in solving the crime, most surely and consistently morally upright, explains to others that all of them "belong to the gang that grew up just after the war and found the place in such a mess that everything had to be a roaring joke, and we laughed ourselves along, trying everything, and finding nothing was very serious . . . as it wasn't then . . . but times have changed. We're old. We're grown up. We're the ruling generation. When we get in a mess now it's real. It's a serious mess. You can't go assing along like this as though we're still back in the nineteen-twenties. It's disgusting as well as being dangerous." The same shift takes place in Dorothy Sayers's fiction, although Peter Wimsey keeps the patina of his 1920s' guises (like his Harlequin costume in *Murder*

Must Advertise) to lead him to the social sources of crime. In Blake, the moral seriousness underneath apparent lightness is omnipresent, the conflicts and balances of good and evil central to the fiction. Writing almost a decade after Day Lewis's death, his eldest son, Sean Day-Lewis thought his father's own motives more ethical and psychological than social. He claimed his father wrote detective fiction to make money, to introduce others to his own addiction, and, because of his own guilt for his lost belief in God [he was a clergyman's son], as a "substitute religious ritual with the detective and murderer representing the light and dark side of man's nature, two sides which could both be identified with by both reader and writer" (Sean Day-Lewis 1980, 86).

In some of Blake's detective novels of the 1930s, applications of good and evil are social, as in *There's Trouble Brewing* (1937), in which the identity of two brothers is confused, masked, switched, and dissolved in the death by drowning and decomposing in a beer vat. The apparent victim, the mercenary capitalistic evil brother, is finally the killer who has disposed of his lazy, amiable, humane brother. The psychological pattern is of sibling identities locked in mutual guilt, the picture of the alter ego, but the novel's emphasis is on the economic and social, the rich capitalist destroying communal unity and simple humanity. Good and evil are seen more simply and lightheartedly in *A Question of Proof,* in which the dead is a repulsive emotional nullity, the murderer a life-denying Puritan who hates the humane and high-spirited pair of illicit lovers, represented as good, who are, for a long time, the principal suspects. A more searching treatment of good and evil, which also uses two sibling pairs, one a set of twins, is developed in *The Case of the Abominable Snowman* (the American title is *The Corpse in the Snowman*—published in 1941, the novel is set crucially in the frozen, static winter of early 1940, the "phony war," socially and morally, for Blake and others, an apotheosis of the 1930s). The novel begins with the assertion, by the brother of the older sibling pair, in the midst of a reflexive discussion of detective fiction, that most such writers "shirk the real problem, the problem of evil . . . the man who revels in evil . . . the man or woman whose very existence seems to depend upon the power to hurt or degrade others." The victim is his sister, an iconoclastic and loving young woman, particularly fond of, and important to, the set of still innocent twins (the children of their brother) who may, when society and time unfreeze, be the eventual inheritors of the country house in which the novel is set. The sister is found dead, by what appears to be suicide, is then thought to be murder, but is finally discovered to have been suicide—pushed by her doctor who corrupted her with drugs when she was a teenager in America (the novel, like many in the 1930s, reveals a melodramatic naïveté about drugs, as if three "sticks" of marijuana led infallibly to lifelong destructive addiction, and Blake does not apparently use the connection later readers would make between "snow" and heroin). The brother, justifiably in the novel, kills the doctor/drug dealer, stuffing his body in the snowman the twins have already made. The snowman lasts for weeks, long enough to accommodate the plot, discoveries of the past, numerous switches, and speculations, and to allow the self-sacrificing brother to get to Germany to damage the Nazis as much as he can before he's discovered.

Throughout the novel, in the discussions about suicide or murder, the consideration and rediscoveries about the suspects, including himself, the brother shows an emotional identity with his sister, not just a sympathy but an incapacity to separate, an insistence that he feels exactly what he knows she felt. They are spoken of as "like twins," just as he speaks of the need to protect his twin nephew and niece from further corruptions by the doctor/drug dealer and from their own exaggerated likeness. The brother's judgments of his sister and himself are similarly dual. "Betty was the most arrant little bitch and the most glorious creature I ever—Oh, God damn it, she was my sister." Incest is implied, an extreme of the destructive symbiosis, not a matter of choice. As a wise, scholarly woman, devoted to the eighteenth century (she is Georgia Cavendish's aunt, Georgia the explorer from *Thou Shell of Death* whom Strangeways married after her guilty brother's death), explains, "what happened to Betty was, for him, the rape of his own innocence. . . . His whole life since that day . . . has been a penance for the sin which, through Betty, was committed against him." We are all, in Blake's world, doubled. Siblings, twins, country houses, communities—all display the two-sidedness of the human creature, good and evil endemic to human nature. Psychological understanding of our dualities that lead to crime can also reveal its nature and its moral locations. Sibling symbiosis is a metaphor for both original sin and the attempts to counter or redeem it.

In 1948, W. H. Auden, more explicitly interested in themes of Christian guilt, sin, and redemption than was his friend Day Lewis, published an essay entitled "The Guilty Vicarage," in part in response to Edmund Wilson's earlier charge that detective fiction was simply a harmless addiction, like that of smoking or crossword puzzles. Auden acknowledged his addiction, but went on to analyze some detective fiction, contrasting the structure with that of Greek tragedy. He pointed out the moral appeal of Christian detective fiction, using Chesterton's Father Brown series as a principal example. Auden asserted that the "typical" reader of detective fiction, like himself, is "a person who suffers from a sense of sin," not from the hubris of Greek tragedy. Developing the structure of detective fiction from the 1930s that appealed to his "typical" reader, Auden wrote: "The magic formula is an innocence which is discovered to contain guilt; then a suspicion of being the guilty one; and finally a real innocence from which the guilty other has been expelled, a cure effected, not by me or by my neighbours, but by the miraculous intervention of a genius from outside who removes guilt by giving knowledge of guilt." For Auden, the reader's fantasy is to be "restored to the Garden of Eden, to a state of innocence," and both guilt and restoration can occur in either Christian or Freudian terms (Auden 1948, 157–58). Auden's formula does not entirely fit Blake's fiction, for Blake's resolutions don't achieve innocence and he is more ambivalent about restoring a Garden of Eden, finding "real innocence," than Auden is. Nevertheless, in the interior focus, the recognition of the sin or crime within a version of the self, or the sense that the social violation of community is a reflection of divisions within the nature of the creature herself, and in the operation of guilt, the feeling that the self should be more or better than it is, Blake's doublings, parallels, and fiction can be given deeper and more cogent meaning through Auden's formulation.

The Blake novel of the 1930s most infused with concepts of sin and guilt is *The Beast Must Die* (1938), which, called by Nigel Strangeways "my most unhappy case," was Day Lewis's own favorite of his detective fiction. The novel begins with the personal diary of Frank Cairnes, a detective story writer who uses the pseudonym of Felix Lane. Before he reveals any hint of the cause, Frank records his misery with quotations that signal interior guilt and doubled identity from two of the poets most widely read by his generation: "We are betrayed by what is false within" from Meredith's *Modern Love* sequence and "hypocrite lecteur, mon semblable, mon frere" from Eliot's *Waste Land*. The specific cause for guilt is that Frank's six-year-old son has been killed by a passing motorist while returning home with a bag of sweets he'd bought from the village store. Although Frank knows that the as yet unknown motorist was flagrantly irresponsible, and that the boy was old enough to be alone on an errand he'd managed safely before, he still feels himself guilty of insufficiently protecting the person he loved most (his wife had died giving birth to the boy, their only child). The guilt is reenforced by harassment from a villager, an older woman who loved the boy. She destroys the prize roses in Frank's garden and sends him an anonymous note urging that he leave the community. In addition, he had always apologized for making his living by writing detective fiction, as if the occupation was worthless, and had told inquisitive villagers he was working on a scholarly biography of Wordsworth.

In an effort to appease his guilts and avenge or redeem his son's life, Frank uses his deductive skills and imagination to track down the killer and plots ingeniously to join the killer's family. Through the agency of the woman who was with the killer in the car (his sister-in-law with whom he was having an affair, and who then falls in love with Frank), Frank manages to join the family as a boarder, using the identity of his pseudonym for his work on a new detective novel, which is his diary. The woman provides the opportunity for Blake's ancillary use of some themes from his earlier novels, such as the vulnerability to Nazism of the overtly or freely sexual woman, as this one casually states, to Frank's silent horror, that "of course all these Jews are in league I must say we could do with a bit of Hitler here though I do rather bar rubber truncheons and sterilization. Well now, as I was saying—." She changes in the course of the novel, however, unlike some earlier opulently sexual women who admire the Nazi's force, certainty, and lack of guilt. Sexuality, in *The Beast Must Die,* is far less than the treatment of good and evil families, seen primarily in the relationship of fathers and sons. In the familial doubling, Frank, the good father who has lost his son, attaches to the evil father, George, a killer and domestic tyrant, and attempts to liberate and redeem George's sensitive and innocent son who hates his father. Frank's reclamation of George's son is, in moral terms, justifiable revenge. Blake details all the political and personal confusion that has created the bullying tyrant: the military officer father who could not burn the farms his mission in the imperialistic Boer War required; the narrow, ferocious mother who raised her son to compensate for what she saw as his weak, inadequate father. The doubling, the parallels, and the differences, are matters of the past and families, including two or three generations. Cain and Abel are the sons of Eve and of Adam as well as brothers, and the morality of the family is also the morality of the human community.

The writer's diary, the first half of *The Beast Must Die,* details Frank's developing plan to kill George. The plan, carefully designed by Frank, an expert sailor, depends on his skill at process, which is always elaborately described in Blake's fiction as a metaphor for knowledge and control, for techniques that mastering the modern world requires. Of course, the apparently foolproof project misfires (this is doubled in the failure of similar plans of process by George's son, morally Frank's worthy heir), and Frank, partly too sensitive, partly incompetent, the fallible good man, fails to kill the evil tyrant. Yet George is killed, and at this point Nigel Strangeways's voice takes over to work out what has happened. George's death throws suspicion on numerous others in the family, son, wife, sister-in-law, mother, but Nigel discovers that Frank is, in fact, the murderer and then allows him to commit suicide and to write a confession designed to rescue the son of the bully who'd killed his son. Allegiance to the moral valences of good families may finally work better than conscious plans or techniques. Hamlet's forms of weakness and indecision, as well as his masks and his ambivalences about revenge, are points of reference for the good characters. As literature shows, there are always good and evil families, always sins and guilts, always questions about the difficult line that can separate good from evil.

The good, vulnerable, weak man experiences guilt because of both his inadequacies and the vulnerability, the humane concern for others, that characterizes his goodness. In trying to destroy or eliminate evil, the good is vulnerable to suicide, locating the evil within the self. This leads to a texture of shading lines between murder and suicide, visible in all of Blake's fiction, though multiplied in *Thou Shell of Death* and *The Beast Must Die,* the reliance among the twists of the plot on the suicide that looks like or is framed to resemble murder and the murder framed to resemble suicide. Strangeways is not Auden's "genius," nor is his thinking magical, but he is a good and rational man whose psychological knowledge and insights enable him, often only after considerable thought, to distinguish murder from suicide, to know the difference between violation of the human community and punishment of the self because all of us are implicated in the potential for evil. In *The Beast Must Die,* the evil is also distinctly Nazism, a brutal totalitarian organization that locates sin in otherness, that glorifies or magnifies an image of supranational self by eliminating others. The good seems weak or helpless, an image of the widespread feelings of defeat, loss, and impossibility endemic in British society of the 1930s, as if hopeless in confronting the brutal efficiencies of totalitarianism. But Blake is far from suggesting that Britain is an insular repository of civic virtue (and his next novel, *The Smiler with the Knife,* 1939, locates evil in an organization of British Nazis smuggling arms into England to fuel a potential revolt); rather, this novel is his most searching treatment of psychological totalitarianism, in which the evil British tradition is military and imperialistic, most manifest in the Boer War. Nevertheless, Blake still suggests a moderate version of theories about the genetic transmission of value, about eugenic theories that so easily encouraged imperialism and, at their extreme, Nazism.

George's son, young Phil, is seen as the genetic inheritor of his grandfather's inability to burn the farms in South Africa, his negative virtue, just as he is seen as the nurtured and nongeneric inheritor of the sometimes weak though positive virtue of humane concern and self-sacrifice he has acquired through his surrogate father, Frank.

Blake's modified allegiance to eugenic theory is far from unusual in 1930s detective fiction, is less than that of some other explicitly non-Nazi writers, such as Margery Allingham whose heroines and heroes always have "well-bred faces," and the best of them, no matter what happened, "would still have strength and breeding in her shapely head, character and sensitiveness in her wide mouth." Nigel Strangeways sees himself much less a product of the well-bred upper classes he comes from, secure enough to laugh at or excoriate its own forms of pride and insularity, its own sins, and he always mocks words like "breeding," its focus on duplicating the values of self. Rather, Nigel's superiority and his morality are in his knowledge, his learning, and his understanding that is both literary and nonliterary. He has nothing of the "magic" or transcendence Auden suggests, just the fullest and most sensitive acquisition of humane and social learning for the always limited and fallible human creature.

Notes

1. In a 1942 preface Blake wrote for Howard Haycraft's *Murder for Pleasure: The Life and Times of the Detective Story,* he asserted that detective fiction served those "who have a stake in the social system and must, therefore, even in fantasy, see the ultimate triumph of their social values ensured." He contrasted this "stake" to its absence in those to whom thrillers appealed, and thought the upper and professional classes more likely to read detective fiction and the "lower-middle" and "working" classes to read thrillers or "bloods." I have written a more detailed essay on the complexities of class and social issues in Blake's fiction of the 1930s (and later) in the chapter entitled "Nicholas Blake's 'Stake in the Social System'" in *British Fiction in the 1930s: The Dispiriting Decade* (London: Macmillan; New York: St. Martin's, 1992). This essay, in contrast, will concentrate on the psychological doubling and moral framework in the fiction.

Works Cited

Auden, W. H. 1948. "The Guilty Vicarage." In *The Dyer's Hand and Other Essays.* New York: Random House.

Blake, Nicholas. 1935. *A Question of Proof.* London: Collins.

———. 1936. *Thou Shell of Death.* London: Collins.

———. 1937. *There's Trouble Brewing.* London: Collins.

———. 1938. *The Beast Must Die.* London: Collins.

———. 1939. *The Smiler with the Knofe.* London: Collins.

Day-Lewis, Sean. 1980. *C. Day Lewis: An English Literary Life*. London: Weiden-field & Nicholson.

A Bibliography of Works by and about C. Day Lewis

Detective Fiction in the 1930s

————. 1935. *A Question of Froof*. London: Collins; New York: Harper & Row, Publishers.

————. 1936. *Thou Shell of Death*. London: Collins; New York: Harper & Row, Publishers.

————. 1937. *There's Trouble Brewing*. London: Collins; New York: Harper & Row, Publishers.

————. 1938. *The Beast Must Die*. London: Collins; New York: Harper & Row, Publishers.

————. 1939. *The. Smiler with the Knife*. London: Collins; New York: Harper & Row, Publishers.

Other Novels in the 1930s

————. *The Friendly Tree*. London: Cape, 1936. Reprint, New York: Harper & Row, Publishers.

————. *Starting Point*. London: Cape, 1937. Reprint, New York: Harper & Row, Publishers, 1938.

————. 1939. *Child of Misfortune*. London: Cape.

Poetry in the 1930s

————. 1931. *From Feathers to Iron*. London: Hogarth Press.

————. 1933. *The Magnetic Mountain*. London: Hogarth Press.

————. 1935. *Collected Poems, 1929–1933*. London: Hogarth Press.

————. 1935. *A Time to Dance and Other Poems*. London: Hogarth Press.

————. 1936. *Noah and the Waters*. London: Hogarth Press.

————. 1938. *Overtures to Death and Other Poems*. London: Cape.

Essays in the 1930s

————. 1933. *A Hope for Poetry*. Oxford: Blackwell.

————. 1935. *Revolution in Writing*. London: Hogarth Press.

————. 1936. *"We're Not Going to Do Nothing: A Reply to Mr. Aldous Huxley's Pamphlet 'What Are You Going to Do About It.'"* London. *Left Review*.

————. 1968. Handley-Taylor, Geoffrey, and Timothy d'Arch Smith. *C. Day Lewis, The Poet Laureate: A Bibliography*. London and Chicago: St. James Press.

Autobiography

————. 1960. Day-Lewis, Cecil. *The Buried Day.* London: Chatto & Windus; New York: Harper & Row, Publishers.

Biography

Day-Lewis, Sean. 1980. *C. Day-Lewis: An English Literary Life.* London: Weidenfield & Nicolson.

Secondary Sources on Detective Fiction

Haycraft, Howard. 1942. *Murder for Pleasure: The Life and Times of the Detective Story.* London: Peter Davies.

Twentieth Century Crime and Mystery Writers. 1980. Edited by John M. Reilly. London: Macmillan; New York: St. Martin's Press.

Julian Symons. 1985. *Bloody Murder: From the Detective Story to the Crime Novel.* London and New York: Viking Penguin.

Detective Fiction: A Collection of Critical Essays. 1988. Edited by Robin W. Winks. Woodstock, Vt.: The Countryman Press.

James Gindin. 1992. *British Fiction in the 1930s: The Dispiriting Decade.* London: Macmillan; New York: St. Martin's Press.

Secondary Sources on Poetry

Dyment, Clifford. 1955. *C. Day Lewis.* London: Longmans, Green, for the British Council.

Stanford, Derek. 1969. *Stephen Spender, Louis MacNeice, Cecil Day Lewis.* Grand Rapids, Mich.: Eerdmans.

Riddel, J. N. *C. Day Lewis.* New York: Twayne.

Maxwell, D. E. S. *Poets of the Thirties.* London: Gollancz.

10

Cyril Vernon Connolly: Inside *The Rock Pool*

CHRIS HOPKINS

A Brief Biographical Sketch of Cyril Vernon Connolly (1903–74)

CYRIL VERNON CONNOLLY WAS BORN IN 1903. HIS FATHER WAS A PRO-
fessional soldier. His education was characteristic of someone from
his background, and the friendships formed at school and in college
were characteristically important for his later career and life. Like
the characters in Anthony Powell's *A Dance to the Music of Time* he
and his school and college friends (and their friends) made up a small
but influential network whose paths frequently crossed during the
rest of their lives. He and Orwell (Eric Blair) attended the same prep
school (the one described so vividly—and according to Connolly
exaggeratedly—in Orwell's "Such, Such Were the Joys"). At Eton
(where Orwell was also a student), Balliol, Oxford, and then London Connolly met (future) literary personalities such as Henry Yorke
(who wrote as Henry Green), Anthony Powell, Evelyn Waugh, and
Peter Quennell, among others (Connolly discussed this phenomenon
of English upper/upper-middle-class life in *Enemies of Promise* and
parodied it in his thirties skit, "Where Engels Fears to Tread").

His actual academic achievements at Oxford were not impressive,
but, as was often the case during the twenties and thirties, his creation of himself as a personality or literary figure stood him in good
stead. When he came down from Oxford, the influential critic and
reviewer Desmond MacCarthy offered him reviewing work for *The
New Statesman*. In 1930 he married an American (Jean) whose relatively modest but secure financial position made frequent travel in
Europe possible until the war.

Connolly published his first novel, *The Rock Pool,* in 1936 (in

Paris, after failing to find an English publisher). In 1938 he published the work—part critical essay, part autobiography—for which he is best remembered, *Enemies of Promise*. In 1939, he and Stephen Spender founded *Horizon,* with the aim of keeping "culture" alive in a period which they felt was soon to be beset by the inevitable pressures of war. Connolly remained the editor of *Horizon* until 1950. He published a number of other works of various kinds (including selections of his articles, reviews, and essays) before his death in 1974.

✳ ✳ ✳ ✳ ✳

Cyril Connolly was unable to find an English publisher who would print his first novel *The Rock Pool*. They seem partly to have felt that there was a danger of charges of obscenity, and may also have thought it not to be a commercial proposition, and, indeed, unfashionable (Peter Quennell gives an anecdotal account of English publishers' reactions in his introduction to the Oxford University Press edition of 1981). The novel was therefore first published by the "avant-garde" Obelisk Press in Paris, in 1936. It was not published in a native English edition until 1947, when Hamish Hamilton brought out a new edition, and was not then reprinted until the Oxford paperback edition in 1981. It was not, therefore, a very widely read book during the thirties. Quennell remarks that the 1936 edition did attract some notice since it was reviewed by some English newspapers.

This is not a very fortunate publishing history, and the novel is again out of print (the Oxford edition was available for only a year). This is a fundamental reason for the highly insecure status of *The Rock Pool* in the "canon" of "thirties novels" (though its apparent lack of concern with politics may also be a factor). Even were the novel itself uninteresting in terms of the decade (which is far from the case), the status of its author as an important literary figure might be thought to lend it some value. In fact, though, it has rarely been discussed either individually or in the context of the thirties, and its complex relation to politics in general and to the politics of writing in particular has remained completely undiscussed.

When it is referred to (as in Valentine Cunningham's *British Writers of the Thirties*) it is generally mentioned only in passing. Richard Johnstone's *Will to Believe—Novelists of the Nineteen Thirties* mentions the novel twice, once to say that in it "Connolly takes the predicament of his generation very seriously indeed" and once to say that its hero resembles other thirties heroes—Tony Last in *A Handful of*

Dust, Pinkie in *Brighton Rock,* and Gordon Comstock in *Keep the Aspidistra Flying*—in that each of them has a choice: "to accept, with resignation or despair, the impossibility of coping, or to confront the conditions of existence and by some means triumph over them" (Johnstone, 4, 44). Apart from seeming rather too general to be useful, this comment does not actually seem to apply very well to Connolly's hero (or rather antihero). At the opening of the novel Edgar Naylor is coping perfectly well with life in his own English way, and shows no signs of wishing to confront any conditions of existence which might prove taxing. He is on a vacation, and intends only to observe the curious life which he lights upon at Trou-sur-Mer: he is not obviously seeking for values in a dramatically meaningless world. He is, initially, seeking temporary escape from an all too ordinary and complacent world, of which he is comfortably part.

There are, though, some more definable ways in which *The Rock Pool* resembles other thirties texts, and which make a fuller discussion of it worthwhile. In particular, it has some resemblances to two other thirties novels which are much concerned with both the value of writing and its impossibility: George Orwell's *Keep the Aspidistra Flying* (1936) and Christopher Isherwood's *All the Conspirators* (1928).[1] Moreover, comparison with these texts might suggest the wider importance of "writing" and notions of "the aesthetic" among thirties novelists (e.g., writing and contested definitions of the aesthetic are major issues in two other neglected yet central novels— C. Day Lewis's *Starting Point,* published in 1937, and John Lehmann's *Evil Was Abroad,* published in 1938.)

Naylor is meant to be writing a book about the "banker-bard," Samuel Rogers, during his summer vacation. During the course of the novel (despite a few desultory attempts), he makes no progress with this project. As a way of comparing this novel with Isherwood and Orwell's "writing" novels, this does not sound a very promising resemblance, since Naylor's ambitions are so much more minor than Philip's ambition to write a novel, and Gordon Comstock's to "be" a writer. However, one might notice that there are things in common among all these characters. All utterly fail to produce any writing (or, at least, fail to finish a single work), and all have in one way or another a deep attraction to the world of artistic bohemia, to a world which can supply values which differ from those of the mundane world. If the novels share a sense that there is value in this kind of alternative order, and if all of them represent characters who fail to attain the necessary token of membership, then it seems likely that Connolly's version of this is significant, rather than incidental.

Though Naylor fails to write, the novel pays considerable attention to the idea of writing. Arriving for the first time at Trou-sur-Mer, Naylor sees some paintings and some old *New Yorkers,* dated 1929 and 1930. He remembers that there had once been an artists' colony here, and immediately thinks of a way of capitalizing on his discovery." "He would be the Goethe of a new Pompeii—and besides this stuff about the twenties was a paying proposition" (*The Rock Pool*, 2). Naylor soon realizes that not only was there an artists' colony here, but that there still is. He therefore changes his project slightly.

> No longer an archaeologist, but an observer, a naturalist. Such a settlement was as good, easily, as a termites' colony—*The Pond I Know, The Stream I Know, The Artists' Colony I Know,* by Edgar Naylor—aquarium similes were the rage now, in Proust, in Gide, and another in *Point Counterpoint.* Why not *The Rock Pool*—a microcosm cut off from the ocean by the retreating economic tide? (*The Rock Pool,* 3)

That Naylor himself appears in a novel which has the same title as the book he thinks of writing is an irony which is developed as he becomes absorbed into the colony (there are also ironies about the relation of Naylor to Connolly's own sense of failure as a writer). The idea of making money out of writing and art is also very prominent in the novel, thought most of the artists at Trou-sur-Mer never produce anything at all. As Naylor becomes one of their number, he also drops the idea of making something out of describing them; there seems to be a certain sense in the novel that actually to profit from art or writing is to conform to the values of a civilization which is left behind in the artists' colony.

Successful artists are in this respect less bohemian than the unsuccessful; thus, as a distinctly narratorial voice says early in the novel, even modernist artists are merely supplying goods which the public want. "We all like obscurity when it is on our own plane: great artists like Epstein and Orpen know how to provide for the public the bewilderment it deserves" (*The Rock Pool,* 2). Here the difficulty of modern art is not something to be wrestled with and that will then change perceptions of the world, but a difficulty which is easily interpretable as difficulty and can therefore be simply left as artistic difficulty. The work of art remains meaningless, and this is the value which its consumers are content to accept as its meaning. A similarly cynical attitude to the meaningfulness of writing is attributed more directly to Naylor after he has been thinking about the title of his book on the colony. "An outpost or a blockhouse would have done

just as well but he preferred the other metaphor." (3) Naylor regards
the metaphor not as having some genuine connection with what he
wishes to express, but as an entirely arbitrary and (as the tone suggests) casual choice.

The notion that art is merely another form of commerce is reminiscent of some of Gordon Comstock's criticisms of modern culture
in Orwell's *Keep the Aspidistra Flying;* however, where Comstock
tries to maintain a distinction between "money"-art, and real art
(such as his own), Naylor is much more ready to accept the values
of commercial civilization: he starts off intending to observe dis-
tantly and slightly satirically these outmoded artists who thought
they could escape from such values. He knows that he speaks from
a position in the "real" world. Indeed, he is what Comstock might
call a moneyed young beast, and it is largely this which gives him
his sense of superiority to the mode of life he is to investigate.

> Naylor was neither very intelligent nor especially likeable, and certainly
> not very successful, and from the image of looking down knowingly
> into his Rock Pool, poking it and observing the curious creatures he
> might stir up, he would derive a pleasant sense of power. Otherwise the
> only power he got was from money. He didn't have a great deal, just
> under a thousand pounds a year . . . but he knew how to be handy with
> it, how to make some people feel that he was paying for them, and
> others, mostly women and artists, that he might be persuaded to. (*The
> Rock Pool,* 3)

Naylor is in many ways thoroughly part of the world as it is: he is
certainly not challenging it, and does not consciously feel any lack
in it. However, there are signs of a distaste for normal work and
channels of advancement even at the beginning of the novel, and
these grow during the course of the narrative. This is detectable in
the description of his normal life:

> he had two jobs, one as a kind of apprentice-partner in a firm of stock-
> brokers, and the other as self-appointed biographer of Samuel Rogers—
> Rogers appealed to him not only because he had lived enormously long,
> but because in that life (1763–1855) everybody else . . . who had been
> interesting at the time, had played a part. He knew that from the most
> accessible biographies of all these he would be able to make up a series
> of chapters more or less concerning his own hero. (*The Rock Pool,* 4)

Neither of his own two jobs as reported here sounds very substantial:
"a kind of" and "self-appointed" do not suggest much status or
commitment. The idea that he has picked his "hero" because his

biography can be easily pasted together from his more famous contemporaries' biographies suggests an equally serious lack of real
commitment. The way in which this information about Naylor, or
in which these thoughts of his, are described (by an inscrutable narrative voice reminiscent of that in Anthony Powell's thirties novels,
such as *Afternoon Men*, 1931, and *Venusberg*, 1932), reinforces this
sense of uncommitedness: the use of "narrative report of thought
act" robs the description of intimacy, but inevitably leaves us with
a feeling that we have had a report from the inside of Naylor's mind
(Leech and Short 1981, 334, 337). The effect is not really satiric
either, because there is no gap between what Naylor knows and
what we know, into which we might insert a "real" reading of his
motives: he (via the narrator) appears conscious of his own motives,
so that there is nothing left for us to interpret. He has told us all
about his biography, and its insignificance, and there seems to be
nothing to add.

Naylor's feelings about the normal world and the world of art
develop at first gradually, and then more sharply (as part of the
"acceleration" noted by Edmund Wilson in his review of the novel).
Soon he begins with some reluctance (and with the help of liberal
doses of Pernod) to take the artists' life more seriously. He begins
to see Juan-Les-Pins as part of a normal and alien world—"a world
of externals, where jewellery and large cars formed the true
background."

> He recognised in Toni an integrity, a total freedom from that interfer-
> ence, that static of the external world which destroys the harmony of
> those who do not live entirely in the imagination. And Rascasse! There
> was a real person—a rugged, honest, single-minded lover of the brush!
> Both in fact had a vocation, and he recognised unwillingly how deeply
> that could compensate for the lack of all other possessions. (*The Rock
> Pool*, 25)

His distaste for the normal ways of filling life practiced by his peers
becomes intense; when he receives a letter from his contemporary
at Oxford, John Spedding, he comments:

> It was a long journey from the security of the class-room to the appalling
> liberty of Trou. . . . Spedding had simply exchanged the Gothic quads,
> dining-halls, gowns, subfusc pleasures and gregarious intolerance of
> Winchester and Oxford for those of the law-courts. He would never
> leave the quadrangle. (*The Rock Pool*, 82)

The way in which this progression is mediated raises an important question about the novel: how are we to react to Naylor? Peter Quennell in his introduction to the Oxford edition says that there was a "strain of emotional ambivalence" in everything that Connolly wrote; he suggests that *The Rock Pool* displays both the "romantic and nostalgic aspects of Connolly's nature" and his "satirical wit" (*The Rock Pool,* x–xi). One is very aware of both sets of qualities in this novel, and that both are focused through or on Naylor. Indeed, there is often uncertainty about the tone of the narrative, whether the romanticism is there in its own right or is being satirized. When Naylor, for example, realizes the integrity of Toni and Rascasse, how are we to react? The language is lushly romantic, and does not seem in itself to undermine a romantic conception of the artist ("vocation," "integrity," "imagination"); on the other hand it seems hard to take this seriously in regard to Toni's behavior in the rest of the narrative (Rascasse is a slightly different case, because he does actually produce art). Nearly all of the romantic passages in the novel (and they are very distinctly "purple passages") could be taken as being satirized, simply because they could be taken as being overdone; equally, though, that overdone quality is an aspect of their romanticism.

The general narrative framework may suggest that the romanticism ought to be undermined, but one wonders whether that necessarily overcomes the local power of such passages. One of the lushest passages illustrates this potentially conflicting use of local effect and wider narrative framework. Towards the end of the novel, Naylor appears to glorify failure

> but he was forgetting Toni. Now she would be putting the studs in her shirt, brushing her hair, tying the laces of her patent leather shoes, arranging her tie. In the Djem el Fna, at Marrakesh, it would also be dark. The Cleuh boys, members of that rebel tribe whose maidens required a French soldier's testicles from every suitor, would be dancing on their dusty pitch, the silver castanets on their fingers, the huge ring on each left ear. The archaic music would be scraped out as they bowed and jingled in their long robes. There was a kind of corrupt dignity in their defeat. (*The Rock Pool,* 132)

This all seems quite seriously intended, but the next paragraph begins: "Next morning his nerves were not so good. Regeneration does not come quickly, and the drafts of night are seldom honoured by the grim cashier of day." To a certain extent this places the high romance of the Moroccan tribe in the bathetic context of a Pernod haze, and relates it both to Naylor's supposed subject, the banker-bard, and to a potentially containing commentary which points to the impossibility of escape from the "ordinary" world of money, causality, and responsibility. It is noticeable, though, that even the placing comment is rather lushly phrased, making the ravages of drunkenness poetic through personification, despite the use of images of bankruptcy. The passage is undercut a little, but the description of the defeated tribe retains some of its power, and thus does dignify Naylor's vision to a degree.

The effect of this mixture of modes which can be variously seen as either satiric or romantic is complex. As in some of Evelyn Waugh's novels, it is difficult to feel sure that either satire or romance is completely straightforward. One often feels that the romantic passages are mock romantic passages, and that they will be placed by what follows or precedes them (and, indeed, they are), but equally it is not clear how much authority the satire has. Neither is dominant, and if anything, it is the romantic vein which is strengthened by this, since the satiric edge allows us to accept the romance without having wholly to believe in it. The satiric mode in the novel is complex in its own right, because the targets keep shifting: Naylor's initially secure sense of ordinary life is often mocked, through his reactions to the artists, but they are often mocked through their failure to conform to his expectations. Neither artistic escape nor social conformity is allowed to have any real substance. The novel is constantly both criticizing the genuineness of the artistic alternative order, and subscribing to it. In not allowing us to commit simply to one or other vision of life, the novel reproduces for the reader Naylor's own constant disappointment in both worlds.

Nevertheless, we are often invited into quite a thorough identification with Naylor's point of view. When John Spedding sends him the letter, for example, we are shown the original text of it and there is no opportunity to react to it, and the world it represents, in any but a hostile way. At the end of the novel, we see things through Naylor's drunken haze. This is comic to some extent, but the drunkenness is elevated at points by poetic language. Against the comically described though compelling drunk's viewpoint must be put the romantically drunken epiphany.

Long walk back to table. Do things carefully. Put the glass down. So. Now sit in chair. One at a time though. Careful. So. Put legs out. Left, right. Big magic. Whoopee. Made three faces turn a kind of red at a distance of several yards. Big magic. (*The Rock Pool*, 137)

> Yes, yes. There were many women, many beaches, many bars. This
> was the soul's February. Outside all was bleak and unpromising, but
> deep within him stirred something unexpected, something noble. He
> considered the rows of coloured bottles—Cassis, Mandarinette, Cordial
> Medoc. A thousand franc note, and in the corner he would write: "For
> my darling Toni."
>   A *ten* thousand franc note!
>   'Hey! GarCON! No use. Just another bum, indeed!
>   I wonder. (137–38)

Again, this epiphany may be being undermined, but it may still
survive this as a form of active romanticism. The last words of the
novel are very curious—with their brief switch to a wholly unlocated
and unexpected first person narrative—and clearly demand some
kind of interpretation. They could be taken as a sign that the implied
author is identifying himself with Naylor—suggesting that *The Rock
Pool* actually was written by someone who, like Naylor, had been
through this kind of experience. This would rescue from irony the
narrator's/Naylor's reflection. "And now that the emotional content
of his mind had been purified, could he not write better?" (*The
Rock Pool,* 131) Alternatively, the "I wonder" could suggest that the
narrator/implied author sees more to Naylor's plight than is covered
by the simple label of "just another bum." It could be a claim for
the general significance of Naylor's experience: given the world of
the thirties, perhaps Naylor's reaction is not merely personal. If so,
it is rather along the lines of Orwell's idea in *Inside the Whale* (1939),
that there is only a choice between irresponsible and "unreal" escap-
ism and an unfaceable real world; the looseness of the explanation—
it is almost nonexistent—resembles the looseness of Father Rothschild's explanation in Waugh's *Vile Bodies* (1932), that the behavior
of the Younger Generation is "perhaps in some way all historical"
(Waugh, 132), as if causes and effects have become nearly impossible
to relate significantly or authoritatively. At any rate, it seems to
suggest some attribution of narratorial sympathy to Naylor (there
seems to be no way of making it a satirical comment, although there
is plenty of room to see Naylor's final comment as having meanings
other than those he intends).

Generally, the novel represents a world where meaningfulness is
seriously problematic (and the novel's own strategies often seem to
be equally caught in a process of meaning which cannot be easily
grounded). It is interesting to observe how a number of comments
about the meaninglessness of English literary life are put into
Naylor's mind, which two years later were to be put into *Enemies
of Promise* under Connolly's own name. Naylor explains to Jimmy

(the idea resuscitated by the "lyricism of his hangover") why he has not written his novel of contemporary London life (the third failed literary project of his of which we hear).

> Why hadn't he written it? Partly because he found he could only write in one language, the dialect of Pater, Proust, and Henry James, the style that is common to mandarin academic circles given over to clique life and introspection. This dead literary English, with its long sentences, elaborate similes and clever epithets effectually blocked any approach to a new vernacular. (*The Rock Pool*, 40)

Interestingly the description of the novel's plot makes its Eliotesque nature very clear.

> A crisp astringent picture of English harlotry, some of it in rhyming slang and Soho English, the rest in the genteel demotic speech of furnished flatlets of the Tottenham Court Road . . . newspapers blowing along the streets in grimy dawns, barrel organs in peeling squares, the expectancy of Charlotte Street, the decay of still-born Pimlico. . . . (*The Rock Pool*, 39)

Thus we have a twofold insignificance—the seediness of contemporary life was to have been the novel's subject, but (in Naylor's hands at least) the literary language available cannot be made to describe anything appropriately. Further, Naylor's idea is, anyway, a highly derivative one.

Naylor then goes on to talk about something which is important in *The Rock Pool,* and which is also dealt with more negatively in *Enemies of Promise.*

> And after all—why should he write it? It is part of the happiness of youth that the sense of power, like the mystical apprehension of goodness, can be enjoyed to the full without the necessity of projecting it into the tainted realm of action. . . . This conviction of intense disponibilite is known as promise and whom the gods wish to destroy they first call promising. (*The Rock Pool*, 40)

In his critical/autobiographical book Connolly discusses all the things which prevent the vital activity of writing; here Naylor feels that the potential to write is as valuable as actually doing so. In this he resembles Isherwood's Philip Lindsay in *All the Conspirators* and Orwell's Gordon Comstock in *Keep the Aspidistra Flying.* Each wants to be a writer, though they cannot actually produce writing. It is also interesting to note that Connolly's idea of "promise" and the "tainted realm of action" is very like Lukacs's notion of "abstract potentiality" over "concrete potentiality." Lukacs argues that this results in a pathological interest in subjectivity and ultimately in a denial that things which actually happen in the world are necessarily anymore real than things which happen only in the mind (*Meaning* 1962, 22). Though Lukacs's argument here dates from 1955, it is based on Marxist ideas about modernism which were already well-developed during the thirties, and certainly familiar to English Marxist critics of the period such as Ralph Fox and Philip Hender-son.[2] This resemblance is not accidental, for Connolly was (as his parody "Where Engels Fears to Tread" (*Condemned* 1945, 136–53) suggests) well aware of the connections between, and counter at-tractions of, aestheticism, modernism, and Marxism. In exploring the attraction of the "aesthetic" life, Connolly is partly making a claim for modernism's playful "escapist" subjectivity against the "mature" commitments to the reality of realism and socialist realism (partly witnessed even in the novel's love of metaphor as opposed to metonymy). As for other English writers of the period the aes-theticism of the 1890s is still a powerful image of the life of the artist, and one which is invariably associated with modernism (which Lukacs, of course, sees as a descendant of the artistic move-ments of the late nineteenth century).[3]

If the novel is a defense of the irresponsible pleasure of "Art" thus conceived, it is, however, a far from committed defense (to be wholly serious and committed would itself undermine the escape from commitment and reality). Naylor does not merely prioritize "abstract potentiality" in books, but in his own life. As an artist who fails to produce, Naylor is subject to irony, but irony itself, and particularly an irony which is difficult exactly to place, is a modernist status symbol (as in Joyce's *Portrait of the Artist as a Young Man* or Woolf's *Mrs. Dalloway*). He is certainly shown as being very thoroughly liberated from the conventional material concerns which were very much part of him at the opening of the novel (concerns with politeness, paying for items actually consumed, social status, and living within one's income). His rebellion may be not only against his respectable English life, but also may stand for a rebellion against the equally pressing demand for responsibility of the domi-nant literary-political ethos of the thirties.

Though Trou is shown as full of inconsequence of various kinds, Naylor comes to see it as being more real than anywhere else.

> England didn't seem such a delightful place to return to. . . . And the unreality of it! Even Juan-les-Pins seemed non-existent after the mysteri-ous jungle atmosphere of Trou-sur-Mer; people there seemed to live an

intense nocturnal secretive life, to be as shy of observation as an Indian reserve near a densely populated city. (*The Rock Pool,* 41)

This "reality" is clearly a highly romantic one, however; here it is associated with the Indian reservation, but on the next page, the exotic Cleuhs are also invoked. In other respects actual life in Trou is highly insignificant (as Naylor is at first able to see), in ways which are familiar from other novels of the late twenties and the early thirties. There is considerable use of inconsequential dialogue, explanations which explain nothing, random comings and goings, the absence of a conventional plot or conventional motivation, and the failure of events which should be significant to be so. There is, for example, a short passage on love making which very much resembles scenes in Powell's *Afternoon Men* (1931) and Greene's *England Made Me* (1935)—there may, of course, be direct influence. In all three accounts climax is presented as anticlimax, and the whole process is seen as a mechanical one particularly in Powell and Connolly's novels (both use the same female name, Lola).

> Naylor was with Lola. It had got to be done; the machinery, obsolete, cumbrous, rusty, by which one got into somebody's bed for a few minutes had to be brought into use again, the noisy gears had to be engaged. (*The Rock Pool,* 51)

Connolly's introductory letter to Peter Quennell explicitly refers to the notion of futility, and so too does Naylor. In the letter Connolly writes:

> Any first book is in the nature of a tardy settlement of an account with the past, and in this case my debt is with the nineteen-twenties. It was a period when art was concerned with futility, when heroes were called Denis and Nigel and Stephen and had a tortured look. I wonder who remembers them now. In any case I think I may claim to have created a young man as futile as any. It also dates because the life it deals with has almost disappeared. . . . The bars are closed, the hotel is empty, the nymphs have departed. (*The Rock Pool,* xx)

The romantic nostalgia (and reference to "The Waste Land") at the end of this is notable, since—part parodic, part serious—it is an attitude associated with Naylor in the novel. Though this letter refers futility back to the twenties, it is clear that in the novel itself, it is also seen as one kind of response to the decade which follows.

> What rendered his Rock Pool so attractive to Naylor, however, was the note of archaism. . . . Here alone a spark of life survived; a life moreover

which belonged to a period when people could still keep out of politics, when a change of government did not recall them to their citizenship by a change of income. (*The Rock Pool*, 58)

At another point Naylor notices some people who he thinks must (ironically) "turn one or two people into Communists almost every time they open their mouths". (42)

Naylor, indeed, actually expresses the paradoxical idea that he is "irretrievably *committed* [emphasis added] to futility.

As well as having a common interest in the idea of writing *The Rock Pool* also resembles *Keep the Aspidistra Flying* and *All the Conspirators* (and other novels by Waugh and Greene) in that it seems to see a paradoxical value in failure, which draws particularly on romantic conceptions of the artist and on nostalgia. In looking back at the twenties, it demurs from the dominant thirties commitment to responsibility and purpose, and does so by picking up on an interest in bohemianism and aestheticism which had formed part of the intellectual background of many thirties novelists, and which continued to contribute to their understanding of being a writer. It thus contributes to a debate about literature and commitment which Connolly approached by other means in *Enemies of Promise*, and which is of central importance to an understanding of thirties literature and politics in England. Though *The Rock Pool* might seem indeed to be a highly marginal text—"a microcosm cut off by the retreating economic tide" (*The Rock Pool*, 3)—it is in fact one which focuses a central concern of the thirties.

Notes

1. I am here counting Isherwood's early novel as a thirties text, since its concerns seem to me to be those of a "thirties writer," even if they are related to the "prehistory" of that decade as a literary-cultural construction. See Valentine Cunningham's *British Writers of the Thirties* (Oxford: Oxford University Press, 1988), 14–15, for a brief discussion of periodization.

2. See Fox's *The Novel and the People* (1937), and Henderson's *The Novel Today—Studies in Contemporary Attitudes*, (1936). For a European version see Lukac's own *The Historical Novel* (first German edition, Moscow, 1937, first English translation, 1962, by H. and S. Mitchell, reprinted (Pelican edition, 1981).

3. See, for example, "Where Engels Fears to Tread," which pretends to review a book called *From Oscar to Stalin. A Progress;* Wilde and aestheticism also provide models for other fictional characters from the period, such as Theo in Day Lewis's *Starting Point*, Mr. Surrogate in Greene's *It's a Battlefield*, and Ambrose Silk in Waugh's *Put Out More Flags*.

Works Cited

Connolly, Cyril. 1981. *The Rock Pool*. Oxford: Oxford University Press.
———. 1938. *Enemies of Promise*. London: Hogarth Press.

————1945, 1985. *The Condemned Playground—Essays 1927–1944.* London: Hogarth Press.

Cunningham, Valentine. 1988. *British Writers of the Thirties.* Oxford: Oxford University Press.

Day Lewis, C. 1937. *Starting Point.* London: Jonathan Cape.

Fox, Ralph. 1937. *The Novel and the People.* London: Lawrence and Wishart.

Greene, Graham. 1934. *It's a Battlefield.* London: Heinemann.

————. 1934, 1968. *Brighton Rock.* Harmondsworth: Penguin.

————. 1935. *England Made Me.* London: Heinemann.

Henderson, Philip. 1936. *The Novel Today—Studies in Contemporary Attitudes.* London: John Lane.

Hopkins, Chris. 1994. *Neglected Texts, Forgotten Contexts: Four Political Novels of the Nineteen Thirties.* Sheffield: PAVIC Publications.

Isherwood, Christopher. 1987. *All the Conspirators.* London: Hogarth Press.

Johnstone, Richard. *The Will to Believe—Novelists of the Nineteen Thirties.* Oxford: Oxford University Press.

Joyce, James. 1924. *A Portrait of the Artist as a Young Man.* London: Jonathan Cape.

Leech, Geoffrey and Mike Short. 1981. *Style in Fiction—A Linguistic Introduction to English Fiction.* London: Longman.

Lukács, G. 193. *The Meaning of Contemporary Realism.* London: Merlin Press.

Orwell, George. 1975. *Keep the Aspidistra Flying.* Harmondsworth: Penguin.

————. 1960. *Inside the Whale.* London: Secker and Warburg.

Powell, Anthony. 1973. *Afternoon Men.* London: Heinemann.

————. 19—(12 vols.) *A Dance to the Music of Time.*

Waugh, Evelyn. 1930. *Vile Bodies.* London: Chapman and Hall.

————. 1934, 1975. *A Handful of Dust.* Harmondsworth: Penguin.

————. 1942. *Put Out More Flags.* London: Chapman and Hall.

Woolf, Virginia. 1925. *Mrs. Dalloway.* London: Hogarth Press.

A Bibliography of Works by and about Cyril Connolly

Primary

————. *The Rock Pool.* 1936. Paris: Obelisk Press. Reprint, London, 1947 and Oxford University Press, 1981.

————. 1938. *Enemies of Promise.* London: Routledge.

————. 1944. *The Unquiet Grave.* London (published under the name "Palinurus").Hamish Hamilton

————. 1945. *The Condemned Playground, Essays 1927–44.* London: Hogarth Press.

————. 1953. *Ideas and Places.* London. Weidenfeld and Nicholson.

————. 1965. *The Modern Movement, One Hundred Key Books from England, France and America 1880–1950.* 1965. London: Deutsch.

Secondary

Bradbury, M. 1959. "'Horizon' and the English Nineteen Forties." *Gemini* 2.

Davis, R. M. 1992. "Waugh's Letters to Cyril Connolly: The Tulsa Archive." *Evelyn Waugh Newsletter and Studies* 26, no. 1 (spring): 1–5.

———. 1993. "Man Overboard: Cyril Connolly in Austin." *Evelyn Waugh Newsletter and Studies* 27, no. 1 (spring): 1–3.

Ewart, G. 1963. "Cyril Connolly." *The London Magazine* 3.

Fisher, C. 1995. *Cyril Connolly—A Nostalgic Life,* London: Macmillan

Kertzer, J. M. 1987. "Cyril Connolly's *The Unquiet Grave:* The Pilot and the Nonday Devil." *Mosaic: A Journal for the Interdisciplinary Study of Literature* 20, no. 4 (fall) 23–36.

Kramer, H. "Cyril Connolly's *Horizon.*" *The New Criterion* 8, no. 1 (September): 5–11.

Lienhardt, R. G. 1945. "From Playground to Grave." *Scrutiny* 13.

Ozick, C. "Cyril Connooly and the Groans of Success." *The New Criterion* 2, no. 3 (March): 21–27.

Pryce-Jones, D. 1983. "Journals (1928–34): Cyril Connolly." *Grand Street* 2, no. 3 (spring): 52–86.

Shelden, M. 1989. *Friends of Promise—Cyril Connolly And the World of Horizon,* LOndon: Hamish Hamilton.

Wilson, Edmond. 1950. "A Cry from the Unquiet Grave." In *Classics and Commercials.* New York: Oxford University Press.

Wain, J. "Lost Horizons?" *Encounter,* 1961; reprinted in his *Essays on Literature and Ideas,* 1963.

11

Rosamond Lehmann: *The Weather in the Streets*

Judy Simons

A Brief Biographical Sketch of Rosamond Lehmann (1901–90)

Rosamond lehmann was born in 1901 to rudolph and alice Lehmann. She was educated privately at home before winning a scholarship to Girton College, Cambridge, and in 1923 married Leslie Runciman. Her first novel, *Dusty Answer* (1924), written during the bleak years of this marriage, describes the passionate education of a young heroine from a secluded background confronted with the glamour of university life. It was an immediate—and scandalous—success. In 1928, after her divorce from Runciman was finalized, Lehmann married the Hon. Wogan Phillips, with whom she had two children. Their home in Oxfordshire became a focus for artists and writers, attracting figures such as the Woolfs, Siegfried Sassoon, W. H. Auden, Stephen Spender, and Augustus John. Lehmann produced some of her best-known novels during this period: *A Note in Music* (1930), *Invitation to the Waltz* (1932), and *The Weather in the Streets* (1936). All address the issue of women's emotional experiences contextualized by the revised and unstable cultural climate of the interwar years.

After the collapse of her second marriage, Lehmann's most sustained relationship, from 1941 to 1950, was with the poet, C. Day Lewis, a relationship that inspired some of her most intense and most technically innovative writing. Her two major works of this period, *The Ballad and the Source* (1944) and *The Echoing Grove* (1953) focus on the troubled nature of passionate attachments and the resulting bitterness that such relationships engender. In 1958, however, after the sudden tragic death of her daughter, Sally, at the age of twenty-four, Lehmann's literary career came to an abrupt halt. She turned to spiritualism for comfort, and produced only one more novel, *A Sea-Grape Tree* (1976), a work which explores the impact of the past on present experience.

In 1982 Lehmann was awarded the CBE for services to literature. She was a vice president of International PEN, a Fellow of the Royal Society of Literature, and a member of the Council of the Society of Authors. At her death in 1990, she was generally acknowledged as one of the most distinguished writers of her age. Recently her work has been rediscovered by a new generation of readers, its frank exposure of sexual and psychological uncertainties a definitive statement of what constitutes the modern.

* * * * *

Rosamond Lehmann's *Weather in the Streets* (1936) is a text which locates its heroine in a psychological no-man's-land of confusion and desolation. Caught between two cultures, that of her parents' generation of the prewar period and that of the postwar avant-garde, Olivia Curtis finds herself rootless and without direction in a world where the moral parameters are constantly shifting. The society that Lehmann depicts in this, for some readers her most powerful and bitter, work is that of a bourgeois culture in crisis, the fractured sensibility of the protagonist itself emblematic of the tensions of the 1930s. As the novel moves between two locations, the urban wasteland of contemporary London and the comfortable but stultified rural environment of the Thames valley, the impression that emerges is that of a divided England, a nation whose incompatible elements serve only to destabilize each other's value systems.

To some extent, the book reflects Lehmann's own position at the time of writing. Brought up in a conventional and highly protected household, she was educated at home, before moving on to Girton College, Cambridge, at the age of nineteen. There Lehmann had encountered for the first time the unrestrained and hedonistic lifestyle of men and women, many of them survivors of the French battlefields, for whom the cult of youth had become virtually de rigueur. Her first novel, *Dusty Answer* (1927), in its account of a young woman's passionate adventures in college, documents the independence and experimentation that characterized this new, "lost" generation. Scarred by the aftermath of the Great War, the characters in *Dusty Answer* seek pleasure without responsibility, careless of others in their pursuit of self. In its intense focus on Judith

Earle's emotional education, the work also examines and reevaluates femininity, a topic which in the new climate of female emancipation came to dominate Lehmann's writing.

That same ghost of the war which haunts *Dusty Answer* is also present in *A Note in Music* (1930) and *Invitation to the Waltz* (1932), both novels which explore the frustrations and the potential of women whose lives are conditioned by a static society, but who are aware of possibilities for fulfillment outside their immediate environment. *Invitation to the Waltz,* the prequel to *The Weather in the Streets,* in particular, suggests a world in transition as it follows the activities of a community populated by those whose lives have been transformed by the war. The blinded war veteran, the lovelorn spinster, the bereaved parents who have lost their son, the returning heroes who avoid mentioning their experiences: all serve as reminders of a devastated world that is struggling to accommodate itself to the forces of change. The teenage Olivia Curtis, similarly uncertain and searching for direction, thus functions as a representative of her age. As her semiformed consciousness tries to make sense of the oblique messages that surround her, she becomes dimly aware of the breaks with tradition that signal a personal future very different from the past that has shaped the previous generation. It is the nature of that future, and the ultimate failure of the promise held out to Olivia in the closing pages of *Invitation to the Waltz,* which form the central subject of *The Weather in the Streets.*

By the time she came to write *The Weather in the Streets,* Rosamond Lehmann had endured an unhappy marriage and a divorce. Her second marriage, to the painter, Wogan Phillips, was already beginning to disintegrate, and the resulting sense of personal disillusionment permeates the novel. This marriage had, however, brought her into contact with an artistic circle whose outlook on life embodied the combination of vision and cynicism that determined much of the creative production of the 1930s. In common with that of other writers during this period, although perhaps articulated less insistently, Lehmann's development is one of increasing politicization. Lehmann has been too easily categorized by critics as a novelist of the emotions, indifferent to the wider impact of social and political movements which contextualize her narratives.[1] Her reputation has been established as a "woman's novelist," and she has been placed firmly within the tradition of the novel of sensibility, as a writer "concerned only with picking over the minutiae of the feminine consciousness" (Coe 1993). While contemporary critics applauded Lehmann's delicate psychological insight and her talent for comedy, they also damned her work with faint praise by suggesting that her scope was confined to a limited compass, and one moreover that occupied an "increasingly insignificant niche in an increasingly materialistic civilization."[2] This criticism of being out of touch with the age in which she lived, a criticism frequently leveled by male critics at women writers, seriously underrates Lehmann's achievement.

For more than many of her contemporaries, Lehmann shows herself sensitive to the impact of historical process on women's lives. For a number of reasons, it is important that the protagonist of *The Weather in the Streets* is a woman, a character who signaly lacks political influence but whose life is fundamentally affected by the external events which shape the national consciousness and which have contributed to the moral decline of a society fashioned by dissatisfaction. To adopt a feminist slogan of the 1960s, in Lehmann's writing the personal *is* the political, and it is her heroine's individual experience of dissolution which stands as a metaphor for the cultural incoherence of the age.

While on one level *The Weather in the Streets* remains fundamentally a love story in its analysis of the doomed relationship between Olivia and Rollo Spencer, it subjects that relationship to a scrutiny which savagely exposes the mechanisms of sexual politics which underlie it. As the poet, Stephen Spender, a close friend of Lehmann's observed, "the 1930s were a perpetual state of emergency for those aware that there was an emergency." Lehmann's depiction of the love affair between Olivia and Rollo discloses the existence of a state of emergency for contemporary women who, despite the apparent freedoms of the postwar years, remain perpetual victims of power structures that threaten their very being. The technical innovations of the text, as it moves between first- and third-person narrative, dramatize the dichotomy between private and public experience in a society founded on deception, and the consequent crisis in personal and social relations that this produces. In presenting Olivia as caught between two irreconcilable milieus, the book also forms an examination of the subtle processes of cultural shift during the first half of the twentieth century, and addresses the means by which contemporary artists confront or evade current issues.

In its realization of psychological fracture, Olivia's story takes full account of the complexities of the modern consciousness and the insights afforded by psychoanalysis into female sexuality. For Olivia as she appears in *The Weather in the Streets* is *the* modern young woman of the 1930s. Educated and independent but retaining the romantic longings of adolescent imagination, she confronts the dilemmas which a sexually liberated climate creates for twentieth-century women. Brought up in an age of Edwardian values and traditions, Olivia retains respect for the past. Yet she is also conscious of the attractions of the new, and the opportunities for release that the modern age has created for women. Her personal experience of the psychological and emotional trauma of an adulterous love affair, the central action of the novel, endows her with the status of a representative of her generation of women, women whose adventurousness in their investigation of their own erotic nature is not necessarily complemented by the economic security of marriage or of genuine professional independence.

The story of *The Weather in the Streets* thus gives a new twist to the familiar "woman's story" of romance and betrayal. Olivia Curtis is twenty-seven when the novel opens. Divorced from her first husband, she is living alone in London, sharing a house with her older and more sophisticated cousin, Etty, and working as an assistant in a photographic studio belonging to her friend, Anna. On a train journey back to the family home in the Thames valley, she meets the glamorous son of a wealthy neighboring family, Rollo Spencer, a man whom she has secretly worshiped since she was seventeen. Falling helplessly in love with Rollo and with the privileged world that he represents, Olivia embarks on a clandestine love affair despite the fact that Rollo is married. The secret life that she enjoys with him, however, has devastating effects on her other relationships, and ultimately exposes the real precariousness of her social and psychic situation. In the process of the affair, Olivia becomes pregnant, undergoes an abortion, and as a result of these unacceptable acts effectively becomes isolated from her family and friends, trapped in a "glass casing" of adulterous passion which paralyzes and destroys her hold on self. The novel's subject matter, the sympathetic treatment given to the plight of the "other woman," and the graphic details of the abortion episode combined to produce a shocked reaction from contemporary readers. The gentle quality of the satire which had characterized *Invitation to the Waltz* was now replaced by a harsh and uncompromising analysis of gender and class politics which stripped away any sense of reassurance from romantic illusion.

The Weather in the Streets is divided into four sections, each monitoring a discrete stage in the love affair between Olivia and Rollo as it moves inexorably from euphoria to despair. The romance scenario of the first section proceeds conventionally enough, but it is important to recognize the levels of irony with which the initial encounters between the couple are presented. Projected through Olivia's perspective, these are tinged with the glamour of fantasy and only gradually does their hollowness become apparent. Self-consciously deploying the discourse of popular fiction, the text ex-

poses the clichéd nature of romantic passion itself as it is filtered
through Olivia's self-delusive memories. Entering her parents' home
after her first kiss from Rollo, Olivia thinks of the double life she
has now embarked on and the mask she must adopt for the benefit
of her family who are oblivious

> to the two forms murmuring, clasping, to me hurrying away alone,
> flying from him, back to my home, back to myself, away from the two
> shapes in shadow, leaving them there, to be there now for ever, clasped,
> as I dreamed in the beginning they would one night be. This is with
> whom it was to be, and this is the night. Now I am back at the begin-
> ning, now begins what I dreamed was to be. (*The Weather in the
> Streets,* 136)

Rollo has seduced Olivia not only physically but into the world
of double standards, deceit, and intrigue which he inhabits. From
henceforward Olivia is condemned to wear a mask, her life shaped
by duality, her only consolation that she believes herself to be loved.
As this extract makes clear, Olivia colludes willingly in the perpetra-
tion of her own downfall, love functioning simultaneously as both
the energizing and the destabilizing factor in her experience. As
Rollo remarks in a moment of supreme narrative irony, "'You were
like a statue. I never thought I'd be able to bring you to life'" (*The
Weather in the Streets,* 156). Yet it is his ability to release her sexual
drive which also traps Olivia in a traditional relationship which in
turn negates her identity. By the end of the novel Olivia is left
stranded, her will broken and her self-respect destroyed. Passion
activates one aspect of the self, but it does so at great cost. In her
impressionistic recall of Rollo's embrace, Olivia's perspective is determined by the edifice of romantic fantasy she has built for herself,
carved from her dreams of adolescent longing.
    The disjunction between the imaginative idealization of romance
and the actuality of sexual passion is brought home forcibly in the
scene in Olivia's London apartment where she and Rollo make love
for the first time. After intercourse, Olivia lies physically close to,
but psychologically distant from, the man at her side and reflects
dispassionately on the experience in terms very different from the
rhapsodic emotionalism with which she had retraced the first kiss

> I thought about it. I had a lover. But nothing seemed changed. It wasn't
> disappointing exactly. . . . The word is, unmomentous. . . . Not won-
> derful—yet. . . . I couldn't quite look at him. . . . Thinking. Aren't I in
> love with him after all then? (*The Weather in the Streets,* 153)

Despite the fact that romance is traditionally thought of as a distinctively female narrative genre, Lehmann shows in *The Weather in the Streets* how romance as a construct continually militates against women. Right from the opening scenes of the novel, Olivia mediates her own subjectivity through received models of the feminine and consequently compromizes her sense of identity in order to conform to the demands of romance. She thinks of herself through a refracted perspective as the object of a judgmental "male gaze," "seeing an image of herself in Rollo's mind" (*The Weather in the Streets,* 13) as a sexually desirable being. Invited to dinner at the Spencers' house, she abandons the Bohemian persona she has acquired during her years of independent living, and dresses to meet her lover in borrowed clothes that she thinks will appeal to his virility. Her mother's fur coat, her sister's white diaphanous dress (reminiscent of one she has seen Rollo's wife wear) are symbols of a conventional femininity which transform Olivia's image into the stereotype of virginal innocence, attractive bait for the predatory male. And indeed the strategy is effective. "'You're so young,'" says Rollo admiringly, as he takes Olivia in his arms, conveniently ignoring the reality of the situation. "'You're like a young, young girl'" (132).

Yet it is Olivia's complicity in the fictive scenario of romance that has set her on the path to self-destruction. As the affair reaches its height, she becomes aware that Rollo will never leave his wife nor his privileged lifestyle. Existing in a no-man's-land of waiting, on the margins of another's life, Olivia gradually realizes that the affair renders her powerless, reducing her to a form of paralysis through the insidious erosion of her individual will. The text is permeated with images of unreality; the "glass casing"; "a vacuum . . . an unborn place" (*The Weather in the Streets,* 144); "a kind of permanent dream" (165); "abandoned in a pestilence stricken town . . . a wasteland" (263). All underscore her exclusion from the economic and emotional centers of contemporary culture. The visit Olivia receives from Lady Spencer when she is alone, pregnant and ill, shows her more clearly than anything that has gone before how the massed forces of the establishment retain the power and influence that has always been their perogative. The interview serves as a reminder of her real vulnerability within the British social structure. As a woman, single and without the protection of affluence or family, Olivia has no ammunition with which to defend herself. Lady Spencer on the contrary assumes authority as her right: age, wealth, and class combine to alienate Olivia from the superstructure that the Spencers represent, whatever the latent dissolution threatening the unruffled surface. As Olivia observes with wry irony:

"I expect monogamy's a tradition in your family. . . ."
A show of it at least. . . . Facades of virtue and principle, as an example
to the lower classes. Anything may go on underneath, because you're
privileged. That Marigold's no good, she's a drunken tart. And what
about old Sir John in his day, I wouldn't be too sure. . . . (*The Weather
in the Streets*, 277)

The Weather in the Streets does not adopt an explicitly feminist
agenda. Lehmann remains, as always, suspicious of women whose
political aggressiveness overrides their femininity. Olivia "loathes
women who . . . hoot about sex-equality." The novel rather explores the ambivalent status of contemporary women in a society
which simultaneously liberates and imprisons them. It is in this context that Lehmann's work addresses issues that are fundamental to
the politics of gender in a patriarchal culture. Olivia, like other
women in her circle, is shown as powerless without male protection.
Her liaison with Rollo has effectively denied her the right to an
individual identity, and she finds herself categorized by others in
terms which are ultimately dehumanizing. She has become variously
the "other woman," "a mistress," "a hot bit," whose meetings with
her lover must take place furtively, snatched encounters in the semi-
darkness of restaurant alcoves or nighttime encounters in her
cousin's rented flat where the real world is kept at bay.

The respite from harsh reality is, however, temporary. The illusion of romance cannot last and Olivia cannot avoid acknowledging
the truth of her position. The novel's emphasis on the fragmentation
of the psyche and the destruction of the self that the love affair
precipitates reaches its climax in the abortion episode, a scene that
Lehmann's publishers had wanted removed from the text. Lehmann
insisted on its inclusion, and indeed it sums up the indignities and
the injustices to which women are subject when they forfeit their
approved role within the social code, and gravitate to the margins.

Olivia's visit to the abortionist, coldly commercial, forces her
to realize both her lack of status and the inescapability of biologic
determinism. Discovering that she is pregnant, Olivia loses any
sense of her individual personality and becomes a generic "female,
her body used, made fertile, turning, resentful, in hostile untouch-
ability, from the male, the enemy, victorious and malignant" (*The
Weather in the Streets*, 230). The loser in both the class war and
the sex war, Olivia is a victim of the system which subsumes such
hostilities. The abortionist, the ironically named Mr. Tredeaven, is
represented as quite simply a dealer in women, his clinical handling
of Olivia's body as detached as his dispassionate fondling of the

statuettes of female nudes adorning his desk. For him, women, whether flesh and blood or cast in bronze, carry no more significance than objects, elements in a commercial transaction which promotes the perpetuation of a materialistic culture to male advantage.

Not only is the myth of romantic love exploded in Lehmann's ferocious attack on Rollo's power over Olivia, but also the fiction of female emancipation. The interwar years might have granted women a superficial license to be educated, to engage in free love, and to taste an independent lifestyle, but without traditional safeguards of home and family women's lives are seen as directionless and sterile. Olivia's lifestyle as a single woman is portrayed as reduced to a series of insubstantial activities typical of her rootless generation:

> lives passing up and down outside with steps and voices of futile purpose and forlorn commotion: draining out of my life, out of the window, in their echoing wake, leaving me dry, stranded, sterile, bound solitary to the room's minute respectability, the gas-fire, the cigarette, the awaited bell, the gramophone's idiot companionship, the unyielding arm-chair, the narrow bed. . . . (*The Weather in the Streets*, 77)

Lured by the magnet of love, women such as Olivia acquire purpose but the consequences of illicit passion reveal the lack of support for those brave or foolish enough to be seduced by the promises of such freedom. For Olivia's narrative is one shared by countless women and her plight is echoed in the half-told stories of her cousin, Etty, and her friend, Mona, who have also been patients of Mr. Tredeaven. Their whispered, guilty secret reveals to Olivia the existence of "a feminine conspiracy," a network of women, vulnerable and suffering beneath the glittering facade of socialite London.

That facade is ruthlessly exposed in *The Weather in the Streets* to disclose a world which is essentially brittle and corrupt. The gaiety of the Bright Young Things of the 1920s has been replaced by a decadence which marks the period as one of inexorable decline. As *The Times Literary Supplement* observed twenty years after its initial publication, "*The Weather in the Streets* . . . exudes an atmosphere of the 1930s almost as pungently as did *Dusty Answer* that of the previous decade." Like Evelyn Waugh's *Handful of Dust* with which it can usefully be compared, it offers a portrait of a "transitional and rather featureless period" (*The Times Literary Supplement* 1953, 252) and its characters are similarly transitional and drifting. Many of the personalities who appeared so exciting and glamorous to the untrained perception of the youthful Olivia in *Invitation to the Waltz* reappear in this novel as faded and hollow. Etty, the sophisticated flapper of the twenties, is shown ten years later, motiveless and pathetic, her apartment littered with sordid debris and mementos of past lovers who have discarded her. Marigold, so beautiful and fresh in the earlier text has become, ten years later, a seeker after sensation and excess, her fashionable marriage a sham as she moves indiscriminately from one lover to the next.

The subtle gradations in the novel's tone from optimism to despair are reflected in the repeated scenes that shift perspective almost imperceptibly. The depiction of Olivia's visit to Meldon, the Spencers' household, in the opening section of the book is projected through her own nostalgia for past stability and glamour, her search for the lost values of her childhood. Entering the grand drawing room for the first time in ten years, she observes its beauty, order, and opulence, "the panels of glass, the screen, the Aubusson carpet, the subdued gleam of porcelain and crystal, the piano painted with light, faint coloured wreaths and sprays" (The Weather in the Streets, 55). Attracted by the traditions and by what one character describes as the "lost art" of living which the evening tries to resurrect, she ignores at first the uncongenial details which impinge on her consciousness: Sir John's illness, the ritualistic conversation of Lady Spencer, and the emptiness which lies behind the surface display. If anything, she is comforted by the sameness of the scene which only subsequently strikes her as petrified. Returning to the drawing room after dinner, however, Olivia is uncomfortably aware of the unreality of it all. Although "change was in the air. The wheels were running down" (90), the characters cling to the past for refuge, and in Olivia's revised perception they appear to take on "a static quality as if anaesthetized" (97).

The moribund atmosphere of the great house where the inhabitants refuse to accept that they are living out "the end of a chapter" (The Weather in the Streets, 84) stands in direct opposition to the creative world of Olivia's artistic friends, Simon, Anna, and their circle. In this environment, at supper in Simon's studio, Olivia gazes round the room which is filled with evidence of energy and productive activity, a marked contrast with the surroundings at Meldon:

wherever the eye fell some mark of liveliness, some kind of wit, selection, invention—the vitality of shape, pattern, colour, making an aesthetic unity—the creative hand, the individual mind mattering—the dirt, untidiness, poor materials not mattering at all. Thinking the room lives; their rooms are dead, full of dead objects. I meant Meldon. (The Weather in the Streets, 147)

Olivia's divided allegiance between the two groups symbolizes her split identity. She is caught between the desire to hold on to her past history and her understanding of the potential of the future, and her personal dilemma, her condition of indecision and stasis, reflects the cultural crisis of the age. As she fluctuates between the two communities, assuming masks and personae, she becomes aware of the process of her own nullification. "Sometimes I wish I could be free again, able to belong to myself" (*The Weather in the Streets,* 203) she reflects, conscious of the irreparable damage the love affair has inflicted on the psyche. She becomes absorbed into an "inward double living under amorphous impacts of dark and light mixed" (144) and the effect is one of disorientation both social and personal. In comparison with Rollo her friends are "a different race altogether," and the division undermines her sense of a coherent self. "Where was I between the two?" (153) she asks herself, confronting the problem of her own dislocation to which there is no apparent solution.

This experience of deracination is underscored in the text's use of oppositional imagery of death and life; Olivia's father's death, prefigured in the opening scenes of the book, indicates the passing of a generation. Her sister Kate's children signal the direction of the new age: lively and careless "they don't know the meaning of the words filial respect" (*The Weather in the Streets,* 243). Olivia is drawn to the past, but it is a lethal magnet, her father's illness acting as the stimulus for her return home: Olivia herself can never recapture the confidence or the stability of that period which has had its day. Denied the safe status of marriage enjoyed by her sister, she has no social role to fulfill: the abortion serves as a symbol of her frustrated potential, her ability to generate thwarted by circumstances. Set between two time zones and two distinct environments, Olivia is a displaced person.

Lehmann's social analysis does not rest with the narrative of her heroine's personal predicament. The satire of both upper-class complacency and Bohemianism is far-reaching, and incorporates an attack on the state of contemporary art which ignores current issues. The Bohemian party to which Olivia takes Rollo epitomizes the decadence of the modern intelligentsia, self-absorbed and refusing to engage with the real world. Outrageously dressed party-goers parody the avant-garde in their theatrically assumed personae, their gaiety reduced to a series of casual and unorthodox sexual encounters and drunken episodes. Olivia, whose vision has inevitably been affected by her contact with Rollo's value systems, looks with fresh eyes on the painters, writers, and intellectuals of contemporary London who were her friends and sees only debauchery and exhibitionism.

Only Simon and Anna appear in the novel to embody genuine artistic potential. It is, however, highly significant that they flee from England to the south of France, to settle in a culture where their creativity can find full expression. Without their sustenance Olivia is bereft, left to a London society which nurtures self-indulgent and frivolous beings who play at the game of art through commercial patronage without ever understanding its capacity for transformation. Toward the end of the novel, finding herself at Mrs. Cunningham's fashionable party, Olivia observes the display of Simon's paintings on the walls of the hostess's salon and notes that they have become little more than monuments to another aspect of materialist ownership. The death of Simon, coinciding with the death of Olivia's love for Rollo, is one further instance of the failure of art to influence the stasis which the novel presents as symptomatic of the modern condition.

The Weather in the Streets is not a text to be dismissed lightly. It is a fiction of both personal and public disenchantment. The divergent worlds that Olivia occupies both cast a fatal spell over her: as Colin warns her, she must beware of their attraction.

> "Dying's so insidious", he said, speaking softly out towards the night."
> It's so easy. Death's catching. We must steer clear of it. . . . Look at us
> all going about breathing it in at every pore because we caught it. . . .
> Carrying death about with us." (*The Weather in the Streets,* 372)

Framed by the imminent death of her father at the beginning of the novel and the irrevocable fact of Simon's death at the end, Olivia is herself unable to find a lifeline. The final scene of the book shows her drawn back to Rollo, impelled by his charm despite her decision to avoid him. The ambivalence of the closing sentence, refusing to spell out the direction of the future, leaves the reader in little doubt that Olivia's fate is predetermined. Her personal crisis of indecision incorporates issues that take the scope of the novel way beyond the remit of the conventional love story. Olivia's paralysis, her drift toward vacancy, and her negation of her individual will have political implications that register precisely the climate of her times.

Notes

1. See especially Diana E. LeStourgeon, *Rosamond Lehmann* (New York: G. K. Hall, Twayne, 1965) for a summary of these attitudes.

2. Clifton Fadiman, *The Nation,* quoted by Joseph Wood Krutch, "All For Love," a review of *The Weather in the Streets, The Nation* (June 1936): 713.

Works Cited

Coe, Jonathan. 1993. "On the Shelf." *The Sunday Times,* 10 October.

Faidiman, Clifton. 1936. *The Nation,* quoted by Joseph Wood Krutch, "All For Love," a review of *The Weather in the Streets. The Nation* (June).

Lehmann, Rosamond. 1981. *The Weather in the Streets.* London: Virago Press.

LeStourgeon, Diana E. 1965. *Rosamond Lehmann.* New York: G. K. Hall, Twayne.

Spender, Stephen. 1951. *World Within World.* London: Hamish Hamilton.

The Times Literary Supplement. 1953. London: Times Newspapers Ltd. (17 April).

A Bibliograhpy of Works by and about Rosamond Lehmann

Novels

————. 1927. *Dusty Answer.* London: Chatto and Windus.

————. 1930. *A Note in Music.* London: Chatto and Windus.

————. 1932. *Invitation to the Waltz.* London: Chatto and Windus.

————. 1936. *The Weather in the Streets.* London: Collins.

————. 1944. *The Ballad and the Source.* London: Collins.

————. 1946. *The Gypsy's Baby and other Stories.* London: Collins.

————. 1953. *The Echoing Grove.* London: Collins.

————. 1976. *A Sea-Grape Tree.* London: Collins.

————. 1977. *The Swan in the Evening.* London: Collins.

Plays

————. 1939. *No More Music.* New York.

Other Nonfiction
————. *A Letter to a Sister.* 1931, New York, 1932.

Secondary Sources

Interviews 1988.

Janet Watts. "Rosamond Lehmann." In Mary Chamberlain, ed. *Writing Lives: Conversations between Women Writers.* London: Virago Press.

————. 1984. Bel Mooney. "Lost Loves of a Soul Survivor." *The Times,* 9 February, 8.

Criticism

Atkins, John. 1977. "Rosamond Lehmann." In *Six Novelists Look at Society: An Enquiry into the Social Views of Elizabeth Bowen, L. P. Hartley, Rosamond Lehmann, Christopher Isherwood, Nancy Mitford, C. P. Snow.* London: Calder.

Day-Lewis, Sean. 1980. *C. Day Lewis: An English Literary Life.* London: Weidenfeld & Nicolson.

Dorosz, Wiktoria. 1975. "Subjective Vision and Human Relationships in the Novels of Rosamond Lehmann," *Studia Anglistica Upsaliena,* no. 23. Stockholm: Acta Universitatis Upsaliensis.

Gindin, James. 1974. "Rosamond Lehmann: A Revaluation." *Contemporary Literature* 15: 203–11.

Gustafson, Margaret T. 1959. "Rosamond Lehmann: A Bibliography." *Twentieth Century Literature* 4, no. 4: 143–47

Kaplan, Sydney Janet. 1975. "Rosamond Lehmann." In *Feminine Consciousness in the Modern British Novel.* Chicago: University of Illinois Press.

LeStourgeon, Diana E. 1965. *Rosamond Lehmann.* New York: G. K. Hall, Twayne.

Simons, Judy. 1992. *Rosamond Lehmann.* London: Macmillan.

———. 1992. "The Torment of Loving: The Inter-war Novels of Rosamond Lehmann." In *Writers of the Old School: British Novelists of the 1930s.* Edited by Hazel Colt and Janice Rossen. London: Macmillan.

Tindall, Gillian. 1984. *Rosamond Lehmann: An Appreciation.* London: Chatto & Windus.

12

Katharine Burdekin: An Alien Presence in Her Own Time

GEORGE MCKAY

A Brief Biographical Sketch of Katharine (Penelope) Burdekin (1896–1963).

KATHARINE BURDEKIN WAS THE ENGLISH AUTHOR OF TEN PUBLISHED novels, including a children's book and other unpublished works, including *The End of This Day's Business,* recently published for the first time, fifty years after being written. Many of her works were published under the male pseudonym of "Murray Constantine," including her best-known work *Swastika Night* (1937), which was re-published in 1940 as one of the Left Book Club's rare forays into fiction. Burdekin had a fairly conventional Edwardian middle-class upringing: educated at Cheltenham Ladies College and an early marriage to an army lieutenant. Within a few years though this marriage was over, and by the late 1920s Burdekin was living with her two daughters and her lifelong female companion, writing novels in short intense bursts of literary activity. Never a central part of a literary scene (living in the English countryside), her friends and admirers did though include Radclyffe Hall, H. D., Margaret Gold-smith, and Frederick Voigt, as well as the Woolfs and Bertrand and Dora Russell. Before writing, she had worked as a nurse in an army hospital during World War I, and she supplemented her income while writing by working in a shoe factory, in a printer's shop, and in a flour mill. Prone to occasional mental problems during her life, in later years she also suffered long-term physical ill health. (I am indebted to the work of Daphne Patai here for much of the bio-graphical material concerning Burdekin.) She published her last novel in 1940, though she continued writing for many years afterward.

✳ ✳ ✳ ✳ ✳

For in the midst of the post-World War One lull in British feminism, [Katharine] Burdekin, like Virginia Woolf and Rebecca West, continued to cast a critical and distinctly feminist eye on her society. But unlike Woolf and West, Burdekin faded from the literary record. This fate may well be related to the very challenge her uncompromising vision posed to her society. There seems to have been no critical standard in Burdekin's own time capable of incorporating her writing. . . . If Burdekin was an alien presence in her own time, to ours she is a precursor.
—Daphne Patai (1989, 161)

Unshakable, impregnable Empire has always been the dream of virile nations, and now . . . it's turned into a nightmare reality.
—Katharine Burdekin, *Swastika Night* (78)

Introduction

In the 1930s, according to Brian Aldiss and David Wingrove, science fiction "is full of *zeitgeist,* mirroring uneasily the forthcoming global conflict with its lost store of lives" (Aldiss and Wingrove 1986, 216). Both a response to, and a product of, what Christopher Isherwood called the "fantastic unrealities" (quoted in Croft 1990, 239) of life in the period, a wide number of nonrealist fictions were written which sought either tangentially to comment on the spread of fascism and Stalinism across Europe, or deliberately to offer non-referential worlds of fantasy. As Andy Croft puts it, "[t]he 1930s was an especially rich period for 'futuristic' writing of all kinds in Britain, fabulous, allegorical, mythic, satirical, time-travelling, utopian and dystopian" (Croft, 220–21). One of the most prolific authors of the political "'futuristic' writing" during this period was Katharine Burdekin, many of whose texts rely on "the broad historical sweep—across thousands of years, encompassing not only the past but also the future" (Patai 1989, 164). While W. H. Auden and other poets were apostrophizing history, in fiction it was being employed by writers like Burdekin for extrapolative purposes, to offer a quick futuristic perspective, to paraphrase Stephen Spender.

The action of Burdekin's 1937 feminist dystopia *Swastika Night* takes place in a far-future Nazi Germany which was formed after victory in the twentieth century. Later the scene moves with the English protagonist, Alfred, to occupied England. The world of seven hundred years in the future is ruled by two totalitarian Empires, the German (which includes Europe) and the Japanese (which includes the United States). The inhabitants of the Nazi Empire are presented as "a people . . . whose ethic is war and whose religion is war" (*Swastika Night,* 76). While this is the case, the world survives in a state of permanent, if uneasy, peace between the two Empires. Women in the Nazi Empire exist within a superpatriarchal society—they are breeding machines for the next generation of Nazi soldiers and imperialists. Repression is systematic. The "Reduction of Women" (70) consists of a number of male laws: complete segregation of women from men, kept in the cages of the Women's Quarters; the right of any Nazi to have sex with any woman, with the result that there is no crime of rape; the "Removal of the Man-child" (9), of male children from their mothers at eighteen months, to be raised by men in a militaristic environment. The plot revolves around a slightly eccentric figure of authority, the Nazi Knight von Hess, who has in his possession a family book which is the only unofficial book surviving in the entire Empire, which was written by a distant ancestor in the twentieth century, and which has been handed down from father to son in the family since then. The hero is Alfred, an English technician, who is recognized by von Hess as an exceptional character, and to whom, since his own sons are all dead, von Hess gives the book. With the book, which contains facts of pre-Hitlerian life, the rebellion will begin, and the Nazi Empire will eventually crumble. What's so significant about *Swastika Night* is that it is an exploration of the connection between power and gender, an uncovering of the operations of patriarchy in relation to fascism.

In spite of its far-future setting, though, there's a timely fascination in the novel with airplanes and flying—an early scene of male bonding between the Nazi Knight and the English hero takes place in an aerodrome and up in the air, which is presented as a source of great privilege and excitement for the Englishman. Burdekin's is clearly not a future text of the type concerned with, for instance, technology and progress. Working within the conventions of nonrealist fiction, Burdekin's historical prolepsis (seven hundred years in the future) and political extrapolation (a victorious and enduring Nazi Reich) functions as what Fredric Jameson terms science fiction's "strategy of indirection" (Jameson 1982, 152). However, Burdekin also employs other conventions of science fiction within *Swastika Night.* First, she is working within the context of feminist utopian fiction—for example, Charlotte Perkins Gilman's *Herland* (1915), Charlotte Haldane's *Man's World* (1926)—in which the social role and construction of woman is interrogated by means of the science fiction strategies of extrapolation and satiric exaggeration. Second, she is working within the staple plot device of what has become known as the "Hitler Wins" narrative (see Clute and Nicholls 1993, 572–73). Possibly even Burdekin *invents* this narrative convention— or at least *Swastika Night* is a very early example of it. In terms of this, it's worth noting that *Swastika Night* doesn't simply extrapolate a Nazi victory in World War II, but actually anticipates the war itself, and its devastating global effects. Burdekin also anticipates other aspects of the coming war.

> When Katharine Burdekin wrote *Swastika Night* she could not have guessed how horrifyingly accurate her vision of the Nazi regime was to be. The Jewish population in her dystopia has been annihilated and the Christians are tolerated as a sub-race but are termed "untouchables". (Russell 1991, 23)

During the 1930s Burdekin wrote at least half a dozen novels, not all published, most of which dealt with her recurring concerns of pacifism, socialism, and feminism, through her favored textual strategy of nonrealism. Her work has been paid increasing attention by contemporary critics not least since her textual approach overtly links genre and gender in ways which feminist science fiction writers of the 1970s and 1980s have themselves explored. Many of her 1930s novels are overtly propagandistic, clear responses to the political issues of Nazism and communism in Europe. Her texts favored a grand historical sweep in which she could examine not only the past and the present, but also extrapolate into the distant future in order to construct a more powerfully historicizing generic defamiliarization. *The Rebel Passion* (1929) moves from a twelfth-century monastery to a twenty-first-century Britain in which there is a degree of feminist utopia. *Quiet Ways* (1930) is a pacifist novel that links masculinity with a discourse of war. (Faced with fighting fascism, she later abandoned her pacifist principles, though not her critical focus on the social effects of masculinist aggression.) *Proud Man* (1934) features a visitor from the future examining contemporary society and its sexual and gender roles. Also in *Proud Man* Burdekin offers something of a critique of the literary practice of other writers of dystopia. Patai notes that "Burdekin criticizes Aldous Huxley's *Brave New World* for its assumption that human beings would be the same even under totally different conditions" (Patai 1984, 87). Burdekin displays here both her development of the genre in particular directions, and her textual strategy of critical interrogation of the genre's practice and expectations. *The End of This Day's Business* was written around 1935, and is set four thousand years in a future England. Basically a sex-role reversal satire, Burdekin represents a utopian matriarchal society for which the price to be paid is the total social repression of men. Her novel *Swastika Night* is dealt with in the chapter. In 1940 she published her last novel, with Margaret Goldsmith as coauthor, *Venus in Scorpio,* a historical narrative about the life of Marie Antoinette. Though she continued writing for many years Burdekin never published another novel.

Interestingly enough, considering her thematic and social interests, many of her novels, including *Swastika Night,* were published under the male pseudonym of "Murray Constantine." *Swastika Night* was originally published in 1937, with a second edition in 1940 as one of the few works of fiction published as a Left Book Club text. A publisher's note informs the Left Book Club readership:

> In reissuing this novel the publishers wish to say:
> 1. It was written and published in 1937.
> 2. The picture painted must be considered symbolic rather than prophetic—symbolic of what would [happen] to the world if Hitler were to impose his will (as he must not) upon it.
> 3. While the author has not in the least changed his opinion that the Nazi idea is evil, and that we must fight the Nazis on land, at sea, in the air and in ourselves, he has changed his mind about the Nazi *power* to make the *world* evil. . . . (quoted in Russell 1992, 37).

This extract touches on a number of relevant points. First, it informs readers of the point just made, that *Swastika Night* was written *before* war broke out. Second, it illustrates the contemporary context that early readers approached the book as a novel by a *male* writer (despite its clear gender concerns; as Elizabeth Russell points out: "the 'Publisher's Note' has failed to mention" that "*Swastika Night* is a conscious debate on gender politics": Russell 1992, 41). Third, it suggests the very real *danger* involved in republishing an anti-Nazi novel at a time when quite feasibly there could be a Nazi invasion (a good enough reason for maintaining a pseudonym, it seems), and foregrounds the propagandistic intent of the text. Finally, it picks up one of the central actions of Alfred and the other English rebels within the novel: "we must fight the Nazis . . . in ourselves," both the identification and the overcoming of what Michel Foucault has called the fascism in our heads.

Text and Reading

A contemporary review of *Swastika Night* in the *Daily Worker* describes it as a "useful book for those who do not take fascism seriously enough to realize its dreadful implications" (quoted in Croft 1990, 229). Perhaps unsurprisingly, bearing in mind the historical context of writing, with Mussolini, Franco, Hitler, and Stalin spreading their brutal grand narratives around Europe, not only is there a propagandistic impulse within *Swastika Night,* but also the very operation of propaganda itself is explored. One way in which this takes place is through the formal aspect of the book-within-the-book, the von Hess book which is handed on to Alfred and which he reads. By definition, propagandistic fiction seeks to move between the fictive text and the real world, and transgresses the distinction between the two. Fiction using documentary forms questions the distinction between fiction and nonfiction. Michael Wilding argues that the twin modes of political fiction—which he identifies as romance and realism—have formal attributes. The romantic mode is associated with the fantasy, the fable; the realist mode is associated with the documentary.

> These are not decorative, aesthetic, abstract conflicts; the aesthetic clash carries the force of ideological clash. (Wilding 1980, 11)

Swastika Night suggests a mix of the two modes Wilding identifies, introducing into the fantastic future the apparent realism of the written document—or rather, references to this realistic document and odd quotations from it, and description of the reading process of it by Alfred. Further, there is a "dialectical tension" between the two modes (Wilding, 6), so that, following Wilding's argument, the very referential form of the text exhibits the dynamic structure of political struggle, which is one of the sites of action it seeks to explore.

Before going further, I should emphasize that it's not simply though that the text constructs a tension between the fantasy of the future-set narrative and the realism of the von Hess book read by Alfred. The von Hess book is a *history* book, read in future times when history has officially ended, or is only official. It tells of a different social situation, and has power by virtue of that fact. It's a textual challenge to the familiar dystopian "campaign against the Past," as Aldous Huxley puts it in *Brave New World* (Huxley 1932, 50). Not only historical by virtue of its age, it is also a book that deals with "the history of human beings" (*Swastika Night,* 87), written clandestinely in reaction to the systematic destruction of all books by the Nazi regime. (Burdekin is writing only a few years after Kristallnacht, the infamous Nazi night of book-burning.) The Nazis have an overwhelming "fear . . . of Memory itself" (79), of the memory in particular of a less oppressive treatment of women, and of the ascendancy of other nations. Such memories would challenge their construction of a superior subjectivity, and would contradict their infinite narrative of victory. They are quite conscious about this erasure of memory, as seen when, in an almost doublethinkful way, the original organizer of the destruction of the archive, of the campaign against the Past, is named by von Hess as "the Father of Lies" (80). Against such institutionalized (and gendered) mendacity Alfred will lead "[t]he rebellion of disbelief" (26). Elizabeth Russell notes that "it is not the truth which [Alfred] possesses at the end of his pilgrimage—it is the knowledge of lies" (Russell 1992, 40). Indeed, before he is even aware of the book's existence Alfred has been thinking in archival terms. He describes himself to Hermann: "I am the repository, the place where a very old human idea is kept" (*Swastika Night*, 30). He both *is* atavistic, and he comes to be the protector, the reader, of the history book.

Alfred's action of rebellion revolves around the book; more specifically, around the activity of reading the book. Here, in describing a reader's process of engagement with a political text, Burdekin explores the operation of propaganda. The actual reading event of the von Hess book takes place in "an old gas chamber or dug-out" (*Swastika Night*, 140) under Stonehenge, the entrance of which is guarded by skeletons with a machine gun, that have been dressed by Alfred to resemble soldiers and to scare off any superstitious Nazis. The inexplicable but monumental sense of the past can be experienced by Alfred only through fleshing out the bare bones of an old man's ancient memories. Burdekin also uses the landscape of southern England, of Stonehenge itself, as a significant site for the historical struggle of her characters and plots, as seen elsewhere in another thirties novel, *The End of This Day's Business*. This both adds an extra historical dimension and a strong sense of the *situatedness* of her England. Further, it contributes to the markedly contemporary feeling her novels possess—New Age mysticism combines with a mythical England and a clear ideological slant focused around gender and aggression to resonate with contemporary interest. Now reader and critic, Alfred subjects the book to a close textual analysis.

[He] carefully considered every sentence to try to draw from it its deepest meaning. . . . [H]is head full of confusion and glory, . . . he could get

in touch with lost civilizations and the thought-mechanisms of complex
human beings. (*Swastika Night,* 156, 172)

Through being able to get in touch with these, Alfred's own
"thought-mechanism" is provoked and inspired, and he becomes
himself a more "complex human being." Alfred's is an act of *self-
reading:* he reads a sense of himself into or out of the von Hess
book. Following the initial destabilization, he is now able partially
to construct and resituate a subjectivity which was never possible
and barely imaginable until he saw the book with his own eyes, and
read it with them too. By "carefully considering every sentence,"
Alfred's analytical activity is highlighted as significant for the 1930s
(or 1990s) reader of *Swastika Night,* who presumably would do well
"to try to draw from [*Swastika Night*] its deepest meaning," too. In
this way the focus on the reading process of a clearly oppositional
historical text has the function of allowing Burdekin not only to
propagandize in her text but also to explore the modes of operation
of propaganda in fiction. Not only does she write political fiction
in the 1930s, this period of fervent commitment by a whole range
of literary and cultural practitioners, but also Burdekin explores the
way in which political fiction operates on the reader. It may be taken
further than this, to suggest that Burdekin *idealizes* the reading process of political fiction with Alfred (if only all readers of these texts
worked with such consideration and attention!). Yet there is a coun-
terbalance to this argument in Alfred's lover, Hermann, who (like
Julia being read to by Winston in Orwell's *Nineteen Eighty-Four*) falls
asleep when the von Hess book is read to him. Some readers are
reconstructed in terms of subjectivity, others simply narcotized.
Burdekin privileges the active, involved reader in this metafictional
focus: Alfred's act of reading is his action of rebellion. Literary production is both emphasized and justified as a political activity by
events within the text.

Text and Gender

The human values of this world are masculine. There are no feminine
values because there are no women. (*Swastika Night,* 108)

The main focus of social comment in the novel is less that directed
explicitly against fascism, than that which explores oppressive social
institutions and customs directed against women. Burdekin examines the operation of patriarchy by looking at some of the most
extreme manifestations of it in her time. Thus patriarchy is directly

connected with fascism and war, which are read as discourses of masculinity to be critiqued within the text. *Swastika Night* represents a world concerned with "Men's Business" (*Swastika Night,* 13), with "the Holy Mystery of Maleness" (9), in which women are the significant absence. When they *are* introduced they are described in terms of negative representations of the body, the female body. As Daphne Patai observes:

> Male egos and female bodies; male persons and female animals—these are the extremes of which an ideology of male supremacy is capable. (Patai 1984, 87)

Indeed, a repressive fragmentation, a sinister synecdoche, is used in the text: "a woman is of herself nothing but an animal, just a collection of wombs and breasts and livers and lights" (*Swastika Night,* 105). In the first few pages of the novel women are compared to worms, cattle, dogs, puppies, and kittens. Descriptions of women's bodies are channeled through the perspectives of male characters, contributing further to the distaste of the vision. For example, Hermann thinks back to an occasion when he saw a mass of women as a young boy.

> He was terrified. . . . [T]heir small shaven ugly heads and ugly soft bulgy bodies dressed in feminine tight trousers and jackets—and oh, the pregnant women and the hideousness of them, and the skinny old crones with necks like moulting hens, and the loathsome little girls with running noses. . . . (*Swastika Night,* 90)

Von Hess thinks of women as "an intolerable ugliness" (*Swastika Night,* 11). Women must stand in church during their three-monthly Women's Worship because "[w]omen's rumps were even more defiling to holy places than their little feet" (8). They even have "unclean ears" (12) that are unfit for receiving the Holy narratives from the Hitler Bible. Russell links body and text, arguing that women "have no possibilities of creating their own texts because they cannot write their bodies" (Russell 1992, 38). There is though one woman who has the ability to create her own text, wise "old Marta," but significantly she is utterly marginalized, and in fact desexed: "She was not a man, no, but not a woman either, something more like an old incredibly ugly tree. Not human, but not female" (15). The problem for Marta, the only woman of all who can see through the authority of the knight, is that she is held in contempt by the other women, too, since they have totally internalized their subjection: "all the other women despised her. Ugly as they were they could see she was uglier" (15). Ironically, Marta's nearest ally would be von Hess. "The Knight would have found himself in a certain amount of sympathy with her, had he been in psychic contact" (16). In fact, the pair are connected, both through age and through the loss of their children.

Russell suggests that "the regime reduces language and fixes meaning into absolute truths" (Russell 1992, 38). For example, the word "married" cannot be comprehended (*Swastika Night,* 69), it has no social referent—indeed it contradicts the social norm, since it implies a man and a woman living together rather than the woman kept in the cages of the Women's Quarters. Interestingly, Burdekin offers as a linguistic example here a word which might be seen as representing an institutionalized version of her contemporary patriarchy. This illustrates the extent to which Nazi patriarchy has developed, even while its origins are clearly signaled. There's an occasion when Alfred informs von Hess (and the reader) about the ancient origins of Nazi patriarchy, of the "Reduction of Women" (70). Referring to the distant past—such as the twentieth century—Alfred explains that women then

> were living an imposed masculine pattern, just as ours do now. They were no more *women* than ours. . . . (*Swastika Night,* 109)

A quite clear correspondence is identified here between the extrapolated future and Burdekin's present. In fact, Burdekin suggests that there is no difference in the way that women are socially constructed in the symbolic order between the superpatriarchy of the Nazi Empire and her own times in the 1930s: as Alfred says, "[t]hey were no more *women* than ours."

The extreme of patriarchal activity as viewed by Burdekin is male violence, and, ultimately, war between men, and rape against women. According to Andy Croft, the "thesis of *Swastika Night,* that fascism was originally misogynist and ultimately self-destructive, that it had its popular roots in sexual hysteria and that the institutional oppression of women was the key to its support among men, makes it the most original of all the many anti-fascist dystopias of the late 1930s" (Croft 1990, 238). Patai notes that in her 1934 novel *Proud Man* Burdekin defines a soldier as "a killing male" (Patai 1984, 89). Burdekin answers the question in *Swastika Night:* "what *is* a man? A being of pride, courage, violence, brutality, ruthlessness" (*Swastika Night,* 28). With always a marked pacifist impulse in her novels, it is significant that "Alfred is emphatically not a warrior . . . [he] realizes that the Hitlerian notions of violence, bru-

tality and physical courage can never make a 'man', but only ageless
boys" (Patai 1984, 89). Male violence toward women is the social
norm, reflected in the acceptability of rape:

> there was no such crime as rape except in connection with children under
> age. . . . Over sixteen, women's bodies were well-grown and womanly,
> that danger was past, and as rape implies will and choice and a spirit of
> rejection on the part of women, there could be no such crime. (*Swastika
> Night,* 13)

As I've suggested, Burdekin's strategy is to focus on the specificity
of extreme moments, and to generalize outward from there, in—as
here—a powerfully defamiliarizing movement. The pleasure of male
sexuality is largely confined to the male attraction to male: homosex-
uality is the normalized sexual state of men in Nazi Germany. In-
flamed with sexual passion for a beautiful choirboy, Hermann (his
name itself signals an ambivalence) beats the boy to death because
he finds the boy with a girl. Hermann has also been Alfred's lover
in the past, and would "adore" to be so again: "to be his slave, to
set his body, his strong bones and willing hard muscles, between . . .
Alfred and all harm, to die for him" (*Swastika Night,* 31). Burdekin
connects even male *love*—"the Holy Mystery of Maleness" (9)—
with domination, subservience, and self-annihilation. Homosexual-
ity isn't represented as a sign of Nazi depravity, though, but as a
symptom of the totalizing power of patriarchy, of its institutionalized misogyny.

Russell notes that "the feminine principle has been totally destroyed and the victory of the male over the female seems to be
absolute" (Russell 1991, 25). This reckons without two possibly
more positive factors in the novel, though, only the first of which
Russell discusses. The feminine principle has *not* been totally destroyed; there remains a biologic protest by women as mothers
against the regime. The end of the Nazi Reich is within sight, since
there is a fertility problem: identified originally by the Nazis of the
novel as justification for their repression of women, birth capacity
now holds the key for a future liberation. As it's put in the narrative,
"If a woman could rejoice publicly at the birth of a girl, Hitlerdom
would start to crumble" (*Swastika Night,* 14). This is particularly
interesting because it seems to go against Burdekin's otherwise very
strong materialist reading of gender construction. On the one hand,
as we have seen, the social conditioning of patriarchy is emphasized
throughout ("Women will always be what men want them to be,"
explains von Hess with great confidence [70]). On the other hand,

the race is coming to extinction. The men are committing suicide, but the women, whose discouragement is entirely unconscious, are not being born. (*Swastika Night,* 70)

Women's social protest here, an "entirely unconscious" response to overwhelming oppression, seems to be caused by a biologic essentialism, in which women's bodily functions, the sole aspect for which they are valued, refuse to operate. Second, there is the question of nation, a positive angle offered through the role of the Englishman Alfred. (It's worth noting that Burdekin does relate nation to gender: women are "beings without nationality" [*Swastika Night,* 113].) In terms both of his reading of the von Hess book (and passing that knowledge and the book onto his son) *and* of his partial shift in attitudes toward women—he does what no man has done for centuries, holds his baby *daughter* in his arms—Alfred too offers a way forward. Burdekin suggests both a female and a male possibility of change. For Patai, the possibility of hope in the dystopian genre is itself made a focus of gender criticism, as she compares Burdekin with the male "despair" of George Orwell.

Burdekin allows the reader to hope—that knowledge will somehow survive, that the secret book will be passed on, that a girl child will be raised with a smattering of pride. But Orwell offers only the bleak prospect of perpetual domination. . . . Orwell's despair and Burdekin's hope are linked to the degree of awareness that each has of gender roles and sexual polarization. (Patai 1984, 87)

Swastika Night is an examination of power and sexual difference, and of the relation between the two, in what is commonly understood as the pessimistic genre of dystopia. Yet, as Patai shows, there are positive aspects to the quite shockingly negative scenes of women that Burdekin projects. In an earlier thirties novel, the pacifistic *Proud Man,* Burdekin again focuses on the problems of the social construction of gender, and again offers the suggestion of a potentially affirmative path. She declares that women and men

must stop being masculine and feminine, and become male and female. Masculinity and femininity are the artificial differences between men and women. Maleness and femaleness are the real differences. (quoted in Patai 1985, ix)

Note

A short section of this chapter also appears in my article "Metapropaganda" in *Science-Fiction Studies.* The reader is directed toward this for further discussion of the operation of propaganda within *Swastika Night*.

Works Cited

Aldiss, Brian W., and David Wingrove. 1986, 1988. *Trillion Year Spree: The History of Science Fiction*. London: Paladin.

Armitt, Lucie, ed. 1991. *Where No Man Has Gone Before: Women and Science Fiction*. London: Routledge.

Burdekin, Katharine. 1935, 1989. *The End of This Day's Business*. New York: The Feminist Press.

———. 1937, 1940, 1985. *Swastika Night*. London: Lawrence and Wishart.

Clute, John, and Peter Nicholls. 1993. *The Encyclopedia of Science Fiction*. London: Orbit.

Croft, Andy. 1990. *Red Letter Days: British Fiction in the 1930s*. London: Lawrence and Wishart.

Huxley, Aldous. 1932, 1977. *Brave New World*. London: Granada.

Jameson, Fredric. 1982. "Progress versus Utopia; or, Can We Imagine the Future?" *Science-Fiction Studies* 9, no. 2: 147–59.

McKay, George. 1994. "Metapropaganda: Self-reading Dystopian Fiction: Katharine Burdekin's *Swastika Night* and George Orwell's *Nineteen Eighty-Four*." *Science-Fiction Studies*, 21 pt. 3: 302–314.

Patai, Daphne. 1984. "Orwell's Despair, Burdekin's Hope: Gender and Power in Dystopia." *Women's Studies International Forum* 7, no. 2: 85–95.

———. 1985. Introduction to *Swastika Night*, iii–x.

———. 1989. Afterword to *The End of This Day's Business*, 159–90.

Russell, Elizabeth. 1991. "The Loss of the Feminine Principle in Charlotte Haldane's *Man's World* and Katharine Burdekin's *Swastika Night*." In Armitt, *Where No Man Has Gone Before*, 15–28.

———. 1992. "Katharine Burdekin's *Swastika Night*: The Search for Truths and Texts." *Foundation: The Review of Science Fiction* 55: 36–42.

Wilding, Michael. 1980. *Political Fictions*. London: Routledge.

A Bibliography of Works by and about Katharine Burdekin

Primary

Burdekin, Katharine (or Kay). 1929. *The Rebel Passion*. New York: William Morrow.

———. 1930. *Quiet Ways*. London: Thornton Butterworth.

———. 1935, 1989. *The End of This Day's Business*. New York: The Feminist Press.

———. 1937, 1940, 1985. *Swastika Night*. London: Lawrence and Wishart. (pseud. Constantine).

Constantine, Murray. 1934a. *Proud Man*. London: Boriswood.

———. 1934b. *The Devil, Poor Devil!*

Constantine, Murray, and Margaret Foster. 1940. *Venus in Scorpio*.

Secondary

McKay, George. 1994. "Metapropaganda: Self-reading Dystopian Fiction. Katharine Burdekin's *Swastika Night* and George Orwell's *Nineteen Eighty-Four*." *Science-Fiction Studies,* 21, pt. 3: 302–14.

Patai, Daphne. 1984a. "Orwell's Despair, Burdekin's Hope: Gender and Power in Dystopia." *Women's Studies International Forum* 7 no. 2: 85–95. This is a special issue of the journal, devoted to "feminist science fiction," edited by Marleen S. Barr.

————. 1984b. *The Orwell Mystique: A Study of Male Ideology.* Amherst: University of Massachusetts Press.

————. 1985. Introduction to *Swastika Night*. London: Lawrence and Wishart, iii–x.

————. 1989. Afterword to *The End of This Day's Business*. New York: The Feminist Press, 159–90.

Russell, Elizabeth. 1991. "The Loss of the Feminine Principle in Charlotte Haldane's *Man's World* and Katharine Burdekin's *Swastika Night*." In Lucie Armitt, ed. *Where No Man Has Gone Before: Women and Science Fiction*. London: Routledge, 15–28.

————. 1992. "Katharine Burdekin's *Swastika Night*: The Search for Truths and Texts." *Foundation: The Review of Science Fiction* 55: 36–42.

13

Montagu Slater and Theater of the Thirties

STEVE NICHOLSON

A Brief Biographical Sketch of Charles Montagu Slater (1902–56)

CHARLES MONTAGU SLATER WAS BORN IN 1902 IN MILLOM, CUMBER-
land. He received a scholarship to Oxford, and subsequently wrote
poetry while working as a journalist in Liverpool and London. He
had three daughters with Enid, whom he married in 1929. In 1931
Slater published his first novel and became a free-lance writer; he
became increasingly interested in dramatic writing, producing stage-
plays and puppet plays as well as large-scale pageants for the Communist party and the cooperative movement. Slater was a founding
editor of (and frequent contributor to) the *Left Review,* and worked
with both the professional Left Theatre and the nonprofessional
Unity Theatre.

After the 1941 Anglo-Soviet alliance, Slater found himself more
within the political and cultural mainstream. Rejected from active
service because of ill health, he wrote a pageant celebrating links
between Britain and the Soviet Union, and became involved with
the Films Division of the Ministry of Information. He helped found
the Communist cultural journal *Our Time,* and was theater critic for
Reynolds News. Slater had a strong friendship with Benjamin Britten,
who had written music for several of his prewar plays. He supported
Britten at a tribunal investigating the composer's conscientious objection to the war, and they cooperated on writing the opera *Peter
Grimes;* however, the creative process was full of conflict and, to
Slater's disappointment, Britten did not invite him to collaborate
again.

In 1946, Slater tried and failed to help establish a new theater movement to be funded by the trade union movement. He published further novels, and continued to explore the boundaries between fiction and factual documentation; in *Englishmen with Swords,* for example, he invented the diary of an actual historical figure during the English civil war. Though he continued to write stage plays which remained unperformed and unpublished, Slater became increasingly interested in film and television. In 1948 he spent time in Nigeria among the Ibos, and one of his African films, *Daybreak in Udi,* received a British Film Academy award as documentary of the year.

Though his work was rarely didactic propaganda, Slater's longstanding commitment to the Communist party, which he had joined in the late 1920s, almost certainly hindered his career opportunities. He died in 1956, leaving sketches for many uncompleted projects.

* * * * *

In a short script written for Punch and Judy puppets in 1934, Montagu Slater satirized contemporary attitudes to theater; first Punch is prevented from throwing the baby out of the window:

> No, no. I won't have that. Public wouldn't stand it . . . It is unrealistic. Worse, it is alarming. ("Prologue for Punch" 1934)

Then the hangman arrives before his cue, explaining

> We've been cut to make room for the news reel.

When Punch raises his stick in anger, he is interrupted by a warning voice from offstage:

> No violence, Punch. Art is never violent.

Punch manages to subvert the catechism of repentance which he is forced to swear for disturbing the peace. In both form and content, Slater's theater work during the thirties also disturbed the peace by challenging theater conventions and by confronting the expectations of the establishment on both aesthetic and political levels.

Acknowledgment of Slater's contribution to the political culture of the 1930s usually centers on his editorship of *Left Review;* indeed, he not only contributed numerous articles and reviews to the journal, but largely defined its role and political stance. Yet Slater also produced fiction, poetry, several stage plays, scripts for puppets, and a series of spectacular political pageants to be presented by huge casts in large arenas. He contributed to Unity Theatre's Living Newspapers, and as a leading exponent of "reportage" was commissioned to document life in a struggling Welsh mining village. The research for this became the basis of Slater's best-known play, *Stay Down Miner* (1936).[1]

Slater's work is informed by his long-standing commitment to the Communist party, which he joined in the late twenties, well before membership became almost de rigueur for all artists with the slightest degree of political consciousness. He viewed art and culture as part of a political struggle, insisting it was

> the job of literature to influence readers, to work a change, and to record change both in reader and writer. ("The Purpose of a Left Review" 1935)

But his political convictions owed little to the reality of practice in the Soviet Union, deriving rather from a humanism which defined the injustices and repressions of contemporary society as a function of capitalism's emphasis on money and profit.

> The great reason for being communist is that, above all things . . . we value the human individual. We claim that complete freedom is only possible with the full community of minds and possessions which is communism. ("Ann as I Remember Her" 1954)

Slater's writing repeatedly bears witness to the iniquities of capitalism, and assumes the inevitable evolution of a future socialist society; but its strength is that it hardly ever descends into the simplistic propaganda and sloganizing which were at the center of the agitprop form from which so much political theater was derived.[2]

Slater was saved in part by his commitment to factual details. It was not that he professed objectivity or detachment.

> Let our slogan, then, be that we are going to utilize history . . . for the purposes of the class which is going to build socialism. ("Writers' International" 1935)

But though his interpretation was consciously defined by his ideological standpoint, the decision to root his scripts in actuality allowed for a creative tension between documented events and his own political convictions.

He was driven equally by a poetic imperative; indeed, one of his criticisms of capitalism was that it abolished the very essence of culture.

> Literature concerns human relationships. Capitalism destroyed these . . . substituting money or commodity relationships. ("Writers' International" 1935)

His obligation to the aesthetic as well as to the functional role of art overcame any inclination toward delivering simplistic messages. In many left-wing plays, characters were two-dimensional, manipulated by writers as marionettes to embody abstracted ideology and principles. By contrast, Slater's writing is layered with complexity, even when his actual medium, as in *Old Spain,* is puppets.

In raising the issue of the struggle of the Spanish people against fascism, *Old Spain* deals with a subject of absolutely contemporary relevance; here, surely, one might expect directness and transparency. Yet both the language and the ideas are elusive, and bemused critics complained that puppetry was suitable only for singing and dancing, and not for dealing with ideas:

> the little people had to express sentiments which sometimes seemed too large for their diminutive mouths.[3]

The program notes for *Old Spain* suggested that "the effect intended is sombre and dream-like," and the opening image reveals a sleeping man with three kneeling women "calling to him from an invaded country" (*Old Spain* 1946). The narrative spotlights the agony of bereaved Spanish women, and the outside world's procrastination over offering assistance:

> 3rd WOMAN. If you dare not understand
> Pain as an invaded land
> Let it be transfigured
> To your own finger.
> Think of Spain as the limit of
> Your private love . . .
> ALL.   We are caged in death.
> Bring knives to free us with.

Yet *Old Spain* is not structured around any straightforward and didactic moral. Rather, the performance was defined and promoted by its creators as primarily "a sincere attempt to explore the theatrical possibilities of the medium."

Only in his scripts for pageants, where both form and convention discourage ambiguity, is Slater's commitment to communism explicit. These pageants represented if not a new form for dramatic communication, then at least an appropriation—and a reworking for radical purposes—of a traditionally conservative one. André Van Gyseghem, who directed several such events, suggested that words were often irrelevant.

> It was vital to reduce the amount of speech to a minimum and concentrate on the visual impression . . . not a subtle performance, but simple, straightforward, and visually effective . . . living pictures do make an impression on the mind of an audience, and that was our aim. (Van Gyseghem 1979)[4]

However, pageants were not uniform in the space and significance they allowed to verbal communication, and Slater's scripts also made extensive use of a visual language to convey ideas.

In *Towards Tomorrow* (1938), presented at Wembley Stadium by three thousand performers, the emphasis remained strongly on spectacle.[5] A spoken text contrasted competitive existence under capitalism with the potential of a society based on cooperation, but the climax was a lengthy procession round the stadium of groups in national dress representing every country in the cooperative movement. The depiction of a preindustrial community through traditional folk dancing tended toward an idealizing of the past, and the image of two huge silk-hatted capitalists receiving bags of gold was typical of the simplified imagery favored by the Workers' Theatre Movement. Nevertheless, the scale of the spectacle was impressive; the enactment of war, shown as the inevitable result of capitalist competition, was particularly striking.

> Lines of soldiers and bomb-throwers, backed up by tanks and machine-guns, moved slowly across the enclosure . . . in the centre of the arena girls danced a ballet of war. (Daily Worker, July 1938, 5)

But in such a context, and with the speeches relayed through loudspeakers, any real complexity of thought or narrative was impossible.

By contrast, *Heirs to the Charter: A Pageant of Chartism,* combines visual effects with a much richer text.[6] Written for a 1939 Communist party rally, its main ideological thrust is to define communism as the direct descendant of Chartism; rather than being alien to British traditions, as its enemies frequently argued, communism is seen to derive directly from British radicalism of the nineteenth century. At one point Karl Marx addresses a Chartist convention:

The Chartists of England are the real democrats, and the moment you carry the six points of the Charter, the road to liberty will be open to the whole world. Effect this grand object, you working-men of England, and you will be hailed as the saviours of the whole human race.

The first half of the pageant is an episodic account of the development of Chartism, culminating in the first halting and uncertain use of the term *Communists* to link the Chartists with their European allies. A worker, nicely identified as Cradle-Rocker, explains to a radical M.P.:

EGREMONT. But what are Communists?
C.R. It is a word people use.
EGREMONT. But what do they believe in? What IS Communism?
C.R. It is a word—and a good deal more than a word.
EGREMONT. But *WHAT* more?
C.R. I find it difficult to say.

The act ends with references to the Party Manifesto, actual copies of which are then sold in the interval. The second half dramatizes events leading to the formation of the British Communist party, again collapsing the border between a represented past and an actual present by building to the arrival of Harry Pollitt.

We, who have presented here a pageant of the Chartists and their heirs make way now for one who can speak of our own generation of the history that is around us, and of what lies ahead.
THE COMMENTATOR STEPS DOWN. HARRY POLLITT TAKES HIS PLACE

Slater's particular achievement in *Heirs to the Charter* is the successful integration of aesthetics and politics, through the combining of dense, verbal narrative with highly charged visual imagery. A series of small-scale and episodic scenes, requiring an essentially naturalistic style of performance, are set within an almost operatic framework. The style is established from the opening image; a choir sings a Chartist anthem in darkness, then

In the centre of the Arena two separate Spotlights pick out the Workhouse Master (W.M) and the Assistant Workhouse Master (A.W.M.) Behind W.M. in the shadow a semi-circle of men picking oakum. Behind A.W.M. a semi-circle of women scrubbing the floor.

There follows a predominantly realistic workhouse scene, which is punctuated by the choir's anthem, and interwoven with a tapestry of vocal and percussive effects.

Heirs to the Charter employs several stages and a large arena, creating a flexibility which allows for short scenes, juxtapositions, and a simultaneity which is reminiscent of staging within both medieval tradition and Soviet postrevolutionary theatrical experiments. While Van Gyseghem's experiences were crucial, this staging is precisely conceived within Slater's script. Scene 9, for example, consists of a nineteen-line dialogue at a central podium, in which the prime minister instructs a general to be ruthless in his use of force against the Chartists. In the following scene, "the light moves over to the Rich Man's Stage" for eight lines in which we see the lord mayor banning the Chartists from the Town Hall. Then in another acting area a Chartist announces that the group will assemble outside, and immediately a torchlight procession of banner-carrying Chartists

> goes round the Arena and comes finally to the Central Platform where there are a number of speakers. During the procession the Choir sings one of the Chartist songs.

Policed by soldiers, the procession gathers around the platform for a lengthy address culminating in elections to a People's Parliament, before retracing its steps, again accompanied by the choir, while "the Soldiers are marched to and fro . . . in the Arena"; by the end of this sequence, the Chartist delegates have assembled on the central stage, and the Convention begins. This combination of an almost cinematic cutting with large groups occupying and moving between several spaces was far removed from the contemporary performance language of British theater.

For Slater, the foregrounding of working-class history and experience and the placing of "real life" on the stage is necessarily a political statement.

> To describe things as they are is a revolutionary act in itself. ("The Purpose of a Left Review" 1935)

In *Out of Liverpool,* a verse play set on board a ship traveling between Liverpool and Australia in 1852, shipboard life functions partly as a metaphor for a broader society; there are occasional moments when the text directly addresses political issues:

> Capn', the men who write the laws
> Leave themselves a get-out clause *(Out of Liverpool)*

But the play is really political only in that it focuses on, and pays tribute to, the realities and dangers of working-class life. As Left

Theatre, which presented two of Slater's plays, had declared in its manifesto:

> Politics, in its fullest sense, means the affairs of the people. In this sense the plays done will be political.[7]

The subject matter of Slater's best-known play, *Stay Down Miner*, is more directly confrontational; a group of miners occupy their shaft to protest against exploitation by their employers and the hiring of blacklegs. Yet even given such classically explicit material, Slater again refuses to present two-dimensional exploiters; instead he allows his ideological points to emerge through a broad portrayal of life in a Welsh mining village, and his own position on the violence of the strikers remains ambiguous. The equivocation of the Left's response to this play is revealing; *Left Review* demanded "a somewhat greater explicitness" to help explain "uncertainties," regretting that

> in several respects the play was confusing, both politically and emotionally. On the question of direct action, for instance.[8]

Ironically, the Conservative press criticized Slater on similar grounds; *The Times* specifically complained about "the omission of any serious representation of the powers of capitalist darkness," while the *Daily Telegraph*

> found it quite impossible to discover what he was driving at . . . did Mr. Slater approve of the strike weapon or didn't he?

It seems the establishment preferred to know its enemy, perhaps finding it easier to deal with explicit propaganda than with ambiguity. Indeed, the *Telegraph* stipulated that "clarity is a dramatist's first virtue".

It is not that *Stay Down Miner* fails to identify exploitation; as one miner observes:

> You don't trust the roof not to fall in, or the endless rope not to break, or the shot not to fire back, or the cage not to fall—but you do trust . . . people . . . somewhere to have limits . . . You've got to trust that in the long run men see and think fairly. (*Stay Down Miner*, 8–9)

But Slater's characters are individuals as well as symbols, and neither the problem or the solution is seen to lie with individuals. The local manager, ostensibly the villain, is himself an oppressed victim.

Rhys is a kind man . . . But there is figures behind him . . . bankers behind wire netting, smooth as Judases, and London behind them all, to which Mr. Rhys is saying "Yes, sir." (*Stay Down Miner,* 7)

The same is true of the only blackleg whom we see, a reluctant strikebreaker who is so tortured by his conscience and the judgment of his fellows that he not only repents but ultimately leads the call for the audience to support the miners.

There are at least three elements of formal experimentation which Slater explored in his stage plays; first, the use of a chorus and aural effects to juxtapose realistic situations with a heightened poetic style; second, the integration of visual imagery with spoken text; third, a blurring of the gap between the fictional world on-stage and the reality of the audience. For much of the time, *Stay Down Miner* replicates realistic speech patterns and settings; but at significant moments Slater introduces nonnaturalistic devices. In one scene, two of the miners occupying the pit are in darkness for a page and a half, until "a bluish light slowly reveals them" (*Stay Down Miner,* 47). Their discussion, mundane enough on the page, is significantly mediated in performance, as the following stage direction indicates:

The stage darkens. A metronome set at largo is in the orchestra pit. A drum takes up the rhythm, various percussions die away into the sound of the metronome again. This continues through the scene. (*Stay Down Miner,* 46)

A later dialogue in the same setting is punctuated by a dimly lit chorus standing on either side of the stage; in blank verse they recite a philosophical meditation concerning time, mines, change, and the differences between the worlds above and beneath the ground (*Stay Down Miner,* 55–57).

If Slater's writing was political partly because of the emphasis given to working-class existence, it was not only through the spoken language that he achieved this. *Stay Down Miner* was originally played with a permanent set of a pithead and its workings which dominated the stage; even though it was not specifically lit during interior scenes, everything was seen against—and in the shadow of—that unchanging image. Similarly, *Out of Liverpool* not only demanded part of a ship on stage, but directly integrated the audience with the action.

The auditorium is the rest of the ship, and as the action develops it is important we should feel this. . . . we want to get the audience to feel the motion of the ship . . . the audience should be conscious of the ship's motion and hear the sea. (*Out of Liverpool*, 8)

Stay Down Miner also makes use of its audience by projecting onto them specific, sometimes surprisingly negative identities. In one especially powerful scene they are accused and cataloged as blacklegs imported to steal the jobs of striking miners:

> GWEVRIL. *(Facing the audience.)* You, you, you, marching on our mine, invaders. You're not even Welshmen. You've got English faces.
> BRONWEN. Twelve, fourteen, sixteen, eighteen, twenty . . .
> GWEVRIL. *(Facing the audience.)* You look mean as if you've been robbing the poor box . . . You're robbing our jobs. D'you hear? You're robbing our jobs.
> BRONWEN. Twenty-two, twenty-four, twenty-six, twenty-eight, thirty. (*Stay Down Miner*, 31)

By contrast, in the final scene they are appealed to as jurors in the court and, in defiance of the establishment, as fellow-workers with important (and not wholly fictional) obligations:

> BRONWEN. *(To the audience.)* You people of Cwmllynfach—
> MAGISTRATE. No more speeches, please.
> BRONWEN. *(With great emphasis.)* Tell the world.
> MAGISTRATE. Please.
> BRONWEN. Tell England and Scotland.
> MAGISTRATE. I said no speeches.
> BRONWEN. Tell them to join Wales.
> *CURTAIN* (*Stay Down Miner*, 70)

Valuable insights into establishment attitudes to political theater can be gained from the responses of the Lord Chamberlain's Office to texts submitted for license, since any stage play performed in a public venue required his approval. Though official guidelines did exist, the Lord Chamberlain retained a remarkable degree of discretion to grant or refuse licenses, and was not required to justify his decisions. While relatively few plays were banned outright, many had words, lines, scenes, or characters removed, while others were licensed only because it was feared that suppression might attract more attention to them.[9]

In the case of *Stay Down Miner*, the license was granted with a lingering reluctance:

> This is a Left-Theatre and anti-capitalist play, but as it is unlikely to endanger the peace we can hardly object to it on that score.[10]

Distaste was expressed for the court scene in which the accused "make socialist speeches in their defence," while the play's experiments in nonnaturalistic stylization were patronizingly dismissed.

> This is a formless and at times obscure play: want of experience on the part of the author, I expect . . . there are some of the usual irritating tricks, actors among the audience, and efforts to bring the audience into the action and so on.

However, the only actual changes demanded were the removal of a "bloody" and of a barely noticeable reference to Queen Victoria's bottom.[11]

Easter:1916 (1936) had caused greater anxieties when selected for performance by Left Theatre, a group of professional practitioners whose challenge to the establishment was unequivocal.

> The commercial theatre is limited by its dependence on a small section of society which neither desires, nor dares, to face the urgent and vital problems of to-day. The theatre . . . must of necessity reflect the spirit of the age. This spirit is found in the social conflicts which dominate world history to-day . . . The Left Theatre realises that the very class which plays the chief part in contemporary history . . . is debarred from expression in the present-day theatre.[12]

Slater's ostensible subject in *Easter:1916,* his first play to be published, was the Irish uprising of 1916; however, the Lord Chamberlain's Office was sensitive to its broader implications.

> The story, has of course, a moral for English revolutionaries, but in the circumstances of English politics I think I need hardly discuss that.[13]

Following consultation with the Home Office it was decided that the play as a whole need not be banned since

> except among the more extreme socialists and communists, who always love our enemies best, the Southern Irish get little sympathy over here any more; so that the play should not rouse any very violent passions on this side of the Irish sea (except perhaps in the Irish quarters of such places as Liverpool).

Reluctantly, it was deemed inappropriate to interfere with a scene debating possible strike action.

> This scene is topical in view of the possible coal strike and T.U.C. support, but as such arguments are to be heard at any socialist meeting it seems difficult to object here.

But the final scene in which Connolly, lying wounded on a stretcher, is shot dead by an English soldier in cold blood, was another matter. The truth of the incident was neither denied or regretted, but to show it on stage was unacceptable.

> The shooting of a helpless man is abhorrent to one's instincts and, although justified legally, is a tragedy best forgotten by both sides. The scene is unnecessary to the play and is only dragged in here to sew hatred of the upper classes. I should cut this out completely.

Slater reworked the ending, arguably creating a version which was equally powerful; but this should not blind us to the implications of the determination to control political theater through censorship. It seems unlikely that a license could ever have been granted to Slater's unperformed *Domesday,* in which a Fascist dictatorship takes power in Britain and is opposed by a People's Parliament.

In nineteen episodic scenes, *Easter:1916* chronicled the events leading to the Dublin uprising, and the British army's overturning of the Irish declaration of independence. It mixes fact with deliberate inaccuracies, invented characters with historical ones, and jumps from one significant event to another. A mainly chronological structure is occasionally disrupted by flashback and dream sequences, while an unadorned, realistic prose is juxtaposed with passages of verse and rhetorical variations, spoken by a two-person chorus. The stage represents a variety of places in quick succession, as we cut between locales for sometimes very brief exchanges. The theater audience is assigned a variety of roles, and the gap between stage and auditorium, between fiction and reality, is deliberately blurred.

Audience involvement is established through direct address in the Chorus's opening speeches:

> To-night we present a play about YOU *(points to the audience),* all of you sitting there. *(Easter:1916, 9)*

Since the Left Theatre was committed to performing in working-class venues this could be seen as a statement of fact rather than as an invitation to the audience to fictionalize themselves; the point is immediately reenforced when audience members apparently come on stage and perform.

> MAN. We want a few of you to come on the stage to act. Now—don't get shy. We don't want people who've been trained in the Royal Academy of Dramatic Art . . .
> WOMAN. We want a tram-driver and a conductor. Come now. All

you need know is how to drive a tram. (*Two men get up in the audience.*) (*Easter:1916, 9*)

Actors emerge from the auditorium to perform "their own lives" (*Easter:1916,* 12), and though the device of plants may seem labored now, in 1935 it was innovative; here, it also carries an ideological comment on whose lives and history the theater should stage, and who should be doing the staging.

At the climax of the Dublin revolt, a fictional scene confuses the boundaries further. In a brilliantly conceived coup de théâtre, Slater's actual audience becomes a fictional Dublin audience watching *Cinderella,* while guns are fired from the stalls and rebels fight their way out of the theater. The scene was theatrically powerful, but it also made a calculated political point; *Easter:1916* begins and ends with the chorus accusing the audience of complicity, through willful ignorance, with the forces of British oppression; in between we witness events from an Irish perspective, and at this moment we lose our detachment completely and become actual participants in the rebellion. As Cinderella sings of her wish to go to the ball, an off-stage shout silences the orchestra and an armed member of the IRA enters to address both audiences.

Houselights. (*The houselights go up.*) Ladies and gentlemen. I am sorry to disturb what may have been a well-meaning play. I must ask you to keep your seats for a moment and listen to what I have to say. An Irish Republic has been proclaimed . . . .
(*Another comes on the stage. They whisper.*) (*Easter:1916,* 71)

It is announced that Irish forces are trying to hold the area outside the theater against British forces.

If we can't hold it we're going to draw our men off through the theatre here. We're trusting you because we think you're Irishmen. If any of you are not Irishmen there'll be shooting. (71)

The audience, now performing the role of an audience, is urged to remain seated, and the pantomime recommences, with the sound of the orchestra punctuated by machine-gun fire. The performers in *Cinderella* lead the audience of *Easter:1916* in singing "The Wearing of the Green," while volunteers crowd onto the stage from different parts of the auditorium. Finally there is an explosion, the theater is plunged into total darkness, and the audience hears people running along the gangways and out of the theater.

Suddenly, with the audience surrounded by realistic action and hardly able to tell what is happening, we cut to the most obviously artificial element of Slater's play, the chorus:

> Sure bullets quiver
> And shriek whenever
> The warm flesh stops them. . . .
> Your thoughts are bullets
> And hearts their targets.
>
> (*Easter:1916*, 73)

Abruptly, Slater disrupts the flow again by switching the chorus into a different register; now it summarizes key events of the uprising, in urgent but unemotional and journalistic staccato.

> GPO successfully seized by the rebels. Every window broken. Sandbags piled. Supplies seized from the adjoining Metropole Hotel. (*Easter:1916*, 74)

With another twist, Slater contradicts what we hear by showing British soldiers on sentry duty and in command of the situation. Then the chorus again changes tone and role to describe the ensuing struggle, employing understatement to heighten the emotional impact.

> MAN. Monday! *(Gong)* There has been a fierce battle at the Canal Bridge.
> WOMAN. It would have been a holiday. We should have taken the children to Bray.
> MAN. Tuesday! *(Gong)* Will the people rise? The rebels say that the capitalists will not wish to use artillery on buildings which they consider their own . . .
> WOMAN. I should have been washing the clothes . . .
> MAN. Wednesday! *(Gong)* Will they bombard the post office?
> WOMAN. I should have been ironing . . . I should have been puzzling what to serve for dinner, making do with what little we had, waiting for pay day tomorrow . . . And what's the use of a week's work if your man's brought home with a bullet through him? (*Easter:1916*, 74–75)

A habitual problem for left-wing playwrights was how to avoid instilling an audience with defeatism by showing uprisings which ultimately fail to change anything. In *Easter:1916,* Slater implies that the failure of the rebellion has rectifiable causes since it is the result of lack of working-class support, tactical errors, and the overruling of Connolly's advice. He also insists that, despite its immediate failure, the uprising has raised awareness, making inevitable a future, successful rebellion. This recognition is expressed in Connolly's dying insistence that "the cause can't die now" (*Easter:1916*, 77). Slater's decision to mediate Connolly's dying hopes through the voice of his daughter retelling them, crucially protects them from becoming mere cliché.

The revised ending, in which the three women who have worked with Connolly await news of his death, also treads a fine line; the incursion of the chorus, accusing and incriminating the audience in what they have seen, saves the climax from descending into sentimental melodrama.

MADAME. Did he say . . . when it would . . .
NORA. They said—at dawn.
HELEN. And now it's beginning to get light.
(*Day begins to brighten the window. They stand and watch the dawn grow red.*)
WOMAN. Think of this city
By Moody Liffey . . .
MAN. (Quietly.) You—and you—and you—and you—
Sitting there pretending that you never knew.
WOMAN. Maybe you'll learn
What way you earn.
(*From behind the curtain, the voice of an officer*)
    Take aim. Fire!
    (*Shots ring out*) (*Easter:1916*, 78–79)

Easter:1916 is a significant political text. It is not without weaknesses; the humor has dated badly, and there is a tendency to the idealizing of Connolly on a human as well as a political level. But Slater, as concerned with theory as with practice, was conscious of some of the pitfalls; in reviewing a popular film about the life of Henry VIII, he agonized over the problem for the Left of how to inspire people without pandering to a cult of the individual as hero.

What's the opposite of *Henry VIII* is what I keep asking myself? What is our left to its right?.. Fables insist on such a ridiculous spot-lighting of the leading man. What is to be done about it? Can we permit the spot-lighting? ("Private Life of Henry VIII" 1935)

Easter:1916 could also be charged with seducing its audience through emotional blackmail rather than relying on rational argument. Again, Slater recognized the danger; while wary of emotion too easily gained, he defends it wholeheartedly as long as it "involves a man's intelligible and thought-out actions" rather than "mystical or instinctive gropings." He tells a hypothetical left-wing theatergoer who absolutely rejects emotion in political theater that this limited view results from unfortunate precedents.

> You, like the rest of us, have never been accustomed to meet in the theatre an emotional situation with which you could be whole-heartedly in accord . . . this is something so unfamiliar that the reaction is first shyness and then carping. ("Enter from the Left: A Dialogue on the Theatre" 1935)

Slater's work invariably combines a broad brushstroke approach to political issues with a focus on individual lives and details. He warns against the playwright who "forgets his human beings and thinks only of sublime, unbending forces" ("Enter from the Left"), and was ahead of his time in creating characters who are both genuinely individualized and simultaneously representative of social and political groupings. It is his discovery of appropriate forms which makes this possible; while actors inhabit their characters as fully as possible within particular scenes, theatrical devices constantly remind audiences of a broader context. These devices include the visual frameworks placed around those scenes; the use of simplified or representational settings; narrative juxtapositions and dislocations; intercutting between short scenes in different locales or—in the pageants—on different stages; the use of doubling, which requires actors to move in and out of parts; the omission of personal details which demand an empathetic response; the use of a chorus with a variety of functions and speech registers.

After the 1930s, Slater's writing for theater became more sporadic, partly due to his involvement with film and television. A wartime but unperformed adaptation of Hasek's *The Good Soldier Schewyk* reads well, and in 1942 he scripted a pageant commemorating the first anniversary of the Anglo-Soviet alliance.[14] During this period he became involved in film work with the Ministry of Information, and was a significant contributor to *Our Time,* a Communist cultural journal. After the war, there were further, less spectacular pageants written for the Communist party, though *Peter Grimes* remains his best-known achievement.[15] All his postwar playtexts, unpublished and unperformed, seem far less radical than his experiments of the 1930s. However, the fact that one of the films he made in Africa combined the documentary with the fictional suggests that while Slater's focus may have shifted geographically, and into a different medium, he continued to explore a form which had been at the center of his writing since the 1930s.[16]

Wryly summarizing his career from the supposed hindsight of the

1950s, Slater includes a cynical comment on his achievements in the thirties; at that time, he says, he had labored under "the mistaken idea he was exploring the frontiers of drama."[17] By the fifties, both the frontiers and Slater's professional interests had shifted considerably; but in the context of British theater in the thirties, the earlier optimism was more accurate.

Notes

1. See *Stay Down Miner,* "Number One in a series of REPORTAGE books." This was the first of several reports on industrial conditions in Britain. The play *Stay Down Miner* was first presented by Left Theatre at the Westminster Theatre on 8 May 1936. The rewritten version was performed and published as *New Way Wins* (1937). For this revised text see also Slater (1978).

2. For key texts and discussion of agitprop see in particular Samuel (1985), Stourac and McCreery, (1986), and Chambers (1989).

3. All quotations relevant to the production of *Old Spain* have been taken from a Production File in the archives of the Theatre Museum, London.

4. Van Gyseghem had participated in experiments in mass theater in the Soviet Union, and in 1937 had directed a pageant in South Africa. For further discussion of the politics of pageants in the 1930s see Wallis (1994).

5. *Towards Tomorrow* was presented as part of a six-hour festival celebrating the cooperative movement and the Sixteenth International Cooperative Day. There is a film of part of the event.

6. The unpublished manuscript of *Heirs to the Charter,* from which all quotations are taken, is in the archives of the British Communist party.

7. The manifesto was printed in the program for *Stay Down Miner.*

8. See *Left Review* (June 1936). Other reviews cited are from *The Times,* 12 May 1936, and the *Daily Telegraph,* 11 May 1936.

9. Censorship probably operated most effectively through the fact that plays which were likely to be rejected were never submitted, or even written. For a discussion of censorship in relation to specific political texts, see Nicholson (1992).

10. Quotations are taken from the Lord Chamberlain's Correspondence File on *Stay Down Miner.*

11. The original line "That was when Queen Victoria was warming the seat" was changed to "That was in Queen Victoria's Reign."

12. The longer term aim of the *Left Theatre* was to establish a Repertory Theatre in a working-class district, which could both act as a cultural center for the working class, and give a more solid foundation for work in "the artistic socialist fight." Funding was never forthcoming.

13. Quotations are taken from the Lord Chamberlain's Correspondence File on *Easter:1916.*

14. The unpublished and apparently unperformed manuscript of *The Good Soldier,* adapted from Jaroslav Hasek's *The Good Soldier Schewyk,* is at the University of Nottingham. *An Agreement of the Peoples* was performed in June 1942 at Earl's Court to mark the first anniversary of the Anglo-Soviet alliance. The script was published in *Our Time.* For a discussion of this and other wartime pageants, see Nicholson (1993).

15. It is not difficult to see how this libretto built on aspects of his earlier work. Donald Mitchell (1983,42) notes that the opera was "born out of the tradition of

social realism with which Slater was so closely associated and of which he was a leading proponent." Similarly, Humphrey Carpenter (1992,181) argues that "in Slater 's hands, *Peter Grimes* became a story about a community, much like Slater's own left-wing plays of the thirties, with Grimes, the poor working-class fisherman, being driven to violence by an iniquitous class system."

16. *Daybreak in Udi* was filmed in Nigeria and won the British Film Academy's annual award for the best British documentary of 1950.

17. From a note in his papers in the Manuscripts Collection at the University of Nottingham.

Works Cited

Carpenter, Humphrey. 1992. *Benjamin Britten: A Biography*. London: Faber and Faber.

Chambers, Colin. 1989. *The Story of Unity Theatre*. London: Lawrence and Wishart.

Mitchell, Donald. 1983. "Montagu Slater (1902–1956): Who Was He?" In *Benjamin Britten, Peter Grimes*. Edited by Philip Brett. Cambridge: Cambridge University Press, 22–46.

Nicholson, Steve. 1992. "Censoring Revolution: The Lord Chamberlain and the Soviet Union." *New Theatre Quarterly*, 8, no. 32:305–12.

———. 1993. "Theatrical Pageants in the Second World War." *Theatre Research International*, 18, no. 3:186–96.

Samuel, Raphael. MacColl, Ewan, and Cosgrove, Stewart 1985. *Theatres of the Left 1880–1935*. London: Routledge and Kegan Paul.

Slater, Montagu. 1934. "Prologue for Punch." *Left Review* 1, no. 3:59–61.

———. 1935. "Writers' International." *Left Review* 1, no. 4:125–29.

———. 1935. "The Private Life of Henry VIII." *Left Review* 1, no. 4:144.

———. 1935. "Enter from the Left: A Dialogue on the Theatre." *Left Review* 1, no. 5:173–76.

———. 1935. "The Purpose of a Left Review." *Left Review* 1, no. 9:359–65.

———. 1936. *Easter:1916*. London: Lawrence and Wishart.

———. 1936. *Stay Down Miner*. London: Martin Lawrence.

———. 1937. *New Way Wins*. London: Lawrence and Wishart.

——— 1946. "Old Spain." In *Peter Grimes" and Other Poems*. London: John Lane the Bodley Head, 71–75.

———. 1954. "Ann as I Remember Her." In *Nothing Is Lost:Ann Lindsay 1914–1954*, Edited by Edgell Rickword. London: Communist Party Writer's Group, 5–8.

———. 1978. "Stay Down Miner." In *The 1930s: A Challenge to Orthodoxy*. Edited by John Lucas. Hassocks: John Spiers, The Harvester Press Limited, 201–64.

Stourac, Richard, and Kathleen McCreery. 1986. *Theatre as a Weapon: Workers' Theatre in the Soviet Union, Germany and Britain, 1917–1934*. London: Routledge and Kegan Paul.

Van Gyseghem, André. 1979. "British Theatre in the Thirties: An Autobiographical Record." In *Culture and Crisis in Britain in the 30s*. Edited by Jon Clark Heinemann, Margot, Margolles, David, and Snee, Caroll. London: Lawrence and Wishart, 209–18.

Wallis, Mick. 1994. "Pageantry and the Popular Front: Ideological Production in the 'Thirties." *New Theatre Quarterly,* 10, no. 38:132–56.

A Bibliography of Works by and about Montagu Slater

Publications

———. 1931. *The Second City.* London: Wishart & Co.

———. 1934. *Haunting Europe.* London: Wishart & Co.

———. 1936. *Easter 1916.* London: Lawrence and Wishart.

———. 1936. *Stay Down Miner.* London: Martin Lawrence.

———. 1937. *New Way Wins.* London: Lawrence and Wishart.

Two of Slater's puppet-plays which were written and performed in the 1930s were subsequently published in *"Peter Grimes" and Other Poems,* John Lane, The Bodley Head, London, 1946.

Slater also contributed on a very regular basis to the *Left Review* and less frequently to other journals.

Unpublished Material

Stage Plays

———. *Domesday.* (The manuscript is in the collection of Slater's papers in the Library at the University of Nottingham.)

———. *Out of Liverpool.* (The manuscript is in the collection of Merseyside Unity papers at the Liverpool Maritime Museum.)

———. *I Want a Hero.*

———. *Cock-Robin.*

Puppet Plays

———. *Seven Ages of Man*—"A processional piece in which . . . the plot is simply the passage of time."

———. *The Station Master*—"A Farce."

———. *The Forest*—A "little ballet".

———. *Old Spain*

All four of these marionette plays were performed at the Mercury Theatre in 1938.

Seven Ages of Man and *Old Spain* were later published in *"Peter Grimes" and Other Poems.* London: John Lane, 1946.

Another puppet script—*Prologue for Punch*—was published in the *Left Review,* December 1934, but was probably unperformed.

Pageants

Pageant of Empire, performed at Collins' Music Hall, London, 28 February 1937.

Towards Tomorrow, performed at Wembley Stadium, 2 July 1938. The manuscript was lost, but a film of part of the event is available through the Cooperative Society.

Pageant of South Wales, performed 1 May 1939, simultaneously in three different Welsh towns.

Heirs to the Charter: A Pageant of Chartism, performed 22 July 1939, at the Empress Hall, London. The manuscript and a program are in the archives of the British Communist party.

Material about Montagu Slater

There have been no full-length studies of Slater's writing, though some discussion frequently occurs in general analyses of the culture and theater of the 1930s. There are also references to him and his work in almost every study of the life or work of Benjamin Britten. Significant items include the following:

1978. *The 1930s: A Challenge to Orthodoxy.* Edited by John Lucas. Harvester Press.

Mitchell, Donald. 1983. "Montagu Slater Who Was He?" In Philip Brett, ed. *Benjamin Britten, Peter Grimes.* Cambridge: Cambridge University Press.

———. ed. 1991. *Letters from a Life: The Selected Letters of Benjamin Britten, 1913–1976,* London.

Rattenbury, Arnold. 1976. "Total Attainder and the Helots." *Journal of Renaissance Studies* 20 (reprinted in Lucas, *The 1930s*).

Slater, Montagu. 1954. "Ann as I remember her." In Edgell Rickword, ed. *Nothing Is Lost: Ann Lindsay 1914–1954.* London: Communist Party Writers Group.

14

The Novels of Rex Warner

JOHN COOMBES

A Brief Biographical Sketch of Rex Warner (1905–86)

BORN IN BIRMINGHAM IN 1905 TO A CHURCH OF ENGLAND CLERGYMAN and his wife, a schoolteacher, Warner's education followed faithfully the norms which convention decreed for those of his epoch, gender, and social class. Attendance at an undistinguished boarding school, St. George's, Harpenden, was followed by studies in classics and English literature at Wadham College, Oxford, in which Warner distinguished himself as well as achieving notable successes at rugby football.

Classical studies were to be, for Warner's subsequent intellectual life, an even more continuous point of reference than the Marxist materialism around which his thinking developed in the 1930s (together with that of his near-contempories Auden, Upward, Isherwood, and Day Lewis). After leaving Oxford, he contributed regularly to the *London Mercury, New Statesman,* and *Saturday Review,* and taught in schools in Egypt and England, eventually becoming director of the British Institute in Athens from 1945 to 1947. It is in the late 1930s and wartime years that his best-known novels were written.

From the mid-1940s on, Warner produced—in addition to novels and works of criticism—a large number of translations from the Greek and Latin. He subsequently taught at various institutions in the United States, and lastly at the University of Connecticut from 1964 to 1974, after which he retired to rural England. He died in 1986.

Rex Warner had two sons and two daughters; he was married three times: once to Barbara, Lady Rothschild and twice to Frances Chamier Grove.

* * * * *

Ever since someone once noticed the absence of any direct reference to the Napoleonic wars in the novels of Jane Austen, it has been customary in certain schools of English literary criticism to value works of fiction in inverse proportion to their degree of engagement with the history of their times. Were we to adhere to this arbitrary and questionable scale of values, we should have, indeed, to characterize Rex Warner's novels as antipodean to Austen's work. Written between 1936 and 1943 they, perhaps even more than other contemporary fictions of the committed Left, bear and rearticulate the imprint of their time. Warner's novels confront, with varying degrees of explicitness, rapidly succeeding moments in the European history of anti-fascist struggle (the establishment of the Popular Front in France, the Spanish civil war, and the Moscow purge trials; the vicissitudes of appeasement and the approach of victory over fascism in the Second World War). They thus appear as forms of expression of the contradictions which activated the Left in the late 1930s (and which arguably have never ceased to inhabit it). This is evident, notably, in the discursive conflicts they show, between an articulation of the project of the revolutionary Left as imaginative and political liberation, and the authoritarian ordering of those energies with the coming of Stalinism; but they also bear witness to the exigencies, in Western Europe, of the compromise of revolutionary potential with established liberalism in a problematic common project of antifascism.

I would contend that the most notable of Warner's novels is his first, *The Wild Goose Chase* (1937), and I shall suggest that all his subsequent fiction represents to some extent a decline from this initial achievement. *The Wild Goose Chase* is an extensive epic, a modernist allegorical fantasy in which an unlikely trio of brothers—Rudolph the man-about-town, David the aesthete and intellectual, and George the "ordinary" man—succcessfully cross the unspecified frontier in search of the Wild Goose. They find a land in which the Town oppresses the mass of the people by means which are chronicled with ceaseless inventiveness. Rudolph and David are incorporated into the mechanism of repression (though David is subsequently redeemed), whilst George eventually organizes its overthrow (narrated thus baldly, the plot seems like a militant masculinized version of Cinderella). The novel has frequently been compared to the work of Kafka—unprofitably, to my mind. For whereas *The Trial,* for example, tells of the progressive interiorization by the protagonist, K., of the (absent) values and authority of the court (so that he effectively constructs his own ideological imprisonment), George's movement in *The Wild Goose Chase* is from innocence to knowledge, from subjective experience to collective action. A more suitable comparison would possibly be with the typical structure of the picaresque novels of the age of the Enlightenment, and more particularly with those intriguingly aberrant instances of the genre, Diderot's *Jacques le Fataliste* and Voltaire's *Candide*. Both of these works, like *The Wild Goose Chase,* may be characterized as paradoxical voyages of discovery in which, moreover, dialogue and rational discourse (in the form of stories within the story) emerge as the key to fulfilment.

The Wild Goose Chase is very much a revolutionary novel of its time; yet its complexities and internal discrepancies outrun the limitations of its moment. The initial, fascinated, centralizing on the trope of the "frontier" is of course characteristic of the 1930s—we remember here the crossing into Germany in Isherwood's *Mr. Norris Changes Trains,* the approaching transition in Upward's story "Journey to the Border," the grotèsque mirror images from both sides of Auden and Isherwood's *On the Frontier.* It very often, in the literature of the period, betokens a reflexive, indeed anguished, preoccupation on the part of the privileged writer with the problematic of political commitment itself, of transition from one *class*-interest to another. Yet significantly in *The Wild Goose Chase* the frontier between bizarre archaic homeland (England *ad absurdum*) and the lands ruled by the modern totalitarian Town is never shown; George's first realization of an effective demarcation is of that between oppressed countryside, with its recognizable affinities with the world he has left, and the tyrannizing Town itself.

Just as the Frontier (which we might, initially, assume to be heavy with allegorical significance) is effectively displaced, lost, dissolved, and supplanted by stress on collective political action, so is the symbolism of the Wild Goose only presented in order to be discarded, and sporadically resurrected—notably in a cursory instance at the very end of the novel. We are reminded again, here, of the optimistic materialism of Diderot's novel in which the purpose of the journey undertaken, never stated, comes to appear as the journey itself; just so is the Wild Goose progressively deflated as a bearer of intrinsic and abstract "Meaning" and eventually figured as, at most, a catalyst to action—and a fairly arbitrary one at that.

More than those of the contemporaries with which he is associated—Auden, Upward, Isherwood—Warner's narrative bears the marks of 1930s Soviet aesthetics, of socialist realism with its declared aim of depicting humanity in the revolutionary stage of its develop-

ment. George, of course, as well as a Cinderella figure, is a positive
hero in the Soviet mold both in his "ordinariness" (manifest in his
initial choice of humble push-bike in contrast to his brothers' mo-
torbikes and, it has to be said, in his casual relationships with
women) and in his organization of the final successful revolution.
Certainly his transformation from innocence to experience, into "a
strong man . . . browned by the sun, hardened by wind and work,
tightlipped now, a master. . . ." (*The Wild Goose Chase*, pt. 2, chap.
6) has more in common with the romantic hero figures of contemporary Soviet fiction than with the perennial hesitations of so many
fictional characters of the 1930s English Left. A contrast is observ-
able, too, in the designation of the army and revolutionary vanguard
party which he largely organizes: "an army of leaders, not of followers, who would take the town" (part 2, chap. 5).

At times, indeed, narrative dynamic becomes locked into the exemplary, the emblematic. Thus the description of the country girl
who marries and redeems the blinded and repentant Rudolph has all
the archaic monumentality of Soviet sculpture:

> Andria's sister, a giantess. . . . On straight legs she stood, and upraised
> her brown arms were powerful. She was deepchested, a generous being,
> and when she spoke to them her voice was low." (*The Wild Goose Chase*,
> pt. 2, chap. 6)

The revolution achieved, its politics sometimes hint at those of
the contemporary Soviet Union. Shortage of food is ascribed to
sabotage by technicians in a direct echo of the anti-Trotskyist state
propaganda of the late 1930s (*The Wild Goose Chase*, pt. 2, chap. 17).
Hitherto, moreover, the building of the revolution has been occluded
in terms which, like those of much socialist realism, seem both aes-
thetically conservative (concern for the "proper" subject matter of a
novel) and politically élitist (representation of political will through
a few leaders):

> They went on to speak of the revolutionary organization then existing
> in the country, its weaknesses, and their plans for making it into an
> instrument capable of overturning their enemies; nor is it either necessary
> or possible here to describe the results of this discussion or of subsequent
> discussions. It will be enough to say that before many months had passed
> the organization had been transformed. (*The Wild Goose Chase*, pt. 2,
> chap. 5)

In view of all these tendencies, it might be supposed that George's
speech to the mass demonstration which concludes the novel would

be conventionally exhortatory and heroic in the Soviet mould. This element is indeed there, but is prefaced by a denunciation which is, to say the least, intriguingly eccentric:

> What our old leaders most respected we chiefly despise—the frantic assertion of an ego, do-nothings, the over-cleanly, deliberate love-making, literary critics, moral philosophers, ballroom dancing, pictures of sunsets, money, the police; and to what they used to despise we attach great value—to comradeship, and to profane love, to hard work, honesty, the sight of the sun, reverence for those who have helped us, animals, flesh and blood. (*The Wild Goose Chase,* pt. 2, chap. 18)

Though the progress of the novel represents the victory of a rational "normality" (the country, the revolutionary party) over the "fantasy" of the fascist town, it is for the critical confrontation and interpenetration of the two modes, rather than for the schematic replacement of the latter by the former, that Warner's text is memorable. The Town is indeed *unheimlich,* "Kafkaesque" in tone (though not, as we have seen, in tendency), in its figuration through introductory sentences which are sometimes tortuous, even labyrinthine (Warner was of course a classical scholar)—and which are then deflected by the laconic narration of the most extraordinary events; here, moreover, the purposive and the gratuitous are shown to coexist, in act and gesture, in an apparently random and promiscuous confusion whose effect is to perpetuate dominance.

The intertextual relations of this world are many and various; George's first recognition of its values through his encounter with the mad philosopher, Don Antonio, and his two slave women, kept in a perpetual state of animality (*The Wild Goose Chase,* pt. 1, chap. 3) has notable affinities with H. G. Wells's *Island of Dr. Moreau* (as well as with its more recent film derivative, the little known but notable predecessor to their *King Kong,* Cooper and Shoedsack's *Hounds of Zaroff* [1932]). Similarly, opposition to the régime is, initially, expressed with an attractive, quasi-naïve directness which recalls Shaw: "Call me Pushkov. I am an agitator" (pt. 1, chap. 4). More generally the Town has much in common with the *Metopolis* of Fritz Lang—at least in its ceaseless revelation of one layer after another of bizarre and cruel significance (though in Lang's film a final liberal reconciliation is produced which is the very antithesis of *The Wild Goose Chase*). In many aspects, too, Warner's text recalls elements of *Alice in Wonderland.* It has been suggested that Carroll's caucus race represents, in its Brownian indeterminacy, the modalities of unregulated capitalism. Warner's description of a state where physical measurement depends on the whim of the government (pt.

1, chap. 4), where time and memory can be reversed and where, accordingly, determinism is tantamount to High Treason (pt. 1, chap. 14) suggests the development of that analogy into the structural confusion of twentieth-century fascism, where historical and rational consciousness is supplanted by a continuing incoherence, an endless repression by the arbitrary.

And it is, indeed, for the manifold instances of this bizarre interplay of differences that the text remains in the memory. The giggling policemen who ceaselessly reappear throughout the novel and who, it is rumored, have been known to tickle political prisoners to death, are all the more sinister when we take into account their probable origin in the 1930s comic song, Charles Penrose's *The Laughing Policeman*. And similar effects are achieved through the character of Bob, the lively yet timorous itinerant singer who attaches himself to George and then abandons him to become incorporated in the mechanisms of the town: a figure out of Conrad's *Heart of Darkness*, adapted to the 1930s, endlessly prolific in the production of trite lyrics, his mastery of what he appealingly styles the "do-do-de-o business" inescapably recalling the facility and the fragile commitment of so much "committed" poetry of the period.

On first encountering the Town, George is invited to give an instant lecture on "the Heroic in Shakespeare" to the hermaphrodite students of the Convent. The scene, nightmarish in its gradual disintegration into inattentive chaos, is not merely a chronicle of the disruptive irrationality of fascist totalitarianism; for to this it comically juxtaposes George's—at this point—surviving naïve liberal humanism. The ineffectuality of "humane letters" in themselves—a trope with which the liberal mind, after Auschwitz, was to become much preoccupied—has already been demonstrated to George by the Convent's Professor Pothimere, who follows the frank avowal that "I shall never forget my agreeable perturbation when I first saw a woman roasted" with a flawless recitation of Hugo's poem "Booz endormi" (*The Wild Goose Chase*, pt. 1, chap. 13). Nonetheless, George continues doggedly with his hopeless pedogogic project in spite of the laughter which the very mention of Othello provokes— "and finally, I hope, we shall have a general discussion"—and concludes in naïve puzzlement: "Was this the education at the Convent? If so, he reflected, he was in a much more dangerous position than he had contemplated. . . ." (pt. 1, chap. 13).

A still more pathetic contrast between the ineffectuality of liberal humanism and the strategies of fascist totalitarianism is charted in what is, perhaps, the most brilliant imaging of the text's political preoccupations, the football match between the Pros (the resistance team) and the Cons (representing the régime). The scoreboard announces victory to the latter before the match begins; when the Pros look like scoring, the goalposts are moved by a vast unseen mechanism; finally the opposition are all massacred. As referee—"I want to see a clean open game . . . remember the advantage rule"—George initially shares the idiom of the public school with the captain of the doomed Pros—"Chaps! he was saying, 'We're up against it all right'" (*The Wild Goose Chase, pt. 1, chap. 15*). The language, with its inapt ideological assumptions of "fair play" is immediately parodied by the captain of the victorious Cons: "'Keep it clean, fellows. We know the final score.'" Moreover, it chronicles, derisively, the last stage of George's liberal illusion, its moralism to be supplanted by the evolution of collective action—in a language both more laconic and more resonant—throughout the second part of the novel, "The Many Change." Significantly, the episode ends with George swamped in feathers from the spectators' cushions—"unconscious, softly inhumed, having wasted crying"—an Alice-like moment of oneiric transition, from extinction of the liberal consciousness to the ambiguous possibilities of rebirth.

Notably, the vicissitudes of collective action intercalate, in quasi-absurdist fashion, the totalitarian and the quotidian. (Just so was Orwell later, in *Animal Farm,* to realize the dictatorship of the pigs by having them read the *Daily Mirror* and send out for crates of brown ale.) Thus the traitorous President of the "Free State" of Lagonda, besides being a more sinister version of Groucho Marx's Rufus T. Firefly, is both an apparent futurist—"'Next to Freedom and Glory', said the President, 'I revere Speed'" (*The Wild Goose Chase,* pt. 2, chap. 2—and a Fabian believer in the "inevitability of gradualness" (pt. 2, chap. 3). The banality of the odes which he sends to his "uncultured" fellow-revolutionaries before betraying them is a predictive counterpart to the punishment inflicted on the aesthetic Rudolph, condemned—as a "great poet"—to eternal infinitesimal description of his room. (bk. 2, chap. 8). The incident, indeed, foreshadows Borges, whilst it both confirms and denounces the perennial tendency of fascist art toward pleonasm, toward the self-enclosed and absolutistic affirmation of the status quo.

Nowhere is the horror more pertinently intensified than in the scene (bk. 2, chap. 11) where the revolutionaries confront a series of giant automata bearing down on them just like the assailants in H. G. Wells's *War of the Worlds.* Yet here the frisson of horror is achieved less by the size of the monsters than by the realization that they are engineered by a police car in each giant foot: the technical is only a fantastic cover for human violence and degradation.

By contrast, the incongruities with which the revolutionaries are sometimes characterized bear a sense of dignified, if unorthodox, elegy. Thus George's funeral oration for Joe—

> This man had never aimed at acquiring wealth, had never written a sonnet, standing by the verge of the sea; he had never exacted women, or despised them, never gone into a corner with a dog and a pipe, never perfumed himself. (*The Wild Goose Chase*, pt. 2, chap. 7)

—recalls, in its unorthodox homeliness, in its bridging of social realism and fantasy, Joe's own memories of his wife; not only did she (like Rosa Luxemburg?) lead the revolutionary minority in activating the factories, we learn, but she was "good at tennis" (pt. 2, chap. 4). Such—only apparent—inconsequentiality bears some comparison with Auden's "Spain" in its espousal of the everyday. But whereas in the poem, the future of "bicycle races / Through the suburbs on summer evenings" is set against the present of politics, "the flat ephemeral pamphlet and the boring meeting," such disdain is entirely absent from Warner's narration of the struggle for, and seizure of, power.

To end with the beginning. The introductory chapter, "Far on Bicycles" assumes its full significance only after a reading of the novel as a whole (when, notably, the Wild Goose—initially presented as a kind of Graal-entity—has lost its significance in the course of conscious collective action). Here, a particular, unctuously decorous narration, sinuous in its lower-middle-class hesitations and orthodoxies, recounts the world of "this side" of the frontier as combining aspects of both country and town of the later story. Stock situations and characters emerge, more or less directly, from surrealist films; the Prebendary Garlic (with whose wife, we presume, George has been having an affair) is, in a gesture without consequence which recalls *L'Age d'Or*, suddenly struck in the face by our hero immediately before his departure. These, we realize eventually, are all elements to be organized into political coherence and significance on the "other side" of the frontier—whose effective absence makes its own comment on the relationship between archaic "liberal" tradition and totalitarian repression.

The Wild Goose Chase was indeed a hard act to follow; it cannot be maintained that Warner ever subsequently achieved such an incisive articulation of political insight and literary invention. *The Professor* (completed in October 1938, the month of the Munich agreement) largely abandons the fantastic mode of *The Wild Goose Chase* and remains closely tied to the moment of its writing, in its narration of the last few days in the life of its eponymous hero. A liberal Professor of classics, he is made Prime Minister of his central European country (an amalgam of Austria and Czechoslovakia) before being betrayed, in the course of a putsch, by Fascists sympathetic to the "Great Power" across the frontier, and finally murdered in a scene which bears only the faintest similarity to the end of Kafka's *Trial*. Whereas the politics of *The Wild Goose Chase* were imaginatively revolutionary, here they are, by comparison, constricted into a skillful—but only transiently significant—manipulation of "politics-fiction" (the techniques of the 1930s thriller appropriated for a relatively new purpose). To this may be added elements of socialist-realist satire, largely directed against ineffectual liberalism. But this particular mode, whilst serving its purpose of pointing up the cruel contrast between desperate European circumstances and complacent "English" insularity (the Professor thinks like a conventional Oxford don, the Trade Union leader like a contemporary caricature by David Low), only detracts from the work's fictional coherence, since no Europeans of the Left or Center-Left could credibly be presented as thus naïve. It is as if the stress, ever present in the Popular Front alliance of the 1930s, between defence of liberalism and the necessity for positive anti-fascist action, have, in the moment that the Popular Front has become a literally desperate necessity, broken apart in the very structure of the novel.

By contrast, *The Aerodrome* (1941) marks a partial return to the fantastic mode of Warner's first novel. We are presented with two worlds, two sets of values, two time scales even; that of the English village, initially evoked (significantly through the narrator's drunken awareness) with loving detail as pastoral from a children's storybook (or maybe from Agatha Christie), and that of the nearby aerodrome, gleaming with modern efficiency. The ethos of the former, that of Squire and Parson (the latter the narrator's adoptive father) is however, we gradually discover, degenerate, at once brutal and deferential, quasi-feudal; that of the latter, as represented by the Air-Vice-Marshal (a neat hint that there may be still higher powers operating in the background) is fascist and moreover expansionist, ruthless in its determination to destroy the "culture" of the village. [To the original edition of 1941 Warner rather timorously added a prefatory note, protesting his affection and respect for the "real" villages and Air Force of his country. The operation demonstrated the complexities not only of art and life, but of politics and practice: it can hardly be denied that Britain in the 1930s had many villages still locked in feudality, and an Air Force, many of whose officers held pronouncedly right wing opinions. World War, as ultimate extension of the Popular Front, was to effect a problematic unity of these elements with the political Left.]

Two related series of developments are of particular interest in the novel. Firstly, the development of the narrator (in some sense an extension of the unctuous narrator of whom we are briefly aware at the beginning of *The Wild Goose Chase*). Snobbish to a comic degree (he is capable of expressing his snobbery, even, in terms which come straight from an eighteenth-century novel), arrogant, complacent and deferential by turns, he is moreover brutally inept in his emotional dealings with women, and above all, dim—an average boarding-school boy of his age and time. As such, he slips without difficulty or regret out of the ambit of the quasi-feudal viallage into that of the aerodrome, and eventually back again; his concluding ethical self-judgment suggests, in its inflexible pomposity, the complementary sterility of both worlds:

> The Code under which I had been living for the past year was, in spite of its symmetry and its perfection, a denial of life, its difficulty, its perplexity, and its suffering, rather than an affirmation of its nobility and its grandeur." (*The Aerodrome*, chap. 20)

More particularly, however, the narrator is (in what is in some ways the most Dickensian of Warner's novels) an orphan, the revelation of his circumstance being the first of a series of melodramatic revelations about parentage which activate the text, and which involve most of its major characters. Once all the interlocking relationships have, as in *Dombey and Son,* been established (the dead Air-Vice-Marshal as the narrator's father, the Rector as father of his mistress Bess, etc.), there emerges, it seems, a kind of vapid social and political reconciliation between the "traditionalism" of the village and the "modernism" of the Air Force—between, in effect, feudalism and fascism. Still more significantly, it seems that the children bear this process on behalf of their ancestors:

> We had been talking, I remember, of the lives of our fathers and of ourselves. Nothing of any great profundity was said by either of us, but, as we talked and looked into each others' eyes, it seemed that between those two enemies there was something binding and eternally so. (*The Aerodrome*, chap. 20)

A drab conclusion, indeed; rather than, as in *The Wild Goose Chase,* one series of values *transcending* another, here, it seems, two negativities merely merge. They may be seen, retrospectively, to move towards Warner's last work of original fiction *Why Was I Killed?* (1943)—a "dramatic dialogue" in which a series of narrative life-histories are linked by the ghostly dead airman/narrator. The overall effect, here, is one of a flat panorama in which naturalism of presentation—ranging from nostalgic evocation of a genteel country house to, perhaps, the most graphic description available in English (at the time of writing) of a Nazi concentration camp—comes to confirm a generalized and pessimistic liberalism, seeking, as would later the writing of Camus, to transcend inevitable evil by focusing on personal value:

> There's nothing in my heart but love, and not only love for you and the baby we're having, but for everything and everyone. (*Why Was I Killed,* chap. 7)

Most particularly, *Why Was I Killed?* seems largely parasitic on Warner's own former work, a compaction of elements from *The Professor* and *The Aerodrome.* Its effect is largely of inertia, engendered not only by the monotonous succession of brief life stories, but also by the fact that they are filtered through the consciousness of the dead man: a character by definition incapable of refractive consciousness, of interaction, or of imaginative energy.

It is, then, difficult to avoid viewing the process of Warner's fiction as, to some extent, a continuous decline. Undoubtedly, this has much to do with the confused political exigencies of the epoch in which the novels were written—the desperately eclectic appropriation of popular fictional forms in *The Professor* as a reaction to the prewar series of fascist victories; the lapse into an ideologically hospitable sentimentality in the last two works as an accommodation of anti-fascist politics to homely nationalism. Yet fragments of these later works rise obstinately in our consciousness, confirming at least their partial affinities with their predecessor, one of the great revolutionary novels of the century.

Works Cited

Warner, Rex. 1937. *The Wild Goose Chase.* London: Boriswood.
———. *The Professor.* 1938. London: Boriswood.
The Aerodrome. 1941. London: John Lane.
Why Was I Killed? 1949. London: John Lane.

A Bibliography of Works by and about Rex Warner

Primary

———. 1937. *Poems.* London: Boriswood.
———. 1937. "Education." In *The Mind in Chains. Socialism and the Cultural Revolution.* Edited by C. Day Lewis. London: Muller, pp. 19–37.

———. 1937. *The Wild Goose Chase*. London: Boriswood.

———. 1938. *The Professor*. London: Boriswood.

———. 1941. *The Aerodrome*. London: John Lane.

———. 1945. *The English Public Schools*. London: Collins.

———. 1947. *The Cult of Power Essay*. London: John Lane.

———. 1949. *Why Was I Killed?* London: John Lane.

———. 1949. *Men of Stone*. London: The Bodley Head.

———. 1950. *John Milton*. London: Max Parrish.

———. 1950. *E. M. Forster*. London: British Council.

———. 1950. *Views of Attica and its Surroundings*. London: John Lehomann.

———. 1951. *Greeks and Trojans*. London: MacGibbon and Kee.

———. 1951. *Escapade*. London: The Bodley Head.

———. 1953. *Eternal Greece*. London: Thames and Hudson.

———. 1954. *The Vengeance of the Gods*. London: MacGibbon and Kee.

———. 1958. *The Young Caesar*. London: Collins.

———. 1958. *The Greek Philosophers*. New York: New American Library.

———. 1960. *Imperial Caesar*. London: Collins.

———. 1963. *Pericles the Athenian*. London: Collins.

———. 1967. *The Converts*. London: The Bodley Head.

———. 1972. *Men of Athens*. London: The Bodley Head.

Also many translations from the Greek and Latin.

Secondary

Churchill, T. 1967. "Warner: Homage to Necessity." *Critique* 10.

De Vitis, A. A. 1960. "Warner and the Cult of Power." *Twentieth Century Literature* 6.

Drenner, D.V.R. 1952. "Kafka, Warner and the Cult of Power." *Kansas Magazine*.

Maini, D. S. 1961. "Warner's Political Novels: An Allegorical Crusade Against Fascism." *Indian Journal of English Studies, 2.*

Mason, R. 1945. "The Novels of Warner." *Adelphi* 21.

McLeod, A. L. 1960. *Rex Warner: Writer*. Sydney.

———. ed. 1965. *The Achievement of Warner*. Sydney.

———. eds. Rajan, B. and A. Pearse. 1945. "Symposium on Kafka and Rex Warner." *Focus One.*

15

At the Frontier: Edward Upward's *Journey to the Border*

Patrick Quinn

A Brief Biography of Edward Falaise Upward (1903–   )

Edward falaise upward was born on 9 september 1903 in Romford, Essex. The son of a doctor who attended college with the father of W. H. Auden, Upward was raised in the solid, upper-middle class, and at fourteen attended Repton School, where he met his lifelong friend Christopher Isherwood, who describes their friendship in his book *Lions and Shadows.* After a six-month stay in Rouen, Upward was admitted to Corpus Christi College, Cambridge, where he received his degree in English in 1925.

At Cambridge, Upward was reunited with Isherwood and the two undergraduates devised the fantasy world of Mortmere to escape from both the pretentiousness and emptiness of college life. While at Cambridge Upward came under the influence of I. A. Richards, whose attitudes directed him away from writing poetry (despite having won the Chancellor's Medal for English Verse). After graduating, Upward began a teaching career which led to positions throughout the United Kingdom, but he continued to write Mortmere stories along with Isherwood. After various personal and philosophical crises, Upward read Lenin's *Material and Empirio-Criticism* and began to examine the working of the capitalist system. The result was that in 1931 Upward decided to become involved in the work of the communist party. He became a member in 1934. His writing appeared in left-wing journals such as *New Country, The Left Review,* and *Penguin* "New Writing" and because of his friendship with, and influence on, other writers, he became known as the mysterious influence behind Auden, Spender, and Isherwood.

In 1935, he became an English master at Alleyns School in Dulwich where he remained until retirement in 1961. While at Alleyns, he wrote several essays on the Marxist vision of literature, several short stories, *Journey to the Border,* and a number of reviews and articles for *The Ploughshare*. He had married fellow communist Hilda Percival in 1936, and they worked jointly as ordinary members of the British Communist party until they were deemed to have deviated from the party line. Having invested so much of himself in the communist cause, not surprisingly Upward suffered a nervous breakdown soon after leaving. After a hiatus, Upward was able to rekindle his interest in political issues and joined the Campaign for Nuclear Disarmament (CND) in the 1950s. His awakened awareness led him to begin the ambitious project of publishing a trilogy, *The Spiral Ascent* (1959–77), which lightly fictionalized his own political pilgrimage since 1930. Upward continued to write about political questions, and in his latest collection of short stories, *The Night Walk and Other Stories* (1985), one finds an interesting mixture of social realism with Mortmere fantasy.

Upward is still writing and now lives in Sandown, Isle of Wight.

* * * * *

Journey to the Border is not only an important experimental modernist novel of the 1930s, but it is also Edward Upward's autopsy on a mind corrupted by the pestilence of fantasy. The novel, which develops the idea of fantasy misdirecting dedication to political ideology, was begun in early 1935 and finished in September 1937, and it was somewhat surprisingly published by the politically moderate Hogarth Press (thanks largely to John Lehmann's effort) in March of 1938. Upward claimed that his initial idea upon conceiving the story was that "[it] should be "A Dream. A Bad Dream," and that "this dream should allegorize the world of the 1930s in which fascism and war were coming ever nearer" (Ross "Back," 6). However, as Upward worked on the final drafts of the book, the impact of socialist-realist ideas from the Soviet Union caused him to rethink whether the use of modern allegory was relevant in a depiction of the contemporary world. He later admitted in 1969 in an interview for *London Magazine* that his "loss of confidence in what . . . [he] was doing is reflected . . . in a decline of vividness towards the end of the book" (Ross 8). In fact, Upward's continued concern about the weakness of the conclusion recently resulted in his rewriting a considerable portion of the final section of the book.

The novel's concern with the origins of fantasy in human consciousness and with the treatment of its manifestations entailed a great deal of introspection on Upward's part—an examination of his own artistic self-motivation. In his inner delvings he discovered how dangerous an adherence to fantasy was, for he found that it deterred him from taking steps toward for positive political action. But this discovery in a writer to whom fantasy was second nature caused undue stress on Upward. In a typically melancholy letter to Isherwood, written during the second year of drafting and just after his marriage to fellow communist Hilda Percival, Upward admitted that "If I manage to avoid becoming as insane as the tutor [the main character] by the time I've finished it I shall have achieved something" (Letter to Isherwood, 7 December 1936). Upward must have felt that by rejecting fantasy he was repudiating his former bourgeois self: the self that had clung to that mode of art as a way of seeking refuge from the urgent problems of commitment and action that had to be faced in the real world (Lambourne 1973, 847). So the journey to the border became for Upward not only a psychological journey to the frontier where sanity meets insanity, but also a voyage to the frontiers of avoidance and of dedication.

Escapist fantasy had long been Upward's preferred mode of literary creation. Even as early as 1923 while he was an undergraduate at Cambridge, he wrote the beginnings of a play, *After Six Years,* about the rantings of a frustrated young museum curator who wishes to burn his work place down and to desert the empty world he inhabits.

> You can't imagine my desperation; I know that I have all the means to set fire to this building today. . . . I know that I could leave this town for ever this morning. I passionately wish to do these things. And yet I remain here like a genial paralytic, meekly dreaming of recovery, comforting myself with the luxury of imagined action. That's my one romance—a mental scene in which I stand before a flaming museum and defy the whole town. . . . I know perfectly well that as I talk to you I am merely acting the puff-rhetorician, merely applying the neurasthenic's salve, "getting it off my chest." My whole mind is chequered. (*After Six Years,* 3)

Even in this early work, the nascent themes of inaction and grotesqueness, which were to recur throughout Upward's writing into and beyond the 1930s as symptoms of an overactive imagination, were manifest.

However, a glimpse of Upward's work as a young writer shows that his views took time to develop fully: his undergraduate flirtation with escapist fantasy culminated in the joint creation with Christopher Isherwood at Cambridge of a series of comic stories centered in Mortmere, a traditional English village where everyone is slightly mad and where nothing is quite as innocent as it seems. But the anarchistic world of Mortmere and dependence on fantasy appeared somewhat frivolous in an England where the effects of the Great Depression and political injustices were ubiquitous. In an unpublished letter to Isherwood written on 30 January 1931 from Scarborough, where he had taken on a job as a schoolmaster, Upward gave vent to his frustration with his environment and with the conditions of teaching. The letter sounds a death knell for Mortmere fantasy and a clarion call for political action.

> The seafront is a terrible five-storied sepulchre of bogus leisure. . . . There is no time to be fit for pleasure. Now I understand why maniacs weep when they see birds. Now Proust, Gide, Shakespeare are worthless and only Barbusse and Lenin are relevant. Every stone in this piss-house must be smashed. . . . And in this ruined lodging, where hour by hour the screw of the economy is tightened round our paralysed needs, wireless and voices fray the last decencies to a mere bum-clout. But this time there is a solution outside suicide. The picture is ice-clear, and all that is wanted is the trifling energy to make plans. Every inch must be exposed, deplored, contrasted with the iron future when we shall be pure in mind. It is wicked to try to be pure in heart. That is where Lawrence, St. Francis, Ghandi, all went wrong.

By 1931, Upward had rejected the idea that a simple "change of heart" would transform the world in favor of an adherence to the political determinism of a certain future under communism. The three short stories which he wrote prior to *Journey to the Border* demonstrate a rigorous attempt to find a literary form appropriate to the Marxist ideology which he had by then adopted. W. H. Sellers, in his introduction to the Penguin Upward collection, notices that all three stories describe

> with little or no plot, the intellectual awakening of an individual to the necessity of Marxism. A character, as a result of observing the decadence and deceit of the world around him, makes a poetical decision that promises to lead him away from an aimless passivity that foreshadows the delusory world of Hearn [a leading character in the Mortmere fantasy] and towards purposeful, dynamic social action, towards orientation. (*Journey to the Border*, 18)

Journey to the Border reflects in its title the necessity for the bourgeois intellectual to cross the "frontier" of decision in order to ally himself with the working-class movement. This principle is discussed comprehensively by Hynes, Cunningham, and Bergonzi in their respective studies of writings of the thirties, and it is reiterated in Upward's own "Sketch for a Marxist Interpretation of Literature" (1937), which incorporates his rejection of fantasy writing and his principle that a writer must take the side of the workers in order to write a book which tells the truth about reality. *Journey to the Border* attempts to do this as well as to

> awaken the conscience to the menace of Fascism and the extent of the bourgeois crisis, a preoccupation firmly rooted in the experience and the events of the period. The political polarisation of the epoch revealed . . . the fundamental weakness of the position of the bourgeois liberal: of a tragic liability, in the face of crisis, to political paralysis, induced by his continuous adherence to a "bourgeois objective" view. This theme was understandably close to the conscience of the progressive writer addressing . . . primarily the bourgeois reader or spectator (Harris 1966, 137–38).

In fact, Upward confirmed this necessity for a change of direction at the Literature/Sociology Conference on "1936" at Essex University in July 1978.

> In actual experience I found that a para-religious acceptance of things as they are, was no more possible for me than evasion by means of fantasy. I reached a crisis, in which I was unable to continue writing. I was able to start again only after I had decided that writing must no longer be the most important thing in life for me, and that I must put the struggle for Socialism first. (203)

Journey to the Border, then, besides being an allegory of the 1930s, is also a personal literary record of Upward's struggle to throw off the artistic impulse and to embrace wholeheartedly a political ideology in his work.

As the story is told almost entirely through the tutor's unstable mind, the perspective is completely subjective, and as a consequence critics have struggled with what really happens and what does not happen in the story. They have queried the nature of the dialectic reality represented in conflict between the tutor's delusion and external reality. This explanatory leap from dialectic to Hegel and then to Marx's *Grundrisse* is a common trajectory for critics of the story, but the compulsion to infer from the novel an ideological intent on the part of the author seems like an unnecessary labor. The novel does not make it difficult to discern fantasy from reality, and one does not need a knowledge of Lenin's *Teachings of Karl Marx* in order to follow the development in the tutor's consciousness from escapist daydreaming to political awareness. For ultimately, this is not a political morality play, although the tutor accepts the call to political action; instead, this is an experimental novel set within the framework of a Bildungsroman. It is a celebration of the artistic life which Upward had left behind, and a hope and affirmation that the new life he had chosen would be beneficial for him and for society. Upward's work had begun and remained rooted in the actualities of contemporary life and has for its implicit central value a wholesomely normal life—even if, as Upward feels, "life must always be thwarted and perverted by capitalism" (Barratt 1979, 48). The artistic thrust behind the novel is more Joycean, more Proustian than Marxist.

Since the novel is narrated in the third person, it allows the reader an insight into the tutor's own self-awareness, which is ironic and self-absorbed. Clearly, the tutor is accutely conscious of the bourgeois style of life he is leading, but he also knows that any job he chooses to do would be equally as "dishonest and subservient" (*Journey to the Border,* 204). We are introduced to the unnamed tutor in the first page of the narrative. Restless and frustrated by his post in a country house situated in the north of England, which is presided over by a member of the bourgeois, Mr. Parkin, the tutor reluctantly acquiesces to the demands of his employer, but mentally he escapes into daydreams. The subservience which he must adopt in his role of paid servant, albeit that of a tutor, propels him into depressive mood swings. Unhelpfully, the tutor suffers from a combination of an inferiority complex and an overactive imagination. In a bout of self-pity, for example, he convinces himself that staying alone in a despised pseudo–eighteenth-century house offers greater fulfillment than attending the races and meeting other people of his age including the "cheerful MacCreath girls" (86). Even his exaggerated vision of Mr. Parkin as an capitalist leech cannot withstand the cold water of reality, for his employer is simply an unthinking ordinary member of his class whose design is to dominate people like the tutor. But what the tutor finds most anger-provoking is his own smiling acceptance of his role:

> While his nature, the soul for which he had been so meanly alarmed, had performed its invisible fairy-story acrobatics, he had smiled daily at table, agreed with everything the Parkins had said, drunk their beer and

obeyed their orders, given up his whole time to the boy. Any effort to assert himself in practice he would have considered degrading, petty, a danger to his soul. But he had failed even to save his soul. (*Journey to the Border,* 95)

As the tutor is about to assert himself and to refuse to attend the races according to his employer's wishes, the gentlemanly neighbor, MacCreath, enters. In the circumstances, a refusal is out of the question, but the tutor vents his frustration and hostility on the smooth-speaking MacCreath, who is unknowingly subject to the tutor's acerbic criticism and is judged a "philistine" for wearing "an unassertive tweed overcoat and a milky-tea coloured shirt and collar" (*Journey to the Border,* 97). But this assessment of MacCreath is no more valid than the tutor's attitude toward Parkin, and both judgments are distortions fueled by the tutor's pent-up antagonism. In fact, by failing to act, by refusing to state his intention of not wishing to attend the races, the tutor's rancor distorts his perception of reality in much the same way as a simple, guileless action can evoke a powerful emotional response in someone already in a state of neurosis.

Having failed himself for being unable to voice his own wishes, the sullen tutor decides that he should suppress thinking and feeling in order to be liberated from the consciousness of his serfdom. With great concentration, he is able to alter his perception of a distant marquee at the track with some initial success. The dingy gray tent is transformed into a dazzlingly white, shimmering object in the bright light. This transformation from the mundane into the dazzling is a powerful self-deception, but the tutor's self-hypnotic state is not constant, and the vision erratically comes and goes until he is wrenched out of his daydream by the appearance of a steamroller unexpectedly pulling out in front of Parkin's chauffeur-driven limousine.

Soviet films and the art posters of social realism, influenced by Futurist painters such as Boccioni and poets like Marinetti, have prepared us well for the vision of machines as progress. So the image of the steamroller thumping confidently down the road appears representative of an unbridled power in and of itself (*Journey to the Border,* 112). The driver's insouciant attitude, which he demonstrates by pulling out in front of Parkin's car, pleases the tutor immensely. For the tutor, the message is clear: nothing can stand in the way of the mechanical progress engendered in the new-world vision. To emphasize the contrast between new and old, the physical nature of the steamroller is in direct opposition to the radiant marquee; the steamroller is a tangible symbol of progress while the insubstantial marquee is but the romanticized delusion of a diseased imagination.

At the end of the first part of the novel, the tutor has not yet been spurred into action. He is a voyeur in life, knowing that change will come, but he is still apprehensive of becoming actively involved. Or as George C. K. Thayer puts it, "He must learn how to transform intellectual understanding into purposeful and effective action in order to break the pattern of passive failure and escape" (Thayer 1981, 55). The second part of the book sketches the obstacles that deter the tutor from positive movement.

The second chapter presents the tutor with a series of options, all of which suggest possible means of escape from his present dilemma: each offering would seem to have both positive inducements and negative consequences for him. The tutor moves sequentially from one option to the next, rejecting each after contemplating its merits and disadvantages. MacCreath, for example, offers the tutor a satisfactory job which will lead to bourgeois comfort and respectability, but upon reflection, the tutor feels that if he tried to live a comfortable life, he would become complacent and selfish like MacCreath and Parkin (*Journey to the Border,*134).

On cue, a carful of young people of his own class pass by, and the tutor answers to the longing to participate in their world of sensuality and adventure. Ann MacCreath, who calls him over to the car, invites him to join her; it is not long before he has been swayed by her youth, intelligence, and manner and soon proposes a romantic elopement. But MacCreath's daughter herself has embraced socialism, so she resists his unrealistic offer. Ann understands intuitively what is ailing the tutor.

> The strange thing about you is that you see quite clearly what is wrong with the system under which we are living. More clearly than I do. But you take no action. You are content to hate and despise your life . . . . You think you can get a better job. Perhaps you can. A better-paid job, with fewer petty restrictions on your leisure. You may even have a liberal-minded employer. But unless you fight against capitalism you will feel just as servile as you do now. You will never be free in your mind and heart so long as all your actions, your real life, are still wholly in the service of the rich (*Journey to the Border*, 138–9).

The tutor declines Ann's call to immediate action to thwart the Fascist hordes, for her ideas seem abstract and irrelevant in the context of the race course. For the tutor, the real world is what he sees around him, and that is clearly a world of attractive young men and women, like Tod, the driver of one of the cars.

Another of the tutor's options is promulgated by Tod, who has himself already been a participant in imperialistic exploitation in Nigeria and is shown to be a racist as well as an anti-Semite. Many critics have seen Tod as a portrait of "Truly Weak Man," a type developed by Christopher Isherwood in his *Lions and Shadows* and exposed by Auden and Isherwood in the character of the Fascist Michael Ransom in *The Ascent of F-6,* but it may also be true that Tod is representative of the face of the totalitarianism that is so tantalizing to those lost in the entanglements of modern social and political dilemmas. Tod's world is starkly devoid of uncertainties; his answers to social and political problems quickly appall the tutor with their callousness, but the tutor, like so many Europeans in awe of fascism, is unable to contest Tod's will. "The monstrous bulk of Tod's body dazed him, made him as helpless and lethargic as a frog squatting in the shadow of a cobra. He could not even find the energy to look once more at the marquee" (*Journey to the Border,* 150). When Tod finally departs to join the preparations for the appearance of the Master of the Hunt, the tutor finds himself weak at the knees from the force of Tod's charismatic power.

Still recovering from Tod's onslaught, another philosophical alternative presents itself to the tutor in the character of Gregory Mavors, who introduces him to the teachings of Homer Lane as interpreted by John Layard, whose intellectual and physical relationship with Auden has been open to much speculation. Mavors tells the tutor that

> Every disease is a cure if we know the right way to take it. Disease is a result of disobedience to the inner law of our own nature, which works by telling us what we want to do and has no use for "don'ts." From childhood up we are taught that our natural desires are evil, that we must control them, deny them room to grow. But they will not be denied. Twisted, clogged with moralizings, driven back from all normal avenues of development, they nevertheless find a way of asserting themselves, appear in disguise, take on unexpected and abnormal forms— malaria, murder, neurosis, joining a Storm Troop, and whatnot. (*Journey to the Border,* 156)

According to Mavors, then, bridled desire and externally imposed rational behavior lead directly to dissatisfaction; however, when the baggage with which society burdens them is shed, the fortunate, liberated few reach a state of enlightenment which allows them a new perspective of life. Upward was clearly attacking the psychological contention that to promote positive change one must alter oneself from within rather than make efforts to change the world from without. One of the themes of *Journey to the Border* is that

Auden's "change of heart" was not an answer to his dilemma: this type of self-gratifying psychology could easily lead to the romantic allurement of fascism. The realization is confirmed when the tutor observes Mavors listening, enraptured, to Tod's jejune fascist speech in the marquee; he knows then that liberated desire alone cannot bring about meaningful change.

Despairing of answers and feeling more isolated than ever, the tutor is saved from utter resignation by a young woman who remembers him from a tryst which they had experienced at Cambridge six years previously. Ironically, she appears to offer the same kind of mindless romantic escape that the tutor had offered to Ann earlier in the afternoon. She is attracted to the tutor's creative mind because he promises to enliven her empty, conventional life of bourgeois complacency. Her sexuality is ardent, but "simultaneously menacing and trivial" (Thayer 73). The tutor cannot satisfy her zealous passions, and before long she has deserted him in favor of her fiancé, who is actively participating in the Fascist theatrics in the tent. When the tutor looks in at the spectacle, he is horrified by his glimpse into the heart of darkness.

> Horror of the future alone supported him, kept his consciousness alive. He would be gassed, bayoneted in the groin, slowly burned, his eyeballs punctured by wire barbs. . . . And such extremes of torture could not last long, could not compare in persistence with the other slower horrors which he *was* able to imagine. The horror of isolation among a drilled herd of dehumanized murderers. The death of all poetry, of all love, of all happiness. Never more to be allowed to use his brain (*Journey to the Border,* 184).

It is here, at the end of part two of the novel, that the tutor recognizes that the public world of outside events will and must violate the private world. But more than this, he realizes that the public world is full of corruption and illusion, and that to survive, he must cross the border of disillusionment and begin to take action. The second book closes with that awareness.

Parallels can be drawn between the closing section of *Journey to the Border* and Upward's semiautobiographical novel, *In the Thirties* (1962), which illustrates the difficulties which lay ahead for one brought up in the middle class to immerse himself fully in the worker's movement, no matter how great a commitment to political equality he felt. Having walked by the entrance of the movement's warehouse headquarters, worried about looking too bourgeois in his coat or being thought of as a middle-class interloper, a police spy, or a madman, Alan [the Upward figure] returns and still hesitates to enter.

> Perhaps his best course, now that he had located the rooms, would be to go back to the hotel where he was staying the night and come back here again tomorrow, or if doing this might make him feel even less prepared tomorrow than he was this evening, surely there would be no risk of walking up and down the street once more now? (*In the Thirties*, 46)

In the final part of *Journey to the Border*, the tutor is still a remove away from opening the door to the party headquarters. Upward does not suggest that the tutor's journey will be an easy one. In fact, the tutor's first thought after looking into the exposed face of fascism is to seek escape in suicide, but on reflection, he realizes that he does not have the courage for such an action. All options have seemingly closed for the tutor, and he is figuratively anaesthetized, frozen to inaction when suddenly "A noise, a voice. Ghostly and distinct, it came from high up among the fir trees. It spoke into his left ear. It said: ' . . . But you *are* walking. You have not failed'" (190).

The voice tells the tutor that his escapist fantasies cannot change the external world, but that the horrors and madness that he observed were actually manifest in the external world. He now must learn to take an active part in his world, beginning with what he should do about his job at the Parkins'.

One lesson that the tutor has learned is that decisions can no longer be taken in private isolation; in weighing up the options, whether to take up another post, therefore, he must include his responsibility to the public world in the equation.

> You would, whether you liked it or not, have made your money indirectly or directly out of armaments and out of swindling the working class. And don't comfort yourself with the notion that when you retired you would be able to enjoy yourself. The builders might construct a gas-proof shelter with a ten-foot concrete roof in the basement of your country mansion, and it might save you from being murdered by aircraft, but it wouldn't help you do anything worth while in your leisure. Your whole life, your thoughts, your actions, your feelings, would be poisoned by the life outside you (*Journey to the Border*, 196–97).

To ensure that this particular prophecy does not come about, the tutor comes to acknowledge that he must deny his bourgeois entitlements and have faith in the inevitable progress and victory of the worker's cause. Armed with this new conviction, the tutor refuses the ride home with Parkin and resolves to walk into town, where contact with the workers' movement will ensure his participation in the establishment of a just future for all men.

In spite of Upward's exploration of the temptations of capitalism as an evil force in *Journey to the Border,* the novel was rather late in the decade for proclaiming the virtues of communism to a disillusioned public, and seemed anachronistic, "touching the springs of nostalgia with its romantic notion of conversion and its depiction of the anguish and exhilaration of young leftists six years earlier in 1932 (Willis 1992, 332). After the publication of *Journey to the Border,* Upward feared that the allusive modernist style used in the novel would make his work inaccessible to the working-class intellectual, and for Upward, the artistic quality of the work had to be judged by its appeal to the working-class reader. He felt the need to develop an objective style and yearned to write primarily about the external world and the workers' movement within that external world. Importantly, he wanted to have his imaginative prose reflect the selflessness of Wilfred Owen's poetry. Owen, according to Upward's unpublished lecture given at the University of Paris at Vincennes in 1978, "was deeply concerned with the lives and deaths of other people. That is how I hoped to write about communism and about the revolutionary struggle, unself-centeredly" (quoted in Thayer 1981, 96).

The value of Upward's *Journey to the Border* is not only as an interesting predecessor to his *Spiral Ascent* trilogy, or as a quintessential novel of the 1930s, but also as an interesting experiment in narrative technique. The judicious critic Walter Allen points out that "the voltage of imaginative excitement created is very high, . . . It remains a brilliant experimental novel of a very unusual kind" (Allen 1964, 270–71). Further, *Journey to the Border* reiterates Upward's anxiety for the loss of individual freedom well before he was aware of Marxist ideology. For even in the fragment of *After Six Years* that remains, through his committed writings in the early thirties, his brief pieces during the Second World War right through to his writings in the last three decades, Upward shows that he was preoccupied by the need to shatter the constraints imposed on the individual by a repressive society and to find his way toward some method of positive response, whether that response was to shock the bourgeois in "After Six Years," to respond positively to an hallucination in "The Colleagues," to advocate joining the communist party in *Journey to the Border,* or to rededicate oneself to the struggle against imperialist bullying in the more recent "The Night Walk." Upward's confidence in the individual's need for freedom remains his tantamount concern.

Works Cited

Allen, Walter. 1964. *Tradition and Dream: The English and American Novel from the Twenties to Our Time*. London: Phoenix.

Barratt, Daniel. 1979. "The Novels of Edward Upward." *The Compass*, no. 7 (autumn):47–58.

Harris, Henry. 1966. "The Symbol of Frontier in the Social Allegory of the Thirties." *ZAA*, no. 14:127–40.

Lambourne, David. 1973. "The Novelist Between the Wars: Postmodernist Fiction from 1918–1939 in Its Social, Political, and Historical Context." Ph.D. diss. University of Hull.

Ross, Alan (reviewer). 1969. "Back from the Border: An Interview with Edward Upward." *London Magazine* 9, no. 3 (June):5-11.

Thayer, George C. K. 1981. "Aestheticism and Political Commitment in the Works of Edward Upward." Ph.D. diss., University of Tulsa.

Upward, Edward. "After Six Years." Manuscript, British Library.

———. 1978. *In the Thirties*. London: Quartet Books.

———. 1988. *The Railway Accident and Other Stories*. Introduction by W. H. Sellers. London: Penguin Books.

———. 1937. "Sketch for a Marxist Interpretation of Literature." In C. Day Lewis, ed. *The Mind In Chains*. London: Muller.

———. 1979. "Statement for the Literature/Sociology Conference on '1936' at Essex University, July, 1978." In *1936: The Sociology of Literature*. Edited by Francis Barker et al. Colchester: University of Essex.

Willis, J. H. 1992. *Leonard and Virginia Woolf as Publishers: The Hogarth Press, 1917–1941*. Charlottesville: University Press of Virginia.

A Bibliography of Works by and about Edward Upward

Primary

———. 1933. "The Colleagues." In Michael Roberts, *New Country*, London, 174-82.

———. 1935. "The Island." *The Left Review*, no. 4 (January):104–10.

———. 1938. *Journey to the Border*. London: Hogarth Press.

———. 1937. "Sketch for a Marxist Interpretation of Literature." In *The Mind in Chains: Socialism and the Cultural Revolution*. Edited by C. Day Lewis. London: Frederick Muller, 41–55.

———. 1933. "Sunday." In *New Country*. Edited by Michael Roberts. London: New Signatures, 79–84.

Secondary

Bergonzi, Bernard. 1978. *Reading the Thirties*. London: Macmillan.

"A Conversation with Edward Upward." *The Review*, nos. 11–12:65–67.

Cunningham, Valentine. 1990. *British Writers of the Thirties*. Oxford: Oxford University Press.

Griffin, Ernest. 1977. "Conversation with Edward Upward." In *Modernist Studies: Literature and Culture 1920–1940*, 19–35.

Hynes, Samuel. 1976. *The Auden Generation: Literature and Politics in England in the 1930's*. London: Bodley Head.

Isherwood, Christopher. 1938. *Lions and Shadows: An Education in the Twenties*. London: Hogarth.

Lambourne, David 1973. "The Novelist Between the Wars: Post Modernist Fiction from 1918 to 1939 in Its Social, Political, and Historical Context." Ph.D. diss., University of Hull.

Lehmann, John. 1955. *The Whispering Gallery*. London: Longmans.

Lucas, John. 1969. *The 1930's: A Challenge to Orthodoxy*. London: Harvester.

Mensen, Dieter. 1976. "Leben und Werk von Edward Upward: Ein Beitrag zur Literatur des Thirties Movement in England." Ph.D. diss., Freie Universitat Berlin.

Murthy, U. R. Anantha. "Politics and Fiction in the 1930's: Studies in Christopher Isherwood and Edward Upward." Ph.D. diss., University of Birmingham.

Thayer, George C. K. 1981. "Aestheticism and Political Commitment in the Works of Edward Upward." Ph.D. diss., University of Tulsa.

16

Religion and Popular Culture: Charles Williams's *Descent Into Hell*

Elizabeth Tilley

A Brief Biography of Charles Williams (1886-1945)

Charles Walter Stansby Williams was born in London and lived within fifty miles of the city all his life. Educated at St. Albans and University College, London, family finances forced him to leave college before graduating. A clerk's post in the Methodist Book-room in London led to a job at Oxford University Press, where he remained for the rest of his working career, first as a proofreader, then as an editor. In 1917 Williams married Florence Conway; they had one son, Michael.

Williams's life revolved around the Press offices, but he also lectured extensively on poetry and spirituality at Evening Institutes around London and later in Oxford at the behest of C. S. Lewis. In 1917 Williams was initiated into the Order of the Golden Dawn (whose members also included W. B. Yeats) but little information about either the rites or expressed purpose of the Order remain. Certainly the idea of magic and its connection with Christianity finds its way into both his poetry and prose, and the practice and presence of evil remains an important theme in his work.

When the Second World War broke out, the offices of the Press were moved to Oxford, and Williams came into close contact with other members of a loose group of friends that has come to be known as "The Inklings." They met roughly two times weekly in order to read from works in progress and to discuss common concerns. Many of Williams's works, and those of Tolkien and Lewis first saw the light of day at these meetings.

In 1943 Oxford University awarded Williams an honorary M.A.

In May of 1945 he was operated on for adhesions in the digestive
system; he never recovered consciousness.

Williams's list of publications is extraordinary both for its length
and for the diversity of his interests. He wrote masques and plays,
poetry and novels, works of theology, and a history of witchcraft.
Remembered as a forceful personality, he seems to have inspired
either instant dislike or devotion; perhaps this is the best tribute a
writer could have.

* * * * *

The 1930s were a time of political desperation and cultural up-
heaval for most of Europe, but the same cannot be said either of the
cloistered world of Oxford University or of its Press. Humphrey
Carpenter begins his collective biography of "The Inklings" (the
informal Oxford literary group comprising C. S. Lewis, J. R. R.
Tolkien, Owen Barfield, and others, to which Williams contributed)
with the following: "I have tried to show the ways in which the
ideas and interests of the Inklings contrasted sharply with the general
intellectual and literary spirit of the nineteen twenties and thirties"
(Carpenter 1978, xii). These ideas: religious, Arthurian, and highly
reactionary, make it difficult to place Williams in the modernist
tradition and account to a certain extent for his present obscurity. He
seems to have felt himself totally outside current artistic movements,
much closer in preoccupation and belief with pre-World War I verse
and Dantean poetics than with Eliot or Greene.[1] His novels are supernatural thrillers, popular fiction highly charged with classical literary allusions and idiosyncratic Christian principles.[2]

Like those of his friends, Williams's attitudes toward women,
African Americans, Jews, and the "colonies" are often highly sus-
pect, and there is a definite streak of sadism in his dealings with his
youthful followers (and there seem to have been a good number of
these). Nevertheless, his concerns: the nature of evil, the function
of power, and the place of the artist in society are shared by most
other writers in the 1930s, even if his conclusions are eccentric.

Descent Into Hell is a tightly woven novel that depicts the tortur-
ous, Dantesque journey of two souls, one toward paradise, the other
towards hell. The cast of characters includes Margaret Anstruther,
a "Paradise-bound" old woman who acts as a narrative sybil, and
Lawrence Wentworth, perhaps Williams's most complete portrait
of a doomed soul. Margaret's granddaughter Pauline is chosen as
Williams's initiate into coinherence in this novel, and her spiritual

advisor is Peter Stanhope, a playwright whose words reveal for Pauline the realities behind language.

The novel deals with the living, the dead (one of the subplots discusses the twilight world in which a suicide walks) and the dead-in-life, for here the ancient legend of Lilith is reborn. All times become one in this fictive world, so that Pauline, who is haunted by a doppelgänger, is able to use her fear of her double to aid an ancestor of hers as he struggles to find the "Way," and Margaret discovers the existence of the suicide and shows him how to escape from his desolation.

The words spoken by Pauline in connection with her fear of meeting her double form the focal point around which the movement of the novel revolves: she quotes part of a passage from Shelley's *Prometheus Unbound:*

> Ere Babylon was dust
> The Magus Zoroaster, my dead child,
> Met his own image walking in the garden.
> That apparition, sole of men, he saw.
> For know there are two worlds of life and death:
> One that which thou beholdest; but the other
> Is underneath the grave, where do inhabit
> The shadows of all forms that think and live
> Till death unite them and they part no more;
> Dreams and the light imaginings of men,
> And all that faith creates or love desires
> Terrible, strange, sublime and beauteous shapes
> (Zillman 1959, vol. 1, 193–204)

In this one reference, Williams calls forth biblical echoes of the fall of Babylon, as well as providing a foretaste of the coming theme of supernatural forces impinging upon the natural world. The idea of the "terrible good" to be found in art and theology is evoked and the connection between the two is established. The doppelgänger that haunts Pauline is here, together with the Magus Zoroaster, the priest/magician who will lead the haunted girl toward unity with herself and with the greater good. It is, in all, a marvelous beginning, and though Williams cites only the second and third lines of the passage, it is clear that the whole is to be recalled in the unraveling of patterns in the novel.

In each of Williams's seven novels, there is one character who acts as interpreter—a magus figure—for the rest of the cast, one who explains the theological implications of events in each story. In *Many Dimensions* (1931), the Hajji Ibrahim is the only one present who is able to discern the inner light in Chloë, and to interpret the mystery of the Stone to both the other characters and to the reader. In *The Greater Trumps* (1932), Sybil elucidates the theology of love for her niece Nancy, and in doing so empowers Nancy with that love. In *The Place of the Lion* (1931), Anthony Durrant is given the strength and courage that accompany wisdom, and the power to use that wisdom to save creation. In a sense then, the magus figure functions much like an informative chorus, commenting and acting to a certain extent as narrator. In *Descent Into Hell,* Peter Stanhope fills this role, and I think it significant that Williams chose to employ the name as a pseudonym for himself on more than one occasion.[3] It is significant also that the artist/magician is part of the community rather than outside of, or opposed to it. Williams's ideas of coinherence and the city plot this figure in the center of what could be termed the Great Dance, which includes not only the present (more or less static) world, but also the world of the dead and that of the still unborn. These figures are all characterized by a quiet strength and determination, an easiness and seriousness tempered with an awareness of the ironies in life—in fact, a Christ-likeness, though Williams would never so boldly point out the comparison.[4]

The drama of this novel takes place almost exclusively in a suburb of London: Battle Hill, the site of numerous battles, as its name suggests, as well as the burnings of martyrs, and, more recently, the suicide of a workman engaged in constructing the present development. It is further presented as a space in which the existences of the living and dead are played out in such close proximity as to be inevitably overlapping. Whereas in *Many Dimensions* (1931) the Stone of Solomon is used as the door through which the supernatural enters or is summoned, here the element of the supernatural, with its weight of history, of tragedy and of pain, all contained within the Hill, is portrayed as simply overflowing into the present. Peter Stanhope inhabits a manor house that reaches back through the centuries of blood and futile warring to medieval times. It is in itself a more compact version of the movement of history on the Hill, as Peter is the latest in a long line of Stanhopes and holds within his history the history of his line, including the history of the poor whose labor and starvation provided for his security:

> From other periods of its time other creatures could crawl out of death, and invisibly contemplate the houses and people of the rise. (*Descent Into Hell* 1937, 25–26)

Williams is, of course, suggesting that time does not exist along a continuum—that there is only an eternal now. The passage in the novel beginning with "But if the past. . . ." (25) offers this as a premise which might possibly be entertained, though the rest of the novel is then built on that premise. Events move along at a pace that does not allow one to notice at exactly what point the offered possibility has become an asserted reality.

The Hill, then, is both a physical and a metaphoric space, the backdrop against which the drama is to be played out. It also becomes emblematic of the spiritual heights and valleys that will be traversed by various members of the cast. The suicide, the first spiritual pilgrim presented, is set adrift on a hill which is for him entirely bereft of life, and for a time it is all he asks. The scene of his walking the streets of Battle Hill in an eternal twilight is duplicated to similar effect in *All Hallows' Eve* (1945) where Lester wanders through what appears to her to be a deserted London, under the eye of an unfeeling universe or "republic." Images of light and darkness abound in both novels. The wanderings of the suicide take place under an unwaning moon. Wentworth, too, as Williams's only complete portrait of an individual totally lost to the "Mercy," shrinks from the light more and more as his soul descends on its spiritual ladder. The moon as allied with illusion and evil—the false light of darkness—is continually contrasted with the sun and with its suggestions of truth and goodness. Williams demands that one choose light or darkness eventually, but the suicide is given, for a time, and in recompense for the hell of his life, the luxury of twilight, of a purgatory where the absence of all life is construed as peace for this particular soul. Later on in the novel Margaret Anstruther's climb toward the light and truth that she sees in her visions is conceived of as just that: a physical hauling of oneself up over the rocks, out of the shadows toward the sun. Aspects of this climb will be examined in the following section. The novel's title would seem to suggest that it is wholly concerned with chronicling Wentworth's slow and tortuous descent into his personal version of hell. Like Milton's Satan, Wentworth chooses obstinately to forge for himself a hell—a personal prison. In fact, the novel is neatly balanced in terms of the number of damned and saved. For every Wentworth or Adela there is a Pauline or Margaret. For every descent into the self there is a rise to the world of coinherence and love.

I have mentioned the appropriateness of the name of the suburb in which the novel takes place. The battles here are historic and contemporary, external and internal; much of the imagery used to describe them is conceived of in military terms, most often by Wentworth, who is a military historian. In the battle against Hugh Prescott for Adela, Wentworth is Pompey, willingly blind to the threat

of Caesar. Tortured by his suspicion that Adela and Hugh have fore-
gone an evening with him in order to be by themselves, and consequently unable to concentrate on Pauline's halting attempt to speak
about her doppelgänger, Wentworth tries to turn the defeat into a
triumph by fantasizing that the greater the time she and Hugh spend
together, the more Adela will appreciate Wentworth's superiority.

> He curvetted on that particular horse for a while, and while curvetting
> he took no notice of Pauline's remark until the silence startled his steed
> into nearly throwing him. (*Descent Into Hell,* 48)

Wentworth's language reflects his movement toward self-deception.
In this novel, as in *All Hallows' Eve,* spiritual desolation is revealed
in the breakdown of syntax. Adela herself is drawn into conceiving
of the struggle in terms of war and strategy as she speaks of her
"militant blood" and Hugh is similarly aware of the jostling for
position in this mock battle, though his conception of strategy in
clear, dry terms, without an overabundance of emotion (the narrator
calls him a "brutal realist"), is perhaps what saves him in this and
other contests.

Again, the inference is that it is the atmosphere on the Hill, the
proximity of the dead to the living there, that somehow releases
and intensifies the spiritual struggles going on. It is interesting that
Williams offers the interpretation that these characters suffer from
ordinary neuroses. Even Pauline's double could conceivably be the
result of adolescent fear and loneliness. The lines from Shelley about
the Zoroaster's double were set as a punishment for her at school.
After reading the poetry, Pauline has nightmares and is ill for days.
When as a young girl she had tried to speak to her mother about
her fear of the apparition, her mother's coldness and loathing make
mutual understanding or forgiveness impossible. The question of
whether or not Pauline's apparition actually exists is perhaps an academic one. What is real is Pauline's fear and the paralysis she feels:
"she could respond but she could not act" (*Descent Into Hell,* 52).
The point is that Williams does not insist on a supernatural explanation for this novel. No overt claims about the occult (or about Christianity for that matter) are made, and as a result one is much more
receptive to Williams's narrative persuasion, which allows for doubt,
even while attempting to overcome it.

Kathleen Spencer, in her article on Williams's narrative technique,
suggests that this is accomplished through Williams's "control of
narrative point of view and narrational authority—the reliability of
the source through which readers learn of or experience the fantas-

tic" (Spencer 1987, 66). That is, we are invited to share the characters' incredulity at the events they see. Since those who relate these events have clearly established their position as reliable interpreters, one is apt to accept their views. This does not preclude an explicating of phenomenon in different terms. In fact, a Jungian interpretation has been applied to the work of Williams as a whole with success. Diane McGifford suggests that Pauline's visions of her doppelgänger are a symptom of her psychic immaturity, of her inability to face her other self. Consequently, she lives in terror, without the power of that "other" self. Glen Cavaliero says essentially the same thing when he notes that Pauline's doppelgänger "represents a rejected self . . . [but] . . . there are no sexual or guilt-ridden connotations" (Cavaliero 1983, 81). I am convinced neither of Pauline's guiltless state nor of Williams' innocence in the matter of women and sexuality, but it does seem clear that Pauline's problem is one that concerns existential dread. The choice of Stanhope—the magus figure—as Pauline's savior (or "psychic integrator" or object of sexual desire, depending on one's orientation) is clearly deliberate.

C. N. Manlove, in an article entitled "The Liturgical Novels of Charles Williams," suggests that the formalized action in the novels resembles liturgy "in the sense of 'a form of public worship'" (Manlove 1979, 161–81). This is an intriguing idea in the light of Williams's concentration on art and the artist or priest-figure that has been mentioned earlier. The artistic representation of the cosmic dance in *The Greater Trumps,* the portrait of Simon Le Clerc in *All Hallows' Eve,* and the writers who hold central parts in *War in Heaven* and *Descent Into Hell,* all attest to Williams's belief in the place of art and its alliance with ceremony in working out the mysteries of God. Though Manlove does not says so, it is clear as well that the play in *Descent Into Hell,* and Peter Stanhope as its originator, are to be diagrammatic of the larger context of the novel itself, and of the still larger dance of all existence. The passages in which discussion of the play appears will bear closer scrutiny.

As might be expected, Margaret Anstruther and Peter Stanhope share the same reverence for, and understanding of, the mystery and power contained in poetry. The early scene in which Lily Sammile, Myrtle Fox, Peter Stanhope, Pauline, and her grandmother are all together and discussing Stanhope's play illuminates not only the particular viewpoints of each but also the central importance of the play and each person's involvement in it. Mrs. Sammile, whose name identifies her as a horrifying combination of Lilith and Samael (the personification of evil in rabbinic legend), scoffs at the importance of verse. For her, the only meaning of art is illusion. One "tells oneself tales" in order to deny the importance and effect of reality on the self. "Now if I've a nightmare I change it as soon as I can" (*Descent Into Hell*, 63) she says as she looks at Pauline.

For Myrtle Fox, Williams's rather unkind parody of the typical Evening Institute student, the purpose of art is to console. She objects to Stanhope's refusal to give individual members of the chorus the names of trees and thinks:

> we want to realize that Nature can be consoling, like life. And Art— even Mr. Stanhope's play. I think all art is so consoling, . . . Art ought to be beautiful, don't you think? Beautiful words in beautiful voices. I do think elocution is so important." (*Descent Into Hell*, 62–63)

Myrtle fancies herself a Wordsworthian. "I'm rather mystic about nature" (*Descent Into Hell*, 16) and the passage clearly draws attention to Myrtle's inability to comprehend the meaning of poetry—especially its function as a Way of Affirmation, the way of the poets to God. It is an expression of the truths of existence. Myrtle can hear only the sounds of words; the reality behind the words is lost to her. Stanhope's refusal to "name" his trees seems to me to indicate his desire to expose the *meaning* behind his poetry directly, without language as an intermediary. The cries of the trees are inarticulate; they are direct representations of experience. Pauline's reply to Lily Sammile's offer of perpetual oblivion expresses a similar determination to explore the possibilities of art in the pursuit of truth: "Before she told herself tales, it was needful to know what there was in verse" (65).

Only Margaret and Peter understand fully the implications of the play. It is, as I indicated earlier, simply a graphic representation of the Dance—a perfectly orchestrated movement. And, as Thomas Howard notes, "the name of the dance is Charity, and only the saints really understand it. All evil represents some violating of the steps" (Howard 1983, 185). It expresses the unity that rolls through all things, including the idea of the "terrible good" as perceived by Stanhope. It includes

> the Princess and her lover and the Grand Duke and the farmers and the banditti and the bear; and through the woods went a high medley of wandering beauty and rejoicing love and courtly intelligence and rural laughter and bloody clamour and growling animalism, in mounting complexities of verse, and over all, gathering, opposing, tossing over it, the naughting cry of the all-surrounding and overarching trees. (*Descent Into Hell*, 93)

Williams admired greatly the work of Evelyn Underhill, editing her letters and utilizing some of her theories in his work, especially her attempt to place in context the relation of art to liturgy. In *Worship,* Underhill states:

> When man enters the world of worship, he enters a world which has many of the characteristics of an artistic creation. . . . the poetry and music which enter so largely into expressive worship [should be] recognized as indications of its essential character. The true object of our worship cannot be directly apprehended by us. "No man hath seen God at any time." The representative pattern, the suggestive symbol, the imaginative projection too—all these must be called into play and their limitations humbly accepted if the limited creature is to enter into communion with the Holy and so develop his capacity for adoring love. But the difficulty of our situation is this: none of these devices will be effective unless the worshipper takes them seriously, far more seriously indeed than in their naked factualness they deserve." (Underhill 1962, 37–38)

Stanhope's play is both an offering to God and a means of comprehending his works. When Pauline understands this, she is well on her way to psychic unity—a unity which must include belief in the Mercy (if, like Williams, we are shy of an overtly Christian identification as being an oversimplification). Pauline is the only member of the chorus to be named. She is Periel, presumably a combination of Shakespeare's Ariel and her own name.[5] Indeed, there are structural parallels between the *Tempest* and *Descent Into Hell*. Stanhope/Williams, cast in the role of Prospero/Shakespeare, creates in his masque, through his art, a world in which the poles of human and natural behavior are brought together in the dance. The artist conjures up a vision of things as they *really* are, stripped of the impedimenta culture imposes. In both works the artist acts as the creative moral intelligence. In both, art is a means of bringing men to a realization and acceptance of moral goodness.

For a substantial part of the novel, Pauline is outside the community, rejecting Stanhope's offer of coinherence. But unlike Ariel, she does take part in the final integration of society; as Periel she is akin to Ariel in being a woodland spirit, belonging to "a magic world of song, music, illusion which the artist borrows for his use but which exists externally outside of him" (Craig 1973, 1249). But as Pauline, she ends her part in the play fully integrated and clear about her role.

By the conclusion of the novel, which, appropriately, coincides with the first performance of Stanhope's masque, Pauline understands her place in the drama: "Some great art was in practice and the only business anyone had was to see that his part was perfect" (*Descent Into Hell,* 147) Along with this high joy at the completion of what has become a series of intricate mathematical movements comes a realization of darkness and death. As in *The Place of the Lion* and *War in Heaven,* solutions to the mysteries posed in the novels themselves will be found in literature, by literary characters. It is only Pauline's participation in the *text,* in the reality underlying the words, that brings about salvation for Struther. Contemplating the trumpets of the guards and the shining of their uniforms in the sun, she remembers the woodcut she has seen earlier in Foxe's *Book of Martyrs,* portraying the execution of her ancestor, and experiences the dark night of the soul: "she had been lost in a high marvel, but if that joy were seriously to live it must somehow be reconciled with the agony that had been; unless hollow and shell were one, there was only hollow and shell" (*Descent Into Hell,* 148). That is, unless joy is integrated with fear, the soul's unity will remain in peril.

In an essay on Williams and his relation to Dante, entitled "Charles Williams: a Poet's Critic," Dorothy L. Sayers stresses the importance of the connection between the two strong emotions described in the last quotation.

> In general it remains true that a very strong awareness of horror attends upon any very strong awareness of joy. Note that I say "joy," and not "happinesss"—they are by no means the same thing. Indeed it would scarcely be untrue to say that people of a happy temperament are seldom capable of joy; they are insufficiently sensitive. The word "joy" is a favourite word with Williams, as is the word "gioia" with Dante; beneath the coruscations of that joy, the blackness and squalor of the pit open, and run down to the centre. (Sayers 1963, 84)

The joy Williams speaks of encompasses this dual awareness of the "awefulness" and "terror" encountered in the contemplation of the Ultimate. In fact, Stanhope opens *Descent Into Hell* with a discussion of "terrible goodness," the literal meaning of the Omnipotence.

It was very much in order for Sayers to invoke the name of Dante: Williams's fascination with him is well-known. His books and articles on the *Divine Comedy* are perceptive commentaries on a work which influenced his own development of image patterns and themes. Dante's graphic representation of hell as a funnel with an almost infinite number of gradations, each succeeding the last in depravity, is paralleled in Williams's chronicling of the descent of Wentworth into his personal funnel, as well as in the journey of Margaret over the rocks to the sunlight. Similarly, Williams's development of Lily owes something to his meditations on Dante's Siren in Canto 18 of the *Purgatorio*. Sayers remarks that the song of the Siren mimics Beatrice's later "Look on us well, we are indeed, we are Beatrice" (Sayers 1957, 39).

The Siren is in fact the false Beatrice, "so like the truth that it may deceive the very elect; 'the ape of God'—*diabolus simius Dei*."[6] Wentworth's succubus is of course the false Adela, as Lily Sammile is a false mother—whose promises of safety and happiness are lies. C. S. Lewis suggests that there is a connection between Arthur's incest with his sister Morgause and Wentworth's creation of his succubus. Lewis says that Arthur had met Morgause

> as a "man without eyes" so as not to see that the woman's face was the image of his own face. For that is the horror of incest: it offends against the law of exchange, the strain gives itself not to another strain but only back to itself. It is a physiological image of that far more abominable incest which—calling it Gomorrah—Williams studies in *Descent Into Hell*: that final rejection of all exchange whereby the heart turns to the *succubus* it has itself engendered. (Lewis 1947, 314)

Wentworth's succubus fulfills his every desire and talks to him in his own language with apparent lucidity, but not because it is a separate entity with intelligence and beauty of its own, but simply because it is *himself*.

Wentworth's journey toward "Eden" with his hellish guide forms an ironic parallel to Dante's journey with Virgil toward enlightenment, and Williams deliberately points out this correspondence as he describes Wentworth's demented anger at seeing the form of the suicide plodding toward him. The presence of the suicide here denies Wentworth's creation of a perfect, static world. But the tormented form comes on "inexorably advancing as the glory of truth that broke out of the very air itself upon the agonized Florentine in the Paradise of Eden: 'ben sem, ben sem, Beatrice.' . . ." (*Descent Into Hell*, 88). The two forms are linked by their habitation of the same house. Wentworth's home is the house the suicide was building when he took his own life. The rope he hanged himself with appears in Wentworth's dreams, and Wentworth's progress down its length becomes emblematic of the extent of his spiritual desolation. The suicide is helped toward heaven by Margaret and Pauline; Wentworth is helped toward damnation by Lilith.

Williams carries forward the image of the false creation of a new "eden" in both the title of chapter 5, "Return to Eden"—and in his diction throughout the novel. The opening sentence of the third paragraph in this chapter is a direct borrowing from Gen. 1:5 ("The evening and the morning. . . ."). Biblical imagery and language are so prevalent that the entire novel can be seen on one level as a biblical epic which includes a Creation myth, an Armageddon (the hill of Megiddo), the passage of souls both to Heaven and to hell, the fall of Babylon, and the Second Coming and Revelation of God, together with a description of the last plagues. The allegory falls apart if looked at too closely; it is the essence of Christian quest narratives that remains.

Wentworth's "Adela" leads him into the "faint green light, light of a forest" (*Descent Into Hell,* 85), into a secret garden whose gate he shuts and bolts against the "outside," saying "I won't go back" (85).[7] This Dantean image heralds Wentworth's decision to enclose himself in an "eden" of his own devising, with Lilith, Adam's first wife, as companion under the watchful moon. Dante's dark wood becomes Wentworth's refuge from coinherence, his death-in-life. It is significant that Wentworth cannot call his succubus "Adela," since "the name [is] something actual, sacramental of reality" (*Descent Into Hell,* 136). Again, the name *is* the object; somewhere beneath Wentworth's dementia he realizes that to call his creature "Adela" is to admit his crime, his lie against reality.

Dorothy Sayers quotes John Heath-Stubbs's remark concerning the place of nature in Williams's poetry: "landscapes are always emblematic of states of mind" (Sayers 1963 76). In Williams's prose, too, this tendency is apparent. So Wentworth's experience in the depths of the hill, winding down ever further under the earth, is linked with his spiritual movement toward madness and parallels his dream of climbing down an endless, coiling rope to an unknown destination.

The image of Battle Hill in its various forms is one that pervades and unites the narrative: an investigation of one character's experience of the hill will serve as an example of Williams's keen ability in exploitation of image/symbol. Margaret Anstruther (Anstruther, appropriately enough, is Scots-Gaelic for "stream") feels most acutely the proximity of the dead to the living on the Hill, being so close to death herself and understanding the ideas of death and life as simply stages on the Way rather than concepts worlds apart. As she moves closer to death, temporal and spatial distances converge, and "by a natural law Margaret's spirit exercised freely its supernatural functions and with increasing clearness looked out on to the growing company of the Hill" (*Descent Into Hell,* 69). She sees the Hill as a microcosm—sees in her visions its populace scurrying about, though it is significant that the only one of her acquaintances that she does not see is Lily. The Lilith figure is clearly not a part of the movement toward salvation or damnation; she is "other."

The linear movements Williams describes in this novel exclude Lilith, who scurries (patters) in a diagonal motion from one crevasse to another, constantly seeking out the "dark places."

Margaret sees, then, a mountainlike terrain and a light which is self-radiating. She hears small sounds of climbing over the natural sounds of streams and the roar of wind in the chasms. The clock strikes one, dawn breaks, and the light gathers over the mountains— and as it does the sounds of climbing grow louder, Margaret differentiating between those climbing toward the light, as she does, and those who hide from it.

The passage ends with Margaret determining to crawl toward the light, to meet the beams coming to meet her. The process is a humbling, tortuous, frightening one. Williams imagines the souls, belly to the earth, making their slow way over the rocks, but what is more striking is the description of the souls who hide from the light—as Wentworth undoubtedly does from the outset. Margaret is given a vision of the past, of the present and of the future, in fulfillment of Williams's idea of all time existing at one point of eternity: "time is not the most important element in existence; it is rather the subservient element by which man 'becomes'" (Underhill 1962).

Margaret hears footsteps in the first of Dante's circles, hurrying, pattering with hard heels upon the sidewalk. They are clearly those of Lily/Lilith, forever searching and restless in random movement upon the threshold of that "other" world,

> hurrying, hurrying for fear of time growing together, and squeezing her out, out of the interstices, of time where she lived, locust in the rock; . . . (*Descent Into Hell*, 89)

Williams's language reflects the frantic activity of Lilith. His short phrases and repetitions of words evoke the terrified being, forever moving, and inevitably moving downward, deeper into hell. The image of hurrying footsteps is expanded to include Wentworth sitting tensely, torturing himself with listening for the mocking sound of Hugh and Adela walking together on the pavement, until the intolerable knowledge of their relationship is replaced with the sound of the footsteps of Lily/Adela, the false comforter.

Margaret's journey over the rocks continues as she observes the confused but hopeful wanderings of the suicide and the form of Pauline which will help to release him by taking literally St. John's advice to his followers: bear ye one another's burdens. Again, this spiritual terrain is employed by Williams as an extended metaphor for the passage of the soul, regardless of time and space, toward salvation or damnation. Near the close of Margaret's journey the narrator relates her sensation of lying on the surface of the mountain, aware of Pauline "coming over the rock through a door of great stones like Stonehenge" (*Descent Into Hell,* 121) and of the necessity of clinging to the surface of the mountain. The Stonehenge note draws together the idea of worship, of passage into another state, of rock and ancient mysteries, of the search for light and truth associated with the ancient priests of Stonehenge, as well as the recurring image of one figure or another being confronted with a gate which symbolizes a movement toward salvation or damnation. The same idea appears again in *The Place of the Lion* and in *War in Heaven* and is intimately connected with the idea of Christ being the "gate and the light." The marvelous thing in these images is not their originality; they are, after all, standard images, easily recognized, but they are so clotted, so packed together that their sheer weight is impressive.

Chapter 5 ends with the moment of salvation of the suicide, blended by Williams with an echo of Christ's suffering and atonement made immediate and real. Glen Cavaliero comments: "Nowhere does Williams more boldly express his belief in the interpenetration of physical and spiritual. The hill of Golgotha, Battle Hill and the mountain on which Margaret moves are one with the place of exchange where hangs the central mystery of Christendom" (Cavaliero 1983, 89). Similarly, Pauline's experience in confronting her own fears as she confronts her ancestor, Struther, provides Williams with one more opportunity to demonstrate the profundity of the doctrine of coinherence.

As Margaret makes her deliberate way across the rocks, Wentworth moves in ever narrowing circles down the hill toward darkness and oblivion. He begins to walk at night with his Adela through the low, dark streets of the Hill. His dreams of descending on his rope explode with the terrible groaning of the abyss below and above him; one is surely to be reminded of the void so powerfully evoked in Dante's *Inferno*. The groaning is of Prometheus and of Christ and of the suicide, and contains within it all the pain of atonement and regret for the lost. By the conclusion of the novel, the assimilation of Battle Hill into the metaphoric hill of Margaret's journey is complete: Pauline sees Margaret smile at her across the surface of the rocks, shadows engulf the streets, and roads lie like great slashes down a mountain. The earthquake that accompanies this groaning parallels the earthquake Dante hears in Cantos 20 and

21 of the *Purgatorio,* where the sound signals the release of a soul from Purgatory:

> But when some spirit, feeling purged and sound,
> Leaps up or moves to seek a loftier station,
> The whole mount quakes and the great shouts resound.
> The will itself attests its own purgation;
> Amazed, the soul that's free to change its inn
> Finds its mere will suffice for liberation;
> (Sayers 1955, 58–63)

There are areas of darkness, but the sun seeks out those who hide. The earthquake marks both the passage of the soul through purgatory, and the groaning of souls left to languish in the lower realms. Again, the duality of the novel's imagery reflects the duality inherent in the basic tenets of Christianity.

Descent Into Hell is remarkable for the coherence of its vision, and here too Williams manages a relatively clear explanation of his own attitude toward language and art, which he expands in his next novel, *All Hallows' Eve* (1945). Caught up in Stanhope's verse, Pauline

> recognized the awful space of separating stillness which all mighty art creates about itself, or, uncreating, makes clear to mortal apprehension. . . . That living stillness had gathered the girl into her communion with the dead. . . . (*Descent Into Hell,* 80)

An appropriate quotation with which to end this discussion; Williams's belief in the efficacy of language, in its sacramental power embodied in poetry, is what facilitates Pauline's return to health, and what ensures the final damnation of Wentworth.

Valentine Cunningham in *British Writers of the Thirties* is quite right when he accuses the thirties' Christian artists of a refusal to engage with the politics of the time (if they do so, it tends to be Fascist politics). Writers like C. S. Lewis, Tolkien, and Williams (and Eliot, Greene, and Waugh more successfully) were more interested in what they regarded as the fundamentals of spirituality and therefore of life itself: how to perceive and articulate the propensity for evil in society. Williams especially makes palpable the thin curtain separating "good" from "evil," Christian charity and modern self-serving in a form designed to popularize belief. Not always elegant, much less clear, Williams remains interesting for this reason.

Notes

1. Williams wrote an appreciation of Eliot's poetry in a volume entitled *Poetry at Present,* while declaring his inability to understand it. There is evidence that Eliot

read Williams's novels, and owes the "still point of the turning world" in *Burnt Norton* to the character of the Fool in Williams's novel *The Greater Trumps*.

2. Williams evolved a personal terminology for certain theological—philosophical concepts: specifically, (1) romantic theology, (2) the city, and (3) coinherence. (1) Following Dante, Williams regards the act of falling in love as one which can, and should, lead the lover to a proper contemplation and acceptance of the love of God for man. What Williams calls the "Beatrician experience," that first blinding realization of the power of love, is the lover's chance to see the world as the poet sees it and "he beholds 'the physiological glory.'" (Glen Cavaliero, *Charles Williams: Poet of Theology* (Grand Rapids, Mich.: Eerdmans, 1983), 134. But if the lover stops there, if the vision turns back on itself, then he risks entering one of Dante's circles of hell—the abode of luxuria. In the novels, romantic, specifically married, love, illustrates Williams's thesis. (2)Williams calls the city "that clear communion of intelligences." (Mary McDermott Shideler, *The Theology of Romantic Love: A Study in the Writings of Charles Williams* [New York: Harper, 1962], 126) What he is referring to is simply the community of Christ. All activity takes place in the city, and the choices men make are in reality choices through which they include or exclude themselves from this city. For Williams, the city of London seemed to take on the external characteristics of his metaphoric city. As a result, his novels take place exclusively within the general vicinity of London. (3) Williams uses as a model the coinherence (exchange) of the Father and the Word, which produces the Son, to explain the intimate interconnection which exists between men. We are all spiritually allied, and it is our duty to recognize and use this alliance to help one another on the journey toward what Williams would call the Unity. In practical terms, coinherence makes possible the literal sharing of psychic burdens between individuals. Thus Peter Stanhope, in *Descent Into Hell,* consciously decides to carry Pauline Anstruther's fear for her, in order that she may be free to carry the terror of her ancestor, Struther. Since all times exist at one point in Williams's universe, coinherence and exchange can be performed forward and backward in time and by both the dead and the living.

3. Alice Mary Hadfield notes that Williams used this name on the title page of *Judgement at Chelmsford,* as well as in personal letters (Hadfield, *Charles Williams: An Exploration of His Life and Work* (Oxford: Oxford University Press, 1983), 142).

4. Dorothy L. Sayers notes that Williams's interpreters are basically ordinary, middle-class Londoners:

> "There is here, in these poets of the Affirmation, a strong resistance to all that conception of the metaphysical which we conveniently call Gnosticism—the idea that the supreme supernatural experiences are confined to particular persons, secret cliques, groups of initiates, addicts of hidden mysteries. The mystery of God is an open secret, available to all, yet manifesting itself with an almost inscrutable singularity to persons chosen, it would seem, almost at random. Sayers, *Further Papers on Dante* (London: Methuen, 1957), 199–200.

5. Williams's naming of characters is very deliberate, and the names often provide individuals with a "readymade background," based on the philosophical or literary connotations embodied in the name. Thus Pauline Anstruther is a "Pauline" character, in that her experience of coinherence and exchange is exactly what St. Paul in the Letter to the Galatians asked his church to cultivate: "Bear ye one another's burdens." As for Periel, Pauline's other name, Colman O'Hare notes that Periel appears as an Archangel's name in Rolfe's *Hadrian the Seventh* (1904), 13. In "Peter Stanhope" one hears echoes of St. Peter, and Christ's declaration that upon the rock

(Peter, st-an) would the church be built, the hope of men. The biblical echoes further reinforce Stanhope's patriarchal, priestly function in the novel.

6. Sayers, *Further Papers on Dante,* 139. In her notes on the Siren in the *Purgatorio* Sayers points to *Descent Into Hell* as "a brilliant expansion and interpretation of the theme of Dante's dream of the Siren." The Siren is, Sayers says, "at first sight unattractive; she only acquires strength and beauty from Dante's own gaze. She is, therefore, the projection upon the outer world of something in the mind: the soul, falling in love with itself, perceives other people and things, not as they are, but as wish-fulfillments of its own: i.e. its love for them is not love for a 'true other' . . . but a devouring egotistical fantasy, by absorption in which the personality rots away into illusion" (Sayers, trans., *The Comedy of Dante Alighieri, The Florentine: Cantica II: Purgatory* (New York:Penguin, 1955), 220–21).

7. Compare Pauline's refusal to go through the gate held open to her by Lily Sammile. "She flung the gate shut, and snatched her hands away, and as it clanged she was standing upright, her body a guard flung out on the frontier of her soul" (*Descent Into Hell,* 111).

Works Cited

Carpenter, Humphrey. 1978. *The Inklings: C. S. Lewis, J.R.R. Tolkien, Charles Williams, and Their Friends.* London: Unwin.

Cavaliero, Glen. 1983. *Charles Williams: Poet of Theology.* Grand Rapids, Mich.: Eerdmans.

Craig, Hardin and David Bevington. 1993. Preface to Tempest in *The Complete Works of Shakespeare,* rev. ed. Glenview, Ill.: Scott, Foresman, 1249.

Cunningham, Valentine. 1988. *British Writers of the Thirties.* Oxford University Press.

Hadfield, Alice Mary. 1983. *Charles Williams: An Exploration of His Life and Work.* Oxford: Oxford University Press.

Howard, Thomas. 1983. *The Novels of Charles Williams.* New York: Oxford University Press.

La Lande, Sr. M. 1963. "Williams' Pattern of Time in *Descent Into Hell.*" *Renascence* 15:88–95.

Lewis, C. S. "Williams and the Arthuriad." In *Essays Presented to Charles Williams.* 1947; Grand Rapids, Mich.: Eerdmans, 1966.

Manlove, C. N. 1979. "The Liturgical Novels of Charles Williams." *Mosaic* 12, no. 2:161–81.

O'Hare, Colman. 1973. *Charles Williams, C. S. Lewis, and J.R.R. Tolkien: Three Approaches to Religion in Modern Fiction.* Diss. University of Toronto.

Sayers, Dorothy L. 1963. "Charles Williams: A Poet's Critic." In *The Poetry of Search and the Poetry of Statement, and Other Posthumous Essays on Literature, Religion, and Language.* London: Gollancz.

McGifford, Diane. 1979. "Eros and Logos: The Androgynous Vision in the Mythic Narratives of Charles Williams." Ph.D. diss., University of Manitoba.

———. 1955. trans. *The Comedy of Dante Alighieri: The Florentine (Cantica II: Purgatory).* New York: Penguin.

———. 1957. *Further Papers on Dante.* London: Methuen.

Shideler, Mary McDermot. 1962. *The Theology of Romantic Love: A Study in the Writings of Charles Williams.* New York: Harper & Row, Publishers.

Spencer, Kathleen. 1987. "Naturalizing the Fantastic: Narrative Technique in the Novels of Charles Williams." *Extrapolation* 28, no. 1:62–74.

Underhhill, Evelyn. 1962. *Worship*. London: Collins.

Williams, Charles. 1981. *All Hallows Eve*. Grand Rapids, Mich.: Eerdmans, 1981.

Zillman, Lawrence John. 1954. *Shelley's Prometheus Unbound: A Variorum Edition*. Seattle: University of Washington Press.

A Bibliography of Works by and about Charles Williams

Major publications in the 1930s

———. 1930. *Poetry at Present*. Oxford: Clarendon.

———. 1930, 1965. *War In Heaven*. Grand Rapids, Mich.: Eerdmans.

———. 1931, 1965. *Many Dimensions*. Grand Rapids, Mich.: Eerdmans.

———. 1931. *The Place of the Lion*. Grand Rapids, Mich.: Eerdmans.

———. 1932. *The English Poetic Mind*. Oxford: Clarendon.

———. 1932, 1976. *The Greater Trumps*. Grand Rapids, Mich.: Eerdmans.

———. 1933, 1965. *Shadows of Ecstasy*. Grand Rapids, Mich.: Eerdmans.

———. 1933. *Reason and Beauty in the Poetic Mind*. Oxford: Clarendon Press.

———. 1937, 1965. *Descent Into Hell*. Grand Rapids, Mich.: Eerdmans.

———. 1938, 1984. *He Came Down from Heaven*. Grand Rapids, Mich.: Eerdmans.

———. 1938, 1972. *Taliessin Through Logres*. London: Oxford.

———. 1939, 1980. *The Descent of the Dove: A Short History of the Holy Spirit in the Church*. Grand Rapids, Mich.: Eerdmans.

Carpenter, Humphrey. 1978. *The Inklings: C.S. Lewis, J.R.R. Tolkien, Charles Williams, and Their Friends*. London: Unwin.

Cavaliero, Glen. 1983. *Charles Williams: Poet of Theology*. Grand Rapids, Mich.: Eerdmans.

Davidson, Clifford. 1968. *"All Hallows' Eve:* The Way of Perversity." *Renascence* 20:86–93.

Glenn, Lois. 1975. *Charles W.S. Williams: A Checklist*. Kent State University Press.

Hadfield, Alice Mary. 1983. *Charles Williams: An Exploration of His Life and Work*. Oxford: Oxford University Press.

Holder, Robert C. 1975. "Art and the Artist in the Fiction of Charles Williams." *Renascence* 27:81-87.

Howard, Thomas. 1983. *The Novels of Charles Williams*. New York: Oxford University Press.

Manlove, C. N. 1979. "The Liturgical Novels of Charles Williams." *Mosaic* 12, no. 2:161-81.

Moorman, Charles. 1982. "Sacramentalism in Charles Williams." *The Chesterton Review* 7, no. 1:35–50.

Spencer, Kathleen. 1987. "Naturalizing the Fantastic: Narrative Technique in the Novels of Charles Williams." *Extrapolation* 28, no. 1:62–74.

Tilley, Elizabeth. 1992. "Uncreating Sound: Language in Charles Williams' *All Hallows' Eve*." *Renascence* 44, no. 4:303-19.

17

Jean Rhys: Composition in Shadows and Surfaces

Luisa Maria Rodrigues Flora

A Brief Biographical Sketch of Jean Rhys (1890–1979)

JEAN RHYS ALIAS ELLA GWENDOLEN REES WILLIAMS, BORN 24 AUGUST 1890 in Roseau, Dominica; died 14 May 1979 in Exeter, United Kingdom, was a novelist and short story writer. Daughter of a Welsh doctor and a Dominican of Scottish ascent, Jean always "loved the sound of words." In 1907 she left to go to England and in 1909 started work as a chorus girl. Alone in 1912 after a passionate affair with Lancelot Hugh Smith, she married in 1919 the writer and chansonnier Jean Lenglet with whom she had a son (who died three weeks old) and a daughter. They wandered around Europe, staying mainly in Paris. In 1924 Ford Madox Ford encouraged her to discipline her style, and, after the end of their liaison, prefaced her first book of short stories—*The Left Bank: Sketches and Studies of Present-Day Bohemian Paris* (1927). Her first published novel, *Quartet,* appeared in 1928 as *Postures.* Back in England, she divorced Lenglet (1933) and married Leslie Tilden-Smith. The thirties would be Rhys's most productive period. She wrote and published *After Leaving Mr. Mackenzie* (1931), *Voyage in the Dark* (1934), *Good Morning, Midnight* (1939) as well as several short stories later to be printed. Fighting poverty, alcoholism, and depression, Rhys worked throughout the decade with the occasional *succès d'estime (Voyage in the Dark).* For the next twenty years she would remain silent, almost unable to write. After Leslie's death (1945), Jean married Max Hamer (1947) who died in 1966. The 1958 radio adaptation of *Good Morning, Midnight* reminded the literary world that she was alive, encouraging her to go back to a long-cherished project—*Wide Sar-*

gasso Sea (1966). Its success (W. H. Smith Prize and Royal Society of Literature Award in 1966), guaranteed the reprinting of all her works and two further collections of short stories *Tigers Are Better-Looking* (1968) and *Sleep It Off, Lady* (1976). Rhys was made a Fellow of the Royal Society of Literature in 1966 and a Commander of the British Empire in 1978. *Smile Please, An Unfinished Autobiography* was posthumously published in 1979. *Jean Rhys: Letters 1931–1966* were edited by Francis Wyndham and Diana Melly in 1984.

* * * * *

Walking in the night with the dark houses over you, like monsters. If you have money and friends, houses are just houses with steps and a front-door—friendly houses where the door opens and somebody meets you, smiling. If you are quite secure and your roots are well struck in, they know. They stand back respectfully, waiting for the poor devil without any friends and without any money. Then they step forward, the waiting houses, to frown and crush. No hospitable doors, no lit windows, just frowning darkness. Frowning and leering and sneering, the houses, one after another. Tall cubes of darkness, with two lighted eyes at the top to sneer. And they know who to frown at. They know as well as the policeman on the corner, and don't you worry. . . .
—Jean Rhys, *Good Morning, Midnight* (1939)

"The poor devil without any friends and without any money" probably stands as the typical Rhys figure in any brief study of her fiction and some echo of Ford Madox Ford's remark in 1927 that she had a "terrific—almost lurid!—passion for stating the case of the underdog" (Ford 1984, 24) usually comes next. The assertion is then qualified by adding that the underdog is more often than not an "underbitch", possibly followed by a celebration of Rhys's work as an impressive case of the war of the sexes as fought in the battlefields of literature.

While I do not wish to challenge such unquestionable tenets of most criticism on Jean Rhys's fiction, I believe we will do more justice to her talent as a writer if we attempt to reveal what lies underneath the obvious issues.[1] It certainly is undeniable that in her novels and short stories Rhys wrote again and again about the vulnerable passive victimized woman who eventually acquired the position of "paradigmatic" Rhys heroine—what has sometimes been neglected is the technical skill that went into her creation. Helpless and self-absorbed, the fragile isolated female has too easily been taken for the writer herself. Displaced and self-centered as Rhys may have been, her literary voice goes far beyond a disquieting auto-biography. Although there often is a painful closeness between Rhys's troubled existence and her unsettling texts, we should never reduce (as Carole Angier persuasively shows in her biography) the complexity of the writer's plight to an unequivocal depiction of her life. Her heroines will court suicide or at least some form of self-destruction and so apparently did the author, still, as Thomas Staley reminds us,

> Rhys's creative energy is in itself a force against the world which her art depicts. The dislocating and disturbing impulses, the absence of moral order, the failure of the will except for mere survival, these conditions become sources of energy for her art, for rather than repress them she confronts the dark image of life they impose.[2]

By developing "the syntax and vocabulary needed to bridge the gap between the outcast and society" (Wilson 1986, 442), Jean Rhys persisted throughout her work in transfiguring her experience into the spare understated prose which so effectively articulates the long suppressed speech of all those who do not conform to conventional values, all those who seem doomed to drift along life virtually home-less and barely surviving on the margins. She released them from silence and in so doing gave voice to "an area of society, a type of person, not yet admitted to the general literate consciousness" (Lessing 1973, 79).

The cultural and political significance of Rhys's achievement should not be misread as a deliberate effort to open the gates of the literary citadel to deserted women and classless drifters. Her lifelong struggle with words was intimately connected with her own conflict with living. First and foremost she was anxious to cross the wide sea that from earliest childhood she had felt divided her from other people. In stubbornly pursuing her difference, in transforming it into fiction Rhys was seeking her own form of redemption. As she confided to one of her diaries:

> I must write. If I stop writing my life will have been an abject failure. It is that already to other people. But it could be an abject failure to myself. I will not have earned death. (*Smile Please, An Unfinished Autobi-ography* 1979, 163)[3]

The avowed absence of any political intention in Rhys's work does not preclude a reading of her fiction as a critique of sexual and social politics and both *Voyage in the Dark* (1934) and *Wide Sargasso Sea* (1966) have also been studied as novels of postcolonial discourse.[4]

My choice of *Good Morning, Midnight* to represent Rhys's writing in this volume rests on the assumption that her third and last novel of the decade is not only her best work before *Wide Sargasso Sea* but also a powerful metaphor for a cultural situation.[5] Displaying a more mature approach than former texts to the characteristic Rhys style, the novel evokes the nightmarish atmosphere of the thirties' experience. Written under the shadow of war, it conveys both the crisis within the narrator/protagonist and a feeling of widespread neurosis and fatal listlessness.

* * * * *

In the development of the themes and techniques which distinguish Rhys's prose from the very beginning and which Ford so early recognized, *Good Morning, Midnight*[6] stands out as an example of a carefully disciplined narrative capable of building for the reader a coherent puzzle out of the succession of disconnected images and random memories that haunt the narrator/protagonist Sasha Jansen.

> "I unroll the picture and the man standing in the gutter, playing his banjo, stares at me. He is gentle, humble, resigned, mocking, a little mad. He stares at me. He is double-headed, doubled-faced. He is singing 'It has been', singing 'It will be'. Double-headed and with four arms. . . . I stare back at him and think about being hungry, being cold, being hurt, being ridiculed, as if it were in another life than this.
>
> This damned room—it's saturated with the past. . . . It's all the rooms I've ever slept in, all the streets I've ever walked in. Now the whole thing moves in an ordered, undulating procession past my eyes. Rooms, streets, streets, rooms. . . ." (*Good Morning Midnight*, 91)

The "double-headed, doubled-faced" figure of the "old Jew" (*Good Morning Midnight*, 83) and the whole picture in its grotesque expressionistic distortion are adequate images for the first-person narrator's strong feeling of destitution and humiliation as well as for the duality of perception recurrent throughout the novel.[7] Sasha Jansen is a self-consciously neurotic character and the narrative plays on the permanent dissociation within the protagonist's split mind. Zigzagging between consciousness and underconsciousness, between her past life and her present state of imminent breakdown, between flashbacks and flash-forwards, between interior monologue and direct addresses to the reader, Sasha the narrator builds the whole text as a succession of different times (the ghosts of past emotions, "shadows of past selves and spectres of future ones" (Sage 1992, 49), of multiple separate planes whose interaction will eventually structure *Good Morning, Midnight*. As often in Rhys's fiction, there is no linear chronology—episodes flow along the text creating through narrative discontinuity a form of time dissolution and just as often this dissolution is intimately related to the question of identity. Figures with no background, drifting from room to room, never certain of their personal identity, sometimes not even sure of when they have changed their names—"Was it in 1923 or 1924 (. . .) that I started calling myself Sasha. I thought it might change my luck if I changed my name"(*Good Morning Midnight,* 11)[8]—wander through the novelist's pages, friendless moneyless self-exiled beings—in their hand-to-mouth existence these heroines show no control over their destinies, not knowing how to play by other people's rules or knowing "only too well" (88) and putting on a precarious mask, they feel a certain pride in their eternally displaced condition. Living in a world almost totally isolated from any human contact—"The touch of the human hand. . . . I'd forgotten what it was like, the touch of the human hand." (84)—they persistently refuse to abandon their stubborn freedom from social ties. Yet, as Paula Le Gallez successfully proved, Sasha Jansen is totally in control of her narrative and as a character she even "finds the power to inflict pain" (Le Gallez 1990, 135). In spite of her lack of a "proper" social identity—consider, for instance, the episode of the passport (*Good Morning Midnight,* 13–14), the two Russians' initial difficulty in placing her (39–40) or her going back to her family who considered her "as dead" (36–37)—in spite of her inability to "put everything on the same plane" (12), in spite of her impotence to "purchase from sorrow a moment's respite" (97), above all in spite of her gradual descent toward self-destruction, the narrator of *Good Morning, Midnight* does have the capacity to produce out of the chaos of her inner self a text "powered with a (. . .) moral passion strong enough to create order" (Lessing 1973, 80).

The narrative strategy of editing separate time sequences and distinct moments of Sasha's past and present experience as a consecutive whole is clearly reminiscent of the cinematic technique of the montage. In both cases the meaning of the final work does not result from the words or images being used but from the tension established among the diverse elements, from their manifold interaction—the whole is not to be mistaken for the sum of its constituent parts—creating a qualitatively different unity. As Sergei Eisenstein explained:

The point is that (. . .) the combination of two hieroglyphs of the simplest series is to be regarded not as their sum, but as their product, i.e., as a value of another dimension, another degree; each, separately, corresponds to an *object,* to a fact, but their combination corresponds to a *concept.* From separate hieroglyphs has been fused—the ideogram. By the combination of two 'depictables' is achieved the representation of something that is graphically undepictable (Eisenstein 1949, 29–30)

Montage thus functions as a decisive structural principle of film technique and its metaphorical possibilities—"a means of achieving a unity of a higher order . . ."(254)—become evident. Likewise the overall pattern of *Good Morning, Midnight* echoes the basic methods of film montage and its structure could be a novelistic interpretation of Eisenstein's commentary.[9] By valuing the whole instead of the referential quality of each of its parts it refuses any direct or linear interpretation of the text, it enhances the deeper significance of each and every passage within the complete narrative and builds for the reader a novel which is finally much more complex and metaphorically productive than the sum of its (at first seemingly disconnected) fragments. When we finish reading the text all the crucial information is clear enough—"the whole thing moves in an ordered, undulating procession past" the readers' eyes: the time and place of the present action—the modern Paris sequence develops along five days (*Good Morning Midnight,* 9, 154)—the essential background of Sasha since early womanhood, her marriage after the First World War, the death of her infant son (49–52, 116) and the desertion by her husband, her subsequent slow process of disintegration.

> Only, it was after that that I began to go to pieces. Not all at once, of course. First this happened, and then that happened. . . . (*Good Morning Midnight,* 119)

And we get to know her deep-seated resilience which, as it will later be manifest, proves fundamental to the whole narrative.

> Next week, or next month, or next year I'll kill myself. But I might as well last out my month's rent, which has been paid up, and my credit for breakfasts in the morning. (*Good Morning Midnight,* 72)

The "double-headed, doubled-faced" figure of Sasha, her split personality,[10] contributes to structure *Good Morning, Midnight* by creating the essential doubleness of vision that arises as much from the continuous interplay between past and present as from her dual quality as both narrator and character. Her existence as a double also strongly echoes the German expressionist film tradition with its insistence on "Jekyll-and-Hyde" characters (from Caligari to Mabuse) and the recurrent (personal, social, political) menace introduced by insanity. Indeed the whole novel in its imagery, atmosphere, and use of perspective comes remarkably close to expressionism.[11] Walking in the streets of Paris in "late October 1937" (*Good Morning Midnight,* 76) the narrator/protagonist, on the verge of internal disintegration, suffers the urban landscape as a threat: "Then they step forward, the waiting houses, to frown and crush. (. . .) just frowning darkness" (28).

The distorted perspective turns the houses into beasts preparing in the dark their assault on a defenseless prey. As the text makes clear, their menacing quality derives from their paradoxically human attitudes and the personification magnifies the cruelty of society's attack on the helpless victim.

> Frowning and leering and sneering, (. . .). Tall cubes of darkness, with two lighted eyes at the top to sneer. And they know who to frown at. (. . .) as well as the policeman on the corner, . . . (*Good Morning Midnight,* 28)

The narrator's "deformed view" (*Good Morning Midnight,* 41) gives the houses yet another and ultimately more threatening quality: they have a grotesque mechanical character as if they are automata, *man-made* "monsters"—"Tall cubes . . . with two lighted eyes at the top." This sort of imagery often returns in the novel not as the celebration of technological progress or the futuristic joy of the machine but as a defeated statement of a condition where people move like mannequins while dressmakers' dummies "acquire" human prospects:

> watching those damned dolls, thinking what a success they would have made of their lives if they had been women. Satin skin, silk hair, velvet eyes, sawdust heart—all complete." (*Good Morning Midnight,* 18)

This feeling of impending dehumanization and the sweeping atmosphere of artificiality are enhanced by the obsessive recurrence of masks, disguises, and performing acts that accompany Sasha Jansen throughout the novel as she desperately tries to escape the haunting past and to find her way out of the impasse her life has come to. But the machine theme reaches its climax near the end.

> All that is left in the world is an enormous machine, made of white steel. It has innumerable flexible arms, made of steel. Long, thin arms. At the end of each arm is an eye, the eyelashes stiff with mascara. When I look more closely I see that only some of the arms have these eyes—others

have lights. The arms that carry the eyes and the arms that carry the lights are all extraordinarily flexible and very beautiful. But the grey sky, which is the background, terrifies me. . . . (*Good Morning Midnight,* 156)

The mechanical imagery and the ominously seductive quality of the steel beast that allures the heroine, the recurrence of dark gloomy shadows, the distorted perspective that often harries the protagonist, the sinister feeling that comes to pervade the whole physical space, the pessimistic world view, the *huis clos* atmosphere that the novel builds from the very beginning, the premonition of emergent currents of hatred arising from the depths of the human mind, the violent contrast between surface passivity and underneath brutality, the anticipation of destruction and death, all these characteristics support my assertion that *Good Morning, Midnight* establishes a particularly intimate relationship with the tradition of expressionist cinema and offers the readers a disquieting metaphor of contemporary life.

Good Morning, Midnight also shares with the European cultural ethos of the bleak period between the two world wars another legacy which lies close to expressionism—the legacy of Kafka.[12] In Rhys's fiction "all the fools and all the defeated" (*Good Morning Midnight,* 25) share the terrible condition of drifting through life as through a nightmare. The Kafkaesque situation of an innocent person being threatened and persecuted as a criminal is common in her novels and short stories and Sasha Jansen is its most forceful instance.

> I turn to the right, walk along another passage, down a flight of stairs. The workrooms. . . . No, I can't ask here. All the girls will stare at me. I shall seem such a fool.
> I try another passage. It ends in a lavatory. The number of lavatories in this place, c'est inoui. . . . I turn the corner, find myself back in the original passage and collide with a strange young man. He gives me a nasty look. [. . .]
> After this it becomes a nightmare. I walk up stairs, past doors, along passages—all different, all exactly alike. There is something very urgent that I must do. But I don't meet a soul and all the doors are shut.
> This can't go on. (*Good Morning Midnight,* 23)

Houses, passages, stairs, rooms, walls, shut doors, dead end streets—Sasha the "hopeless, helpless little fool" (*Good Morning Midnight,* 25) cannot find her way through life's labyrinth: "North, south, east, west—they have no meaning for me. . . ." (26)

Yet, as I hope will become clear from my interpretation of Rhys's metamorphosis of Sasha the vulnerable passive victim into the violent narrating character that has the power to inflict pain and destruction, the innocent is ultimately as guilty of cruelty and lack of human sympathy as the menacing seductive steel machine.

The montage technique that the author devised to build the whole novel also enables the narrator to form Sasha as a character. As usual in Rhys's style, *Good Morning, Midnight* uses the same spare prose, the same skillful combination of objectively rendered dialogue with the interior monologue of the heroine's consciousness, the broken language, and the accumulation of "orts, scraps and fragments" (Woolf 1978, 156), above all, the dismantling of a traditional presentation of character by the blending of bits of heard conversation with what the protagonist silently experiences. Such narrative strategies convey the heroines' social surface in contrast with the feelings hidden from their passing acquaintances, emphasizing their essential isolation. Sasha is both first-person narrator and character but, as the text moves on, she learns the courage to voice (to narrate) what she had formerly silenced—she faces the wolf within herself and recognizes that she is just as capable of hatred and cruelty as "the wolves outside" (*Good Morning Midnight,* 33). Admittedly, this ability to *act out* what lies *underneath* her passive mask (her makeup as a woman who is dependent on the value men confer on her looks) ends by a Pyrrhic victory over someone who seems just as vulnerable as Sasha—the gigolo René. The price she pays for humiliating him, for wounding another lonely outsider "to get some of [her] own back" (61) and taking revenge on all the "monsieurs" that had walked through her life is the final acceptance of "the enormous effort" (157) to confront her other side and encounter madness. The terrible self-ironical "Yes—yes—yes. . . ." (159) that culminates the text transforms Sasha the character into Sasha the narrator/author who will soon go back to London (36) and presumably edit her "last performance" (154).[13] The protagonist of *Good Morning, Midnight* avoids the self-pity which marred Rhys's earlier heroines by constantly deriding herself and, above all, by reminding the reader of her own capacity to violence and destruction.

> One day, quite suddenly, when you are not expecting it, I'll take a hammer from the folds of my dark cloak and crack your little skull like an egg-shell. Crack it will go, the egg-shell; out they will stream, the blood, the brains. One day, one day. . . . One day the fierce wolf that walks by my side will spring on you and rip your abominable guts out."
> (*Good Morning Midnight,* 45)

Confronting madness Sasha is familiar with the death-bringing machine.

"And the arms wave to an accompaniment of music and of song. Like this: 'Hotcha—hotcha—hotcha. . . .' And I know the music; I can sing the song. . . .

I have another drink. Damned voice in my head, I'll stop you talking. . . ." (156–57)

The character's failure to establish any stable connection with society, her inability to "give [herself] up to people [she likes]" (*Good Morning Midnight,* 51) is the underside of her inescapable need to impersonate a still attractive female, craving for affection and companionship. In dread of old age and the absolute alienation that lies in waiting, Sasha finally learns to accept her long-hidden impulse to hate. After the wound she inflicted on the gigolo she acknowledges that she can be just as bad as any other creature; the former arrogance that has led her to consider sarcastically other people's acts of cruelty toward herself as perfect "close-ups" (75) of human nature now turns into a self-mocking close-up of herself. "I look straight into his eyes and despise another poor devil of a human being for the last time. For the last time. . . ." (159)

The actual *narrative* "transformation act" (*Good Morning Midnight,* 53) is the metamorphosis of the helpless victim into the despairing narrator who—on the edge of madness—is capable of an agonizing tour de force, a (last?) act of coherent discourse. Thus in more ways than one Sasha Jansen prefigures Rhys's next heroine Antoinnette Cosway and her final literary redemption.[14] In transforming the "paradigmatic" heroine from a fragile rejected creature into someone who has the power to act out her inner violence and to admit it while voicing her own story, Jean Rhys goes a long way toward the construction of her last narrator/protagonist.

Through the act of writing Sasha acquires the power, the authority to confront us readers with our own inner divisions. Sasha the character, Sasha the narrator, Sasha the author—they all violently express a vision of the human condition which force us to look straight into the eyes of the dreadful (un)reality of modern life.[15] Distorting mirror of the deformed (personal, social, political) conventions of a neurotic culture on the edge of disintegration, *Good Morning, Midnight* evokes the chaos that (always) lurks beneath the thin veneer of civilization. In its expressionist revolt against the smug artificial values that push the human race into the abyss of imminent military and moral self-destruction, the novel is not only a vital cultural metaphor for the thirties' atmosphere. Disturbing composition in shadows and surfaces, *Good Morning, Midnight* is as much our contemporary as Jean Rhys.

Notes

1. Special mention should be made to Thomas F. Staley, *Jean Rhys: A Critical Study* (London: Macmillan, 1979); and to Paula Le Gallez, *The Rhys Woman* (London: Macmillan, 1990).

2. Staley, *Jean Rhys,* 30. From a different perspective Le Gallez writes in her conclusion:" [T]he 'Rhys woman' has the power to build texts and to articulate her own narratives. In this respect, as the author of her own discourse, she sets herself against the suffocation of her spirit, a suffocation which the traditionally expected 'passivity' would surely bring her." (Le Gallez 176).

3. Listen also to her mother's comment: "You are a very peculiar child, (. . .) I can't imagine what will happen if you don't learn to behave more like other people" (*Smile Please: An Unfinished Autobiography,*92).

4. See, for instance, Gayatri Spivak, "Three Women's Texts and a Critique of Imperialism", *Critical Inquiry* 12, (autumn 1985): 243–61; Helen Tiffin, "Post-Colonial Literatures and Counter-Discourses", *Kunapipi* 9, no. 3 (1987): 17–34; Teresa F. O'Connor, *Jean Rhys: The West Indian Novels* (New York: New York University Press, 1986); and Mary Lou Emery, *Jean Rhys at "World's End": Novels of Colonial and Sexual Exile* (Austin: University of Texas Press, 1990).

5. Although I agree with Staley: "Throughout the thirties Rhys's heroines saw the world from the inside rather than the outside. Her aim was (. . .) not the achievement of an enlarged vision of the contemporary world." (84), I believe that, perhaps *malgré elle,* Rhys's *Good Morning, Midnight* is in its very structure a forceful metaphor of the period. As such it is also a decisive step towards the obviously political implications of *Wide Sargassa Sea* "which finally roots the heroine's suffering in her social and political condition." (Angier, 403)

6. *Good Morning, Midnight,* (1939; London: Penguin Books, 1969). Subsequent quotations are cited parenthetically in the text. Ellipses, unless otherwise indicated, are Rhys's not mine.

7. While Carol Ann Howells refers to "doublings and distorted reflections" she does not explore its central structuring function in the novel. Howells, *Jean Rhys* (London: Harvester Wheatsheaf, 1991), 94.

8. See also pages 36–37 for Sasha on her (real?) name—Sophia and my essays: "'Drunk and Disorderly': Jean Rhys ou a recusa de uma escrita bem comportada," RUNA (Revista Portuguesa de Etudos Germanisticos) nos. 13/14 (1990): 393–403; and" 'Feeding the Lake': Bitter Drops that Matter—The Short Fiction of Jean Rhys." Paper presented at ESSE(European Society for the Study of English)/2, Bordeaux 1993.

9. Montage was a technique widely used by modernist artists as well as by the nouveau roman (particularly by Robbe-Grillet). See Bruce Morrissette, *Novel and Film: Essays in Two Genres* (Chicago: University of Chicago Press, 1985); and Sharon Spencer, *Space, Time and Structure in the Modern Novel* (New York: New York University Press, 1971).

10. "Woman's psyche is split in two by her constructed awareness of herself as a visual object and her resulting double role as actor and spectator (. . .) schizophrenia is the perfect literary metaphor for (. . .) women's lack of confidence, dependency on external, often masculine, definitions of the self, split between the body as sexual object and the mind as subject, and vulnerability to conflicting social messages about femininity and maturity." Elaine Showalter, *The Female Malady:*

Women, Madness and English Culture, 1830–1980 (1985; London: Virago, 1987), 212–13.

11. See, among others, Siegfried Kracauer, *Von Caligari Bis Hitler. Ein Beitrag zur Geschichte des deutschen Films* (English ed. 1947; Hamburg: Rowohlt, 1958); and A. R. Fulton, *Motion Pictures: The Development of an Art from Silent Films to the Age of Television* (Norman: University of Oklahoma Press, 1960). Expressionist film is obviously indebted to early twentieth-century expressionist theater, literature, and painting.

12. Although Kafka's *The Trial* only became available in English in 1937 (when she was probably working on *Good Morning, Midnight,* see Angier, *Jean Rhys,* 368) it is quite possible that Rhys knew earlier (German or French?) editions of his texts. She certainly was familiar with kakfkesque situations as early as *Quartet* (1928)— for instance in pages 23–25 (Penguin ed. 1973) and she deeply admired Dostoevsky. See David Plante, "Jean Rhys: A Remembrance", *Paris Review,* 21 (fall 1979):247.

13. On the ambiguity of both René and the *commis* see, among others, the interpretations of Angier (particularly Angier, 382–85), Le Gallez, 138–40, and Emery, 145–47, 161–63.

14. Antoinette's redemption and probably Rhys's too.

15. As Rebecca West pointed out: "It is doubtful if one ought to open this volume [*After Leaving Mr. Mackenzie*] unless one is happily married, immensely rich, and in robust health; for, if one is not entirely free from misery when one opens the book one will be at the suicide point long before one closes it." *Daily Telegraph,* 30 January 1931, quoted in Angier, *Jean Rhys,* 280. Rhys was (is) definitely not the writer for a consolatory art.

Works Cited

Angier, Carole. 1990. *Jean Rhys, Life and Work.* London: Andre Deutsch.

Eisenstein, Sergei. 1949. *Film Form: Essays in Film Theory.* Edited and translated by Jay Leyda. New York: Harcourt, Brace & Co.

Ford, Madox Ford. 1927, 1984. Preface to Jean Rhys. *The Left Bank and Other Stories.* Salem: Ayer Company.

Howells, Coral Ann. 1991. *Jean Rhys.* London: Harvester Wheatsheaf.

Le Gallez, Paula. 1990. *The Rhys Woman.* London: Macmillan.

Lessing, Doris. 1962, 1973. *The Golden Notebook.* St. Albans: Panther Books.

Rhys, Jean. 1979. "The Trial of Jean Rhys." *Smile Please, An Unfinished Autobiography.* Harmondsworth: Penguin Books.

———. 1939, 1969. *Good Morning, Midnight.* London: Penguin Books;

Sage, Lorna. 1992. *Women in the House of Fiction: Post-War Women Novelists.* London: Macmillan.

Staley, Thomas F. 1979. *Jean Rhys: A Critical Study.* London: Macmillan.

Wilson, Lucy. 1986. "Women Must Have Spunks: Jean Rhys's West Indian Outcasts." *Modern Fiction Studies.* 32, no. 3.

Woolf, Virginia. 1941, 1978. *Between the Acts.* St. Albans: Granada.

A Bibliography of Works by and about Jean Rhys

The primary bibliography does not include several short stories written during the thirties but only published in the late sixties or during the seventies. The secondary bibliography has been selected.

Primary

————. *After Leaving Mr Mackenzie*. 1930, 1971. Harmondsworth: Penguin.

————. *Voyage in the Dark*. 1934, 1969. Harmondsworth: Penguin.

————. *Good Morning, Midnight*. 1939, 1969. Harmonsworth: Penguin.

Secondary

Abel, Elizabeth. 1979. "Women and Schizophrenia: The Fiction of Jean Rhys." *Contemporary Literature* 20:155–77.

Angier, Carole. 1990. *Jean Rhys, Life and Work*. London: Andre Deutsch.

Ashcom, Jane Neide. 1988. "Two Modernisms: The Novels of Jean Rhys." *Jean Rhys Review* 2, no.2:17–27.

Borinsky, Alicia. 1985. "Jean Rhys: Poses of a Woman as Guest." *Poetics Today* 6, nos. 1–2:229–43.

Bowlby, Rachel. 1992. *Still Crazy After All These Years: Women, Writing and Psychoanalysis*. London: Routledge, 34–58.

Brown, Nancy Hemmond. 1986. "Aspects of the Short Story: A Comparison of Jean Rhys's 'The Sound of the River' with Ernest Hemingway's 'Hills like White Elephants.'" *Jean Rhys Review* 1 no.1:2–12.

Byrne, Jack. 1985. "Jean Rhys's *Good Morning, Midnight:* The Boulevard of Broken Dreams." *Review of Contemporary Fiction* 5, no. 2:151–59.

Emery, Mary Lou. 1990. *Jean Rhys at "World's End": Novels of Colonial and Sexual Exile*. Austin: University of Texas Press.

Fido, Elaine Savory. 1991. "The Politics of Colours and the Politics of Writing in the Fiction of Jean Rhys." *Jean Rhys Review* 4 no. 2:3–12.

Gregg, Veronica Marie. 1987. "Jean Rhys and Modernism: A Different Voice." *Jean Rhys Review* 1, no. 2:30–46.

Harrison, Nancy R. 1988. *Jean Rhys and the Novel as Woman's Text*. Chapel Hill: University of North Carolina Press.

Howells, Coral Ann. 1991. *Jean Rhys*. London: Harvester Wheatsheaf.

James, Louis. 1978. *Jean Rhys*. London: Longman.

Jean Rhys Review. Published in the fall and spring at New York: Columbia University Press.

Le Gallez, Paula. 1990. *The Rhys Woman*. London: Macmillan.

Mellown, Elgin W. 1972. "Character and Themes in the Novels of Jean Rhys." *Contemporary Literature* 13, no. 4:458–75.

————. 1984. *Jean Rhys: A Descriptive and Annotated Bibliography of Works and Criticism*. London: Gale.

Naipaul, V. S. 1972. "Without a Dog's Chance." *New York Review of Books* (18 May):29–31.

Nebeker, Helen. 1981. *Jean Rhys, Woman in Passage: A Critical Study of the Novels*. Montreal: Eden Press.

Plante, David. 1979. "Jean Rhys: A Remembrance." *Paris Review*, 21 (fall):238–84.

Roe, Sue. 1987. "'The Shadow of Light': The Symbolic Underworld of Jean Rhys." In Sue Roe, ed. *Women Reading Women's Writing*. Brighton: Harvester, 227–62.

Sage, Lorna. 1992. *Women in the House of Fiction: Post-War Women Novelists.* London: Macmillan, 47–54, 60, 64–65, 70, 83.

Staley, Thomas F. 1979. *Jean Rhys: A Critical Study.* London: Macmillan.

Vreeland, Elizabeth. 1979. "Jean Rhys: The Art of Fiction LXIV." *Paris Review,* 21 (fall):219–37.

Wilson, Lucy. 1986." 'Women Must Have Spunks': Jean Rhys' West Indian Outcasts." *Modern Fiction Studies* 32, no. 3 (autumn): 439–47.

18

"Courage Means Running": William Empson as Poet

DAVID WHEATLEY

A Brief Biographical Sketch of William Empson (1906–1984)

Born a Yorkshire man in 1906, William Empson studied at Win- chester College and Magdalene College, Cambridge, where he read mathematics and English, graduating in 1929. Prompted by the example of Robert Graves and Laura Riding's *Survey of Modernist Poetry,* Empson remarked to his mentor I. A. Richards that "You could do that with any poetry, couldn't you?" Two weeks later, Richards reports, "the central 30,000 words or so" of *Seven Types of Ambiguity* had been completed. The book was immediately champi- oned by the New Criticism; a school whose neglect of biographical and intentional factors Empson later came to deplore. His commit- ment to what he persisted in calling "the story" in literature was stubbornly unshakable: although Empson's poetry, written almost exclusively between 1926 and 1937, is among the most wirily meta- physical written this century, the claim that verse could be appreci- ated without being understood he considered a "lethal formula." Accordingly, though seldom emotionally or politically explicit in his poetry of the 1930s Empson displays a tough historical self- awareness underneath his characteristic "singing line." He lectured, often under difficult circumstances, in Tokyo from 1931 to 1934, during which period *Some Versions of Pastoral* was written, and subse- quently, between 1937 and 1939, at the National University of Pe- king. The Sino-Japanese war saw Empson's flight with his faculty to the southwestern province of Hunan. Here, with scarcely any books at his disposal, Empson astonished his pupils by typing out whole plays of Shakespeare from memory and drafted what he con-

279

sidered his single finest work, a study of the faces of the Buddha (lost in the mail on its way to London). Considering his poetic career over with the outbreak of the war, he returned to England to work as Chinese editor for the BBC, where his office adjoined that of George Orwell. After five further years in China after the war, with summers spent at Gambier College, Ohio, Empson took the chair in Sheffield University that he would keep until 1971. *The Structure of Complex Words* appeared in 1951, and *Milton's God,* with its savage denunciation of the supreme being of Christianity, in 1961. A somewhat isolated figure in his later years, Empson has recently benefited from renewed interest from critics who see in his style of close reading a significant anticipation of more recent structuralist and poststructuralist developments.

* * * * *

The commanding and unmistakable note in the slim volume that makes up William Empson's *Collected Poems* (1955) is intellectual passion. For a sensibility as finely nuanced as that on show throughout his first published work, *Seven Types of Ambiguity* (1930), there is in Empson the poet a peculiar resistance to his own linguistic gifts, amounting at times to almost ascetic proportions. That this resistance, usually manifested under strong emotional pressure, has the effect of convincing us more than ever of these same linguistic gifts only compounds the irony. Christopher Ricks has suggested the term *anti-pun* to describe the effect produced when an unequivocal meaning is reinforced by the use of semantic near misses to heighten the effort required to isolate the single, intended meaning (Ricks 1984, 271); for a poet so preoccupied with evasion and its overcoming, Empson would surely have appreciated the concept. An early poem begins:

> Yet
> To escape emotion (a common hope) and attain
> Cold truth is essentially to get
> Out by a rival emotion fear.[1]

With their skirting of Eliot's celebrated description in "Tradition and the Individual Talent" of poetry as "not a turning loose of emotion, but an escape from emotion," Empson's lines invoke the "common hope" of impersonality only to suggest that this too is another way "to get / Out"—at which point one calls both senses to mind, of getting something "out," as one does a prisoner, and "getting

out" of an unpleasant task, only to find the rest of the line runs—
"to get / Out by a rival emotion fear." In typical Empson fashion,
this last word comes as a double rebuff to the reader. Something
concrete is being "got out," achieved, but that something, so mis-
chievously delayed, is itself an evasion—fear. The sense seems indis-
putable: impersonality may be simultaneously a turning loose of,
and a turning away from, emotion, fear being the mode in which
this is possible. The syntactic cat's-pawing with which Empson
teases out the point serves perhaps to delay his (and our) confronting
what may be an all too unambiguous psychological truth. To see
only the mercurial semantic gadabout of *Seven Types of Ambiguity* in
these lines is to lose most of their poignant inevitability, the force
of the last word tearing off the cloak of ambiguity to reveal the real
terror underneath. The effect on Empson of raw emotion of this
sort, inducing a state of headlong but somehow heroic evasion, does
not make for frankness in his poetry, but neither does it make for
insincerity. The experience of baffled grappling with his emotions
which Empson conveys, emotions whose resistance to articulation
is often as much as the poet can hope to capture in words, is what
John Wain has identified as the "metaphysical" dimension to his
work, associating it with that of such other writers as John Crowe
Ransom and Robert Graves (Wain 1949, 125). In this essay, taking
examples from the poems of the 1930s which rank among his permanent contributions to the language, I would like to explore how
Empson's fascination with what Harold Bloom would call *clinamen,*
the trope of swerving, deflection, and evasion, mirrors his own status as a 1930s poet unaffiliated to either the emerging "neo-
Christian" orthodoxy surrounding Eliot (*Ash Wednesday* having been
published in 1930) or the lefist engagé school grouped around Auden
(cf. his "Just a Smack at Auden" of 1938), but forced to fight his
corner as an individualist, much as Robert Graves or Basil Bunting,
to take two comparable examples, also were during the same years.
How hostile the climate of the 1930s was, in the words of Pound's
Hugh Selwyn Mauberley, to "Mildness, amid the neo-Nietzschean
clatter" of those hectic times can be gauged by the enormous stylistic
resistance which Empson puts in the way of his readers. But beside
the resistance to the writing of any lyric poetry at all which that
decade offered to begin with, perhaps Empson's can, after a little
painless close reading of our own, be safely forgiven him.

Eliot's criterion for a poet, someone able to write authentically of
experiences which have yet to happen to him, could almost have
been devised with Empson in mind. As Christopher Ricks detects
in his thorough account of Empson's poetry (Gill 1974, 145–207),

the most emotionally charged moments in Empson's poetry are
placed under the sign of a tortured anticipation; the most tortured
anticipation of all being reserved for the sexual act and the moral
correctness or otherwise of bringing a child into the world. In his
work on Donne, his favorite English poet, Empson often draws a
parallel between the omnipresent sexual theme and the metaphors
of space travel and astronomy. For Empson no less than Donne the
two themes are intricately related. Just as the Madonna is assumed
into Heaven without bodily decay in "Camping Out," (1929/35), so
the lover's ecstasy "makes physical decay at once unthinkable and
insignificant . . . because the creation of any new life, whether by a
Madonna or not, confutes decay" (Gill (ed.) 1974, 192). Yet, though
few English poets are less monkish than Empson, the sexual threshold on which his poems are habitually to be found frequently opens,
not onto the "new-found-land" of Donne's "To His Mistress Going
to Bed," but onto a world whose alien atmosphere seems scarcely
compatible with human life. "Earth Has Shrunk in the Wash" (1929/
1935) begins:

> They pass too fast. Ships, and there's time for sighing;
> Express and motor, Doug can jump between.
> Only dry earth now asteroid her flying
> Mates, if they miss her, must flick past unseen;
>
> Or striking breasts that once the air defended
> (Bubble of rainbow straddling between twilights,
> Mother-of-pearl that with earth's oyster ended)
> They crash and burrow and spill all through skylights.
>
> There, airless now, from the bare sun take cancer,
> Curve spines as earth and gravitation wane,
> Starve on the mirror images of plants, or
> Miss diabeatic down odd carbon chains.

—the shrinkage of the title having reduced the Earth to the asteroid
condition in which we find it in the third line, its atmosphere having
escaped. "Under the new conditions man is exposed to the dangerous rays of the sun, once cut off by the air, not made to stand up
straight by the tensions of a normal life, and only able to get such
food as there might be on another planet, which we couldn't eat"
as the notes to the Collected Poems informatively paraphrases (the
Doug in the second line by the way is Douglas Fairbanks) (Collected
Poems 1955, 101). Paradoxically, the state of greatest velocity in the
sequence "ships"—"express"—"asteroid," that of the blindly spin-

ning planet, is on another level also the closest to a condition of complete paralysis, its atmosphere no longer being able to support life. Similarly, the sun's normally beneficent rays, when experienced directly rather than in mediated form, assume a destructive force causing cancer. Just as the planet itself suffers without the protective envelope of its atmosphere, all attempts to reach it suffer the fate of "her flying / Mates" that "crash and burrow and spill all through skylights" on trying to approach. Metaphorically then, the poem is richly suggestive of Empson's constant vacillation between a desire for direct statement and a knowledge of the impossibility of such a statement. Rather than resolving the contradiction, Empson puts himself at its mercy, writing a baroquely remote and inflected poem on the dangers, as the notes put it, of "Civilised refinement cutting one off from other people," much as in "Your Teeth Are Ivory Stars" (*The Gathering Storm* 1940) he writes an unmistakably Empson poem about the dangers of writing Empson poems. Like the "mirror images of plants" whose molecules have been reversed so as to make them inedible, or the diabetes that breaks up sugars into an odd number of carbon atoms, "whereas you can only digest those with an even number" (Collected Poems, 101–2) Empson's poems seem as happy to turn themselves inside out stylistically as the poet is unhappy to do so emotionally.

Perched between two equally intolerable realities, the Empson space par excellence is thus what Samuel Beckett's *Unnamable,* describing his bodily condition at one point in the novel of the same name, refers to as the "tympanum"—"neither one side nor the other [. . .] two surfaces and no thickness" (Beckett 1958, 100). In a more obviously erotic context than "Earth Has Shrunk in the Wash," "Arachne" (1928/1935) visualizes man as "King spider" tracing a path "between void and void" along the meniscus of a pond surface:

> His gleaming bubble between void and void,
> Tribe-membrane, that by mutual tension stands,
> Earth's surface film, is at a breath destroyed.
>
> Bubbles gleam brightest with least depth of lands
> But two is least can with full tension strain,
> Two molecules; one, and the film disbands.

The portentous "Birth, death; one, many; what is true, and seems"; of the poem's second line is instantly telescoped in the next verse to the spider's microcosm, while in the second of those just quoted the surface of the bubble—like the toothpaste of "Camping Out"—

forms a globular whole in itself, but is parasitic upon the water without which the soap cannot make a bubble. In its Janus-faced perspective, taking in the infinitely large and infinitesimally small, "Arachne" exemplifies the brusque transitions in which Empson's poems move. The sudden shift of register in the final tercet further illustrates the wider view the poet prefers to construct before permitting himself anything as merely personal as the sly three-word sentence that reveals "Arachne" for the love poem that it is:

> We two suffice. But oh beware, whose vain
> Hydroptic soap my meagre water saves.
> Male spiders must not be too easily slain.

The "saves" of the penultimate line may simply point out the symbiotic nature of the relationship between the soap and the water, but the former being "vain" may also imply a "saving" on the water's part, in the sense of an element with which it cannot mix without undergoing some essential corruption. The physical incompatibility of the soap and the water is what makes the bubble surface in which they meet—however tenuously—so pregnant an image for the sense of alternating erotic fascination and revulsion with which it colors the whole poem. "Male spiders must not be too easily slain" says Arachne, though this may mean no more than her saying that she fully intends to slay the male spider in question anyway but doesn't want it to seem too easy, since she is "a queen spider and disastrously proud" after all.[2]

"To an Old Lady," the poet's salute to his mother, is also virtuosic in the range of phenomena it invokes to offset the intimacy of the subject in hand. With its tag from *King Lear* the poem begins:

> Ripeness is all; her in her cooling planet
> Revere; do not presume to think her wasted.
> Project her no projectile, plan nor man it;
> Gods cool in turn, by the sun long outlasted.

The "conceit" is once again drawn from astronomy. Though one is not to presume "to think her wasted," the poet's mother is nonetheless addressed "in her cooling planet" which no exploratory probe of ours can fully expect to reach (the intellectual sort of "projection" immediately translated in Empson's hands into a concretely suggestive image). As in La Rochefoucauld's well-known maxim, death and the sun are the two things humanity cannot confront face-to-face; and here too, as previously in "The Earth Shrunk in the Wash," the frailties of mortality are favorably contrasted with the inhuman omnipotence of the sun ("Gods cool in turn, by the sun long out-lasted"). The unavoidable ambiguity attaching to the word "sun" reminds us of the projective nature of all astronomy, the planets all having being given names of gods, often with family ties of their own. By seeing patterns of human kinship writ large in the planetary bodies however, we may also be distancing ourselves from their earthly realities—the Earth itself, as the first line of the second verse points out, being the only planet not to be given a god's name:

> Our earth alone given no name of god
> Gives, too, no hold for such a leap to aid her;
> Landing, you break some palace and seem odd;
> Bees sting their need, the keeper's queen invader.

In its very closeness, the earth is unamenable to the "leaping" efforts of the astronaut, although the "landing" of the third line suggests that the astronaut in question may not even be of this world. The violent rejection that he encounters is then visualized in the image of the rejected queen bee. The peculiar role-reversal this denotes, since the speaker is so evidently male, suggests the intrusion of a second female Empson is not directly naming in the poem, but whom we may assume to have supplanted the mother in his affec-tions (Empson's eventual abandonment of poetry, it does not seem irrelevant to note, virtually coincides with his marriage in 1941). While Empson complains, in *Some Versions of Pastoral,* of the ten-dency of fate as a theme to "dignif[y] into bad metaphysics . . . a piece of pastoral machinery" (*Some Versions of Pastoral,* 10), the comparison of such raw human concerns to the icy fixity of the heavenly bodies skillfully outflanks any pathetic fallacy:

> Stars how much further from me fill my night.
> Strange that she too should be inaccessible,
> Who shares my sun. He curtains her from sight,
> And but in darkness is she visible.

The poet's wife is "further from [him]," but not "inaccesible"; the "son" one cannot resist hearing alongside the "sun" Empson has written constitutes a newly forged family unit from which the poet's mother is, to some extent at least, excluded. Her "cool[ed] planet" is therefore "curtain[ed] from sight" without becoming invisible. The astronomical analogy for this process would be an eclipse, or occultation, such as takes place when the satellites of Jupiter vanish on entering their planet's shadow, or cast a dark spot over its surface on reemerging into the light. The coldness of the analogy captures the sense of unbridgeable and inevitable distance between mother and son, but succeeds in doing so without sacrificing the universal basis of its imagery. On the model of Marvell's "Definition of Love," with which it shares its interest in astronomy, Empson has eschewed direct emotional comment in favor of protective verbal artifice. Yet the effect is anything but self-congratulatory in its sheer accomplishment; rarely if ever, and certainly not here, is Empson reminiscent of the pyrotechnics of 1930s Auden.

Nowhere is the resolutely metaphysical economy of Empson's poetry more severely tested than in its engagment with political subject matter. The development that separates the 1940 volume from its earlier counterpart, in the shift from emotional self-enclosure to poems like "Ignorance of Death," "Manchouli," and the long political meditation that is "Autumn on Nan-Yueh," can be seen as a drawing of the poet from his shell. In place of the astronomer of *Poems*, *The Gathering Storm* gives us the cartographer crossing boundaries, drawing and redrawing maps as he goes. The suggestion that a volume, one of whose star turns is entitled "Courage Means Running," simply witnessed Empson's surrender to the genteel defeatism of 1930s verse after the tragedies of Spain, and now the outbreak of war in Europe and the Pacific, drew an angry response from the author. In a conversation of 1963 he told Christopher Ricks that

> The first book . . . is about the young man feeling frightened, frightened of women, frightened of jobs, frightened of everything, not knowing what he could possibly do. The second book is all about politics, saying we're going to have this second world war and we mustn't get too frightened about it. Well, dear me, if you call the first brave and the second cowardly it seems to me that you haven't the faintest idea of what the poems are about. (Ricks, *The Review* 1963, 26)

While metaphors of flight run through *The Gathering Storm* like a refrain, the verb is invariably being tugged between the simple "flight" that is desertion in the face of intolerable reality, and the Icarian "flight" born of poetic genius—"The heart of standing is you cannot fly," as "Aubade" phrases it, "standing" too somehow conveying resilience and limitation at one and the same time. While the 1940 volume does mark a relaxation in psychological tension beside *Poems* (nothing as wiredrawn or recondite as "High Wire" or "Letter IV") the semantic clarity into which the later Empson has emerged has the desperate economy of a man running:

And it is true I flew, I fled,
　I ran about on hope, on trust,
I felt I had escaped from They
　Who sat on pedestals and fussed.
But is it true one ought to dread
　This timid flap, that shirk, that lust?
We do not fly when we are clay.
　We hope to fly when we are dust.

This is from "Autumn on Nan-Yueh" (1940), Empson's longest poem. In an extended squaring off of political evasiveness as a type of "flight" against the physical displacement of the speaker (the poem was written in exile with the Peking faculty) Empson solidly absolves the latter from the charge of cowardice as resolutely as he flails the former. Incapable of ad hoc sloganeering, the political virtue of Empson's position is his refusal to dodge the bare facts of experience even when the "aeronautic" style can be the only genuine response to them—

Verse has been lectured to a treat
　Against Escape and being blah.
It struck me trying not to fly
　Let them escape a bit too far.
It is an aeronautic feat
　Called soaring, makes you quite a star
(The Queen and Alice did) to try
　And keep yourself just where you are.

—the common human decencies, Empson implies, being impervious to simple physical uprooting. Lines like this expose the essential rootedness, for all its aeronautics, of Empson's imagination, as does *in nuce* the audacious remark in a 1940 review of Auden that "What is heartening about people is their appalling stubbornness . . . rather than the ease with which you can convert them and make them happy and good" (*The Royal Beasts and Other Works,* 1986, 73 n, 52). The "make" of that last clause is the key word; Empson can see the point neither in telling the reader what to think nor in assuming the reader should owe him any gratitude for doing so. In the course of the poem, an opening (mis)quotation from Yeats's "Phases of the Moon" is playfully taken up to help the poet walk this treacherous tightrope between public statement and lyric autonomy. "there is no deformity / But saves us from a dream" writes Yeats; the sight of pilgrims being hauled manually "in baskets or in crates" up the side of a "holy mountain" in Nan-Yueh alerts Empson to the resil-

ience of dreams which, on the contrary, bodily weakness or deformity actively encourages—"The pilgrims fly because they plod."
The pilgrims' dogged plod, tested against the realities of physical
frailty, is the tortoise to the Achilles of agitprop political verse: the
pilgrims "fly" *because* they also plod, while the "revolutionary
romp"—

> The hearty uproar that deploys
> A sit-down literary strike;

"flies" because it cannot even walk. Empson's apostrophe to 1937
England, with the specter of Nazi Germany large on its horizon, is
similarly cautious but also guardedly optimistic in its way, for all
the preliminary soul-searching—

> But really, does it do much good
>   To put in verse however strong
> The welter of a doubt at night
>   At home, in which I too belong?
> The heat-mists that my vision hood
>   Shudder precisely with the throng.
> England I think an eagle flight
>   May come too late, may take too long.
> What would I teach it? Where it could
>   The place has answered like a gong.

"Like a gong": the unadorned expression of trust in the political
good faith of the British people in the face of the Fascist terror
imposes itself as a genuine, and in the poetic context, completely
earned expression of patriotic emotion. The verve with which Empson brings off the performance would be remarkable for its un-
apologetic civic-mindedness, if for no other reason; a comparison
with Eliot's "Defence of These Islands" or "To the Indians Who
Died in Africa" shows what poetic disaster Empson was courting
in writing as he did.

With all this borne in mind, the intellectual passion I began by
observing can be described as evasive only insofar as what is evaded
remains extraneous to Empson's strictly poetic needs. *Poems,* with
their so frequently intimate and even painful subject matter conscien-
tiously refuse to surrender the merely personal details in question;
instead, what they give us is a metaphysically lucid primer in emotions normally thought of as private. The gesture itself remains public. The responsiveness of these poems to a close reading of the sort
which I have applied here locally is, I trust, refutation enough of the

charge of obscurity. In the shift of subject matter registered in *The Gathering Storm* the tact and self-restraint of the earlier volume remain unchanged. Refusing to exchange the precarious autonomy of the lyric voice for the advantages of political engagé status, Empson detaches serious political verse from the very gesture of his reluctance to write on political themes. The evasion motif that has figured so prominently is thus Empson's own admission of his own limitations—Empson being by no stretch of the imagination a "great"—but also a vindication of the completely individual voice which his turning his back so resolutely on contemporary stylistic inducements has allowed him to achieve. In the poem with which I began,

> Fearful "had the root of the matter," bringing
> Him things to fear, and he read well that ran;
> Muchafraid went over the river singing,
>
> Though none knew what she sang. Usual for a man
> Of Bunyan's courage to respect fear.

—the reference being to the character in *The Pilgrim's Progress* who accompanies Mr. Despondency singing through the slough of despond and to Mr. Fearing; there is no Fearful. One's first impulse is to take the poet by the sleeve and exact a correction on the spot. In the meantime though the poem itself, having learned its "style from a despair" as the last line of "This Last Pain" advised, simply bustles on regardless. Again, Empson all over. The fear he has in mind, one feels, is already too urgent for the objection to be anything but unworthy. They also serve who only stand and wait; but courage means running.

Notes

1. "Courage Means Running" (1936/1940). Dates of first publication will be given with all poems quoted, followed by the date of their first collection.
2. Notes to *Collected Poems*, 101. Similarly in "Plenum and Vacuum" (1935) a scorpion under a glass kills itself in "suicide defiance" when frightened by fire, while in "To an Old Lady" (1928/1935) the line "Bees sting their need, the keeper's queen invader" is disambiguated in the notes as meaning that queen bees introduced into hives by apiarists are sometimes killed by the bees; the act of violence in both cases centering on an essential boundary somehow violated or trespassed.

Works Cited

Beckett, Samuel. 1958. *The Unnamable*. London: John Calder.
Empson, William. 1986. *The Royal Beasts and Other Works*. London: Chatto and Windus.

Empson, William. 1955. *Collected Poems*. London: Chatto and Windus.

Gill, Roma. ed. 1974. *William Empson: The Man and His Work*. London and Boston: Routledge and Kegan Paul.

Ricks, Cristopher. 1984. *The Forces of Poetry*. Oxford: Clarendon.

The Review. 1963 (June). (special issue on Empson) London.

Wain, John. 1949. "Ambiguous Gifts." *Penguin New Writing*, no. 40.

A Bibliography of Works by and about William Empson

Criticism

———. 1930. *Seven Types of Ambiguity*. London: Chatto & Windus.

———. 1935. *Some Version of Pastoral*. London: Chatto & Windus.

———. 1951. *The Structure of Complex Words*. London: Chatto & Windus.

———. 1961. *Milton's God*. London: Chatto & Windus.

———. 1984. *Using Biography*. London; Chatto & Windus.

———. 1986. *Essays on Shakespeare*. Edited by David B. Pirie. Cambridge: Cambridge University Press.

———. 1987. *Argufying*. Edited by John Haffenden. London: Chatto & Windus.

———. 1987. *Faustus and the Censor: The English Faust Book and Marlowe's Doctor Faustus*. Edited by John Henry Jones. Oxford: Basil Blackwell.

———. 1993. *Essays on Renaissance Literature*. Vol. 1 of *Donne and the New Philosophy*. Edited by John Haffenden. Cambridge: Cambridge University Press.

Poetry and Miscellaneous

———. 1934. *Poems by William Empson*. Japan: The Fox and Daffodil Press.

———. 1935. *Poems*. London: Chatto & Windus.

———. 1940. *The Gathering Storm*. London: Faber & Faber.

———. 1955. *Collected Poems*. London: Chatto & Windus.

———. 1986. *The Royal Beasts and Other Works*. Edited by John Haffenden. London: Chatto & Windus.

Secondary Sources: A Selection

Constable, John. ca. 1993. *Critical Essays on William Empson*. Aldershot: Scolar Press.

Gardner, Philip and Averill. 1978. *The God Approached: A Commentary on the Poems of William Empson*. Totowa, N.J.: Rowan and Littlefield.

Gill, Roma, ed. 1974. *William Empson: The Man and His Work*. London and Boston: Routledge and Kegan Paul. Contributions by, among others, W. H. Auden, Ronald Bottrall, I. A. Richards, L. C. Knights, John Wain, and Christopher Ricks.

Hill, Geoffrey. 1963. Review of *The Review*. June 1963. In *Essays in Criticism* 14 (1964):91–101.

Meller, Horst. 1974. *Das Gedicht als Einübung: Zum Dichtungsverständnis William Empsons.* Heidelberg: Carl Winter-Universistätsverlag.

Norris, Christopher, 1978. *William Empson and the Philosophy of Literary Criticism.* London: Athlone Press.

Norris, Christopher, and Nigel Mepp, eds. 1993. *William Empson: The Critical Achievement.* Cambridge: Cambridge University Press.

The Review. 1963 (June) London (special issue on Empson). Contains an interview of Empson by Christopher Ricks.

Contributors

DEAN BALDWIN was born in Buffalo, New York, and grew up in Ashland, Ohio. He earned a B.A. from Capital University, Columbus, Ohio (1964) and an M.A. (1966) and Ph.D. (1972) from Ohio State University. He joined Penn State Erie—Behrand College in 1975. His books include *H. E. Bates: A Literary Life*, *V. S. Pritchett, Virginia Woolf, A Study of the Short Fiction*, and *The Short Story in English—Britain and North America: An Annotated Bibliography* (with Gregory Morris). He edited *The British Short Story, 1945–1980*, for the Dictionary of Literary Biography Series. His scholarly interests include Shakespeare, Chaucer, and the short story.

JOHN BOWEN was born in Bridlington, East Yorkshire, and educated at Trinity Hall, Cambridge, and at the Centre for Contemporary Cultural Studies, Birmingham. He has been a lecturer in English at the University of Keele since 1983, and writes mainly on topics in literary theory and nineteenth-century literature. He is a member of the editorial board of the *Journal of Victorian Culture* and is currently writing a book about Dickens.

JOHN COOMBES teaches European literature at Essex University. Originally a specialist in French literature, he is now principally interested in the relations between writing, history, and society in Europe since the seventeenth century. He has taught at universities in Tokyo, Silesia, East Berlin, New Mexico, and Algeria. He is at present completing a book on the literary discourses of fascism and is contemplating writing a political biography of Victor Hugo.

JENNIFER FAIRLEY was born in Norwich, Norfolk. She returned to college as a mature student, studying with the Open University and at the University of Leeds. After a B.A. in English, she pursued an M.A. in nineteenth- and twentieth-century literature, with a dissertation on Robert Graves and David Jones. Her Ph.D. thesis explored mythology in the writings and paintings of David Jones. She teaches English literature at the University of Leeds, and creative writing at the University of Huddersfield. She is also a member of the International Arthurian Society.

LUISA MARIA RODRIGUES FLORA was born and educated in Lisbon. She received her Ph.D. in English literature from Lisbon University where, since receiving her B.A. in 1972, she has been teaching mainly English literature and culture of the nineteenth and twentieth centuries. As assistant professor at Faculdade de Letras (Department of English Studies), she has written on Virginia Woolf, Doris Lessing, Iris Murdoch, Jean Rhys, Joseph Conrad, Henry James, and the First World War pacifists. Her research interests include novel and short story theory, contemporary culture, and comparative literature. She is currently working on Rose Tremain.

JAMES GINDIN was a graduate of Yale and Cornell universities and was a member of the Department of English at the University of Michigan since 1956. His previous books include *Post-War British Fiction, Harvest of a Quiet Eye, The English Climate, John Galsworthy's Life and Art,* and *Art and William Golding.* Sadly, Dr. Gindin has recently passed away.

RENÉE C. HOOGLAND was born in Deventer, the Netherlands. She received her M.A. (1986) and Ph.D. (1991) in English, both from the University of Amsterdam. She wrote *Elizabeth Bowen: A Reputation in Writing.* For seven years, Hoogland taught English and Comparative Literature in Amsterdam, and is now working as a postdoctoral fellow with the Netherlands Organization for Scientific Research, and as a lecturer in Lesbian Studies at the University of Nijmegen. She has published essays on postmodernism, lesbian (feminist) theory, film, and modern English literature. She is working on a book on lesbian cultural studies, and Hoogland's current research focuses on the interconnections among sexuality, cultural production, and the embodiment of knowledge.

CHRIS HOPKINS lectures in English at Sheffield Hallam University. He has done research in twentieth-century fiction, especially the novel in the 1930s. He has published on a number of thirties writers: Elizabeth Bowen, Graham Greene, Walter Greenwood, Storm Jameson, Lewis Jones, John Lehmann, Cecil Day Lewis, Edward Upward, Rex Warner, Sylvia Townsend Warner, and Evelyn Waugh. His articles have appeared in journals including *English Language Notes, The Journal of Gender Studies, Literature and History, Literature of Religion and Nation,* and *Notes and Queries.* He is currently working on Welsh writers of the thirties and on the travel writing of Peter Fleming.

GEORGE MCKAY is a Senior Lecturer in the Department of Cultural Studies, University of Central Lancashire. He has a degree from Humberside University and a Ph.D. from Glasgow University. He teaches twentieth-century British and American literary and cultural studies, and has been a visiting lecturer at the University of Southern Maine, USA and at the University of Veliko Turnovo, Bulgaria. He has published articles on science fiction, popular music, and popular culture, and he is the author of *Senseless Acts of Beauty: Cultures of Resistance Since the Sixties*.

STEVE NICHOLSON was born in Surrey and studied English at Exeter University. After working with White Horse Travelling Theatre he received his M.A. at Lancaster University and a Ph.D. at Leeds on the portrayal of communism in British theater between 1917 and 1945. He taught undergraduate and postgraduate courses at Leeds, and is now Senior Lecturer in Theatre Studies at the University of Huddersfield. His publications include several articles on British political theater, for *New Theatre Quarterly* and *Theatre Research International,* and he is currently finishing a book based on his Ph.D. His teaching interests are both practical and theoretical, and focus on contemporary British theater, production analysis, and seventeenth-century theater.

PATRICK QUINN is the general editor of the *Robert Graves Programme for Carcanet Press* and is Professor of English Literature at Nene College, Northampton. He is the author of a study of the writing of Graves and Siegfried Sassoon, *The Great War and the Missing Muse;* he also edits *Focus on Robert Graves and His Contemporaries,* a biennial journal, and has published essays on the writers of the 1930s.

JUDY SIMONS was born in Sheffield, England. She received a degree in English language and literature from the University of Manchester, where she also did postgraduate work. She was appointed as a lecturer in English at Sheffield City Polytechnic. She is currently a Professor in English studies at Sheffield Hallam University. Her books include *Fanny Burney, Diaries and Journals of Literary Women from Fanny Burney to Virginia Woolf, Rosamond Lehmann,* and *What Katy Read: Re-readings of "Classic" Stories for Girls 1850–1920.*

ELIZABETH TILLEY is a Canadian currently teaching in the Department of English at University College Galway (the National University of Ireland). Her areas of interest include nineteenth- and twentieth-century literature, especially Gothic/Speculative fiction.

STEVEN TROUT, a native of Kansas City, Missouri, received a Ph.D. at the University of Kansas in 1993 and is currently an assistant professor of English at Fort Hays State University. He has written several articles on British writers and the Great War and presented papers on H. G. Wells, Evelyn Waugh, Willa Cather, Robert Graves, and Henry Williamson. At present, he is coediting a collection of critical essays on First World War narratives.

DAVID WHEATLEY was born in Dublin. He studied English and French at Trinity College, Dublin, where he has been a Foundation Scholar and is currently doing research on Samuel Beckett. His articles and criticism have appeared in such journals as *The Irish Times, Irish Review, Poetry Review,* and *Bucknell Review.* Also a poet, his work has appeared in many outlets in Britain and Ireland, including *After Ovid: New Metamorphoses,* and in 1994 he was awarded first prize in the Irish National Poetry Competition.

PATRICK WILLIAMS was born in Sunderland, County Durham, and studied at the University of Nottingham. He has taught at the University of Marrakesh, the University of Strathclyde, the Open University in Scotland, and Nottingham Trent University, where he is currently a Senior Lecturer. He has published on twentieth-century literature and literary theory, as well as various aspects of colonial and postcolonial theory and texts. His books include *Colonial Discourse and Post-Colonial Theory* and *An Introduction to Post-Colonial Theory.*

JERALD ZASLOVE is a professor of English and humanities at Simon Fraser University, Vancouver, British Columbia, and writes in the area of aesthetics and politics, social history of art, and cultural theory. He has written most recently on modernity and the self in *Public;* coedited *Federalism in the Making;* authored a monograph, *Jeff Wall 1990* and is currently editing, with David Wallace, a book of essays on Arnold Hauser and modernism; and is completing a book on Herbert Read and the failure of British modernism which is part of a study on the problem of historical consciousness in Modernism.

CAROLINE ZILBOORG is a professor of English at Lake Erie College and a life member of Clare Hall, Cambridge. Born in New York, she received her B.A. from Vassar College and her Ph.D. from the

University of Wisconsin. Her books include *Richard Aldington and H.D.: The Early Years in Letters* and *Richard Aldington: Essays in Honour of the Centenary*. Her *Richard Aldington and H.D.: The Later Years in Letters* appeared in 1995. She is currently writing a critical biography of Mary Renault, for which she has received a National Endowment for the Humanities Fellowship for the 1995–96 academic year.

Index